Mary Baker Eddy

MRS. EDDY IN 1886

MARY BAKER EDDY

The Years of Trial

Robert Peel

Holt, Rinehart and Winston

New York   Chicago   San Francisco

Acknowledgments

For permission to reprint copyright material, grateful acknowledgment is made to the following:
Trustees under the Will of Mary Baker Eddy for quotations from the writings of Mrs. Eddy;
Trustees of The Christian Science Publishing Society
for quotations from works published by them;
Harper & Row for passages from Karl Barth, *The Word of God and the Word of Man*,
Werner Heisenberg, *Physics and Beyond*, and G. B. Caird, *The Revelation of St. John the Divine;*
International Publishers for a quotation from Joseph Stalin, *Leninism: Selected Writings;*
A. D. Peters & Company for a quotation from Arthur Koestler,
The Sleepwalkers (Hutchinson);
Routledge & Kegan Paul Ltd. for a passage from Michael Polànyi, *Personal Knowledge;*
The University of Chicago Press for a quotation from Charles E. Rosenberg,
The Trial of the Assassin Guiteau © 1968 by The University of Chicago;
Harvard University Press for a quotation from
Learned Lady: Letters from Robert Browning to Mrs. Thomas Fitzgerald 1876–1889,
ed. Edward C. McAleer;
George Braziller, Inc. for a quotation from Chadwick Hansen,
Witchcraft at Salem © 1969 by Chadwick Hansen;
America (weekly) for passage quoted in Herman S. Hughes, "All Them Witches"
(November 9, 1968);
Sharing Magazine for quotation from John Gaynor Banks article in July, 1965, issue;
Little, Brown and Company for quotations from *The Journals of Bronson Alcott*, ed. Odell Shepard;
Holt, Rinehart and Winston, Inc. for passage from Deltus M. Edwards,
The Toil of the Arctic Seas; and
Trustees of the Longyear Foundation for permission to quote from documents and publications
of the Longyear Historical Society.

Frontispiece: 1929, © 1957, The Christian Science Publishing Society.

Published simultaneously in Canada by Holt, Rinehart
and Winston of Canada, Limited.

ISBN: 0–03–086700–2

Library of Congress Catalog Card Number: 66–14855

Published November, 1971

Third Printing April, 1972

Printed in the United States of America

Contents

Prefatory Note
Page vii

I
No. 8 Broad Street
Page 1

II
The Year of Trials
Page 29

III
Church Militant
Page 59

IV
Exit from Lynn
Page 89

V
The Faces of Janus
Page 119

VI
Pulpit and Podium
Page 151

VII
Culture and Probity
Page 181

VIII
Acclaim and Dissent
Page 213

IX
Exit from Boston
Page 245

X
The Face of Autumn
Page 273

Appendices
Page 303

Notes
Page 314

Index
Page 383

Prefatory Note

This book carries forward the story begun in *Mary Baker Eddy: The Years of Discovery*. It is independent, however, of the earlier volume. I have written it from the point of view of one encountering Mrs. Eddy for the first time in 1876 when she was still Mrs. Glover of Lynn, the little-known author of a recently published book called *Science and Health*.

The story begins as a Victorian idyll, middle-aged in cast, provincial in setting, obscure in significance. Yet by force of the plain facts it plunges quickly into critical issues. One cannot examine seriously the fifteen years of Mrs. Eddy's life that followed the publication of her first book without being brought up against the great existential questions of life and death, the self and the void—revelation, absurdity, purpose, commitment, pain.

It was a crucial period of trial and error for the Founder of Christian Science, barely hinted at in her own restrained statement in *Science and Health* (p. 39): "We must have trials and self-denials, as well as joys and victories, until all error is destroyed." At the end of it, in 1891, she was seventy years old, ripe in experience and ready to begin what by most people's reckoning would be a lifetime's work. The story of those last twenty years lies beyond the scope of the present volume, but the knowledge that they are there casts its own oblique light on "the years of trial."

This characterization of the stormy middle years of test and experiment is drawn from Mrs. Eddy's repeated references to the "trials" of the period. The word as she uses it strikes a sympathetic note to an age that values experience above dogma, experiment above security, venture above arrival. For in the lexicon of Christian Science, a trial of faith has a special significance: it is the theological equivalent of a laboratory test.

ROBERT PEEL

Boston, Massachusetts

Chapter
I

No. 8
Broad
Street

It was plain to be seen that Mrs. Godfrey of Chelsea, Massachusetts, was a descendant of Yankee sea captains who had stoutly held to their course through hurricane, blizzard, and typhoon.

Accidentally running a needle deep into her finger, she found herself with an increasingly painful infection. It could, the doctors warned her, lead to the loss of her entire arm unless she allowed them to amputate her finger. But the daughter of mariners who had braved the roaring seas around Cape Horn stood firm. Matter-of-factly she wrapped the hugely swollen finger in a homemade bandage, tried to stop the "putrefaction"[1] by applications of tar, bore the pain with stoic resignation, and carried on with her housework.

In the midst of this septic crisis an SOS arrived from Mrs. Godfrey's favorite nephew, William Nash, foreman in a shoe factory in the nearby city of Lynn. His wife was ill; he needed help, and Mrs. Godfrey rallied to the challenge. Disregarding her finger and bundling her seven-year-old daughter along with her, she hurried off to her nephew's home.

Young Nash and his wife were living on the second floor of a modest house at 8 Broad Street, Lynn.[2] At supper the first night—a meal which Mrs. Godfrey energetically set about preparing as soon as she arrived—they were joined by the owner of the house, a Mrs. Mary Baker Glover, who took her meals with the Nashes. At one point she reached over and touched Mrs. Godfrey's hand, asking what was wrong with her finger; then the conversation turned to less dispiriting subjects.

That night Mrs. Godfrey slept peacefully. When she woke in the morning, her finger was almost normal. Years later her daughter described how her mother gave a little scream, jumped out of bed, and ran into the next room in her nightgown, calling out to her nephew, "William, look at my hand!" William's laconic response was: "Guess Mrs. Glover has been trying her works on it."

To his aunt's blank question as to what *that* meant, he explained that Mrs. Glover had an incomprehensible new method of healing which she called Metaphysics or Christian Science. At the breakfast table that morning Mrs. Glover herself offered to complete the cure through her method. This involved entire reliance on God, she emphasized. Within a few days the last vestige of the difficulty had disappeared except for a slight malformation of the nail, and that too was corrected as soon as Mrs. Godfrey drew Mrs. Glover's attention to it.

The young Nashes were great admirers of their landlady-boarder and had named their four-month-old baby Flora Glover Nash in her honor.[3] But they felt no interest in her ideas and, when it came to their own ills, preferred the known evils of nineteenth-century medicine to the unknown hazards of relying on God. Thus Mrs. Nash had a doctor attending her during her sickness and little Flora had a medical nurse for her own diminutive but distressing ailments. Mrs. Godfrey took strong issue with the nurse's judgment on occasion and appealed to Mrs. Glover for support, but the latter refused to be drawn into any interference with the Nashes' private arrangements. With a few quiet words, however, she calmed the domestic squalls.[4]

To Mrs. Godfrey this was "the most wonderful woman that ever was," and from that time on she relied on her absolutely and unfalteringly for healing. But lacking the instinct to generalize from particulars, Mrs. Godfrey developed no interest in Christian Science itself, nor did she evince any great confidence in the ability of other Christian Scientists to heal. Mrs. Glover urged her to study in a class she was soon to hold, offering to teach her free of charge, but Mrs. Godfrey was satisfied with the comfortable liberalism of her own Universalist Church and declined the offer.

To her, as to her small daughter Mary, Mrs. Glover was simply an utterly unique woman with a gift of healing. When they returned to Chelsea after a month or six weeks in Lynn, she was outspoken in her new friend's praise. Her husband, George Llewellyn Godfrey, who had spent several weekends at Broad Street while she was there, shared much of his wife's enthusiasm and confidence,[5] but a sister, Mrs. Nancy Benson, who had never met Mrs. Glover, denounced her works as obvious witchcraft.

Mrs. Benson was particularly scandalized by an incident that occurred a little later. Mary Godfrey had suffered all through childhood from severe attacks of membranous croup, much to her parents' alarm. On the occasion of the next attack Mrs. Godfrey decided grimly to take the child to Lynn for healing. Wrapping her in a warm blanket she started off in a snowstorm. Mrs. Benson, shrill and Cassandra-like, accompanied her as far as the railroad station, prognosticating doom all the way.

Arrived at 8 Broad Street, the two Godfreys were met at the door by Mrs. Glover, who took in the situation at a glance. Cheerfully she told the little girl to run upstairs to the Nashes' apartment and play. That was the end of the trouble. A sort of instant certainty seems to have communicated itself to both mother and daughter, and before the latter had even reached the next floor she was healed. When George Godfrey arrived the following day to take his wife and child home, Mrs. Glover told him crisply that what really needed healing in order to prevent a recurrence of the disease was the parents' fear.[6]

There were other visits to Mrs. Glover, who would often take Mary on her lap and talk with her about matters of interest to a small girl. Occasionally the child was even allowed to come up to Mrs. Glover's little attic room where the final pages of her book *Science and Health* had been written.

"I remember," Mary Godfrey wrote years later, "being filled with awe and secret delight at being taken up there where she never allowed anyone to come." She recalled particularly the skylight which gave the room its only light and a small haircloth rocker in which Mrs. Glover would sit, rocking her in her arms.[7]

Part of Mary's childhood devotion was reserved, however, for another friend of her parents, who was soon to play a wholly unexpected role in Mrs. Glover's life. Asa Gilbert Eddy was a salesman for the Singer Sewing Machine Company. He had first become acquainted with the Godfreys several years before when he sold Mrs. Godfrey a machine, and now he was a regular visitor at their home. In later years Mary Godfrey wrote of him:

> As a child I did not take to people quickly, but was immediately won to him. Undoubtedly his own fondness for children drew me to him, for he was kind to me, was a jolly playmate in a quiet way, taking me on his knee and entertaining me with all kinds of stories. . . . There was always a sweet smile on his face and his eyes were so gentle you could not imagine him hurting anything in the world.

Though he himself had grown up on a Vermont farm and had led a dullish life since then, Asa Eddy liked to listen to the tales of nautical adventure that he heard at the Godfreys' house. George Godfrey, like his wife, was the descendant of Maine sea captains and shipowners, and before his marriage he had sailed on a brother's ship to Greenland and Iceland. His seafaring brothers and cousins would often visit the Chelsea house, swapping salty yarns to which Asa Eddy listened with silent but intense attentiveness. "Possibly," Mary wrote later, "the philosophy of these dauntless seamen appealed to him, for . . . they were fearless, courageous, honest, God-fearing men, who faced danger in the unshaken confidence that if they did their best and trusted the Lord things would come out all right."

With Mrs. Godfrey, Asa Eddy shared a special friendship. She was a well-educated woman, who had taught school for several years and put some stock in "culture." He had only a common-school education, distinguished chiefly by his cultivation of a fine Spencerian hand, but she recognized and admired both his character and his unpretentious mental honesty. After her first encounter with Mrs. Glover she urged him to go and be healed of the heart trouble that in recent years had been making it increasingly harder for him to carry on his daily work. But she also advised him to study with Mrs. Glover, apparently recognizing that he was not the sort of man who would be able to accept healing without understanding it.[8]

So Asa Eddy went—it was March, 1876—and, after two visits to Mrs. Glover, found his health so improved that he took her three-week course of instruction. The class,[9] like all of Mrs. Glover's in those years, was held in the Broad Street house, either in the little parlor she reserved for herself on the second floor or in the regular classroom downstairs.

The instruction was based on her essay or treatise entitled *The Science of Man, By Which the Sick Are Healed, Embracing Questions and Answers in Moral Science.*[10] This work had been copyrighted in 1870 when she first started teaching, but it was not actually printed until February, 1876—and then in a version greatly changed from the manuscript copies used by her earlier students. Although her book *Science and Health* had been published meanwhile, in October, 1875, it was not then used in the classroom. There the Bible and *The Science of Man* were the sole texts studied.

A brief passage from the latter gives something of the tone of Mrs. Glover's early teaching:

> In the nineteenth century I affix for all time the word, Science, to Christianity, and error to personal sense; and call the world to battle on this issue. I know the revelation and discovery of this science has arrayed mankind against me, for notwithstanding it heals the sick, etc., it dishonors the schools! But I also know it honors God, and I shall perform this my mission on earth without fear or dissimulation, for to be well done, it must be done unselfishly. . . . New positions of thought have already gained a hearing; one is, that all is matter; the other, that all is mind. Prof. Tyndall entertains the first, I the

last; let us then, according to the saying of a great general, "fight it out on this line."[11]

Asa Eddy, who had listened so quietly to tales of mariners battling the elements (while Mrs. Godfrey bustled about the parlor with cookies and hot punch), now sat in another parlor and heard the call to action. In his middle forties, unmarried, untrammeled, a mild man but not a weak one, cautious but not without an astonishing courage on occasion, he accepted the challenge with a total commitment which seems never to have wavered. Leaving behind his job, his bachelor quarters in East Boston, his earnest activities in an evangelical church, he embarked on a course that was to take him to landscapes of the mind more singular than Greenland's icy mountains.

The *Lynn Directory* for 1876 lists a new resident: "Eddy, A. G., 'Christian Scientist,' 46 Market." It was Mary Baker Eddy who later pointed out that he was the first person to so announce himself in public.

2

The big religious news of the early spring of 1876 was not that Mrs. Glover had taught one or two more people Christian Science but that the evangelist Dwight L. Moody was packing the New York Hippodrome every night and "saving" sinners by the thousand. Heaven, Moody assured his delighted listeners, was just as much a place and just as much a city as New York, Paris, or London, and it behooved them as prudent travelers to make their reservations in advance.

To the small group of Christian Scientists in Lynn, heaven (like hell) was a state of consciousness. It could be experienced here and now, Mrs. Glover explained, in proportion to one's grasp of reality. Some of her students felt they already had exchanged a good deal of hell for at least an effective glimpse of heaven. Wasn't every healing an outward evidence of the implicit structure of things, a sign of the kingdom of heaven within?

As to New York, Paris, and London, copies of *Science and Health* had at least been sent to these places, to Oxford and the Victoria Institute, to the universities of Heidelberg and Halle.[12] There were few acknowledgments in return, but one voice from another world than Lynn brought encouragement. A. Bronson Alcott, the Concord philosopher, had come to visit Mrs. Glover in January and had returned on February 16 to meet with the whole group. His journal for that day carried the entry:

> *5* P.M. *Leave for Lynn. Dr. Spofford takes me to The Falk-*
> *land House, where I take tea, and meet, afterwards, Mrs. Glover's*
> *circle at her house in Broad Street. The evening is passed in*
> *discussing metaphysical problems. I find her followers thoughtful*
> *and devout, without cant or egotism, students of life rather than*
> *of books, and a promising company. The slight touch of mysti-*
> *cism mingling with their faith renders them the more interesting,*
> *and Mrs. Glover's influence appears to be of the happiest char-*
> *acter. Our conversation continues till near 11 o'clock. I sleep at*
> *The Falkland House.*[13]

There were also reviews of *Science and Health* appearing here
and there, some of them surprisingly favorable in view of the radical
novelty of the book's ideas, not to mention the difficulty of its language. To those that were less than favorable Mrs. Glover wrote
vigorous, even peppery, rejoinders, for she was by no means passive
in the face of criticism. At some of the Broad Street meetings there
was lively discussion of the issues raised by the critics, particularly by
speakers in local pulpits.

One minister, for instance, declared of *Science and Health:*

> *This is a singular book. It is like nothing else ever written*
> *. . . is attracting the attention of marvel seekers and excitable*
> *persons. . . . [The author] seems to believe that she knows more*
> *about the "Science of Soul" than all other people of the earth,*
> *because she professes to have God for her soul, and to be His*
> *idea.*[14]

Mrs. Glover, in actual fact, maintained that God was the Soul or
Principle of all men, not in any neo-Platonic sense that would make
human personality a debased expression of Deity but in the Pauline
sense that "in him [God] we live, and move, and have our being."
The ministerial critic made no attempt to understand or even note
such distinctions. Let good ladies who wrote metaphysical disquisitions
remember that older and wiser masculine heads had long ago settled
the intricate questions of soul and immortality and a God who was
a single substance but three persons. It was one thing for Thomas
Aquinas to divide theology into two disciplines—Divine Science and
the Science of God—and to write of God as Principle. It was quite
a different matter for Mrs. Glover of Lynn to set forth a Science of
Soul and to describe the essential relation of God to man as that
of Principle to idea.[15]

A similar tone of slightly exasperated masculine amusement is
to be found in a criticism of *Science and Health* by a Swedenborgian

clergyman of Boston. "Its style is the oracular," he writes; "the author does not give opinions nor elaborate theories, but announces laws and principles. This saves the reader a great deal of trouble though it imposes a severe tax upon his faith." With a kind of ironic generosity he concedes that the author may be "a great and good healing medium," but there are "healing mediums in Boston to be reckoned by the score." Then, having consigned her to that lowly status, he advises her "to devote her remaining years to healing the sick, and leave the writing of books upon philosophy and religion to others."[16]

Mrs. Glover disregarded the advice. When the second edition of *Science and Health* appeared in 1878, it would include a chapter, "Reply to a Clergyman," which was her answer to her clerical critics. A century later when they and the healing mediums of Boston had long passed into oblivion, the chapter—in revised, expanded, and generalized form and renamed "Some Objections Answered"—would be analyzed in doctoral dissertations and studied by readers in Polish, Dutch, Greek, Norwegian, Portuguese.

Mrs. Glover was in fact determined to withdraw from healing and devote her entire time to writing and teaching. This was especially necessary, and especially difficult, since *Science and Health* was now drawing inquiries and requests for help from other parts of the country. The great need was to teach more people who could become practitioners, but while there were many readers who wanted healing, there were only a few who were ready to undertake the discipline of class study.

Then there were some like "H. Dexter, M. D." of Dundee, New York, who had written her after reading her book: "I have demonstrated in a number of instances. I have cured myself of a chronic disease of long standing and of an acute inflammation of the eyes."[17] Dr. Dexter wanted to come to Lynn to study with her, as did his friend Colonel J. M. Letts, a former consul at Haiti and present justice of the peace at Dundee, but neither was able to get away from his home duties.[18] While Mrs. Glover greatly reduced the price of instruction in view of the continuing financial depression in the country and taught many students free of charge, she still had only five in her class in June, 1876, and seven in the following October.[19]

Yet by her own scale of judgment it was not numbers that counted,[20] and the mood of her small group was one of boundless determination. Something of this mood is suggested in a letter from George McLaren of Boston to

. . . *my Dear Sister Mary of Lynn, Author of a* Wonderful Book . . . *making strange statements, causing poor bodies to*

cringe & writhe with sledge hammer blows . . . down comes
the metaphysical sword, cutting & slashing. . . . And you have
thrown down the gauntlet to Prof. Tyndall. And you have called
the world to battle on this issue. Who is to be your Armour
bearer in this battle of Life?[21]

Asa Eddy might well have asked the same question as he looked
around at the veteran students in Mrs. Glover's circle—simple people,
for the most part, drawn from the shoe industry of Lynn.

First there was Daniel Harrison Spofford, the most successful-
practitioner next to Mrs. Glover herself.[22] Spofford was a thoughtful,
idealistic man in his middle thirties, deeply devoted to Mrs. Glover
and ready to accept any responsibility she laid on him. On the face
of it, Spofford might well have been both armor bearer and heir
apparent.

Then there was fresh-faced young George Barry, who had recently
become engaged to another student, Florence Cheney, with Mrs.
Glover's blessing. The blessing was essential to him, for his horizon
had been totally bounded by his relation to Mrs. Glover in the five
years since he first studied with her. When Bronson Alcott, who took
rather a fancy to the young man, asked him how old he was, he
promptly replied, "Five years old, sir." The remark was a tribute, but
it also revealed something a little unformed and childish about Barry.
After a visit he made to Alcott at Concord, the latter in his journal
described Barry as an "interesting young gentleman, bearing favorable
testimony to the faith and purity of the school," but gave him several
copies of *The Journal of Speculative Philosophy* for the improvement
of his mind.[23]

Samuel Putnam Bancroft, often called Putney, was an intelligent
young businessman whose outspoken common sense comes across in
his later accounts of the period. But although he had brought his
younger brother Henry into the ranks and had made a brief attempt
to set up as a full-time practitioner, he lacked the stamina and perhaps
the audacity to outface the storms that lay ahead.

Two women students who were successful in the healing practice
but unremarkable in the qualities of leadership were Miss Dorcas
Rawson and her sister, Mrs. Miranda Rice. Among the remaining
students, new and old, none was of notably high caliber. They were
leaners more than leaders—more, even, than followers. Through Mrs.
Glover life had taken on for them the dimension of miracle, of
boundless possibility; but they were not, one would have said, the
material from which a new religious force could be forged.

Even so, Mrs. Glover made the best of what she had. On July 4,

1876, when the whole country was in a delirium of patriotic fervor over the centennial celebration of American independence, she took a step toward welding her small band into an effective group. A year earlier they had formed themselves into a loose organization with a president, secretary, and treasurer. More than a year later they would adopt a formal constitution and rules of order. At this midpoint she found an appropriate name for them: "The Christian Scientist Association."

Here was the nucleus of the organization which in ten years would have grown to national proportions. It both belonged and stood in contrast to the America of 1876, of the Whiskey Ring and Belknap scandals then shaking Washington, of Custer's greatly overrated last stand and the overblown start of the Buffalo Bill legend, of the simplistic Moody-Sankey revivals and convoluted Hayes-Tilden election. In its Lynn beginnings, Christian Science could easily be accounted one more transient phenomenon of the Gilded Age and Mrs. Glover be written off as a lively but minor period figure.

When she managed, for instance, to get down to the Centennial Exhibition in Philadelphia before it closed on November 10, her enthusiasm overflowed in an article which she described as being composed of jottings from her centennial journal—one of the fugitive pennings in prose and verse she contributed to the Lynn papers from time to time. The comments were exactly what might have been expected of an exuberantly patriotic lady just back from the big show of the century. "Having returned to gushing," she wrote, "we deem it prudent to use our pen for a safety-valve."[24] The article was obviously just that, and it gave not a hint of the reserve powers at her command.

Earlier in the autumn the great T. H. Huxley, speaking at the inaugural of the Johns Hopkins University, had taken a critical look at America's future:

> *I cannot say that I am in the slightest degree impressed by your bigness, or your material resources, as such. Size is not grandeur, and territory does not make a nation. The great issue, about which hangs a true sublimity, and the terror of overhanging fate, is what are you going to do with all these? What is to be the end to which these are to be the means?*[25]

Huxley, the popular apostle of nineteenth-century science, saw the answer in a system of education that would foster the scientific spirit in all aspects of life. In the free air of scientific experiment, in the white light of scientific truth, men would become as gods. Freed from inhibiting religious superstitions, they would seek salvation by works and justification by verification.

Mrs. Glover, in a "Hymn of Science" published in the *Lynn Transcript* a week after her centennial effusion, likewise hailed Science as the Saviour—but it was an eternal rather than an empirical science, a truth to be lived rather than a methodology to be worshiped. Science as the revelation of divine law was both insight and power, the Word made flesh, and her poem asked with deceptive simplicity:

> Saw ye my Saviour? heard ye the glad sound?
> Felt ye the power of the Word?
> 'Twas the Truth that made us free,
> And was found by you and me,
> In the Life and the Love that are God. . . .[26]

Later she revised the last line of the stanza to read, "In the life and the love of our Lord." The change in wording from the metaphysically absolute to the historically concrete is significant. Science, as generally understood, is antihistorical, in the sense that it seeks validation in present experience rather than in past authority. Christian Science, as Mrs. Glover understood it, required both.

Either way, however, the poem spoke with an assurance hardly to be anticipated among lady versifiers in the Lynn press.

3

Mrs. Glover, to say the least, was a resilient woman. Widowed in 1844 after only six months of marriage, permanently parted from her son a few years later, unhappily married a second time to a well-meaning but irresponsible man whom she later divorced, she still had a sort of buoyant femininity at fifty-five. Most people assumed that she was many years younger.

"She was a very attractive woman," wrote a young man whose cousin occupied part of the house at Broad Street a little later, "with a lovely face and a very good figure."[27] The cousin herself described Mrs. Glover as always beautifully dressed, often with flowers pinned to her gown, and added that she never seemed to be without flowers in her sitting room.[28] Indeed, her one extravagance seems to have been her patronage of the local florist.[29] In the summer she sometimes took refuge on a little balcony at the side of the house where morning glories and moonflowers made a natural screen and she could look out briefly on the world through stacks of calla lilies.[30]

The room on the first floor where she received students and inquirers was decorated in plain gray paper with gold cornices, a crimson carpet covering the floor, white lace draperies looped back over high gilt arms at the windows, black walnut furniture, and of course vases of cut flowers.[31] These may have been the "Parian marble vases" which little Grace Choate, who lived in the house for a time, considered a mark of wealth "and perhaps more beautiful than they really were."[32]

Eleven-year-old Grace, her mother, and her infant sister were among the tenants at 8 Broad Street who came and went with the speed and mobility already characteristic of American life.[33] Mrs. Glover, she wrote later, greatly loved the baby and "would come downstairs and hold her in her arms. She seemed hungry for children and the affection children expressed."[34] This love of children is a constant theme throughout her life.

It is illustrated in an incident recorded by a Mrs. Helen M. Grenier who, as a small girl in Lynn, was seized one day with agonizing pain. Because of an intense fear of doctors she tried to conceal the pain from her mother, who nevertheless noted her pallor and told her that she must go to the doctor the next day if she was no better.

The little girl had often noticed the sign at 8 Broad Street which read,

Mary B. Glover's
Christian Scientists' Home

and she had heard that Mrs. Glover was a doctor. Childlike she reasoned: "If I must have a doctor I will go to the lady on Broad Street. The sign shows she is a Christian, and a Christian—even if she is a doctor—wouldn't hurt a little girl."[35] So off she took herself to the room with the crimson carpet and the gilt cornices where a pleasant-faced lady chatted with her a minute or two, closed her eyes for a few more minutes, then took her hand and said, "If you are not better tomorrow, come and see me again." Nothing was said about Christian Science either by Mrs. Glover or by Asa Eddy, who met the child at the door, but the pain was gone and the child ran all the way home. "I was filled with wonder," she wrote later, "at the loving kindness of the people who were so good to a little girl."

Yet many of the reminiscences of this period speak also of a certain reserve Mrs. Glover had, a reserve that could sometimes amount to severity. A Mrs. Mary Gatchell who, with her husband, moved into the ground-floor apartment in April, 1876, many years later made the ambivalent comment: "She was a crank, but the purest-minded woman I ever knew." Asked to explain the epithet, Mrs. Gatchell replied that Mrs. Glover wanted the house kept unreasonably quiet for her writing and urged her to keep the neighborhood boys from climbing on the back fence and pounding.[36]

Whether this pounding was the expression of high spirits or of neighborhood sentiment against Mrs. Glover is uncertain, but what is clear is that Lynn gossip did its best to bring her into disrepute. For a woman to preach, lecture, write for the newspapers, challenge the doctors and the clergy, claim a new religious revelation and a new scientific discovery—all this was in itself enough to make her an object of suspicion to cautious Yankees. But for a divorced woman to do these things—even though the husband had been the guilty party—put her clearly outside the pale of provincial acceptability. The touch of the miraculous about her activities was the final invitation to every extravagance of speculation.

Mrs. Glover was charged with rouging her cheeks and dyeing her hair, with teaching "free love" and practicing witchcraft, with being a loose woman, a despoiler of homes, a medium, a fraud, a termagant. The coming and going of men students at 8 Broad Street was given the most sinister possible significance; the respectable women in her circle were said to be held to her by a sort of hypnotic spell. It is small wonder that credulous parents hurried their children past her house as though it were a den of arcane iniquity.[37]

It required courage to live at 8 Broad Street then, according to Grace Choate. Grace's mother—described by her as a strong Episcopalian, intelligent, broad-minded, and given to original thinking—stood up vigorously for Mrs. Glover against the aspersions and innuendos of her friends.

Deeply though Mrs. Glover herself felt the hurt of such criticism, she tried to make light of it and on one occasion remarked laughingly to another tenant, Mrs. Elvira Newhall, "Of course I believe in free love; I love everyone."[38] But the degree to which such charges distressed her is evident from the extraordinary vehemence with which she launched a newspaper attack on Victoria Woodhull when that flamboyant exponent of free love, spiritism, and the marriage of Marx and Wall Street lectured in Lynn.[39]

If Mrs. Glover herself was an object of intense local interest, the same could not be said of her book *Science and Health*. Six months after its publication, not many more than two hundred copies out of a printing of one thousand had been sold. George Barry and Dorcas Rawson had been taking the book from door to door, trying to interest people in it, but with only limited success. Daniel Spofford was in charge of advertising and publicity, but most of his time was necessarily given to his own large healing practice, which he carried on not only in Lynn but also in Newburyport and Amesbury farther to the north.

As soon as Asa Gilbert Eddy started in to heal and proved his effectiveness as a practitioner, Mrs. Glover suggested that Spofford turn over to him a large part of his practice and devote his own time to promoting the book. This was done, and on April 11, 1876, Spofford took over the "Christian Scientist Publishing Company"— the rather grandiose name used to designate young Barry and another student, Elizabeth Newhall, who had jointly paid for the publication of the first edition.[40]

Six days later a legal agreement was drawn up between Mrs. Glover and Spofford by which he rashly guaranteed the sale of not less than one thousand copies annually and agreed to pay the author, who up to now had received no royalties, ten per cent of the net list price.

In a speech the preceding winter Susan B. Anthony had argued: "Women must be educated out of their unthinking acceptance of financial dependence on man into mental and economic independence. . . . Whoever controls work and wages controls morals."[41] And in her chapter on marriage in *Science and Health*, Mrs. Glover, drawing on her own unhappy experience, had written:

> *If a dissolute husband deserts his wife, it should not follow that the wronged and perchance impoverished woman cannot collect her own wages, or enter into agreements, hold real estate, deposit funds, or surely claim her own offspring free from his right of interference.*

But it was still hard for a man to accept direction in business matters from a woman. Mrs. Glover wrote Spofford that what he most needed in his work for the book was love, meekness, and charity. "These things would increase your success."[42] But Spofford was more concerned with the practical economics of the problem and with the fact that the book still did not sell.

A more immediately disruptive effect of the new arrangement was the rebellion of young George Barry, who had been used to having Mrs. Glover call on him for all the small services—and some of the large—in which she needed masculine assistance. He had apparently taken the gradual ascendancy of Spofford with good grace, but Asa Eddy was the catalyst that caused him suddenly to "chemicalize"—to use Mrs. Glover's word for emotional reactions which she believed to be provoked by developments and demands beyond the individual's immediate ability to cope with.[43]

Barry, who appears to have seen himself in the role of her gallant champion, was now confronted with the fact that the arrival of a rank newcomer was turning everything upside down and leaving him only a minor part to play in a mounting drama. Almost overnight the young man decamped with his fiancée, to reappear a year later in a role of active hostility.

4

There was no mistaking the fact that Mrs. Glover was increasingly relying on the support of Asa Eddy, whom she called Gilbert. Spofford she addressed as Harry from his middle name of Harrison, but after the custom of those *laissez-faire* days[44] the two men were commonly referred to in the little group as "Dr." Eddy and "Dr." Spofford.

About this time Mrs. Glover gave evidence of feeling rather keenly the burden of her responsibilities as well as certain mental undercurrents which she believed to be disturbing the peace of the group. As early as February 24, 1876, she had written her cousin Hattie Baker in Boston, "I feel the weight of sick folks terribly since my book is at work,"[45] but this was only the cloud as big as a man's hand which portended the storm to come.

On July 14 she wrote the same cousin that recently she had had a "violent seizure" and had fallen unconscious. Gilbert Eddy had been called and immediately had brought her out of it. He was so "calm, clear and strong, and so kind," that she felt a sudden upwelling of affection for him. "Never before had I seen his real character, so tender and yet so controlling. Hattie, you would change your views of him if you were to read him spiritually."[46]

Nevertheless Spofford at this time still seemed in some ways the more promising student of the two, and she wavered between her reliance on Gilbert Eddy's character as a man and Spofford's promise as a metaphysician.[47] To the latter she wrote on October 1:

> *My joy at having* one *living student, after these dozen years of struggle, toil and defeat, you at present cannot understand, but will know at a future time when the whole labor is left with you. . . . God bless you; and He will bless us and carry us through. Let us lean there only; the students make all their mistakes leaning on me.*[48]

At this time Mrs. Glover was working on a revision of *Science and Health* and considering the possibility of having a picture of Noah's ark stamped on the cover of the new edition. The symbolism of the ark seems to have been much in her mind during the next few months, as well as in Spofford's. It was not inapt, for a flood tide of scientific materialism was inundating the religious assumptions of the past, and she seems to have realized how presumptuous her claims would seem to the spreading skeptical spirit—as well as to an implacable but frightened orthodoxy. It was one thing for philosophical idealists, Hegelian or Platonic, to challenge the reality of matter; this could be accommodated as theory by the scientist and the theologian, even when rejected by them as fact. But to put it forth as a proposition with radical practical consequences—as a revelation that included both a coherent metaphysic and a successful therapy—was to defy equally the established order of nature and the traditional faith in special miracles. For the claim to be advanced by a woman with no philosophic credentials made it all the worse. There were times when Mrs. Glover seemed to confront not merely the establishment of her day but the current of modern history as it rushed in angry haste toward total materialism.

On October 22 she wrote Spofford:

> *The mercury of my mind is rising as the world's temperature of thought heats and the little book "sweet in the mouth" but severe and glorious in its proof, is about to go forth. . . . But my student, in my lonely chamber I read the coming storm. I feel it gathering. . . .*
>
> Press on; *You know not the smallest portion, comparatively, of your ability in science. Measure your stature in Christ; do not count on your powers as man, and do not rob God by denying them. . . .*
>
> *I feel like a tired and wounded soldier of the cross, taken to the rear; but my wounds are enlivening my soldiers, I do believe; if so, God give me more—and teach me all I need— and make me more of a blessing; poor, weak and unworthy, on one hand, august and glorious on the other! Pray for me dear student.*[49]

Although she could write to Spofford with this sort of intimacy, Mrs. Glover reacted sharply from the element of idolatry in his affection. "Don't make a Dagon of me as Dr. Spofford does," she warned Putney Bancroft on one occasion.[50]

While Spofford's feeling may have been largely the expression of an intense human idealism, there was another element in it, and a surprising one. Despite the disparity in their ages—he was twenty years younger—Mrs. Glover was by all accounts a very attractive woman, a fact sufficient in itself to explain the speculations of the Lynn gossips. In Spofford's case, he gave them something to cluck about. His marriage having broken up some years before, he brought suit for divorce in 1876, charging his wife with repeated adultery. There is evidence[51] that he hoped to be able to offer his hand to

Mrs. Glover in marriage as well as in more intimate support of her work. But when the case came up in court in November, one of the witnesses suddenly and inexplicably changed her testimony and he lost his suit.[52]

Mrs. Glover felt that there were obscure influences at work which she did not understand.[53] Spofford, in an emotional turmoil, showed a growing resentment at the way she turned to Gilbert Eddy for support.[54] Finally the situation reached an unexplained crisis on December 30 when he received from her a letter written in evident anguish of mind and body:

> *Dr. Spofford won't you exercise* reason *and let me live or will you* kill *me? Your mind is just what has brought on my relapse and I shall never* recover *if you do not govern yourself and* TURN YOUR THOUGHTS *wholly away from me. . . . It is a* hidden *foe that is at work read Science and Health page 193 1st par.*
>
> No student *nor mortal has tried to have you leave me that I know of. Dr. Eddy has tried to have you stay you are in a* mistake, *it is God and not man that has separated us and for the reason* I begin *to learn. Do not think of returning to me again I shall never again trust a* man *they know not what manner of temptations assail. God produces the separation and I submit to it so must you. There is no cloud between us but the way you set me up for a Dagon is wrong and now I implore you to turn forever from this error of personality and go alone* to God *as I have taught you.*[55]

Into this unhappy situation stepped Gilbert Eddy with a humble but earnest proposal of marriage.[56] In later years Mrs. Eddy told a student of a dream she had that night after going to bed with a feeling that she must rely wholly on God:

> *She seemed to be standing on one side of a beautiful field of wheat. As she was rejoicing in its promise, dark swinish forms seemed to move underneath it; their uprooting instincts were destroying thought. She could not cross the field as she intended. Terror and abhorrence chained her to the spot. Then on the other side of the field she saw Gilbert Eddy's manly form. "Come on, Mary," he said, "I will help you."*[57]

In the morning she accepted him.

The astonished Spofford, the day after receiving her long letter of dismissal, was handed by Gilbert Eddy the following short missive:

Dear Student,

For reasons best known to myself I have changed my views in regard to marrying and ask you to hand this note to the Unitarian Clergyman and please wait for his answer.

Your Teacher

M.B.G.[58]

The next day the Unitarian clergyman, the Reverend Samuel B. Stewart, united Mary Baker Glover and Asa Gilbert Eddy in marriage. The date was January 1, 1877.[59] Many years later Putney Bancroft wrote:

> *I believe she married, thinking she had found a man who would be of great help to her, not in one, but in many ways, in this labor. . . . She had been sought in marriage by several since obtaining a divorce from Dr. Patterson . . . but had refused, thinking her work would be retarded, hoping her students would afford her the assistance needed; but now that her pupils, one after another, had failed her, and her burdens were heavy and hard to bear, she thought it the part of wisdom to accept the offer of this good man, to share them with her. As one of those who failed her, could I blame her?*[60]

Some of the students, however, did.

5

Four weeks later, after recovering from their own surprise, the students held a surprise party for the Eddys. The occasion turned out to be an interesting mixture of social jollity and metaphysical gravity. A newspaper account in the *Lynn Reporter* concluded:

> *One of the most elaborate gifts in silver was a cake basket. A bouquet of crystallized geranium leaves of rare varieties encased in glass was charming, but the presents were too fine to permit a selection. Mr. S. P. Bancroft gave an opening address —a very kind and graceful speech, which was replied to by Mrs. Glover-Eddy with evident satisfaction. . . . The happy evening was closed with reading the Bible, remarks on the Scriptures, etc. Wedding cake and lemonade were served, and those from out of town took the cars for home.*[61]

Nevertheless there were murmurings among some of the students. A woman who was at that time on the outer fringe of the group wrote later:

This [disapproval] was no new thing, for these earlier students objected to nearly every movement Mrs. Eddy made along progressive lines . . . and this flutter of dissension appeared under the least . . . provocation of progress, or reform. . . . My own thought of both Dr. and Mrs. Eddy was started with a personal prejudice against them, tinctured with a fear that Dr. Eddy might absorb Mrs. Eddy's ways of doing and of teaching into his own personal views or divert her work for the cause.[62]

This fear, which was doubtless shared by others, was soon put to rest. Gilbert Eddy gave up his private practice at once and devoted himself wholeheartedly to helping his wife. This extended even to his taking over the domestic duties, for he had been brought up in a farm family where the boys and girls alike had learned to cook and sew and look after themselves.[63] But although he might run the household, his role in the group turned out clearly to be that of Mrs. Eddy's lieutenant rather than of her mentor.

According to those who knew him at that time Gilbert Eddy possessed an equable temperament and a certain quiet strength. Less charitable later writers have called him a dull little man. Everyone seems to be agreed that he gave his wife total support in her decisions, although he apparently did not hesitate to advance his own views in discussion and when she scolded the students for what she considered to be a dereliction of duty, he would sometimes remind her with a glint of amusement, "Mary, they are not all you."[64]

He could also be stubborn as a mule on occasion. *Science and Health* frowned on the recording of ages, and Gilbert Eddy took this with a literalness that could not be shaken. In a letter twenty years later Mrs. Eddy wrote: "My last husband in a humorous way gentle but firm as his character, declined to answer legal authority on this question, and finally the magistrate laughed and gave it up."[65] She may have referred to his procuring a marriage license, when the clerk ended by putting down forty for the age of both bride and groom.[66]

Two highly subjective descriptions by students who knew them during these years throw light on the quality of emotional loyalty that each inspired. Both these students were young men at the time, both were later separated from Mrs. Eddy by difference of opinion or circumstance, and both wrote these descriptions in later life after years of separation.

The first is of Mrs. Eddy:

She was a little above average height, well-formed but slender. Her hair was very dark and her pale complexion presented a marked contrast. Her most prominent features were the eyes, dark blue with a wonderful lustre, but sad, very sad at times, yet with a glory shining through. . . . I can see now it was the shining through of soul, a striving to give birth to secrets of great moment, while lamenting over the unwillingness of those whom she loved to receive her message. . . . I should say she was naturally joy-loving and light-hearted, but the desertion of her friends and relatives had saddened her.[67]

The second is of Gilbert Eddy:

He was of light florid complexion and had large blue seriously expressive eyes whose liquid light inspired one with the trustworthiness of the man, the deep and abiding purity of the hidden fires of his nature. . . . The hermit-like life he had been compelled through circumstances to lead before coming into Christian Science happily had not confirmed him in stoicism, for he greatly enjoyed congenial company and was especially fond of young people's society and pleasures. . . . In his class and public lectures he seemed to convey the impression that it was more important to understand God than to agree with his personal presentation of the subject.[68]

Two days after the marriage Mrs. Eddy had written Spofford, "I have done what I deem the best thing that could be done under the circumstances, and feel sure I can teach my husband up to a higher usefulness, to purity, and the higher development of all his *latent noble* qualities of head and heart."[69] The evidence suggests that Gilbert Eddy developed considerably during the next few years. He may never have had the personal and intellectual flair of Spofford, but it is hard to see how Mrs. Eddy could have got through the critical period that followed without the qualities of head and heart he brought to her support.

Something of the uneasy situation that still prevailed is apparent in a letter Spofford wrote her in February:

I told the Dr. I should like to see you perhaps ten minutes . . . but your reply to that request indicates that I am too repulsive for you to endure my presence[;] if such is the case certainly you cannot wish me to go into practice . . . but I do propose by a cultivation of Christian virtues and an understanding of "Science and Health" to attain unto the example set before [me] although you perhaps will think [that] is a long distance off. I acknowledge it and let me say for now and all time that whoever speaks against you is and has been my enemy that your foes are my foes and I wish this damnable place was sunk. If you have a husband that

*will make you happy from the bottom of my heart I say thank
God for none need help and comfort more than my teacher; it is
true I did hold you as a personal God and my idol had to be
torn away. . . . I also had a* fear *that* mesmerism *had been used to
produce certain recent results and can you wonder at a momentary hatred? I felt that I should like to sink from out of existence for I knew if such had been the case Truth might perhaps
again be buried beneath the accumulating dust of centuries by
the stopping of your labors. . . . The* world *may love a Judas
better than a Jesus but I do not intend that it shall love me.*[70]

The differences were patched up. Gilbert Eddy turned over his
practice at Newburyport and vicinity to Spofford, and Mrs. Eddy again
wrote to the latter in a tone of confidence and appreciation as she
pushed forward her plans for a revised edition of *Science and Health.*

In February, 1877, she taught a small class which she thought
might be her last one, as she hoped to have Gilbert Eddy take over
the future teaching.[71] For his aid in this purpose she had a stenographic
report of the class sessions made, but the report so failed to catch their
spirit, she felt,[72] that ever afterward she forbade the taking of any
notes whatever in her classes.

Just as the spirit of her teaching escaped the "chemicalizing"
stenographer's busy squiggles, so the deeper currents of Mrs. Eddy's
life seem all but lost to view in the welter of small harassments and
dismal trivia which arose about this period. One of her later critics has
written, "The great ideas of God, of immortality, of the soul, of a life
penetrated by Christianity, were never far from her mind."[73] She had
need of them. Putney Bancroft noted that her favorite hymn in those
years was to the effect that when the winds and waves are raging on the
upper ocean there is settled calm and quiet in the depths below.[74] This,
he said, she considered emblematic of her life. Certainly there was no
want of squalls on the surface.

In March, George Barry brought suit against her for $2,700 and
secured an attachment on the house at 8 Broad Street. His bill of
particulars itemized the various services rendered during his five years
of discipleship, years when he had called her "mother" and had been
eager to fill the place of her absent son.

Chief among these services was the copying of various manuscripts,
including early drafts of *Science and Health,* but among other things
he listed running errands for her, carrying a bucket of coal upstairs,
"aiding in buying and caring for the place 8 Broad St. aiding in selection of carpets & furniture; helping to move, putting down carpets etc.
and working in the garden."[75] In her appearance on the witness stand,

Mrs. Eddy added ironically that he had also bought her a bottle of ink and had taken her for walks for which she had not paid. She further testified that she had healed him of tuberculosis, had reduced his tuition by half (although he later insisted on paying her the full amount), and had made him the chief beneficiary of her will. He had begged, she testified, to be allowed to copy her manuscripts so that he could become more familiar with them.

His bill of particulars makes melancholy reading in the light of a poem he had addressed to her several years earlier:

> O, mother mine, God grant I ne'er forget,
> Whatever be my grief or what my joy,
> The unmeasured, unextinguishable debt
> I owe to thee, but find my sweet employ
> Ever through thy remaining days to be
> To thee as faithful as thou wast to me.

The case was to drag on for more than two years, with a final judgment which awarded Barry $350. Since it was highly doubtful that any of his services had been performed with the expectation of money payment, the reward was limited to his services as copyist. It is hard not to believe that the factor which goaded him into bringing suit in March, 1877, was the intolerable thought of Gilbert Eddy's new stewardship of a household where he himself had laid the carpets, hung the pictures, and carried up coal for the fire.

6

Mrs. Eddy was pushing ahead meanwhile with her revision of *Science and Health*, hampered not only by the Barry suit but also by a mental struggle she only half understood. In this phase of development she felt acutely the sufferings of those who looked to her in a personal sort of way for healing. It seemed to her that, instead of leaning on the Science she had taught them, her students and their patients were too often looking to her spiritual vitality to save them and were seeking to draw on it without telling her. This constituted a species of robbery, in her view, and her letters of that period are filled with extraordinary anguish, which she attributed to this cause as well as to persecution by hostile minds.

To Mrs. Eddy consciousness was primary and matter was a false mode of consciousness—the way in which the human mind represented to itself symbolically its present sense of reality, substance, and energy. The body, like everything material, was a construct of consciousness, but Mrs. Eddy held this view on the basis of experience more than of theory. The primacy of the spiritual, as expressed in the phenomenon of Christian healing, was a fact of being rather than a philosophical postulate or a mystical presentiment. She arrived at her position not by way of Berkeley or Fichte, Parmenides or Shankara, but through the concrete example of the New Testament Jesus, for whom matter was an impossible limit on spiritual power. Viewed in this perspective, the whole material creation could be recognized as a limited and faulty interpretation of reality, rather than reality itself. The real locus of experience was the mind. There it was that the crucial battles must be fought between reality and appearance, understanding and belief.

It was blind belief, Mrs. Eddy held, that so often called out for help and then resisted the enlightenment that would dispossess it of its illusions as well as its vexations. This is an irony familiar to every psychologist and educator, but it leaped into central importance as soon as all human experience was seen as the externalization of conscious and unconscious thought. Attitudes of mind that might be merely annoying in a world posited on matter, or physical causation, could become suddenly of gravest import in a world where mental energy was recognized as determinative.

Here again Jesus was the operative example of a man who moved in a universe of wholly mental forces. There was, for instance, the occasion on which he asked, "Who touched me?" after the woman with an issue of blood had touched the hem of his garment and had been healed. The rather scornful common-sense objection of his disciples, "The multitude throng thee, and sayest thou, Who touched me?" missed the point, Mrs. Eddy held. As she explained it, he was responding to a mental call rather than to a physical touch.

At a deeper level, even the crucifixion of the flesh was for Jesus the objectification of a mental struggle—the life-and-death struggle between his recognition of Spirit as reality and what she would later call "the atheism of matter."[76] In the revision of *Science and Health* which she was then preparing, Mrs. Eddy wrote of the lonely fight at Gethsemane:

> *In the garden night-walk, that hour of gloom and glory, the utter error of supposed life in matter, its pain, ignorance, superstition, malice and hate, reached [Jesus] in their fullest sense. His students slept. "Can you not watch with me one hour?" was the supplication of their great spiritual Teacher, but receiving no response to this last human yearning, he turned forever away from earth to heaven, from sense to Soul, and from man to God. . . . The weight of mind bearing on him at that hour from the throng of disbelievers in the great Principle for which he was*

crucified, weighed heavily. . . . The world's hatred of Truth, caused that agony, harder to bear than his cross up the hill of grief.[77]

Another part of the Bible to which she turned increasingly at this period was the twelfth chapter of Revelation. In the great apocalyptic drama of the woman clothed with the sun, the dragon who stood by to devour her child as soon as it was born, the man-child caught up to heaven and the mother driven into the wilderness to be persecuted by the dragon, she found a revealing metaphor of a timeless spiritual phenomenon. Christianity at its deepest level of insight had always emphasized the resistance of entrenched materialism to every new influx of spiritual light which threatened the ancient hegemony of darkness.[78] To see the trials of her own experience within this impersonal framework was a source of evident and deepening comfort to Mrs. Eddy.[79]

After Lucretia Brown, one of Spofford's patients, went into convulsions on April 13 and "was not expected to live, but came out of it saying she felt perfectly well," Mrs. Eddy wrote Spofford, "I thought at the time if she was not 'born again' the Mother would die in her labors."[80] The next day she wrote him from Boston:

> *This hour of my departure I . . . write you a line to say I am at length driven into the wilderness. Everything needs me . . . the book lies waiting but those who* call on me mentally *in suffering are in belief killing me. . . . If the students will continue to think of me and call on me I shall at* last *defend myself and this will be to cut them off from me utterly in a spiritual sense by a bridge they cannot pass over. . . . I am going* far away *and shall remain until you all do your part and give me some better prospect.*[81]

The next five weeks she and Gilbert Eddy spent at Fairhaven, Connecticut, the home of Gilbert's brother Washington, their address unknown to the students. Yet an incomprehensible shadow still seemed to hang over Mrs. Eddy. She worked a little on a "Key to the Scriptures" to be added to *Science and Health*—although it was not added until six years later—and wrote to Spofford about business details connected with publishing the long-deferred second edition. But when she returned to Lynn toward the end of May, nothing seemed any better within or without.

Then on May 30 the storm broke.

The occasion was a letter she had sent Spofford outlining the terms on which the new edition was to be published. "If you conclude not to carry the work forward on the terms named," she had written, "it will have to go out of edition as I can do no more for it, and I believe this hour is to try my students who think they have the cause at heart."[82]

Spofford's reply started off baldly: "Mrs. Eddy." *Science and Health,* he announced, had been written by inspiration and Mrs. Eddy had "no more right to walk over it rough-shod" than had anyone else. The world was suffering from lack of the revised edition:

> It is not [just] healing a few sick or teaching a dozen students a year but the preparing of the "ark" for the saving of God's people. Nineteen months since the book was first issued and not corrected yet . . . and the "writing on the wall" is . . . "you have proven yourself unworthy to be the standard bearer of Christian Science," and God will remove from you the means for carrying on this work. . . . I consider that I have a perfect right to appoint meetings, or place in practice those you have taught. . . . I suggest that you give that book and the copyright unconditionally to some one, any one; and see if God will not prosper it. . . . You have said "if you only had two to stand by you you would carry this cause." I propose to carry it alone expecting no one but God to stand by me.
>
> Daniel
Lamentations IV, 6, 7, 8[83]

In the letter he had written her back in February explaining the temporary disaffection he had felt at the time of her marriage, he had asked, ". . . can you wonder at a momentary hatred?" Something more than a momentary hatred seems visible in the ferocity of the epigraph he chose from Lamentations:

> For the punishment of the iniquity of the daughter of my people is greater than the punishment of the sin of Sodom, that was overthrown as in a moment, and no hands stayed on her. Her Nazarites were purer than snow, they were whiter than milk, they were more ruddy in body than rubies, their polishing was of sapphire: their visage is blacker than a coal; they are not known in the streets: their skin cleaveth to their bones; it is withered, it is become like a stock.

The differences over the terms of publication seem inadequate to explain the violence of his reaction.[84] Ironically enough, if Spofford had accepted Mrs. Eddy's terms and had remained her publisher through subsequent editions, he would have found the position highly profitable. But it is now clear that in 1877 he was nagged to distraction by deep-lying doubts of her capacity and worthiness for leadership. To doubt her, as he had written her in February, was a kind of torture and called for desperate expedients. The only way he saw to escape this torture was to repudiate with some violence her claim to a unique spiritual mission. Characteristically, one of his first acts after breaking with her was to write and publish a pamphlet denying the virgin birth.[85] But the symbolic defiance of this act is apparent only if one appreciates the place held in Mrs. Eddy's theology by the article of faith he now repudiated.

In her writings she had drawn a basic distinction between the personal Jesus and the impersonal Christ, or Truth. The Christ, she taught, had been expressed in varying measure by prophet and sage and apostle; as the true idea of God it was still available for all men to express in the measure that they followed the example of Jesus, thought as he did, drew on the same inexhaustible source of good which he called "Father." Nevertheless, though she emphasized the universal availability of the Christ-power and the Christ-spirit, she held that Jesus had embodied them with unique perfection, and this fact ensured his role as Exemplar, or Way-shower, till the end of time. This uniqueness she attributed to the spirituality of Mary's conception of him, and the virgin birth played a key role in her Christology.

Spofford's pamphlet was clearly aimed against the idea that anyone could be set apart, in a spiritual sense, to play a special role in history. Jesus, he wrote, like anyone else found the Christ through being "born again." There was nothing unique about his birth. Ergo, there was nothing unique about the birth of Christian Science—the modern appearing of the Christ, as both he and Mrs. Eddy believed it to be—and therefore no reason why he should not supersede her as leader of the movement.[86]

Actually, no one followed Spofford out except a few of his patients. At the beginning of July he turned over to Barry and Miss Newhall the remaining money from the first edition. Later that month he signed an agreement with Barry that if at any time he should "receive control of the said book 'Science and Health,'" he would pay Barry some $400 more. Finally, at the end of September, when Barry's suit against Mrs. Eddy came up for trial, Spofford testified as a witness for the plaintiff. It may have seemed to him that if Barry could win his suit the financial pressure this would bring on Mrs. Eddy would force her to turn *Science and Health* over to him for future handling.

Mrs. Eddy's own reading of the crisis is expressed in a letter she wrote to Colonel Eldridge J. Smith of Philadelphia on October 19:

> *At this hour in a spiritual vision I was directed to the 12th chap. of Revelations to explain the hour and I also saw the*

terrible jargon of false students and their fatal power through mesmerism that I learned was the "Old Dragon" . . . and that it was best to pause in our labors at present and await the future direction of our Father. Truly the "Devil and his angels" which are Mesmerism and the messages it sends forth from mortal mind are fighting "to devour the child as soon as it is born."[87]

All work on the second edition stopped. There were no more classes taught that year. Late in November the Christian Scientist Association asked Spofford to return to it the funds he still held as treasurer. Five days before Christmas he was formally expelled from the association and four days later he returned the funds, together with various books and papers he had hopefully held on to.

As the year 1878 dawned, the severance was complete, but the drama had only begun. Apocalyptic or parochial, a tempest in a teapot or a blast in a cyclotron, there were forces here whose implications reached far beyond a vaguely bewildered Lynn.

Chapter II

The Year of Trials

The Year of Trials

One day in 1878 Robert Browning, perennial optimist though he was, put down his newspaper and wrote a friend: "What horrors fill the *Times* . . . !I don't remember such a generally disastrous year as the present."

Almost a century later a conscientious Browning editor pointed out that the particular issue of *The Times* which the poet had been reading included reports of

> . . . *a collision in the Thames of the* Princess Alice Saloon Steamer (*476 persons drowned*); *the worst colliery explosion in the history of South Wales* (*280 men dead*); *a railway collision at Sittingbourne, and a fatal fire in Birmingham. Abroad, eighty persons died of yellow fever in one day in New Orleans; 115 in Memphis. In Catania, a high wind blew the campanile down upon a dormitory for females. At Verkinodensk, 175 houses were burnt, the charred remains of thirty-five persons found in the ruins. At Pesth, Mohammedans beheaded the Chevalier Perrod; the Mafia was especially zealous in Sicily, and the Russians were rearming.*[1]

It was Browning's Pippa who had sung so blithely: "God's in his heaven,/ All's right with the world!" Yet how could optimism rationally encompass the needless and savage horrors of a single day— including those disasters traditionally characterized as acts of God?

The amiable Emerson had tried to save God's reputation by insisting that the first lesson of history is the good of evil, as the Deists before him had cheerfully held that all partial evil is universal good. This was bleak cheer indeed for the mourners at Birmingham and Verkinodensk, and there was not much more solace in the traditional Augustinian view that evil is mere privation, as darkness is only the absence of light.[2] Such a doctrine did not diminish greatly the terrors of the dark. Augustine himself had believed in a devil who was the prince of darkness as well as the ape of God.

Nineteenth-century religious liberalism tended to dismiss the devil as an outmoded fiction. But that left one with a powerful lot of evil unexplained—and all too often unexamined, even unsuspected. Carlyle had marched Emerson around London to look at one example after another of misery, squalor, degradation, and each time had asked whether *now* he believed in the devil, but Emerson had only shaken his head in tranquil obduracy.

There were lessons closer to home for those who, like William Dean Howells, believed that the smiling aspects of life were the most American. The annual reports of the Massachusetts Bureau of Statistics of Labor, examining the housing of laborers in Lynn, Salem, Chelsea, and other cities of the commonwealth, pointed up that form of degradation which subsequent generations have increasingly attributed to the iniquity of an economic system rather than to the sinfulness of the human heart:

> *In a single building . . . thirty-two feet long, twenty feet wide, three stories high, with attics, there habitually exist thirty-nine people of all ages. For their use there is one pump and one privy, within twenty feet of each other, with the several sink-spouts discharging upon the ground near by. . . . In a locality recently inspected, the foul and broken sink-pipe of a tenement discharged its contents almost immediately into a well, from which the inmates of this and surrounding houses drew their water-supply, and which was also freely used by passersby or those employed in the vicinity. To this well-water were traced nineteen cases of typhoid fever.*[3]

Natural evil, social evil, psychological evil—there were depths and areas of experience far removed from the prevailing blandness of the age. Writers as different as Rimbaud, Zola, Dostoevsky, Ibsen, and Nietzsche were plunging into the demonic and disheveled aspects of human existence, and, as usual, life kept well ahead of letters. Mrs. Eddy found all the challenge she needed in her own immediate circle.

Paradoxically enough, she started from a vision of good that involved a categoric denial of evil.

At the heart of her teaching was the conviction that being is wholly good. This conviction had come to her with a power that transformed and transvalued the whole of human experience. It had come as insight into a realm of spiritual values which was at the same time the true order of being. It was, one might say, a God's-eye view of the universe, in which the true nature of every created thing was seen as an expression of the divine Principle, or Spirit, from which it drew its being.

This view of reality differed from the enraptured visions of cosmic mystics and the abstract constructions of philosophical idealists by its Christian emphasis on *incarnation*. In the nature of things, absolute truth must be capable of incarnation or demonstration in relative human experience. Accepted as supreme fact, it must necessarily be operative, regenerative, meliorative—reshaping the phenomena which constitute a finite "material" world, not merely providing an ecstatic or theoretical escape from them.

To Mrs. Eddy's students the uncompromising metaphysical thrust of her teachings came with revolutionary impact. Many of them have told of their feeling that they were stepping into an entirely new universe, as fresh as though it had just come from the hand of God. With wondering eyes they saw the evils rooted in the mortal condition begin to slip away from the unsuspected world opening up before them. It was not a new theory but a new life which they seemed to be encountering.

Yet Mrs. Eddy did not simply reclassify evil as good in order to get rid of it; instead, she redefined it as error, demanding correction. The metaphysical logic of Christian Science left no place for evil to operate in the perfectly ordered universe of Spirit. But in the relativities of human life this logic was confronted daily by the empirical evidence of evil. Mrs. Eddy's answer to the riddle was that the false evidence, not the true logic, must go. To minds trained in formal philosophical disciplines such an answer was almost incomprehensible. This was feminine logic with a vengeance! But it was, Mrs. Eddy explained calmly, the basis of Christian healing—and the logic lay in the healing.

It might well seem irrelevant, if not absurd, to deny the existence of a particular evil which was obviously a part of human experience, whether or not one allowed it ontological reality. But if one's very acknowledgment of its lack of absolute (*i.e.*, spiritual) reality resulted in wiping it out of relative human experience—possibly in contradiction of all known physical law and psychological explanation—then a "demonstration" of a different order had been offered. One such demonstration, Mrs. Eddy held, implied the answer to the whole nightmare of evil—and in that lay the significance of the life of Jesus Christ.

Nevertheless, Mrs. Eddy differed from many of her followers in recognizing the immensity and complexity of the challenge before her. She did not need to go into the slums of Lynn to look for evil. Old habits of thought in the students themselves, the obstinacy as well as the hostility of the human mind committed to its own world of material appearances—there was enough here to reveal Armageddon right in middle-class Broad Street.

The first necessity was to get thought moving, as she sometimes put it. Too many of the students failed to close the gap between the ideal spiritual order they glimpsed through her teaching and the discipline it demanded of them. A young man who studied with her a year or two later has left a high-flown but graphic account of a psychological experience common to many of these students when they left her class:

> We go forth from this unfolding of Truth and Intelligence with elastic hope and strong confidence, and we are ravished with the sunshine and gladness. The mind . . . waking from its dream in non-realities . . . springs to power. In this sudden surprise of might, there opens to the student's mind new possibilities, with a dazzling consciousness of the greatness of possible achievement. . . .
>
> [But suddenly] there is an unlooked-for experience. Straightway, a mist rises from below; . . . all beauty and blessedness vanish; the heart feels sunken. . . .
>
> We were not wholly pure. What was seen through the merits of another had not yet become our own. In moments of mental confusion, error has been whispered into thought. We should lose no time in retracing our steps toward Truth.
>
> If we had gone directly to the field of action, and begun at once to do good, by healing and uplifting the race . . . those wrong thoughts could not have seduced and deluded us.[4]

The same writer goes on to speak of the Christian Scientist's moral responsibility to demonstrate the truth of his convictions for the sake of others—at no matter what cost of "suffering and work." In this emphasis on responsibility, he may have put his finger on an element in Mrs. Eddy's teachings that allies them with mainstream Christianity rather than with mystical and quietist thought. Although there was little to relate Christian Science to the drums and trumpets of the Salvation Army, then in its booming infancy, the two movements at least shared in common the sense of a Christian fight to be fought—fought with discipline, energy, and persistence.

Through much of 1878 Mrs. Eddy felt that she was literally battling for the life of her movement, and in retrospect it seems something of a miracle that it did escape obliteration at that time. The period was one of almost continuous trials, but with some notable advances also. Among the latter was her outgrowing of the belief that she took on the sufferings of her students. By 1881 she could write, using the editorial "we": "In years past we suffered greatly for the sick when healing them, but even that is all over now, and we cannot suffer for them."[5]

In her exploration of unmapped mental territory, however, a new and greater challenge awaited her. Since the defection of her early student Richard Kennedy in 1872, she had been greatly concerned with the problem of "mesmerism." Increasingly she was to see all evil as hypnotic in nature, a temptation to accept as actual and inevitable what was only perceptual and contingent. But because of her experience with Kennedy she had given special attention thus far to what she saw as the hazardous use of suggestion growing out of old-fashioned mesmerism or animal magnetism.

By his own account, Kennedy in his practice had completely abandoned her metaphysical basis of healing but had retained the manipulation of his patients' heads which she at first had permitted. Without throwing them into the trance state, he used this traditional mesmeric technique to increase their suggestibility. In the first edition of *Science and Health,* Mrs. Eddy had expressed her deep concern at the possibilities thus opened up of one mind's dominating another. In a rather startling way, Kennedy's practice seemed a counterfeit of spiritual healing—an imposition of the operator's will rather than an actualization of God's will. This sort of subliminal domination, Mrs. Eddy warned, could all too easily be used for evil as well as for good purposes.

In a world compounded of thought and moved by mental forces, there was great peril, it seemed to her, in the exercise of unbridled mental power by an unscrupulous operator skilled in the telepathic transmission of thought. The unwary recipient could be led to accept induced states of mind as the product of his own thinking, just as the skillful advertiser can make impressionable consumers believe that they passionately desire products of little use or value to them.

Now to Kennedy's settled hostility was added Spofford's. She warned her students against both of these mentally active individuals, as "malpractitioners." But Spofford, unlike Kennedy, had never manipulated his patients physically, so she added a paragraph to the chapter entitled "Mesmerism," which she was preparing for the new edition of *Science and Health:*

> *Mesmerism is practised through manipulation—and without it. And we have learned, by new observation, the fool who saith "There is no God" attempts more evil without a sign than with it. Since "Science and Health" first went to press, we have observed the crimes of another mesmeric outlaw, in a variety of ways, who does not as a common thing manipulate, in cases where he sullenly attempted to avenge himself of certain individuals.*[6]

This was strong language to use against the estranged Spofford, and even stronger followed. To the "criminal mental marauder, that would blot out the sunshine of earth," she addressed a jeremiad which matched in opulence the curse from Lamentations he had hurled at her. "Behold," she concluded, "the 'cloud no bigger than a man's hand,' already rising in the horizon of Truth, to pour down upon thy guilty head the hailstones of doom."

It has sometimes been said that Mrs. Eddy ruled Satan out of her metaphysics only to let him back through the doctrine of "aggressive mental suggestion" or "malicious animal magnetism." It would be more exact to draw a distinction between her "absolute" metaphysics and her "relative" psychology. In the realm of absolute Truth, evil was absolutely powerless; in the human situation it had only as much power as belief gave it, in somewhat the same way that a mathematical error had power to produce wrong results only so long as it remained undetected and uncorrected.[7]

Later she would warn her students against being overwhelmed by a sense of the odiousness of sin when it was brought to light by truth; but there is plenty of evidence that at first she herself was almost overwhelmed by what she felt she was discovering about the operations of mental evil. Putney Bancroft has described her attitude at that time:

> *The difference between malicious animal magnetism and sickness would seem to be that one was premeditated wickedness, and the other merely a false belief with which it was comparatively easy to contend. I do not claim that Mrs. Eddy made this distinction in giving instruction to her pupils. On the contrary, she shows no lines of demarcation in her teachings, excepting between Truth and error, Mind and matter, the Soul of man and personal sense. Nevertheless, her attitude seemed to be this; she was absolutely fearless in sickness, and lenient with those who erred through ignorance, while she suffered intensely from a belief that her work was being retarded by some of those with whom she had shared this knowledge of the power of mind over matter. She seemed to feel that she had put a dangerous weapon into their hands, which they were using against her and those who were loyal to her.[8]*

This is the background of the struggles that harried and almost destroyed Christian Science in 1878. In the perspective of time Mrs. Eddy was to see these battles as a necessary, even an invaluable part of her experience, forcing her to a higher level of thought and action.

2

Through the month of January, the battle centered on Newburyport, where Spofford had now withdrawn.

At a meeting of the Christian Scientist Association on January 3 the motion to expel him for unworthiness was reconsidered; it was then voted, with Putney Bancroft dissenting, to expel him for "immorality."[9] Two weeks later the members decided that public notice should be given of this expulsion, and an announcement was accordingly made in the *Newburyport Herald*.

To this startling charge of immorality Spofford made an equally surprising reply. Taking no notice of the unusual use of the word, he simply furnished the newspaper a statement to the effect that he could hardly have been expelled from the Christian Scientist Association since he had never belonged to it. This disingenuous answer somewhat embarrassed George Barry, who had entered into a brief alliance of interest with him. Barry wrote Spofford a day or two later that he assumed the statement was based on the fact that the association had no legal existence.

Statements and counterstatements continued to appear in the *Newburyport Herald* through the month. Barry and Elizabeth Newhall issued a protest against "certain malicious statements" being circulated about Spofford's business transactions with them, and Miranda Rice replied by imputing to Barry himself the statements in question. An article by Spofford on "Truth and Health" was answered by Mrs. Eddy in the *Ipswich Chronicle*.

During this time an effort was made by Benjamin F. Atkinson, the respected ex-mayor of Newburyport, to effect a reconciliation. He, his wife, and his daughter Adelma, or "Dell," were all students of Mrs. Eddy. Mrs. Atkinson was also a patient of Spofford's.

On January 15 Atkinson wrote Mrs. Eddy of his family's continuing esteem for her and their unwavering faith "in the Science of Mind as taught by you," but he went on to say, "We think it becomes us as students having only borrowed light to leave the very intricate matter of separating the tares from the wheat to our Teacher," trusting that "the inspiration which has enabled her to discover so great a Truth will not forsake her in her hour of trial." The same day Spofford wrote Atkinson a letter warning him to avoid Gilbert Eddy, who was "making a business of coming to Newburyport" to turn Spofford's patients against him.[10]

On the seventeenth Mrs. Eddy informed Atkinson that she approved his desire to effect a reconciliation but doubted the possibility of changing Spofford's purpose at this time. "Guard well your own and your dear family's symptoms," she wrote, "and when you feel doubts of me, or physical ailments, take [Spofford] up with the contradictions of his arguments and the symptoms will disappear."[11]

What she may have meant by the last part of the statement is suggested in a letter to another student, George Prescott, a week later: "Take up Spofford thus: He cannot affect his Teacher or her students to make them sick or turn them away from Truth and their Teacher."[12]

A later age would have no difficulty recognizing the psychosomatic relationship which might exist in that intense atmosphere between the students' faith in Mrs. Eddy and their mental and bodily health, but her warning extended to the possibility of accepting another person's doubts and rancors as one's own. As to the effect of the struggle on her well being, she wrote Atkinson on the twenty-fifth, "Let me own dear Mr. Atkinson that I have been so besieged for a whole year that my *native* sense at times seems almost yielding and I almost fear the end my besiegers desire will come, unless I have an armistice."[13]

Spofford, however, rejected the idea of an armistice and wrote Atkinson that he hoped the subject of reconciliation "may never again be mentioned."[14] The latter passed the word along to Mrs. Eddy and commented himself, "When the time comes that we can meet you as of old in friendly communion, the faults of other students having been forgiven or forgotten so they may not come up to mar the pleasure, we shall be pleased if permitted to call on you at your home."[15]

Cordial relations were actually resumed in April when the Christian Scientist Association voted to admit Dell Atkinson as a member and her parents as honorary members; but meanwhile another figure had loomed up who was to provide the nearest approach to sheer melodrama in Mrs. Eddy's life and to Gothic romance in Dell Atkinson's.

Edward J. Arens (pronounced Ahrens and frequently mispelled Arnes) was a Prussian cabinetmaker who had come to Lynn some years before as a young man, limited in education but mentally restless, ambitious, and above all pugnacious. His powerful personality made a considerable impact on the little group and particularly on Gilbert Eddy, whom Mrs. Eddy had just described in a letter to Atkinson as being a trifle too passive in the present emergency. Arens at least had all the masculine drive that one could ask for.

The first mention of him occurs enigmatically in a letter written by Mrs. Eddy to George Prescott on February 22, referring to an unspecified incident:

> . . . *the effect I saw on Mr. Arens when you were here was owing to the influence of Mesmerism, as I will explain when I see you. . . . I wish you could see what a nervous desire he has to do us good and you would like him.*[16]

The Eddys at this time were without any substantial funds to carry forward the movement. During March, 1878, Gilbert Eddy taught a class of four in Salem, for which he received a total of $250, but a month later he wrote Prescott that "the bank has failed in which I had deposited nearly all I had and has left me bare as an egg."[17] At the same time Barry's suit hung over them and it was a question whether they would even be able to retain the house on Broad Street.

In this dilemma Arens energetically proposed to collect various moneys that were owing to Mrs. Eddy. He was one of the four who studied with Gilbert Eddy in Salem, but instead of paying for his tuition, he undertook to bring suit in Mrs. Eddy's name against several renegade students who, as he saw it, had not discharged their contractual obligations to her. A year or two later, using the editorial "we," she was to write:

> We have suffered great losses and the direst injustice rather than go to law, for we always considered a lawsuit, of two evils, the greatest. About two years ago the persuasions of a student awakened our convictions that we might be doing wrong in permitting students to break their obligations with us, refuse the payment of their notes, and to deny their consideration when they were filling their pockets by their claims to be practising that for which they refused to pay us.[18]

The first of the suits promoted by Arens was filed in February against one of Mrs. Eddy's earliest students and probably the most seriously disaffected of them all. Richard Kennedy, who had opened an office with her in Lynn eight years before, had signed a note which read:

> February, 1870.
> In consideration of two years' instruction in healing the sick, I hereby agree to pay Mrs. M. B. Glover one thousand dollars in quarterly installments of fifty dollars commencing from this date.
> Richard Kennedy.[19]

He now alleged that when he had signed the note, Mrs. Glover told him that she would never collect it, but wanted it only to show to prospective students; somewhat contradictorily he also stated in his answer that she had

> ... obtained the promissory note declared on by pretending that she had important secrets relating to healing the sick which she had not theretofore imparted to defendant, and which she promised to impart after the making and delivery to her of said note, and she then had no such secrets and never afterward undertook to impart or imparted such secrets.[20]

The correspondence between Mrs. Glover, Kennedy, and their joint friend Sarah Bagley in 1868–72 indicates, on the contrary, that Mrs. Glover had never laid claim to having special esoteric knowledge to impart.

When the case came up before Judge William Parmenter in the Boston Municipal Court on March 14, 1878, judgment was awarded the plaintiff for the sum she claimed, plus interest and costs but minus $250 for that part of the indebtedness which was covered by the statute of limitations. Kennedy immediately appealed the case and a month later filed a new answer with the Suffolk Superior Court, in which he declared

> . . . that he is ignorant of ever having signed the agreement and denies ever having received consideration and . . . says that in the Spring of the year 1872 said plaintiff had a full settlement of all accounts existing between them. . . . The defendant requests a trial by jury.[21]

The possible significance of this appeal was not to be apparent until the case was heard in November, when it would provide what may be the most likely key to the bizarre events of that period.

Meanwhile Arens, encouraged by the favorable decision in *Glover vs. Kennedy,* brought two new suits for Mrs. Eddy—one against Spofford, to recover unpaid tuition and royalty on his practice, the other against two of her earliest students, George H. Tuttle and Charles S. Stanley, for unpaid tuition. The Spofford case was dismissed on June 3 because of defects in the writ and insufficient service. *Eddy vs. Tuttle et al.* came up in the Supreme Judicial Court in Salem on May 17 but was completely overshadowed by the much more dramatic hearing in the same court on the same day of a suit which had arisen as the misbegotten climax of Arens' passion for litigation.

3

This was the trial that came to be described—naturally enough, in view of its setting—as the "Salem Witchcraft Trial" of 1878. Spofford was again the defendant, and he was charged with using mesmeric power to injure one of his former patients.

In the years since then, the case has been interpreted on the one hand as a reversion to the superstitions of 1692 and on the other as a sort of rude advance shock of awareness of criminal possibilities in the use of suggestion—possibilities that were to receive serious scientific attention in the 1880's and reveal new dimensions in the twentieth century. The psychological bombardment of personality first revealed in its full horror in Hitler's Germany, not to mention the more sophisticated techniques of suggestion developed since his day, still bear a genetic resemblance to the primitive spells of the witch doctor, and the Salem trial of 1878 may stand halfway between what Mrs. Eddy herself was to call "ancient and modern necromancy."[22]

In his essay on "Demonology" Emerson had written:

> How slowly, how slowly we learn that witchcraft and ghost-craft, palmistry and magic, and all the other so-called superstitions, which, with so much police, boastful skepticism, and scientific committees, we had finally dismissed to the moon as nonsense, are really no nonsense at all, but subtle and valid influences, always starting up, mowing, muttering in our path, and our day.[23]

An interesting if casual contribution to the still largely unexplored area between the superstitious and the scientific was made in 1892 by Barrett Wendell, Harvard professor and biographer of Cotton Mather, in a paper—"Were the Salem Witches Guiltless?"—read before the Essex Institute.[24] After investigating with some distaste the current spiritism (particularly the phenomena of materialization, mediumship, and automatic writing), he had come to the conclusion that it was a variable mixture of conscious fraud, self-deception, genuine states of psychopathic excitement, hypnotic or autohypnotic influence, and possibly telepathic communication, with a generally demoralizing tendency to blur sharp distinctions between truth and untruth even when the participants were honest people. Struck by certain analogies with the evidence given in the Salem witchcraft trials of 1692, he speculated that the witch-hunting hysteria of that early period may have been induced in part by a serious epidemic of genuine witchcraft.[25] In other words, he asked tentatively whether some of those found guilty may not actually have considered themselves to *be* witches and have tried to impress susceptible people with their powers of occult persuasion.

Although students of abnormal psychology and of social pathology have concentrated their attention on the "bewitched" rather than on the accused in that episode of history, there is little reason to doubt that Salem in 1692 contained at least the normal modicum of people addicted to experiments in those subliminal and/or extrasensory forces which psychology and parapsychology today are exploring within a wholly different frame of reference.[26] Wendell hypothecates the presence of a few such experimenters among both the accused and the accusers, and he suggests that within the seventeenth-century theological framework it would have been natural for them to think of themselves as having made a pact with the devil. On these terms the psychic explosion of that year would be attributable to a diabolism that was no less actual because a later age would reclassify its demons and incubi as neuroses and psychoses, its witches and warlocks as dabblers in hypnoidal suggestion.

Mrs. Eddy had written in the revised edition of *Science and Health* that was almost ready for publication by the time of the trial: "The peril of Salem witchcraft is not past, until that error be met by Truth and science; Metaphysical Science will show the need there is for law to restrain mesmerism when it is injuring another knowingly in person or property."[27] If the words strike a chill into the modern reader who remembers the religious inquisitions of the past, they reflect accurately the crisis atmosphere through which the new movement was then passing. Mesmerism was the "great red dragon," and for a time it looked as though this whole question might swallow up Mrs. Eddy's conviction that good alone was absolutely real. It was the measure of her perplexity that she looked to human law for what, according to her own theory, divine power alone could accomplish: the restraint of a malign mental influence consciously exerted on susceptible people.

This was illustrated by the events that culminated in the Salem trial.

Miss Lucretia L. S. Brown, a maiden lady of some fifty years' precarious existence, had studied with Mrs. Eddy and had been healed by Spofford of a severe spinal injury received in girlhood. With her mother and sister she lived in a spotless little house facing the green in Ipswich, between Salem and Newburyport. It has been said that Essex was the cleanest county in Massachusetts, Ipswich the cleanest town in Essex, and the Browns the cleanest people in Ipswich. Miss Lucretia conducted a crocheting agency, and everything she did was marked by maidenly delicacy, scrupulous neatness, and a rather fluttering modesty. Recently she had been elected secretary of the Christian Scientist Association.

After Spofford's defection she turned to Dorcas Rawson for treatment whenever she needed it, although she also did a little healing work of her own. Miss Rawson, a good-hearted, strong-minded woman who had formerly been a "Holiness Methodist," was puzzled to have her patient subsequently suffer an unaccountable relapse. Daniel Spofford at that time was known to be calling on former patients and warning them of the dire effects of continuing in the Eddy camp. While it is impossible today to judge the exact state of his mind in 1878, it almost certainly was at an unhealthy pitch of hostility. In a pamphlet written forty-four years later he insisted that intentional injury could not be mentally directed, but conceded that an evil or a sick person might cause another "to be afflicted merely through causing the mind to rest upon them without intending injury."[28] As

Miss Rawson and her patient thought about the situation, it seemed to them that something more than unintentional harm was resulting to the latter from Spofford's mental influence.

Miss Lucretia's worst fears were confirmed when one day, out of the blue, Spofford presented himself at the front door of the little Ipswich house and told her that he had come to have a talk with her. Agitatedly she made her excuses and he left without entering, but the mischief was done. If he really had wanted to wreak grievous bodily injury on the good lady, he could hardly have devised a better method. Her own fears did the rest.

The wording of the bill in equity in which Miss Brown then besought the Supreme Judicial Court of Massachusetts to restrain Spofford from using his mesmeric powers against her shows the dangerous hysteria which threatened the new movement:

> *The plaintiff humbly complains that the said Daniel H. Spofford of Newburyport, is a mesmerist, and practices the art of mesmerism, and that by his power and influence he is capable of injuring the persons and property and social relations of others, and does by said means so injure them. That the said Daniel H. Spofford, has at divers times and places since the year 1875, wrongfully, maliciously, and with intent to injure the plaintiff, caused the plaintiff, by means of his said power and art, great suffering of body, severe spinal pains and neuralgia, and temporary suspension of the mind; and still continues to cause the plaintiff the same. And the plaintiff has reason to fear and does fear that he will continue in the future to cause the same. And the plaintiff says that said injuries are great and of an irreparable nature, and that she is wholly unable to escape from the control and influence he so exercises upon her, and from the aforesaid effects of said control and influence.*[29]

The wording suggests that the temporary suspension of mind was not only on Miss Lucretia's part. The complaint was probably drawn up by Arens who, unable to find a lawyer who would take the case, acted as counsel for the plaintiff and was prime mover as well as chief publicist of the whole affair. Mrs. Eddy, who has been described by one of her critics as "by nature polemical, but not litigious,"[30] was apparently not in favor of the suit, despite her theoretical endorsement of legal action to restrain malpractice. In a letter to her three years later Miss Brown wrote:

> *I am ready to give my testimony under oath that you did not advise me to bring the case of malpractice against Spofford, and objected to it when it was first mentioned in my hearing.*

Later, E. J. Arens interviewed me upon the subject and gave me to understand that you approved of the measure, being thus misled, I was overpersuaded to take the part assigned me by Arens. I was myself utterly opposed to such a step.[31]

Once the suit was launched, however, Mrs. Eddy went along with it and even received power of attorney to appear for the plaintiff. On May 14, attended by what one Boston paper called "a cloud of witnesses,"[32] she turned up at the Salem courthouse to hear Arens, with his heavy German accent, present his petition for a hearing on the bill of complaint. Judge Horace Gray heard Arens' exposition of the case, ordered that a notice be served on Spofford, and appointed the following Friday, May 17, for the hearing.

When that day came, the defendant's counsel, Amos Noyes, filed a demurrer which was immediately sustained by the judge, who simply commented that it was not within the power of the court to restrain Spofford's mind.[33] On the same day the case against Stanley and Tuttle for unpaid tuition came up and their counsel likewise filed a demurrer, which was, however, overruled by the court, and the case postponed to a later date.[34] What had promised to be a day of sensational news for the press turned out to be rather an anticlimax. For Mrs. Eddy it was a confirmation of her original instinct against litigation, and Arens was never again allowed to initiate a suit on her behalf.

For the moment, the atmosphere became more tranquil. At Gilbert Eddy's solicitation, Bronson Alcott had accompanied the Eddys to the preliminary hearing of the case at Salem. Instead of being alienated by proceedings as foreign to Concord Transcendentalism as to Boston rationalism, he appears to have had his interest in Christian Science revived, for on June 5 he and the Reverend J. A. Dudley attended a meeting of the Christian Scientist Association and engaged in a friendly discussion of metaphysics with Mrs. Eddy and her students. Afterward he wrote that there was "perhaps a touch of fanaticism, though of a genial quality, interposed into her faith."[35]

A fortnight later one "Lawyer Bancroft" was sent by one of the papers to a similar meeting of the group as a result of the interest aroused by the Salem trial. In an article entitled "A New School of Medicine," published on July 2, he recapitulated the facts of the trial, then described the meeting:

[It] was opened by prayer and regularly organized, and conducted with parliamentary precision, and the business and discussions were conducted in a perfectly decorous and intelligent manner. . . . Who knows but that this little cloud no larger than a man's hand, may grow till it covers the firmament? Some of the

greatest developments of philosophy and religion that the world has ever known, have sprung out of smaller and more humble beginnings than this.[36]

Two weeks later in the same newspaper, under the heading "Letter from a Lady," Mrs. Eddy commented on his summary of the Salem case:

> *It is, at least, progress at present to learn that witchcraft can no longer be pinned to the skirts of "spirits," or to his satanic majesty, but is found out mesmerism. . . . The humane and scholarly Chief Justice Gray gave that case all the consideration the law allowed. We understood the Judge to neither admit nor deny the charge in the bill in equity; but, for lack of precedent, or the court's jurisdiction, dismissed the case.*[37]

She then went on to mention the question that still troubled her in connection with human law and mental malpractice. Was there ever a theft or a murder that mind did not plan? Did not the consideration of mental motives enter into the court's judgment? Was its jurisdiction simply over matter and not over mind? These were questions which led to metaphysical speculations well beyond the cautious empiricism of a Blackstone.

4

During the spring of 1878 Mrs. Eddy taught another class. There were only two students in it, but it was the first she had taken for over a year. Gilbert Eddy also taught two small classes in April and August.

His earlier class in February had been held at the house of George and Clara Choate in Salem. Mrs. Choate, then in her early twenties and with a lively temperament that was both promising and unpredictable, described later the passion of enthusiasm her first meeting with Mrs. Eddy aroused in her.[38] The evidence indicates that even through her most troubled times the discoverer of Christian Science was able to kindle this sort of feeling in her students, who constantly flocked to her for encouragement and counsel. To most of them she seemed to be a woman who dwelt in intimate communion with God, and there can be no doubt that a great deal of her time was spent in pondering both the abstruse and the practical aspects of her metaphysical system.

This is evidenced in the new chapter "Metaphysics" in the second edition of *Science and Health,* which was now being printed. For the first time she clearly and repeatedly defined God as Mind, as well as Soul, Spirit, Life, Truth, Love, and Principle. As a correlative step she began to substitute the term "mortal mind" for "personal sense," though not abandoning the latter phrase altogether. Previously she had tended to use "mind" in a neutral sense which permitted it to be identified either with spiritual reality or with material appearances. Now she drew a clear distinction between "divine Mind" and "mortal mind," not merely as two modes of thinking (a true and a false) but as two antithetical starting points (an infinite intelligence and a self-destructive ignorance). The fourteenth postulate in her new chapter read:

> That Mind or Intelligence is the only "I" or "Us," and this "I" or "Us" is bliss, it being infinite freedom and impersonality. Limits impose ignorance and ignorance is not bliss. When being is personality, it is no longer bliss, but bondage. The "I" and the Father must be one. The Truth of being is harmony and immortality, and any other supposed consciousness or Life is a myth.[39]

While there was evidence that her metaphysics was being clarified, the unsettling impact of Spofford's attack on her leadership was suggested in the new edition by one particular. Almost the first thing Spofford had done after breaking with her had been to publish his argument against the virgin birth. In the first edition of *Science and Health* Mrs. Eddy had taken that biblical event as axiomatic; in the third and all subsequent editions she would again write of it with the same unqualified emphasis on its literal truth. In the second edition, for the first and last time, she wrote of it in conditional or problematic terms.[40]

The whole edition was, in many ways, a near disaster. Generally known as the "Ark edition" because of the gilt Noah's ark stamped on the cover, it came close to sinking in a sea of misprints. It was intended to appear in two volumes, but the first volume was so botched in the printing that it was abandoned as beyond rescue. The second, cryptically labeled "Vol. II," contained only the chapters "Imposition and Demonstration" [a critique of spiritism], "Physiology," "Mesmerism," "Metaphysics," and "Reply to a Clergyman"—chapters weighted on the negative side, since most of those setting forth the positive teachings of Christian Science were in the disabled "Vol. I." It is tempting to see a certain symbolism in these facts, especially as a fresh flood of disaster suddenly rose when the book made its appearance in late October.

For some time Mrs. Eddy had indicated that she felt a new crisis to be building up.

The Barry suit still hung over her head and led to a series of complicated real-estate transactions designed to keep 8 Broad Street from being taken away from her if Barry won his case. On September 16 she opened her Bible at random to II Samuel 7:10 (making a note in it to that effect) and read: "Moreover I will appoint a place for my people Israel, and will plant them, that they may dwell in a place of their own, and move no more; neither shall the children of wickedness afflict them any more, as beforetime." It was a promise that evidently spoke to her with the force of a revelation, relating itself literally to her immediate situation.

Again and again in times of crisis she would note down in her Bible[41] a particular verse through which she felt God had spoken to her and given her direction, noting also the date on which she had turned to it. Sometimes it might be a warning, as when she opened to Micah 2 a few days later and read: "Woe to them that devise iniquity, and work evil upon their beds! . . . And they covet fields, and take them by violence, and houses, and take them away: so they oppress a man and his house, even a man and his heritage."

The "heritage" which obviously concerned her above all else was *Science and Health,* and the danger to the mission of that book lay not in Barry but, as she saw it, in Spofford and Kennedy. Moreover, the case that Kennedy had lost and appealed in April was to come up for a new hearing that fall. As the time drew nearer, it seemed to her that some desperate malice was at work, and the sort of climax she felt it to be reaching is suggested by the passage in Psalms to which she turned on September 29:

> *God is our refuge and strength, a very present help in trouble. Therefore will not we fear, though the earth be removed, and though the mountains be carried into the midst of the sea; though the waters thereof roar and be troubled, though the mountains shake with the swelling thereof. . . . The heathen raged, the kingdoms were moved: he uttered his voice the earth melted. . . . Be still, and know that I am God: I will be exalted among the heathen, I will be exalted in the earth.*

On October 8 Richard Kennedy wrote his old friend Sarah Bagley, thanking her for the manuscripts she had lent him for use in the coming trial. Referring to Mrs. Eddy he wrote that "the Devil will never get his own until he has her. She is really malicious in her intentions. She does her wickedness knowingly and hence I have no charity for her."[42]

In many ways Kennedy is the great enigma in the history of Christian Science. Many writers have accepted without question Georgine Milmine's picture of him as a good-natured, sociable young man, later a respected vestryman in the Episcopal Church, going his own way in amused disregard of his early association with Mrs. Eddy. It is difficult, however, to fit all the known facts about him, including his extreme secretiveness, into so bland a picture.[43]

When Miss Milmine in 1907 was writing her sensational *McClure's* articles on the early history of Christian Science, Kennedy wrote her a letter urging her to keep his name out of the story entirely and adding: "I shall rely upon your sense of honor to see it is not inserted."[44] Miss Milmine naturally enough disregarded his request, but she painted a sympathetic portrait of the young man and poured scorn on Mrs. Eddy's charges against him. At the same time Sibyl Wilbur, writing of the identical period for the magazine, *Human Life,* skated lightly and perhaps charitably over the struggle between Kennedy and Mrs. Eddy —a chapter of history for which few inside facts were then available. Lyman Powell, in 1907 a young Episcopal clergyman, wrote Kennedy asking him what he thought of the disparity between the Milmine and Wilbur articles, and Kennedy replied:

> *The two articles evidently seem somewhat contradictory to you. In the main they are not, nevertheless there are misrepresentations in both. The two women who prepared them have been of very necessity obliged to guess at a great deal, as the material which has been concealed from them was so much more than has been disclosed that both articles are very incomplete and in many respects infantile.*[45]

Interestingly enough, Kennedy himself did his part in concealing such material as he did not wish to have disclosed.[46] Some writers, without troubling to consider alternative conclusions, have been satisfied to accept the Milmine thesis that Mrs. Eddy was simply suffering from paranoidal delusions of persecution. Yet scientific caution would suggest some attention to the possibility that among the hidden factors in the situation was a psychopathic or, to use the term which has again become fashionable, a demonic strain in Kennedy.[47]

The very year, 1872, which brought to Mrs. Eddy what she later described as the shock of discovering Kennedy's true nature saw the publication of Dostoevsky's *The Possessed.* It was to take both abnormal psychology and conventional theology a good many years to catch up with that subtle study of the demonic in human nature, but its insights may throw some light on the Lynn scene. Mrs. Eddy again and again pictured Kennedy as an *experimenter* in the projection of thought to control other people's minds—as acting from a kind of fascination with evil, a "motiveless malignity"[48] or sheer perversity which in some ways suggests the youthful Stavrogin.

On these grounds, it would be easy to believe that the shock of discovery might cause her at first to exaggerate the extent of Kennedy's actual mental influence. Kennedy the agent might well become Kennedy the symbol and as such loom larger than life. Facts are hard to come by here. The remaining events of 1878 point only to probabilities, not to certainties. Their explanation may lie in a shadowy realm which psychology has hardly begun to look at yet.[49]

On October 8—the same day on which Kennedy wrote Sarah Bagley the letter already quoted—Mrs. Eddy wrote him:

Dr. Kennedy

I do not like to blight the future of a young man, I do not like to see year by year your opportunities to do better passing away never to return . . . and will spare every blow in my power if only you will cease to commit in secret the sins you are committing. Your promise to pay me for tuition is not of as much importance to me, or to you, as your debt to God, to Truth. You have said this Truth has saved your life (or that which is called life) and yet you are making it no returns for all this, by acknowledging in your life that you love Truth and adhere to it sufficiently to do as you would be done by. . . .

Now I come to you again with that spirit of forgiveness which you cannot understand, to ask you, if the world knows more of the error of your past, you will cease to commit the sin against the Holy Ghost by doing in secret what you would not have revealed, by trying to injure the helpless who know not what you are trying, and so stop the terrible malpractice you have fallen into. If you will, you shall not be publicly exposed, and I for one will take back the straying lamb, and help you to prosper, and go on in the path of Truth. . . .

Now do not place the false unction to your heart that any sinister motive, or motive to benefit myself prompts this letter, for it does not. I can take care of myself and the dear ones God has given me and the malpractice is powerless to harm me. . . . I hope God will govern your resolves this time and bless you from that hour.

M. B. Glover Eddy[50]

On the same day she wrote a similar letter to Spofford:

Dear Student,

Wont you make up your mind before it is ever too late to stop sinning with your eyes wide open? I pray for you, that God will influence your thoughts to better issues, and make you a good and a great man, and spare you the penalty that must come if you do not forsake sin. I am ready at any time to welcome you back—and kill for you the fatted calf,—that is, destroy in my own breast the great material error of rendering evil for evil or resenting the wrongs done us. I do not cherish this purpose toward any one. I am too selfish to do myself this great injury, I want you to be good, and happy *in* being good, *for you can never be happy without it.*

I rebuke error only to destroy it; not to harm you *but to do* you *good. . . . Your silent arguments to do me harm have done me the greatest possible good. In order to meet the emergency, Truth has lifted me above my former self, enabled me to know who is using the argument and when and what is being spoken,— and knowing this, what is said in secret is proclaimed on the house top, and affects me no more than for you to come and say it to me audibly. . . .*

Pause, think, solemnly and selfishly of the cost to you. Love instead of hate your friends, and enemies *even. This alone can make you happy and draw down blessings infinite.*

Have I been your friend? have I taught you faithfully the way of happiness? and rebuked sternly that which could turn you out of that way? If I have, then I was your friend and risked much to do you good. May God govern your resolves to do right from this hour and strengthen you to keep them.

Adieu

M. B. Glover Eddy[51]

There was no reply to either letter. A week later the abortive second edition of *Science and Health* was published, Daniel Spofford disappeared suddenly from his home, and Mrs. Eddy formed the most trusted members of the Christian Scientist Association into a Committee of Relief to "take up" the two offenders spiritually and counter their mental influence.[52] The overcharged atmosphere was heating up to a final crisis.

5

On October 26 a newpaper notice headed MYSTERIOUS ABSENCE announced that "Dr. D. H. Spofford, the Christian scientist, had been missing since Tuesday, October 15, and much alarm for his safety is manifested.[53] This was followed by a report that his body had been identified at the morgue. Then on the twenty-ninth Gilbert Eddy and Edward Arens were arrested and the *Boston Herald* declared:

A murderous conspiracy, that at the present has the blackest possible appearance, is now about to be investigated judicially

*through the efforts of State Detectives Pinkham and Philbrick.
The story of this crime, which is almost Borgian, implicates a
number of people who have, during the past three or four years,
figured in the Essex county courts with damaging frequency.*[54]

What sounds a century later like a black joke burst on the Christian Scientists like the end of the world. Over the years, biographers have tended to shrug off the episode as an inexplicable product of seething emotions in the Lynn teapot, but it deserves a closer and more careful look than that.

The *Boston Herald*'s invocation of the Borgias was followed by equally inflammatory stories in the other papers. The next day the *Lynn Item* reported the arrest of Eddy and Arens on the charge of having conspired to murder Spofford—who had now reappeared, having been very much alive all the time in a seedy hideout, while supposedly lying murdered in a morgue. "All three [men]," the *Item* commented coolly, "emanate from the notorious Scientists' home, on Broad Street, Lynn."[55] The *Boston Globe,* without waiting for the formality of a trial, explained to its readers:

> *Finding that they could not dispose of their rival by any
> process of law, the Eddy combination next resorted to stronger
> measures . . . visited Boston and bargained with a Portland
> street "bummer" to put Dr. Spofford out of the way, in other
> words, to*
> MURDER HIM IN COLD BLOOD.[56]

The *Globe* likewise referred throughout to "Dr." Eddy but to Dr. Spofford.

On that same day, Gilbert Eddy wrote his wife a typically uncomplaining letter from the Charles Street jail in Boston where he was held pending a preliminary hearing in the Boston Municipal Court. He suggested that Miranda Rice's brother might be willing to provide the necessary bail, if all the students would stand surety for his appearance at the trial—unless, he added wryly, the world came to an end before then. But his chief concern was to reassure his wife that he was well, comfortable, and even happy to suffer persecution if that was the demand of Christian discipleship:

> *You have doubtless seen the charge and I need not say so to
> assure you that it is wholly untrue. I saw D. H. Spofford when the
> trial was called and he could not look me in the face. . . . Do not
> fear for me or Mr. Arens. God doeth all things well . . . and I
> have enjoyed myself during this experience so far, having as I
> have the assurance of being accounted worthy to suffer persecu-
> tion for the Masters sake. Now Mary Dear be of good cheer for*

though this is not the experience we should have chosen yet the Master who knoweth better than we hath said it worketh out a more exceeding and eternal weight of glory.

Yours in Love,
Gilbert.[57]

Mrs. Eddy, for her part, opening her Bible for guidance and turning to Jeremiah 39:10, read on through a story of deliverance in which every word seemed to promise the safety of her husband. A few days later she made note: "Nov 5th 1878 In my affliction I called on God and opened to the 18th Psalm." The scriptural verses that seemed to her like the voice of God at moments of stress form a suggestive counterpoint to the sordid events into which she was plunged. When things grew even darker a few days later, she turned to Acts 20 and read: "But none of these things move me, neither count I my life dear unto myself, so that I might finish my course with joy, and the ministry, which I have received of the Lord Jesus, to testify the gospel of the grace of God."

She had need of that lofty assurance. At the preliminary hearing in the Boston Municipal Court on November 7,[58] the first witness was James L. Sargent, a saloon keeper with a criminal record. Sargent testified that toward the end of July Edward J. Arens, using the *alias* "Miller," came to his saloon to "tell fortunes" and ended by offering him $500 to do away with Spofford. According to his story, he accepted the offer and later met with "Miller" and Miller's friend "Libby" (whom he identified in court as Gilbert Eddy) to plan the murder. He was explicit as to the date, time, and place of this meeting. Another witness, George Collier, at that time under indictment on several charges, corroborated this last piece of testimony, stating that he had been secreted in a freight car where he could overhear the conversation in question, which allegedly took place in an East Cambridge freight yard. At a subsequent meeting with "Miller," Sargent declared, he received an advance of $75, which he thereupon left with his sister, the keeper of a brothel.

So far his story had the familiar outline of a thousand police-court intrigues, but suddenly it took a highly individual turn of its own. When a petty criminal wishes to collect full payment for a crime he has been hired to do, without risking his neck by actually committing it, he would not ordinarily be expected to take this nice tactical and ethical problem to the police and ask for advice. Yet that, according to Sargent, is what happened next. He went with his story to State Detective Hollis C. Pinkham, whose reaction was as singular as his own. The detective neither reported the matter officially nor took any steps to warn Spofford but allegedly told Sargent to play along with Miller and Libby and see what more he could find out.

Sargent then went on to recount how Miller and Libby pressed him for action, insisting that he produce a corpse before receiving further payment. At that point, he testified, he virtuously decided to call on Spofford and warn him of the conspiracy, referring him to Pinkham for corroboration. The obliging detective not only confirmed the story but also persuaded Spofford, now badly frightened, to participate in a rather unusual subplot. Spofford should disappear and it would be given out publicly that he had been killed. This would serve the benevolent purpose of enabling Sargent to collect final payment from Miller and Libby, after which the "would-be murdered man,"[59] as Mrs. Eddy ironically described him later on, could reappear and the whole plot against him be exposed.

Spofford was in no state of mind to question the logic of the plan, the relationship of Sargent and Pinkham, or the authenticity of the facts as he was told them. Meekly he allowed Sargent to take him to a hideaway in Cambridgeport, where for two weeks he stayed in complete secrecy, reading the newspaper accounts of the anxiety felt by his family and friends at his strange disappearance. Presumably during his stay there he had the company of some of the criminals and prostitutes who constituted the social circle of the Sargent family—hardly a reassuring situation for a man of Spofford's background and character.

This is the story that emerged from the combined testimony of Sargent, Pinkham, and Spofford. The detective also testified that he had seen Arens and Sargent in conversation on the Boston Common, had followed Arens on the train and then to 8 Broad Street, and later had seen Sargent walking toward the door of the same house. Jessie MacDonald, a discharged housekeeper of the Eddys', added the titillating information that she had heard Mrs. Eddy read aloud a chapter from the Old Testament which said that all wicked people should be destroyed. The judge commented that the case was anomalous and the testimony not of the best, but there seemed to be sufficient evidence to show that the parties should be held to appear at the December term of the Superior Court.[60]

Arens and Eddy were released on $3,000 bail. The newspapers had already come out with sensational accounts which could leave no slightest doubt in their readers' minds that the two men were guilty—and that very day[61] the case of *Glover vs. Kennedy*, which Richard Kennedy had appealed back in April, came up for jury trial in Suffolk County Superior Court.

By any normal standard of judgment, Kennedy had not a leg to stand on. Under the circumstances, however, with the newspapers painting uninhibited pictures of the Eddys as mountebanks and criminals, no jury was likely to find for the plaintiff, and the earlier decision was reversed. Mrs. Eddy's attorney at once filed exceptions to the verdict and the exceptions were allowed; but before the case could again come to trial, the promissory note which Kennedy had signed in 1870 and which was the subject of litigation disappeared mysteriously from the attorney's office and Mrs. Eddy's appeal was dropped.

It was probably this sequence of events that led her later to interpret the whole conspiracy-to-murder episode as an elaborate masquerade designed to serve Kennedy's interest. At the time she thought that Kennedy and Spofford had conspired together; later she came to the conclusion that Spofford had been only an unwitting pawn. In his diary Gilbert Eddy listed five people he thought Kennedy might have pressed into the conspiracy, including Spofford's estranged wife, but there is no reason why more than one would have been necessary to set the plot in motion.

Mrs. Eddy's lawyer in the Spofford case was Russell H. Conwell, who soon afterward changed his career to become a clergyman and achieved national fame by his phenomenally successful lecture, "Acres of Diamonds."[62] Thirty years later the Reverend Dr. Conwell, then pastor of the Grace Baptist Church of Philadelphia, described Mrs. Eddy as he had known her—"a woman of striking appearance and great personal magnetism, of strong intellectual powers and keen business insight . . . a woman of excellent character. She is not a schemer, nor is she dishonest . . . and is really sincere in her work."[63]

His personal sympathy for both the Eddys is clear in his 1878 correspondence with them. On his advice they hired detectives and extra counsel at an almost prohibitive fee to get to the bottom of the mystery, but it was as mysterious as ever when the case came up before the grand jury of the Superior Court on December 3. An indictment was found by the jury on two counts. The first read:

> *That Edward J. Arens and Asa G. Eddy of Boston aforesaid, on the 28th day of July, in the year of our Lord one thousand eight hundred and seventy-eight, in Boston aforesaid, with force and arms, being persons of evil minds and dispositions, did then and there unlawfully conspire, combine, and agree together feloniously, wilfully, and of their malice aforethought, to procure, hire, incite and solicit one James L. Sargent, for a certain sum of money, to wit, the sum of five hundred dollars, to be paid to said Sargent by them, said Arens and Eddy, feloniously, wilfully, and of his said Sargent's malice aforethought, in some way and*

*manner by some means, instruments and weapons, to said jurors
unknown, one Daniel H. Spofford to kill and murder against
the law, peace and dignity of said Commonwealth.*

The second count charged the prisoners with hiring Sargent "with
force and arms in and upon one Daniel H. Spofford to beat, bruise,
wound, and evil treat against the law, peace, dignity of said Commonwealth."

Eddy and Arens pleaded not guilty, and the case was continued
to the January term. Meanwhile Mrs. Eddy and Conwell were both
busy. The former obtained a number of affidavits showing that Gilbert
Eddy was teaching a class in Boston Highlands on the afternoon when
he was alleged to have conspired with Sargent in an East Cambridge
freight yard and that it would have been physically impossible for him
to be in the latter place at the time Sargent swore he was.

On December 16 George Collier, who had corroborated Sargent's
testimony about the freight yard meeting, wrote an illiterate but frank
letter to Gilbert Eddy retracting his evidence, and the next day Conwell obtained from him the following affidavit:

> *I, George A. Collier, do on oath depose and say of my own
> free will, and in order to expose the man who has tried to injure
> Dr. Asa G. Eddy and Edward J. Arens, that Sargent did induce
> me by great persuasion to go with him to East Cambridge from
> Boston, on or about the 7th day of November last, the day of
> the hearing in the municipal court of Boston in the case of
> Dr. Asa G. Eddy and E. J. Arens for attempting to hire said
> Sargent to kill one Daniel Spofford, and that he showed me the
> place and the cars that he was going to swear to, and told me
> what to say in court, and made me repeat the story until I knew
> it well, so that I could tell the same story that he would, and
> there was not one word of truth in it all. I never heard a con-
> versation in East Cambridge between said Eddy and Arens and
> Sargent, or saw them pay or offer to pay Sargent any money.*
>
> *(Signed) Geo. A. Collier*[64]

Shortly afterward Conwell wrote Gilbert Eddy, "I think now
that I have direct proof that Spofford employed Sargent and the officer
[Pinkham] and shall be able to convict him, if a confidential communication from one of the State Police is to be trusted."[65] Spofford's
complicity was not substantiated, but Pinkham's was. He was removed
from the detective force, and an affidavit by a Lynn justice of the
peace, David Austin, states that Pinkham confessed to him that "the
testimony of all the parties in this case [including, presumably, Pinkham's] were perjuries."[66]

55

In these circumstances it is not too surprising that the Superior Court record in January reads:

> *This indictment was found and returned into Court by the grand jurors at the last December term when the said Arens and Eddy were severally set at the bar, and having the said indictment read to them, they severally said thereof that they were not guilty. This indictment was thence continued to the present January term, and now the District Attorney, Oliver Stevens, Esquire, says he will prosecute this indictment no further, on payments of costs, which are thereupon paid. And the said Arens and Eddy are thereupon discharged, January 31, 1879.*

Gilbert Eddy and Edward Arens might have protested this *nol. pros.,* but at that time they were still hoping to find evidence of Spofford's guilt and to bring an action against him which would put them on the offensive rather than the defensive. The *Boston Globe* on February 5 commented that "Drs. Eddy and Arens are busy endeavoring to ferret and bring to justice the parties who caused the malicious persecution to be brought against them." The *Boston Transcript* later noted the removal of Pinkham from the detective force and the jailing of Sargent and Collier on previous charges.[67] The changed attitude of the press is illustrated by a further item in the *Globe* on March 18:

> *At the time of the arrest of James L. Sargent, for enticing young girls from their homes, some reflections were incidentally made against Mrs. Dr. Eddy of Lynn, who was once accused of being connected with a conspiracy to murder Daniel H. Spofford. The charge against her was most unjust. The parties accused have been sufficiently vindicated by the facts and by the confession of a man who was a witness in the case to be forever exempt from further annoyance in the matter.*

Yet nearly a century later careless writers would still be repeating Pierre Janet's statement that Mrs. Eddy was tried for attempted murder and released with a heavy fine.[68]

6

The question of who set the plot in motion remains to be answered. It was not a matter of spontaneous generation. Neither Sargent nor Pinkham had the wit or motive to generate such a plan on their own. Spofford would have had to lose his wits completely to plan such a self-defeating operation, as Mrs. Eddy soon came to recognize. Gilbert Eddy, quite apart from his known character, was too clearly a victim to be an instigator.

There remain Arens and Kennedy.

Back in 1876 Arens had been briefly arrested and charged with swindling, then released for lack of evidence.[69] The facts in the case are enough to suggest shady connections. It has also been plausibly suggested that he could have approached Sargent and hired him to beat up Spofford or otherwise throw a scare into him, and that Sargent might then have seen a chance to elaborate on the scheme and make more money. The fatal trouble with this explanation is that Sargent did not attempt to make any money out of Spofford— indeed, paid for his transportation to Cambridgeport and for his "keep" while hidden there. Nor does it explain how or why Pinkham was brought in, or why Sargent implicated Gilbert Eddy by perjured evidence, or what wild creative urge could have caused so petty an underworld character as Sargent to plot so improbably.

E. S. Bates and J. V. Dittemore, who tentatively advance this theory with a gratuitous assumption that, if Arens so acted, it must have been with the blessing of Mr. and Mrs. Eddy, conclude their account with the flat statement: "No one but the lawyers gained anything from the case."[70] This is obviously untrue. One person who gained from it tangibly was Richard Kennedy.

Having entered a plea for a jury trial on the case he had lost earlier that year—and he stressed to Lyman Powell thirty years later his desire to have a jury[71]—it was obviously to Kennedy's decisive advantage to have the conspiracy-to-murder case break into the headlines one day before his own trial came up, juries being notoriously more responsive than judges to states of public outrage. It may have been pure coincidence that Pinkham arrested Eddy and Arens when he did—although he could have arrested them earlier and saved Spofford several days of uneasy hiding in Cambridgeport—but it would be extremely interesting to know whether Pinkham had any connections with Kennedy. So much of the affair seems to have been stage-managed by the detective[72] that it is at least a possible hypothesis that he was the link between an unknown principal with an interested motive and the loutish Sargent who would do as he was told.

Mrs. Eddy's own estimate of Pinkham is apparent from a passage in a sermon she preached a little later:

> *The careful sparrow with household furniture in her bill fashions her house wisely and shelters herself from the sly cat that would catch her in his velvet paw like a dishonest detective that pounces upon the innocent and mars the domestic circle.*

No guardian of the law is this cat detective but a law breaker that moral law should handle and disgorge . . . should cut off those claws that reach forth only for God's innocents; a gleam from the Soul of a mouse would enlarge the nature of a cat.[73]

If Pinkham did indeed act as the agent of an unknown Mr. X, Kennedy may best fit the latter role. He is known to have felt animosity for Mrs. Eddy and probably also for Spofford.[74] He had at stake what for a young man still in his twenties was a considerable sum of money. He had had a chance to size up Arens early that year when the latter had confronted him personally with the promissory note which was afterward the subject of litigation. Still later he profited when the note disappeared from the files of Mrs. Eddy's lawyer, since that effectively put a stop to her appeal for a new trial in a calmer atmosphere.

None of these facts is conclusive; taken together, they are suggestive. The hypothesis of Kennedy's complicity is at least free from the anomalies of the only other hypothesis seriously advanced, though Arens' earlier and later career affords little ground for confidence in his total innocence.

If some of the chief actors in this case had been puppets manipulated by a malicious joker, they could hardly have acted more strangely than they did. E. F. Dakin typically and airily dismisses the episode as "a comic-opera mystery,"[75] but there was nothing comic in it for Mrs. Eddy. It came near to imprisoning her husband and wrecking her cause. As it was, it caused her immense expense, heartache, and adverse publicity.

Something of what the episode cost her is suggested in an incident recorded by Clara Choate. Mrs. Eddy had just returned to Lynn from all day in the courtroom in Boston. Obviously ill, she left Mrs. Choate and Miranda Rice in the sitting room, but a little while later passed through the room again, her face pale, blood on her lips, and shakily bearing in her hands a basin with blood in it. The two women ran forward to her, but she motioned them back saying, "God can heal me, God can heal me," and went into the next room. Later she came out again with what Mrs. Choate characteristically described as a "sweet fearless smile" and an "awe-inspiring" countenance. "I knew God would heal me," she told them, "and he has. . . . Now dear [to Mrs. Choate], go home—be happy for all is well and *we can trust God.*"[76]

Later she wrote in *Science and Health,* "Every trial of our faith in God makes us stronger."[77] By that reckoning the year 1878 should have been a very strengthening one.

Chapter III

Church Militant

Church Militant

On November 24, 1878, while the threat of conviction still overhung her husband, Mrs. Eddy lectured in the Baptist Tabernacle in Boston on "The Art of Healing by Divine Power." That was the first of a regular weekly series of Sunday-afternoon lectures or sermons which she gave in the vestry of the shabby old Baptist Church on Shawmut Avenue through most of the winter of 1878–79. The regular minister, Joseph Williams,[1] usually attended these meetings and spluttered a little in the open discussion that followed the talk.

One of Mrs. Eddy's severest critics has written of her, "Though she walked over thorns, her tread was as light as air."[2] So it was that even while the unhappy court cases of the previous year dragged on, she spoke with such buoyant conviction at those Sunday afternoon services that the congregation soon grew and Christian Science began to strike roots in Boston.

On these occasions Mrs. Eddy was smartly dressed in a fur-trimmed velvet coat, a plumed black velvet hat, and gray kid gloves. A critical nineteen-year-old boy who heard her about that time wrote Georgine Milmine later that she could not have been more than forty-five years old; actually she was fifty-seven.[3] The fervid Clara Choate described her as looking like a queen.

The second meeting in the series was a Thanksgiving Day service held five days before Gilbert Eddy's grand jury trial. Mrs. Eddy's subject was "God," and following her sermon there were spontaneous "testimonies" or expressions of thanksgiving by members of the congregation. The first was by Mrs. Sarah Frothingham, who spoke simply of the fact that she had come into Christian Science not for physical healing but for a clearer insight into the nature of God; she told also of the joy she had found and the satisfaction of sharing it with others. Because Mrs. Frothingham was "a modest woman of few words," according to Clara Choate, her little speech was "quite electrifying" to the group. Other testimonies followed, as well as questions and answers, and Mrs. Eddy spoke with "a new inspiration in her tone and manner, an indescribable power," so that, in the words of the not-altogether-impartial Mrs. Choate, "even the hard face of the Rev. softened as he looked at her."[4]

Mrs. Eddy preached at later services on such subjects as "The New Tongue," "Biblical Healing," "Love," "The Coming of Christ," and early in the new year on "The Imposition and Demonology of Mesmerism Explained." The rough manuscript of one of the sermons shows her in more fanciful mood than was common to her, but it suggests something of her rebellion against the dour pieties of her day and place:

> I wish the means were in my power to build a church for the poor, the sensitive, the refined, the proud who earn their bread by the sweat of honest toil, and I would have for them a change from gloomy walls to frescoed ceiling, gilded balconies, hung with the burnished cages of bright winged warblers singing as if at heaven's gate . . . and a deep throated organ pealing, reverberating, fading in soft cadence. . . .[5]

When her own church did come into existence, it would be very different from this, and yet the glowing color and light suffusing the auditorium of the original Mother Church when it went up in Boston fifteen years later did have a little of the quality suggested here, minus the caged warblers.

As early as 1873 she had predicted "Some day I shall have a church of my own."[6] When, in 1875, her students formed themselves into a little group called simply "The Christian Scientists," they held public services for five weeks, with Mrs. Eddy giving what was variously described as a sermon or a lecture at each of the meetings, but these were soon discontinued as premature. When the group was revived in 1876, as the Christian Scientist Association, public services were not resumed. Formalized by a constitution in 1877, the association remained an organization open only to Mrs. Eddy's students, and its weekly meetings were more for the purpose of continued education and metaphysical discussion than for worship.

In the second edition of *Science and Health,* appearing just as the press was in full tilt against the group, Mrs. Eddy wrote:

> We have not a newspaper at our command through which to right the wrongs and answer the untruths, we have not a pulpit from which to explain how Christianity heals the sick, but if we had either of these, the slanderer and the physician would have less to do, and we should have more.[7]

Now she had a temporary pulpit, and the press had turned respectful for the time being. On January 24 she wrote Clara Choate with a certain racy enjoyment:

I wish you could have been at the meeting at the Tabernacle last Sunday. . . . [Three rose to ask questions] and I beat them every time; one of them said he was satisfied, the others had reason to be for the audience cheered me, clapped and stamped and the clergyman told them he should not have that, and commenced saying that I was "dark as a beetle on some points" and I went to reply to the clergyman but he kept on and the audience called out "let her speak" etc; then Mr. Williams turned to complimenting me but I knew it was all for policy at that time. . . . I have lectured in parlors 14 years. God calls me now to go before the people in a wider sense.[8]

In the middle of February the meetings were moved to Fraternity Hall in the Parker Memorial Building on Berkeley Street. The newspapers carried weekly notices and sometimes accounts of the sermons, and on April 6 a letter to the *Boston Globe* from Benjamin Atkinson, recently elected to the Massachusetts legislature, paid public tribute to Mrs. Eddy as "a lady of pleasing address, high character, conscientious, charitable, and humane."

The atmosphere was clearing and the situation was ripening for Christian Science to emerge as a church, not merely a free-wheeling, knockabout system. The obscure but decisive step is recorded in the minutes of the Christian Scientist Association meeting for April 12, 1879, with nine members present: "On motion of Mrs. M. B. Glover Eddy, it was seconded & unanimously voted, that we organize a church to be called Church of Christ." Further consideration at later meetings led to the name's being changed to Church of Christ (Scientist) and to its description as "a church designed to commemorate the word and works of our Master, which should reinstate primitive Christianity and its lost element of healing."[9] On August 6 a state charter was applied for, and on August 23 it was granted. Boston was given as the seat of the church and Mrs. Eddy as its president. A few days later she accepted the pastorate. By that time there were twenty-six members of the church.

Through the month of June services had continued at Parker Memorial Hall, the Eddys coming from Lynn to Boston by train each Sunday to conduct them. Gilbert Eddy, always faultlessly attired in a Prince Albert, ushered, took the collection, and talked with interested newcomers afterward. One of these, Arthur True Buswell, wrote later:

While Mrs. Eddy, the eloquent, earnest pleader for her infant Cause was the chief object of interest, it was the gentle, yet evidently strong nature of Asa Gilbert Eddy which formed a necessary "background," and seemed to make the meetings altogether complete.[10]

He was to the little band of Christian Scientists, wrote Buswell, what Captain Myles Standish was to the Pilgrims.

The simplicity of those early services is apparent in the general pattern they followed: silent prayer, the Lord's Prayer and Mrs. Eddy's metaphysical interpretation of it, the sermon, questions, and answers. Held at times in private homes in various places, with sometimes only four or five present, there would be readings from the Bible and *Science and Health* when Mrs. Eddy was not there to preach.

While the final steps were being taken during the summer toward the organization of the new church, Mrs. Eddy taught Arthur Buswell and a friend of his, James Ackland, who had both become interested in Christian Science through the weekly services in Boston. The two young men came to Lynn and stayed with the Eddys for some six weeks while they studied, and each was included among the directors of the new church when it received its charter.

Buswell later described the mingled doubt and hope that filled him as he pulled the bell knob at 8 Broad Street for the first time. Since the ground floor was leased to tenants, Mrs. Eddy conducted him up to the second floor, and he was surprised at the modesty of the furnishings. But this only enhanced Mrs. Eddy's appeal, he explained:

> She had the faculty of making one feel it a duty, as well as a pleasure, to fight in the Christian Science ranks. A great principle was at stake and one should naturally be led to its defense for its own sake rather than for any personal reward or worldly renown that might follow its possession. Frankly, I was drawn, irresistibly, to trust her quite as much from her own as from my necessity.[11]

Buswell was a former practitioner of hydropathy and Ackland is said to have once been professor of phrenology—fads as popular in their day as group therapy and mind-expanding drugs in ours. But Mrs. Eddy's instruction brushed aside all such fashions as equally beside the point. The course, wrote Buswell, began, continued, and ended with the study of God; even health was considered *sub specie aeternitatis*. Ackland, who was more of a lightweight than his friend, wrote Mrs. Eddy at the end of their stay:

> They were pleasant meetings—those were precious hours, when Life, Truth and Love uttered their inspirations with a woman's voice—through a form transfigured with earnestness— flooding that little parlor with the inspiration of heaven. We reasoned, we counseled, we chatted, we studied, and there were

friends and music. . . . Nor shall I forget or ignore the silent or spoken, the firm, fruitful, wise, honorable influence of your companion, for how could I possibly have been Eddified without him?[12]

Both men were deeply impressed by the companionable understanding between Mr. and Mrs. Eddy. This was especially noticeable because of the difficult circumstances of their life at that time. The lawsuits of the previous year had been a severe drain on their resources. Buswell could pay them only fifty dollars for his tuition, and Ackland only twenty-five. Gilbert Eddy frequently had to do the cooking, and Buswell was shocked to come in one day and find Mrs. Eddy scrubbing the stairs. When he expostulated at her being subjected to such an indignity, she remarked cheerfully that it made a good change from writing—and anyway, the mesmerists had made it impossible for her to keep a servant.

For even though she might now be engaged in building a church, a good deal of her attention was still given to combatting mesmerism.

2

The case of *Eddy vs. Tuttle et al.* had come up again on June 4, 1879, in the probate court at Salem, although Tuttle had now been dropped from the charge and the only defendant was the *et al.*, Charles Stanley.

The *Boston Traveler* next day confined its report to one quizzical sentence: "This celebrated case was heard yesterday before Judge Choate, and the testimony was very peculiar and decidedly interesting, showing how people may be duped." Some days later the *Lynn Item* commented:

> *It appears that the reports in various papers of the case of Eddy vs. Tuttle in the Superior Court recently did injustice to Mrs. Eddy. . . . In previous reports of the case most of the rebutting evidence, notably that of Mrs. Eddy herself, was omitted, which tended to give readers an entirely erroneous opinion concerning her teachings and belief. No opinion has yet been rendered by Judge Choate.*[13]

Many years later Richard Kennedy wrote Lyman Powell that he acted as advisor to Stanley in this suit, as well as appearing as a defense witness. Writing also of Mrs. Eddy's earlier suit against him (Kennedy), he noted that she "was sorely pressed for funds at the time," but that his own concern was not merely with the gaining or losing of a thousand dollars. "It was my opportunity in a public way," he wrote, "to say I did not value her teachings."[14] The Stanley case gave him a chance to rub the point into the public mind further.

Judge Choate's notes of the trial show that Kennedy testified that all he had ever learned from Mrs. Eddy was to heal by physical manipulation: "This was a part of her system that I had learned—The special thing she was to teach me was the science of healing by soul power—I have never been able to come to knowledge of that principle."[15] Mrs. Eddy, remembering Kennedy's long hours of eager discipleship and the spiritual idealism that overflowed his early letters, must have listened with a sinking heart as he coolly proceeded to discredit her Christianity:

> She told me that she had expelled Mr. Stanley from the class—of his incompetency to understand her science—that it was impossible to convince him of the folly of his times—that his faith in a personal God and prayer was such that she could not overcome it—She used the word Baptist in connection with him because he was a Baptist. . . . Mrs. Eddy requested me to rub Mr. Stanley's head and to lay special stress upon the idea that there was no personal God, while I was rubbing him.[16]

This was well calculated to outrage a respectable, God-fearing court, however deliberately it might misrepresent Mrs. Eddy's actual teaching in 1870. Something of this may have been in her mind when she later defined mental malpractice as "a bland denial of Truth."[17] The *Lynn Item* reported that, on being asked whether she ever told him to rub the religion out of and the science into Stanley's head, Mrs. Eddy with a look of contempt replied, "No," and then went on to point out that most of her students were church members.[18]

Other witnesses testified to healings they had had from her method and to the worth of her teachings. In his decision filed on October 14, 1879, Judge Choate himself noted:

> It appeared that the Defendant [Stanley] has practiced as a physician by various methods, or without methods, and at times has held himself out as a "Christian Scientist," a name claimed by the Plaintiff as belonging distinctly to her and those who practice her method, and it also appeared that at times the Defendant has represented that he was practicing her method, or what she taught him.[19]

This method, the Judge continued, was apparently nothing but "certain manipulations" which the plaintiff claimed were no part of her system, and he found that no instructions or explanations were given by her which appeared intelligible, were of any value to the defendant as a competent practitioner of healing, or justified a decision for the plaintiff.

And so the last of the suits instituted by Arens was lost. Eleven days earlier the Barry case had been settled; nine days later the plaintiff's exceptions in the case of *Glover vs. Kennedy* were waived. Apart from an appeal from the Stanley decision, which was withdrawn in July, 1880, the era of lawsuits was over.

Mrs. Eddy had written in the *Lynn Transcript* back in 1876 of using her pen as a "safety-valve,"[20] and she still continued to do so on occasion. Something of the frustration she felt at trying to explain her metaphysical system under cross-examination found relief in a mordant lampoon written in almost Dickensian vein. Only a fragment of it exists in rough form among her manuscripts, but it throws light—and lightness—on the experiences of this period:

> *First inquiry Have you ever written a book? "yes sir." Show it; the judge takes the book passed to him by the lawyer and this blot upon the bar made eloquent with whiskey holds the book like a cocked pistol drawn upon the plaintiff while he proceeds with a leer—Your Honor, this book is mere bosh, it talks of nothing but God, and how to heal the sick, and how to get rid of sin, and all such nonsense as this. The Judge scowls and lays down the book (the lank lawyer nearly substanceless from the use of tobacco, and the disuse of mind, with ears working ominously) commences again what is your business, aint you a doctor, how do you treat the sick?—through mind is the proud response. What do you do with mind, squeaks the long-eared gentleman? heal the body is the reply. yes oh! yes, fill the body with mind eh! how do you do that? I said heal the body, sir. Yes you did, did you? What's the essence of God? the plaintiff replies slowly I know of nothing higher than God. Then you dare to deny there is any Allmighty? No Sir—I believe in God. You do, do you, then why don't you say it? I thought I did, replied the plaintiff. Answer the lawyers question thundered the Judge—plaintiff replies firmly, I know there is a Supreme Being. Then why dont you use medicine, starts up the learned Lawyer, why dont you give rhubarb or physic instead of giving folks metaphysics? dont the Bible say you must use physic when you have dyspepsea? answer my question / I never saw any such command in the Scriptures. Now do you dare tell me the Bible ain't true? . . . I will not have this evasion put in the court, and down came his foot on the floor.[21]*

Mrs. Eddy could laugh somewhat ruefully in retrospect, but the trials had left very grave problems, especially financial ones. Before the favorable Barry decision Gilbert Eddy even considered whether he might not have to go into bankruptcy. It was definitely decided for a time that they would leave Lynn and Boston and move to Cincinnati, Ohio. The plan was to have Arthur Buswell go first, establish himself, and then report back to them whether the laws there were favorable for the practice of Christian Science.

Buswell left, Gilbert Eddy noted in his diary that their crated goods were ready to ship to Cincinnati, and then on October 24, Mrs. Eddy wrote James Ackland in Philadelphia that everything had taken a somersault; the students were now ready to help, wanted her to stay in Boston, had "worked up to having meetings regularly," and were sanguine of success. Because of the recent newspaper stories and her financial situation, she felt she ought to remain there for the winter and "preach to the Pharisees one season to settle the ferment."[22]

This was not the only time in the years now opening when she was to feel a sort of claustrophobia in the overintense atmosphere of Lynn and Boston. Buswell himself had written her from Cincinnati that it was a relief to be away from the "mental furnace" there.[23] But much though she might desire to start again in a fresh atmosphere, Mrs. Eddy was always held to Boston by her infant church.

One thing she had learned from her lectures in Boston the preceding winter: That city, with its broader cultural horizon, provided a more fertile field than Lynn, with its cramped provincialism. Accordingly she and Gilbert let the whole of 8 Broad Street for the winter and moved into furnished rooms in Boston. By November 30, 1879, Sunday afternoon meetings had been resumed, this time at the Hawthorne Rooms, 2 Park Street, and announced as services of the Church of Christ, Scientist.

On Sunday, December 28, Mrs. Eddy took as her text, "For unto us a child is born." The prophet, she declared, had foretold not only the birth of the infant whose wailings blent with the bleating of goats and kine but also the advent of the spiritual idea he represented— "the idea of Life evolved from Spirit." This was the idea conceived by the virgin mother and brought forth as the human Jesus; but, as Mrs. Eddy spoke, it was clear once again that she was talking as much of the nineteenth century as of the first:

> Here the vision of Mary rose above the maternal instinct, giving place to prophecy, and mutely she pondered the fate of her son. Even a mother's pride and fondness were not blind to the necessities of history when the divine meets the human and the human struggles with the divine. But conscious of the power

of Truth, the supremacy of Spirit over matter, she early made demands upon her idea of God to present this proof, saying to her son at the marriage feast, "They have no wine." He replied, "Mine hour is not yet come," but the persistent mother had a clearer sense that God gives dominion to man and she urged the exhibition of this power and the demonstration that her idea was begotten of Truth, namely, that Mind is creative, causal, and must present its own ideals; therefore she said to the servants, "Whatsoever he saith unto you, do it," and Jesus turned the water into wine.[24]

3

After receiving Mrs. Eddy's letter announcing her decision to stay in Boston, Arthur Buswell wrote her that he was not surprised; he had felt from the first that she should remain. "You seem to be aware," he added, "of 'some trials' awaiting your labors there. I hope our little band—the apostles—will rally around and sustain you."[25]

One unexpected trial was her long-anticipated reunion with her son, George Glover.

Almost thirty years earlier, when she was a young widow without health or means to take care of him, young George, then a lusty boy of six, had been put into the care of a foster family at the insistence of her own family. Six years later his foster parents had moved with him out to Minnesota, leaving his mother desolate but helpless to recover him.

Over the years the two had made various unsuccessful attempts to meet again. For some years Mrs. Eddy had not been able to trace the boy at all, but since the Civil War they had corresponded—though intermittently, for George's foster parents had left him virtually illiterate and he depended always on someone else to write for him. He carried his mother's picture with him in a locket wherever he went,[26] but as he moved from Minnesota to Dakota Territory, married, had children, became a farmer and then a prospector for gold in the Black Hills, his life seemed to grow steadily away from her.

After her marriage to Gilbert Eddy, Glover's letters were addressed to "My dear Mother and Father." On August 12, 1879, he had written them of his moving to Deadwood, a place of legend made doubly celebrated by the shooting of Wild Bill Hickok two or three years before. Mrs. Eddy in turn wrote him of some of the trials she was going through, and it was finally agreed that they should meet in Cincinnati. When she failed to turn up there, he came on to Boston, and for the first time in twenty-three years they were reunited.

Glover was now thirty-five, a rugged, picturesque figure from what was still the Wild West. Young Mary Godfrey saw him one day in a Chelsea grocery store and (with her New England prejudices showing) recalled the incident in later life:

> He stood there calling out his orders in a loud voice, and his manner was so boisterous and his costume so unusual that I could not help telling my mother about it when I returned home. I do not recollect the details of his clothes now, except that his legs were encased in great high boots such as I had never seen before, and his trousers were tucked into these boots. I remember his hair was long and he wore a beard. He seemed entirely out of keeping with the surroundings there.[27]

Unfortunately, despite the strong affection Mrs. Eddy and her son felt for each other, they found little in common during the few months of his stay. On November 22 the Christian Scientist Association extended an invitation to him to become a member. He expressed thanks, but declined the honor, "home being so far away."[28] Deeply impressed though he was by his mother's healing powers, he grasped little or nothing of her teachings. One day when he was demonstrating a metal, forked instrument, somewhat similar to a divining rod, which he had invented for the purpose of discovering gold, Mrs. Eddy sighed that that was the difference between them: George was always looking down into the earth, she was looking up and away from it.[29]

One thing, however, he did catch on to very quickly—the "black arts" of Kennedy. In an interview in 1907 he told of the mysterious influence which had forced the Eddys and him to move from one lodging place to another during the winter of 1879–80. "We would move to a new house and fellow lodgers would be all smiles and friendliness," he stated. "Then in an hour an inevitable change would come." The friendliness would vanish and they would be ordered to leave—once within a week of their arrival. It was, Mrs. Eddy explained to him, the mental influence of the malpractitioners that brought about these sudden reversals, and Glover gathered that the chief offender was Richard Kennedy.

To his simple mind a simple solution at length suggested itself. According to his account, he went one day to Kennedy's office and, finding the young man at his desk, pulled out a revolver, pressed the muzzle against his head, and ordered him to stop his hypnotic tricks. While Kennedy "shook like a jellyfish," Glover told him that if they had to move from one more boardinghouse, "I will search you out and shoot you like a mad dog." His laconic comment to the interviewer in 1907 was: "But it did the business all right. We were not ordered out of another boardinghouse that winter."[30]

When the interview was published Kennedy denied the whole

incident categorically, and there is nothing anywhere else that either supports or disproves it. Whether it was real or a tall tale of the Western variety, it gives some indication of the hopelessness of Mrs. Eddy's looking to George Glover for the sort of intelligent championship she needed—also of why they may have been asked to move.

Meanwhile his family in the West were clamoring for him to come home. In a letter to "Dear Husband and Mother" on January 11, 1880, his wife Nellie wrote that she was sick, everybody was tired of waiting on her, and "little Mary is sitting on her stool with mothers letter singing to herself my papa wont come home and papa will be sorry if he dont come home."[31] So early in February, Glover left for Deadwood, not to return until eight years later.

But he found a welcome surprise awaiting him at home. While in Boston he had mentioned to Mrs. Eddy that his three-year-old daughter, Mary Baker Glover, was cross-eyed, and Mrs. Eddy's quiet response had been, "You must be mistaken George; her eyes are all right." On returning to Deadwood he found that they were indeed all right. The daughter, who in later life became a Christian Scientist, wrote in 1934: "Mother has a picture of me taken before this incident, showing my eyes crossed. This healing was often told me by my father and mother, and is at this time verified by my mother, who is with me."[32]

In that same February, Mr. and Mrs. Eddy moved into a house at 551 Shawmut Avenue, Boston, which George and Clara Choate had leased with the understanding that they would share it. Actually George Choate was off in Portland, Maine, trying his wings as a Christian Science practitioner, during the whole five months that the joint venture lasted. But with Mrs. Choate's five-year-old son Warren and her sister Ida living there, the household provided a kind of family base for Mrs. Eddy.

She "sometimes planned the family dinner, & told me how to cook it & enjoyed these little diversions," wrote Clara Choate. "Our part was to entertain her for we all sang & played the piano, & this caused a sunny vein among the shadows. She once rebuked me for singing 'In the sweet bye & bye' so much, & tried to have us realize the 'now' of things."[33]

None of Mrs. Eddy's students seemed more promising than Clara Choate, but that young woman (still in her twenties) in moments of frankness admitted her own instability. The year before she had written Mrs. Eddy:

> *Your words of love are ever before me and I sometimes wonder what inspiration urges you on to make such efforts for me who feel so utterly unworthy of such love and care. I know*

71

you will always understand me in a way no one else ever can or does.[34]

Mrs. Choate went on to confess that while she was quick to rise and conquer sickness because she was in a hurry to be rid of it, she didn't find it so easy to part with the pleasures of sense. In a later letter she wrote that Mrs. Eddy had always taught her students that if they would follow Jesus, they must take up his cross and deny self—"but my darling I am so weak I do not always do this," and she was overwhelmed with remorse:

> *You have set us an example so grand, so beautiful, so true, even like the "Master," that when some trial or grief comes to shock me and I waken to see where I stand I find myself so faltering so weak so* far away *that I cry out like Peter when walking the wave, save me, save me.*[35]

Clara Choate was by no means always so humble. On many occasions she showed herself to be both ambitious and quick-tempered, and living with her produced its own problems. At the same time George Choate wrote Mrs. Eddy constantly and somewhat grumblingly from Portland for advice on his cases. "Look upon the right side," she wrote him briskly in March, "and then have more *fight* in you, more indignation at such an imposition as disease."[36]

A more promising student was a young bookkeeper, James C. Howard, whose wife had been healed by Edward Arens (now carrying on a thriving practice in Boston). Howard studied with Mrs. Eddy in February, quickly began healing, and played the cornet at church services while Clara Choate led the singing. But Mrs. Choate, whose greatest vice was a superabundance of "personal sense," saw in Howard a rival to her husband in the church, and little love was lost between the two.

In May, Mrs. Eddy taught another class. Among its five members was Hanover P. Smith, a nineteen-year-old boy who had been a deaf mute all his life until she healed him. The slight, unprepossessing youth turned out to have more stamina than might have been expected and was eager to launch out into the public practice of Christian Science. "God will bless that boy," Howard predicted, "in a way that will surprise us."[37]

Yet the hopes of the group remained modest. The minutes of a meeting held on January 2, 1880, to prepare for the first communion service, had struck the keynote for the year: "Although the tone of the meeting was rather sorrowful yet there was a feeling of trust in the great Father of Love prevailing over the apparently discouraging outlook of the Church of Christ."[38] The record for two days later read: "The Church celebrated her communion Sabbath as a Church, and it was a very inspiring season to us all, some being present whom we had not seen for some time."[39]

The church was determined to be a real *church,* with all the fixings. That spring a Christian Science Sunday School was started with only one pupil, little Warren Choate, but Mrs. Eddy announced it as though it were already a flourishing institution and the hearts of the faithful bounded in response.[40] Then, in accordance with the established custom of all the most noteworthy preachers, an especially successful sermon by Mrs. Eddy was published in booklet form. This was *Christian Healing,* the first of her works besides *Science and Health* to be printed for general circulation, and it served a missionary as well as a homiletic purpose.[41]

Nevertheless, progress was slow and on May 23 Mrs. Eddy preached what was announced in the papers as her farewell sermon. She had only postponed, not abandoned, her idea of moving somewhere else to make a fresh start. The dismayed church members passed a unanimous resolution asking her to stay, and she consented to remain and preach through the month of June.

Meanwhile the Choates were "chemicalizing" furiously at the thought of having to pay the rent of 551 Shawmut Avenue themselves. George Choate wrote Mrs. Eddy from Portland, "Are you mad?"[42] and she replied to his "saucy silly letter"[43] that she hoped he was already ashamed of what he had written her. Actually his alarm was needless. When the Eddys did leave the house at the end of June, Mrs. Choate was quickly able to rent part of it for as much as they had paid her.

The fact was that Mrs. Eddy was now at work on another major revision of *Science and Health,* and the book had to come before all else. It was imperative that she find a quiet refuge where she could write; and with both apartments at 8 Broad Street safely let for the summer, she and Gilbert Eddy took off for Concord, New Hampshire, a town she had known and loved since early childhood days.

4

Among the Boston group, only James Howard knew where the Eddys had gone.

Writing with a certain breezy loquacity, Howard reported that Mrs. Choate was agog with curiosity about Mrs. Eddy's whereabouts and health. "I don't know what the woman is after," he wrote, "but she is grinding an axe of some kind."[44] He suspected that she wanted to be president of the Christian Scientist Association. She was, he felt, like wild ivy—"I feel the poison for at least 48 hours after leaving her." At their last meeting she asked after Sarah, his wife. On reaching home he found Sarah had been taken sick five minutes after Mrs. Choate's inquiry. "Can you see through *that* ladder?" he asked.

This was the sort of accusation that came up all too often among the students. To Mrs. Eddy it seemed a deliberately induced state of mind, the result of a malicious purpose to destroy Christian Science —a purpose of which the arch-symbol was Richard Kennedy, with Daniel Spofford a close second. Her reply to Howard was that Mrs. Choate simply acted as the sounding board for Kennedy's and Spofford's mental suggestions.[45]

In some respects the struggles of the little group at that time suggest an analogy with the several polar expeditions of the 1870's and 1880's—even to the bickerings, suspicions, and recriminations which so often sprang up on those desperate ventures. The members of the group were battling toward a goal that must often have seemed to them at least as remote as the North Pole and as hazardous to reach.

To men marooned in Arctic wastes, weak with cold and hunger, a member of the group who treacherously steals their dwindling supplies and sets them in frightened suspicion against each other is a representative of absolute evil, no matter how much of a mediocrity he may be in ordinary life. It is not then a moment for a cool recollection of the many other forms that evil may assume in civilized society—nor was Mrs. Eddy then equipped to deal with a world that contained thousands of Kennedys and Spoffords.

The diary of Captain George E. Tyson, who took command of Charles F. Hall's polar expedition when the latter died after extending the line of Greenland north two degrees of latitude, reads strangely like some of Mrs. Eddy's letters in these years:

> *The bread has disppeared very fast lately. We have only eight bags left. God guide us; He is our only hope. . . . I can only advise the men, and have no means of enforcing my authority. But if we live to get to Disko, there they will have to submit, or I shall leave them to shift for themselves. I will not live as I have lived here. . . . Then, too, there appears to be some influence at work on them. . . . The men are organized now and appear determined to gain control. They were masters of the Polaris and want to be masters here. They go swaggering about with their pistols and rifles, presented to each of them after the death of Captain Hall. I see the necessity of being very careful, though I shall protect the natives at any cost. . . . I must*

say I was never so tried in all my life. . . . The fear of death has long ago been starved and frozen out of me; but if I perish, I hope that some of this company will be saved to tell the truth of the doings of the Polaris. *Those who have baffled and spoiled this expedition ought not to escape. They cannot escape their God! . . . Last night, as I sat solitary, thinking over our desperate situation, the Northern Lights appeared in great splendor. I watched while they lasted, and there seemed to be something like the promise accompanying the first rainbow in their brilliant flashes. The auroras seem to me always like a sudden flashing out of the Divinity; a sort of reminder that God has not left off the active operations of His will.*[46]

It was the active operation of His will, Mrs. Eddy felt, that impelled her in the summer of 1880, as she labored over the third edition of *Science and Health,* to take up the strange "research" she describes in her *Miscellaneous Writings:*

I shall not forget the cost of investigating, for this age, the methods and power of error. While the ways, means, and potency of Truth had flowed into my consciousness as easily as dawns the morning light and shadows flee, the metaphysical mystery of error—its hidden paths, purpose, and fruits—at first defied me. I was saying all the time, "Come not thou into the secret" —but at length took up the research according to God's command.[47]

To James Howard she wrote on July 23, "I have passed into and out of HELL since I saw you last,"[48] and to Clara Choate (who had apologized for her flare-up of temper in June) she wrote on August 5: "I . . . now have mastered one part of this earth-problem. In *all* the different malpractices I *now* see first the individual that comes to me or my husband before they go further. So one step follows another of light in this glorious path if we walk in the light."[49]

Two days later Gilbert Eddy recorded one of the dreams or "visions" that Mrs. Eddy sometimes had at times of special stress. Often they were visions of her struggle with evil; in this case the notation reads simply: "A Vision of passing over the wave without sinking into a particle."[50] But it was to remain a vision rather than an actuality for some time to come. Gilbert Eddy himself would not live to see the day when she would finally write of malicious animal magnetism:

This growing sin must now be dealt with as evil, and not as an evil-doer or personality. It must also be remembered that neither an evil claim nor an evil person is real, *hence is neither to be* feared *nor honored.*[51]

In 1880 Mrs. Eddy still saw the problem in entirely personal terms, and never more so than when she worked on the chapter "Demonology" for the third edition of *Science and Health.* Its explicit enumeration of the crimes of K_____ and S_____, its detailed account of the conspiracy-to-murder case, its jeremiads and lamentations —these were the products of a still raging warfare which she saw in apocalyptic terms. Saint John in his archetypal drama of good and evil had written of the dragon's sending forth a flood to drown the woman who brought forth a man child destined to slay all evil, and Mrs. Eddy wrote in "Demonology":

> *The birth of a great idea comes with pain and travail; in its infancy, we have toil and sacrifice; in its advancing stages, envy and rivalry; but when our nursling is menaced we clasp it more tenderly, and when he is a man he speaks for himself and mother.*[52]

Seen from the vantage point of Mrs. Eddy's mature teachings, her mental probings in the summer of 1880 might be compared to some of the medical researches then taking place. That was the period in which each year saw the discovery of some new microbe —malaria, cholera, tuberculosis, diphtheria—and in which Pasteur advanced the principle of immunization through vaccination. The whole world was becoming germ conscious. Those microscopic bacteria were taking on the fearsomeness of the traditional dragon and sea serpent; indeed, the electron microscope of seventy-five years later, capable of enlargements 300,000 times life size, might suggest that in a molecular world even a virus could qualify as a dragon.

Mrs. Eddy, who was to write of mental molecules, molecules of faith, germs of truth, microbes of sin, the virus of hatred, and other such phenomena of inner experience, was thoroughly convinced that all outward experience is an expression of conscious and unconscious thoughts. As she saw it, the invisible germs of doubt, suspicion, and hostility in unconscious thought were as much to be resisted as the overt evils of common existence. "Choke these errors in their early stages," she would write later, "if you would not cherish an army of conspirators against health, happiness, and success."[53]

Her great fear at that time was that the students would not be sufficiently alert to put these germs under the microscope of mind —detect them, identify them, and destroy them with the specific truth appropriate to each. As the microscope enlarged, so her warnings might exaggerate, but she saw no other course than to sound the tocsin loud and clear.

Her attitude at that time was expressed in *Science and Health:*

> *Evil thoughts reach farther, and do more harm than individual crimes. . . . When malicious purposes, evil thoughts, or lusts, go forth from one mind, they seek others and will lodge in them unless repelled by virtue and a higher motive for being.*[54]

Not until a later edition would this become, with a significant change of emphasis:

> *Evil thoughts and aims reach no farther and do no more harm than one's belief permits. Evil thoughts, lusts, and malicious purposes cannot go forth, like wandering pollen, from one human mind to another, finding unsuspected lodgment, if virtue and truth build a strong defence.*[55]

In this change of emphasis there is a certain analogy with evolving medical theories. At first nearly all medical interest was centered on the microbe as the efficient cause of disease, but increasingly the importance of the *terrain* (the individual constitution, including mind and body) was recognized. The reception given to marauding bacteria by the host organism could be decisive. Pasteur himself on his death-bed declared, "Bernard was right: the microbe is nothing, the terrain is everything."[56]

It may have been his scientific honesty that caused Mrs. Eddy to write in later life that Pasteur was a greater glory to France than Napoleon.[57] She herself suffered the disadvantage of belonging to an age that had not even begun to glimpse, through carefully controlled experiment,[58] the influence of "social expectation" on human, animal, and possibly even plant behavior. The scientific generation of the 1880's would, for instance, have dismissed with scorn the hypothesis that rats in a maze will show more or less learning ability according to whether experimenters are told that they have been bred for brightness or dullness. Yet a series of experiments eighty-odd years later[59] would validate the hypothesis and impel the inference that "suggestibility" operates at nonverbal biological levels to a degree which the mechanistic science of Mrs. Eddy's day would have rejected as magical. It would take decades of clinical research and a later generation's widespread acceptance of a mind-matter continuum in place of the old Cartesian dualism before Mrs. Eddy's emphasis on guarding thought against hostile mental influences could be generally understood as anything but regressive.

But while she hardily explored what Teilhard de Chardin would later call the "noosphere," the summer of 1880 had its less demanding aspects. There were places in Concord from which one could look across to the gentle Bow Hills where Mary Baker had been born in 1821. Seventeen miles to the north lay the small town of Tilton, where her later girlhood had been spent and where her stiff-necked, widowed sister Abigail Tilton was now the great lady of the town.

That was a world from whose tidy complacencies Mrs. Eddy was effectively shut off, but on August 22 she wrote George Glover that she had gone to see Mrs. Tilton the preceding week on business. She was grieved to find that her other sister, Martha Pilsbury, and the latter's married daughter Ellen had returned to Illinois only two days before without troubling to come to Concord to see her. Mrs. Eddy had healed Ellen of enteritis instantaneously in 1867 when the doctors believed her to be dying, as several members of the family recorded with a certain startled wonder; but "Nell" now denied the healing. "God bless them all if they deserve it," Mrs. Eddy wrote George, charitably but cryptically.[60]

Abigail Tilton's business partner had found it strange that Glover did not write more often, and Mrs. Eddy admonished him, "Now George be sure and take his advice and write always in the same hand to your Aunty once a month." On that same day Abigail wrote her about the family lot in the Tilton cemetery, also to "relieve your anxiety with regard to my health by telling you, I am up—have attended Church today," and concluding "Yours affectionately."[61] These mundane details were the small change of Mrs. Eddy's summer, but they are reminders of a family affection which had once been her greatest earthly treasure.

Now she was committed to lonely journeys through unfamiliar landscapes, but her love of domesticity persisted. Shortly before, she had written James Howard suggesting that in the fall he and his wife and children move into five rooms of 8 Broad Street where they might live free of rent while he was getting started as a Christian Science practitioner. She and Gilbert Eddy were also planning to return to Lynn for the winter and they would be a happy family together, "for your wife is good and you are not very bad, and the baby is best of all."[62]

Howard replied with gratitude, but wondered whether Lynn would be a good place to settle. "There is where Kennedy and Spofford have held high carnival and raised Hell generally." Moreover, his wife was afraid—fearful of his ability to heal the sick and afraid of Mrs. Eddy.[63] The latter replied in dismay that she had almost lost courage, since "they" (the malpractitioners) could make his wife doubt. This was the old story she had encountered with her early student George Allen, whose wife, through Kennedy's influence, had also doubted and had turned her husband against Mrs. Eddy when the latter went to live with them for a time. Howard's only course, she wrote, was to "gain the full confidence of your wife by showing her you have full confidence in *yourself.* . . . Good by dear student, good by. May God *help you,* and *you help yourself.*"[64]

5

Early in September she and Gilbert were "back at the old homestead in Lynn fighting the Lord's battles," as the latter put it in a letter to James Ackland.[65] The Howards had decided not to move in with them, at least not for the present. Howard himself was unanimously elected president of the Christian Scientist Association at its first fall meeting. Sunday afternoon services were held at 8 Broad Street, in the Choates' Boston house, and in the houses of several other students in Boston, Lynn, and Charlestown. In December they were again moved to Hawthorne Hall. After the manner made fashionable by Bronson Alcott, they were sometimes announced as "Conversations" on healing.

Mrs. Eddy taught a class of three in October and another in November. In the first was a woman of exceptional integrity, who won her heart immediately. At the age of sixteen Julia S. Bartlett had been left motherless and fatherless, with several younger brothers and sisters to care for, although with ample means and an opportunity to continue her education. Deeply religious, she later endured with resignation many years of suffering and invalidism. Hearing of Christian Science in the spring of 1880, when she was thirty-eight years old, she journeyed to Boston from her home in Connecticut, had treatment from Gilbert Eddy, and was quickly healed. In October she returned to study with Mrs. Eddy.

Shortly afterward Mrs. Eddy wrote her a letter addressed to "My dear Student and 'own child,'" ending it with love from her "Affectionate Teacher and Mother,"[66] and to another student she wrote of Julia Bartlett that "the more she exhibits herself to me the more I love her[;] she seems to me like my child."[67]

Miss Bartlett, who was compounded of New England rectitude and Christian charity, was to be a pillar of the Church of Christ, Scientist, until her death in 1924, but in the early days her charity was sorely tested by Clara Choate, whom she instinctively distrusted.[68]

Mrs. Eddy had no illusions about that mercurial lady. To James Howard she wrote at the end of September, "Be sure and include Mrs.

C_____ in your defence[;] she works fiercely in your direction to turn you against me,"[69] and to Mrs. Choate herself she wrote:

> *I am sorry you are so tried, but God is speaking to us all, either in commendation or rebuke through the things we experience, if we are doing strictly right we shall be blessed for all we endure[;] if not, and we continue to justify ourselves we shall suffer more and more and gain nothing through that suffering. We must be* honest, speak the Truth, *tell things as they are or not tell them, we must be unselfish and not envious, we must do as we would be done by, is what God is saying. . . . May God help and bless my dear student, is my constant prayer, and teach her and lead her up higher.*[70]

That she had need to be led up higher was recurrently evident, as when another student, Carrie Potter, of small education but good voice, explained to Mrs. Eddy why she did not want to join the church and be its soloist: "Mrs. Choate dont recognize and despises me and has brought her little Warren up to dislike me and he wont speak. . . . I can try and do just as near right and will sing for *you* or anything I can do to please *you* with pleasure."[71] Yet no matter how visible Mrs. Choate's shortcomings might be, Mrs. Eddy did not believe in abandoning lightly a student of such marked gifts, and she continued to alternate letters of loving counsel with sterner missives:

> *When O when will you see the work of the enemy to destroy your interest and happiness and success and stop before you step too far to stop. . . . Do you turn the mind or* try *to turn it of an individual in your favor and against another person? . . . Another question, with your sensuality do you contemplate trying to teach for at least fifty years this holy and pure science that my most christian and purest students would not attempt?*[72]

The answer to the last question was that Mrs. Choate hoped most fervently to become a teacher of metaphysics, but it was Julia Bartlett, not she, who reached and held that position through many long years of service. Meanwhile another step was being taken by Mrs. Eddy to dignify the teaching and legitimize the practice of Christian Science.

Back in February a bill had been introduced in the Massachusetts legislature to require all persons who practiced healing to be properly trained. This apparently reasonable but loosely worded requirement would have set up a complete monopoly by orthodox—*i.e.*, allopathic —medicine. While the fate of the bill still hung in the balance, Mrs. Eddy had preached in Hawthorne Hall on the subject "Bill of Rights for 1880," that year being the centenary of the incorporation of a 1780 bill of rights into the Massachusetts Constitution. A week or two later the restrictive bill was defeated.

Since then Mrs. Eddy had been giving thought to how Christian Science could be made more respectable in the eyes of society. In that concern she found help in different ways from two medical men.

Rufus King Noyes, M.D., of Lynn, was a highly respected but heretical physician. A graduate of the Dartmouth Medical School and for many years resident surgeon at the Boston City Hospital, he became president in 1880 of Bellevue Medical College, a new institution just starting up in Boston. In that same year a small book by him, *The History of Medicine for the Last 4000 Years,* was published in Lynn.

The history of medicine, Noyes held, was one of imposture—"a practice of fundamentally fallacious principles, impotent of good, morally wrong, and bodily hurtful."[73] Nature, he insisted, is always the healer. Indeed in his own practice he gave little but water—a practitioner of the placebo before the word itself came into use. In his book he delighted to quote great doctors of the past on the uncertainty and positive harmfulness of drugs in medical practice.

Mrs. Eddy quickly read the book and drew on it for relevant quotations in her chapter "Healing the Sick," as she revised it for the forthcoming third edition. God, it appeared, had raised up a champion from the ranks of the doctors themselves. At some point she came to know Noyes personally and seems to have won his admiration, although his cynicism is evident in his asking her how long it took her to decide to make her healing into a religious doctrine in order to escape "the clubbings from our laws."[74]

The dean of the new Bellevue Medical College was one Charles J. Eastman, a much more dubious character than Noyes. He is not known to have received from any reputable institution the M.D. which he sported, but he had attended as a very small boy the "infant school" Mrs. Eddy ran for a season in Tilton. A shady part of his life that was unknown to her in 1880 was his indictment for an illegal operation, with his subsequent release for lack of evidence.[75]

How he and Mrs. Eddy had become acquainted again after the lapse of thirty-four years is not known, nor is it known how he became associated with a man of Noyes' professional reputation and integrity in conducting the Bellevue College. He is said to have been healed by either Mr. or Mrs. Eddy of a condition that "baffled the doctors" and to have advised one of her students, "Never give up this Christian Science, for you can do more than all of us can with materia medica."[76] But his chief connection with Christian Science was in the starting of the Massachusetts Metaphysical College.

Chapter 375 of the Massachusetts Acts of 1874 provided that "seven or more persons within this Commonwealth" could form a corporation for a benevolent, charitable, educational, medical, religious, or scientific purpose." This was the very broad law under which the Bellevue Medical College was formed. The act did not expressly grant the right to confer degrees, and the rickety Bellevue venture came to grief two years later on that point, the law itself having been repealed a few months earlier.

Sometime in 1880, either before or after she met Noyes and Eastman, Mrs. Eddy decided to form an institution to give weight to her teaching. On June 26 James Howard had given official notice of a meeting to form a corporation to be known as the Massachusetts Metaphysical College. On July 29 Mrs. Eddy wrote him about "the tangle over the Charter," advised him to keep the reins in his own hand and "*look out* for *Eastman*," whom she believed to be honest "but I may be mistaken."[77] Eastman's usefulness to them seems to have been that he knew the commissioner who would grant the charter and knew all the procedural ropes. Also it would help to have an "M.D." on the board of directors of the college.

On October 10 a legal "agreement of association" was signed by Mrs. Eddy, Howard, Eastman, Bancroft, and three other male students. The purpose of the corporation was: "To teach Pathology, Ontology, Therapeutics, Moral Science, Metaphysics and their adaptation to the treatment of disease." And finally on January 31, 1881, the charter was issued, a new sign was hung outside 8 Broad Street, Mrs. Eddy became the president as well as the sole faculty member of a college—and for a year things went on exactly as before.

6

Back in 1878, when the still unpublished second edition of *Science and Health* was foundering at the Boston printer's, Mrs. Eddy had turned for emergency help to John Wilson of the University Press in Cambridge. Wilson was generally accounted to be one of the three outstanding book manufacturers in the United States. He had come to her professional rescue, showed her how enough of the book could be salvaged to make the slim "Vol. II" which appeared shortly afterward, and thereby won her enduring gratitude and confidence.

In April, 1880, Gilbert Eddy wrote Wilson for an estimate of the cost of printing the third edition, then in preparation. Wilson replied that the cost would depend on the quantity of new material and the quality of book desired, but that his firm would require one-half of the amount to be paid before beginning work.

That was the last he heard until one January afternoon in 1881 Mrs. Eddy turned up in person in his office, recalled herself to him, told him of the voluminous troubles she had had with the writing and printing of the first two editions, admitted frankly that it would be impossible for her to advance half the cost then or to pay in full on delivery, but assured him of her confidence that she could sell enough copies to meet the cost if he would go ahead and print the third edition. Instantly, in the face of all his Scottish caution and ingrained business conservatism, he agreed. "I *knew* that the bill would be paid," he explained in later years, "and I found myself actually eager to undertake the manufacture."[78]

Mrs. Eddy immediately fished the full manuscript out of her handbag and gave it to him. When he asked her in astonishment, "You brought this on the chance of my accepting it?" she replied with some amusement, "No, not on a chance. I never doubted."[79]

The friendly and fruitful relationship that followed stands in ironic contrast to Spofford's rupture with her over a similar issue. Looking back on it, William Dana Orcutt, Wilson's successor as head of the University Press wrote:

> *I doubt if John Wilson absorbed many of Mrs. Eddy's religious doctrines during that early conference, although he later became distinctly interested in Christian Science, but during that long afternoon he did receive an indelible impression of a great spirit, and a faith in Mrs. Eddy's unwavering devotion to her destiny that always characterized their long friendship.*[80]

At their first meeting in 1878 he had given her a copy of a book by his father—"an advanced Unitarian, but regardless of sect, a verra Godly man"[81]—entitled *A Treatise on English Punctuation.* Mrs. Eddy never did master the rules of punctuation, as she ruefully admitted,[82] but she marked some of the examples that interested her, one of them being: "All great discoveries, not purely accidental, will be gifts to insight; and the true man of science will be he who can best ascend unto the thoughts of God,—he who burns before the throne in clearest, purest, mildest light of reason."[83]

The third edition reflected the author's desire to give a more fully reasoned and "scientific" statement of her subject. It included for the first time her famous "scientific statement of being." This was part of the latest revised version of her treatise *The Science of Man,* which was now incorporated into *Science and Health* as "Recapitulation"—the chapter which in a still later version is the basis of Christian Science class instruction today. It had already moved a long way toward its present form, as can be seen in its answer to the question, "What is substance?"

> *That only which is eternal and incapable of discord and decay. Truth, Life, and Love, are substance, as the Scripture defines this word, "The substance of things hoped for, the evidence of things not seen." Spirit or Soul is substance, for God is the only real substance. The universe and man are shadow or idea.*[84]

Here only the word "shadow" belongs to the early period when she habitually used it to describe man. Now man was emerging from the status of shadow to that of clear-cut idea, as set forth in the uncompromising terms of the scientific statement of being.[85] In a sense, that quintessential statement of her metaphysics would gradually remove many of the relativisms of the early editions.

An often-noted example is the first sentence of the preface, which still read in the third edition: "Leaning on the sustaining Infinite with loving trust, the trials of to-day are brief, and to-morrow is big with blessings." Later, to its spiritual and grammatical betterment, this would become: "To those leaning on the sustaining infinite, to-day is big with blessings."[86]

Among the trials that cast a shadow over the third edition and over the year 1881 was the activity of Edward Arens.

That energetic gentleman, burning more with fanatic zeal than with the light of mildest reason, had steadily drifted away from the Eddys after the court cases of 1878. He had set up as a healer in Boston, developing his own ideas and methods, and had no part in the formation of the church in 1879. Conscious of the growing separation, Mrs. Eddy had written him sometime in that year:

> *Now dear Student, I am taking this forenoon to do you good . . . is this "minding my own business and staying at home as you requested"? . . . we can say naughty things but we must not do them. I shall have patience with your temperament because I like it. . . . Does the stream separate from its fountain and not dry up? Dick [Kennedy] knows, and so does Spofford that if they can turn you into their channel and against us . . . you are without any fountain until you rise higher than you now are, and then nothing could separate us.*[87]

On Christmas of that year Arens paid her a visit which she described in the chapter on demonology in the third edition:

> *After a mutual exchange of kind congratulations tears filled his eyes, and he said: "I have been hating you dreadfully, Mrs.*

Eddy, and am here to confess it, for I now know the cause. When I was feeling so hard towards you it occurred to me it was the aforesaid mesmerist [Kennedy] producing this effect, and when I met it as that metaphysically, it destroyed it, my feelings changed at once, and I feel the same friendship for you as before." We assured him that we should have the same interest in his welfare as ever, so long as he did right, and hoped he would always escape the snare of the spoiler. He has mentioned this circumstance to another student, Mr. James Howard.[88]

But the separation continued and deepened.

Sometime in 1880 Arens married Dell Atkinson. In May of that year Benjamin Atkinson had written the Christian Scientist Association, asking that his name, his wife's, and his daughter's be dropped from membership. This was impossible. Joining the association in those days was like enlisting in the army in time of war; an oath of loyalty had to be taken at the outset, after which a resignation was tantamount to desertion, calling for a court-martial. The usual procedure was for the association to "expel" a member who asked to resign. Because of the special esteem in which the Atkinsons were held, their request was simply tabled.

A week later, on June 2, the case of Arens came up. Joseph Morton, a student who had roomed with him a short time previously, told of the antagonism Arens had expressed to the Christian Scientists and of his plans to pirate material from *Science and Health*. Others spoke in his defense and Mrs. Eddy asked not to be consulted on the matter, but the meeting ended with a unanimous vote for his expulsion.

Late in 1880 an anonymous pamphlet was published by Alfred Mudge & Son of Boston with an enormous title, the first part of which read: *The Science of the Relation Between God and Man and the Distinction Between Spirit and Matter.* It bore a strange resemblance to Mrs. Eddy's writings, and on closer examination it proved to be an almost verbatim transcription of whole pages of *The Science of Man* and *Science and Health,* muddied with a little original matter and a touch or two of Zoroastrianism. A Germanic background for the "author" might be suspected from the way capital letters ran wild through the pamphlet.

The method of its composing was described by Joseph Morton. While he was living with Arens, the latter would read him a statement from *The Science of Man,* then ask him "to state it in different words but not to change the meaning."[89] This would continue for sentence after sentence, and in that assiduous way Arens became an author.

Morton had finally left him and studied with Mrs. Eddy; it was his information about these literary shenanigans that had led to Arens' expulsion from the Christian Scientist Association. The public reason given was his alleged "immorality," a term which Mrs. Eddy used freely for all manner of moral and ethical transgressions.

Arens had long been teaching metaphysical healing as he understood it, using particularly Mrs. Eddy's "Private Direction for Treating Disease Metaphysically." Early in 1881 she had this manuscript printed by James Ackland in Philadelphia and then copyrighted, but copyrights were unimpressive to Arens, who continued to sell to his students copies of her manuscripts as well as of his printed pamphlet.

Several of these students, dissatisfied with his teachings (mystified by them, as one or two of them said), came to Mrs. Eddy for instruction in the spring of 1881. Among these were Elizabeth G. Stuart, an intelligent, strong-minded woman, and her friend Jane Straw. On April 15, after completing a class which Mrs. Eddy still held for seven women, Mrs. Stuart and Mrs. Straw signed a joint statement:

> *We studied Mrs. Eddy's system of metaphysical healing of Edward J. Arens but he did not understand it as we have since learned. And we did not learn of him how to heal the sick according to metaphysics.*
>
> *Elizabeth G. Stuart*
> *Jane L. Straw*[90]

A month or two later a revised version of Arens' pamphlet was published with a different title. *The Understanding of Christianity, or God.* This time it was explicitly attributed to him, although once again it was made up almost wholly of material from Mrs. Eddy's writings. A brief introductory paragraph explained with a curious blend of ingenuousness and disingenuousness:

> *In preparing this work for teaching, I have made use of some thoughts contained in a work by Eddy. In some cases the arrangement of the sentences is altered, and in others the meaning is changed by substituting capital letters for small letters, etc., rendering it impossible to properly make use of the quotation-marks in many* [i.e., in all] *instances.*

And now Gilbert Eddy rose up in righteous wrath and strode to his wife's defense. It was he who had taught Arens early in 1878, who had admired his zeal and trusted his judgment in that year's legal adventures, who had stood in the dock with him under an unjust criminal charge brought on them by the hidden malice of a common enemy—and now Arens was looting and sabotaging his former allies.

As publisher of the third edition of *Science and Health,* Gilbert Eddy at the eleventh hour inserted a vigorous foreword "To the Public," which, without naming Arens, gave examples of his plagiarism and denounced his character.

The plagiarist, Eddy asserted, was at one time telling people that "he learned metaphysics in Germany," at another that "he was Mrs. Eddy's pupil, and paid five hundred dollars for his tuition," and again that "Mrs. Eddy was his pupil." Where he had not directly copied his metaphysics from Mrs. Eddy, they were contradictory and puerile; where he copied without credit, he showed his unfitness to be a spokesman for Christianity:

> *If simply writing at the commencement of a work, "I have made use of some thoughts contained in a work by Eddy," walks over copyright, any fool can aspire to be wise, commence a book with the announcement that "I have taken some thoughts from Ralph Waldo Emerson," and then copy verbatim, without quotation marks, from thirty to three hundred pages of his works and publish them as his own. . . . Mrs. Eddy's works are the outgrowths of her life. I never knew so unselfish an individual, or one so tireless in what she considers her duty. It would require ages and God's mercy to make the ignorant hypocrite who published that pamphlet originate its contents.[91]*

At one point the Eddys apparently considered taking legal action against Arens for infringement of copyright, though their earlier experience in the courts made them hesitant. A letter from Elizabeth Stuart on July 8 advised Mrs. Eddy against going to law "with such a fool or crazy head" as Arens. Personally she wouldn't soil her fingers with the scamp:

> *Keep quiet, dont give things to the* Public, *work* silently *and we will work with you; vanquish him that way, for he is daring, at the same time, with the smoothest face and most angelic expression, praising you when he knows it will tell in his favor.[92]*

It was decided not to take legal action, but neither Mr. nor Mrs. Eddy agreed with Mrs. Stuart's further recommendation: "I would not even append to my Book what your husband has written, true as it is, but reserve all that for some other time and place [;] dont place [it] within the same covers, with that which is so sacred." But it did appear within the same covers at the beginning of Volume I, and the chapter "Demonology" appeared at the beginning of Volume II. The third edition was going to appear in full battle dress.

Chapter IV

Exit from Lynn

Exit from Lynn

Among the Gnostics of the early Christian era was a sect which held that Jesus of Nazareth had no fixed form, but was shaped by each man's perceptions. To one he might appear to be a withered hunchback, to another a handsome athlete.

The myth is fanciful but shrewd. It applies as well to, say, a Joan of Arc—tomboy, witch, campaigner, dreamer, crank, messiah, general, saint. The fact is that historically she was all these things to her contemporaries but was, at the same time, her unique and incommensurable self.

Mrs. Eddy likewise was many strangely diverse things to the people of Lynn. To twelve-year-old Nadia Swartz, for instance, who had just come from Russia to live with her aunt Fannie Phillips, she was a vision of loveliness, gentle, understanding, and kind.[1] To others who experienced the quick lash of her rebuke she seemed a tyrant or a shrew.[2] Mrs. Lavinia Felt, with whom she had boarded ten years before, remarked once after such a rebuke, "That woman is either a saint or a devil; I'm sure I don't know which."[3]

Young Nadia, newly arrived, was hanging out baby clothes in the Phillipses' backyard and singing a Russian song when Mrs. Eddy in the adjoining garden motioned to her to come over. The girl knew no English, but was immediately captivated by this amiable neighbor. When she reported the incident to her hard-bitten aunt, she was told sharply that Mrs. Eddy was a wicked woman, not right in the head, who preached against medicine and let people die. She, Nadia, should have nothing to do with her.

Nevertheless, every time the girl hung clothes on the line after that she sang at the top of her lungs to attract her neighbor's attention. Soon she was slipping away to 8 Broad Street whenever opportunity offered, sitting quietly on a stool beside Mrs. Eddy while the latter read and wrote—content simply to be near the woman she considered to be a paragon of kindness.[4] Mrs. Eddy taught her English sentences, sent her on little errands, heard her faltering confidences, and awoke in her a needed assurance in her own abilities. When

Nadia moved to New York seven months later, she took with her a photograph of her friend and a book of poems by one of Mrs. Eddy's students, a young man of Russian parentage; but the greatest gift by far was the affection that had warmed the young immigrant's heart.

To James Howard and his wife, who finally moved into 8 Broad Street in the spring of 1881, the situation did not seem idyllic. A letter from Mrs. Eddy to young Mrs. Howard on March 8 showed some impatience at the couple's continued indecision about moving in, and after they had made the move, Mrs. Howard was far from happy. She had been healed by Arens a couple of years before, but had never taken to Mrs. Eddy or shown any desire to study Christian Science. Furthermore, she was terrified that her husband would not be able to provide for his family by his healing work. To live rent free at Broad Street was a help, but the high-powered atmosphere there made demands on her beyond her capacities.

For one thing, it was probably not easy to play Martha to the Mary around whom the household necessarily revolved. Mrs. Eddy spent hours of study and prayer in her room. Mrs. Laura Jane Smith, who was one of a small class that studied with her in October, described the sort of incident which filled the students with awe but lay beyond the scope of Mrs. Howard's sympathies:

> One day during her class period Mrs. Eddy spent several hours in her sky lighted attic room. When she came down and stood before Miss Prime and me, her face was radiant, she seemed to be carried away of the Spirit. She spoke of the dear Jesus and the beauty of the incarnate idea and said, "O I wish I could have known Mary."[5]

Preoccupied with the practical problems of motherhood, Mrs. Howard was probably no more enchanted with Mrs. Eddy's new emphasis on the motherhood of God.[6] This emphasis appeared in an extended interpretation of the first chapter of Genesis in the forthcoming edition of *Science and Health*. For the first and last time in her career Mrs. Eddy in this part of her book identified Spirit, or God, by the pronouns She and Her. Later she would refer on many occasions to God's motherhood and write of Deity as Father-Mother, but without using pronouns so disconcerting to the ear.[7]

Typical of that early chapter was her interpretation of the last verse of the first chapter of Genesis:

> "And God saw everything that he had made, and, behold, it was very good. And the evening and the morning were the sixth day."

And Spirit comprehends every idea that She creates before it is evolved, and they are perfect even as their Principle is perfect. Nothing is new to Spirit. She rests from her labors, and the hush and stir of thought is the order of scientific evolution.[8]

It was the alternating hush and stir at 8 Broad Street that made life so difficult for the Howards. To Mrs. Eddy it seemed as though the publication of each successive revision of *Science and Health* caused her new anguish,[9] and never was this truer than in the case of the third edition with its personal diatribes against Kennedy, Spofford, and Arens. When one of the Howard children was seized with convulsions, it seemed almost like a reflection of the convulsions the little group went through under Mrs. Eddy's repeated urgings to resist "the enemy" more vigorously.[10]

By 1881 Spofford had pretty well faded out of the picture,[11] but Arens had more than taken his place.

Mrs. Stuart, who had only recently dropped her association with Arens, told them how that gentleman would order his students to "take up" Mrs. Eddy mentally.[12] Mrs. Stuart herself pooh-poohed the whole thing; but Mrs. Eddy, who at that time had several severe gastric attacks from which she found relief only by handling them as mental assaults from the Arens camp,[13] insisted that malpractice of this kind must be recognized and spiritually counteracted. Some of the students were growing restive under her exhortations, but when one of them asked her one day whether she didn't feel that the time had come to say less about animal magnetism, Mrs. Eddy sprang to her feet, struck her hands together, and cried, "Leave me at once."[14] At times she would take the students to task with a severity that left some of them shaken and contrite, others smarting and resentful.[15]

Yet she could be remarkably patient with them, too, as her many letters to Clara Choate show. "Wont you dear be a good girl," she wrote that young woman, "and *love Mrs. Hart* and show her that you are a christian under all circumstances." And again, "Won't you be careful not to give Mr. Howard occasion to think you malpractice."[16]

On September 11 Mrs. Choate wrote her:

Have felt you quite consciously with your gentle loving thought today and thank you for all your care and wisdom and hope I shall merit your labors in my behalf for I do realize they have been many and great and the greatest fear I have is that you will get disheartened in your attempts to bring out in me what you wish to[;] however I will persevere and sometime your reward will come and then in your joy will I be repaid.[17]

Another student, Sarah T. Prime, who suffered from a great sense of unworthiness, wrote her years later:

> *I remember how vehemently, even sternly, you rebuked the error which seemed at the time to be greater than my understanding of Truth, but I never shall forget the loving kindness with which you told me the next morning that I was not only "called" but "chosen." That assurance from you, and another in a letter a few years later, have stood by me in many dark hours. . . . Could those whom you rebuke see and feel the love back of the seeming severity, they would not murmur at Love's chastening.*[18]

On another occasion Clara Choate wrote Mrs. Eddy about calling on a Miss Brooks and finding her, like many of the other students, "mentally drowsy." She had told Miss Brooks the cause and cure of her condition (*i.e.*, the aggressive mental suggestions of the malpractitioners, to be recognized and rejected as such) and commented to Mrs. Eddy, "The usual sign 'displeasure of you' was first presented but soon wore off and the more I worked the faster it disappeared."[19]

Such "displeasure of" Mrs. Eddy might be explained by the rigorous demands she made on her students, but the peculiar violence of the hostility that burst out among them from time to time shows how explosive were the forces below the surface.

There was unmistakably a kind of violence in the third edition, which was finally published on August 17, 1881. For Lynn people who had known Richard Kennedy as a popular young "doctor," the shock of reading the detailed accusations in the chapter on demonology must have been considerable:

> *Carefully veiling his character, through unsurpassed secretiveness, he wore the mask of innocence and youth. But he was young only in years; a marvellous plotter, dark and designing, he was constantly surprising us, and we half shut our eyes to avoid the pain of discovery, while we struggled with the gigantic evil of his character, but failed to destroy it. . . .*[20]

Identified in Kafka-esque fashion simply as K_____, Kennedy finally emerged as an archetype of the hidden demonism in the world, a Lucifer figure foreshadowing the Rasputins, Streichers, and Duvaliers of the next century:

> *The Nero of to-day, regaling himself through a mental method with the tortures of individuals, is repeating history, and will fall upon his own sword, and it shall pierce him*

through. Let him remember this when, in the dark recesses of thought, he is robbing, committing adultery, and killing; when he is attempting to turn friend away from friend, ruthlessly stabbing the quivering heart; when he is clipping the thread of life, and giving to the grave youth and its rainbow hues; when he is turning back the reviving sufferer to her bed of pain, clouding her first morning after years of night; and the Nemesis of that hour shall point to the tyrant's fate, who falls at length upon the sword of justice.[21]

James Howard, a young man of less imposing proportions, was presented with the first copy of the third edition and put in charge of the book's sales and promotion. It was perilous freight for unsure hands to carry.

By October he and his family had moved out of 8 Broad Street. What Mrs. Eddy had foreseen more than a year before had come to pass: Mrs. Howard's plaintive opposition had been having its gradual effect on her husband, augmented by the trials and demands of what was essentially a kind of garrison life. Disturbing doubts were rising in Howard's mind at the very time he was commissioned to launch the powerful third edition.

Putney Bancroft reported at a meeting of the Christian Scientist Association on September 14 that he had recently visited George Barry, "who acknowledged that he had done wrong and hoped sometime to undo that wrong."[22] Yet now James Howard was about to start along the same path Barry had taken five years before. To Mrs. Eddy, when the break with Howard came, it would seem part of a common pattern that went back to the original defection of Kennedy. But this time it was only one element in an outburst that would leave in apparent ruins more than ten years' work in Lynn.

2

On the evening of October 26, 1881, a regular meeting of the Christian Scientist Association and a special business meeting of the Church of Christ, Scientist, were held at 8 Broad Street. In the absence of Howard, who was president of the association, Putney Bancroft served as president pro tem. At both meetings the following letter was read:

We, the undersigned, while we acknowledge and appreciate the understanding of Truth imparted to us by our Teacher, Mrs. Mary B. G. Eddy, led by Divine Intelligence to perceive with sorrow that departure from the straight and narrow road (which

*alone leads to growth of Christ-like virtues) made manifest by
frequent ebullitions of temper, love of money, and the appearance of hypocrisy,* cannot *longer submit to such Leadership;
therefore, without aught of hatred, revenge or petty spite in our
hearts, from a sense of duty alone, to her, the Cause, and our-
selves, do most respectfully withdraw our names from the Christian Science Association and Church of Christ (Scientist).*

> *S. Louise Durant,*
> *Margaret J. Dunshee,*
> *Dorcas B. Rawson,*
> *Elizabeth G. Stuart,*
> *Jane L. Straw,*
> *Anna B. Newman,*
> *James C. Howard,*
> *Miranda R. Rice.*[23]

Although the letter had been signed five days before, it exploded
with all the unexpectedness of a concealed time bomb. None of the
signers was present. Up until the very hour of its reading they had
given no outward sign of disaffection in their attitude toward Mrs.
Eddy.

The really shattering thing was the presence of Mrs. Rice's and
Miss Rawson's names among the signatures. These two sisters had
studied in Mrs. Eddy's second class in 1870, the same class to which
Putney Bancroft and George Barry had belonged. They had stood by
her through her darkest hours[24]; they were both good practitioners
and devoted workers. It is not surprising, perhaps, that people like
Mrs. Stuart and Mrs. Straw—newcomers with strong prior ideas of
their own on mental healing—should defect; but that Mrs. Rice and
Miss Rawson should do so seemed virtually unthinkable to most of
the students.

Only three months before, Mrs. Rice had visited Arthur Buswell
in Cincinnati and he had written Mrs. Eddy of the inspiration he
drew from her account of affairs in Boston. She had shown him, he
wrote, how much they needed Mrs. Eddy where she was and what a
mistake it would have been for her to move to Cincinnati and leave
them leaderless.[25] Now, in the twinkling of an eye, all this had
changed, and in future years Miranda Rice would speak of her former
teacher with unqualified bitterness.[26]

To Mrs. Eddy the whole thing was clearly the working of
aggressive suggestion. It was Howard, she believed, who had turned
Miss Rawson and Mrs. Rice against her (largely on the issue of her
continued support of Clara Choate[27]), but Howard himself she saw

as the victim, not the source, of a directed, conscious animosity toward Truth lying behind the whole affair. As Buswell put it in a letter to Ackland when he heard with dismay of the rebellion, it "all goes to show the unknown power of thought."[28] To the students who remained faithful it seemed as though something deeply and mysteriously malign was at work.[29]

For the moment Mrs. Eddy was too stunned and hurt to say anything. She withdrew from the church meeting after the twenty members there had voted to send a copy of the following resolution to each "rebel":

> *That your unchristian communication of Oct. 21st 81 renders you liable to Church discipline as you have broken our covenant in that you went not to the individual whom you abused. To tell her that you had aught against her. That you had assumed the appearance of full fellowship with her. . . . You are liable to expulsion. You are hereby notified to appear before the Church of Christ (Scientist) . . . on Monday Oct. 31 at 5 P.M. to answer for your unjust proceedings.*[30]

After passing the resolution the subdued and solemn members quietly dispersed, leaving Mrs. Eddy with her husband. The only others to stay behind were two new students, Abbie Whiting and Calvin Frye. All through the night these four talked over the situation. Then, as the morning broke, Mrs. Eddy, who had been sunk in thought for a while, began to speak as though to herself. The phrases she uttered were fragmentary, exclamatory—the punctuation of a suddenly released flood of thought. All her life she had fled to the Bible in moments of need, and now the vivid phrases welled up from that capacious reservoir. The others with her listened with startled awe. Intermittently they would try to take down what she said, but the recorded words do little today to convey the visionary power they apparently had for the three listeners:

> *Is this humiliation, the humility the oppressor would heap upon me! O, the exaltation of Spirit! . . .*
>
> *One woe is passed, and behold, another cometh quickly; and no sign shall be given thee. . . .*
>
> *And the false prophet that is among you shall deceive if possible the very elect, and he shall lead them into forbidden paths. And their feet shall bleed upon the jagged rocks. And the briars shall tear the rags from them. For they are not clothed with a garment of righteousness.*
>
> *And I will give to thee, daughter of Zion, a new heritage*

and a new people. Her ways shall be ways of pleasantness and ways of peace.

Oh, blessed daughter of Zion, I am with thee. And none shall take my words out of thy lips. Thou art my chosen, to bear my Truth to the nations, and I will not suffer another messenger to go before thee.

And this Absalom shall perish and this backsliding Israel shall eat the bread of bitterness.

And I will lift thee up Oh daughter of Zion. And I will make of thee a new nation for thy praise.

Get thee up! Depart, depart. This people are a stiff necked people.[31]

At the end she stepped forward with rapt face and said wonderingly, "Why, I haven't any body."[32] Then, as though becoming conscious of her surroundings again, she sat down.

At that moment Julia Bartlett arrived. Stopping temporarily in Salem, Miss Bartlett had heard of the secession of the students the night before and had taken the first train to Lynn, with the hope that she could comfort her teacher. As she came into the room she found Mrs. Eddy still luminous from her vision, the two men silent, with tear-filled eyes, and Mrs. Whiting kneeling by the sofa, sobbing. Quietly Mrs. Eddy began to talk with them again, and at one point she said, "I want you three to stop with me three days." Miss Bartlett's comment many years later was:

Those three days were wonderful. It was as if God was talking to her and she would come to us and tell us the wonderful revelations that came. We were on the Mount. We felt that we must take the shoes from off our feet, that we were standing on holy ground. What came to me at that time will never leave me.[33]

Mrs. Eddy had surmounted the immediate crisis, but like a comet it had a tail. On October 31 the Christian Scientist Association, refusing to accept the right of the rebels to withdraw voluntarily from membership, took action to expel Howard, Mrs. Rice, Miss Rawson, and Mrs. Stuart, merely tabling the other names.[34] At the same meeting, however, another prominent Lynn member, Mrs. Mary A. Damon, and a Miss Draper withdrew, to be followed within the next few weeks by several others.[35] It was retirement to the safe lowlands from an exhilarating but exposed height.

On November 9 the loyal remnant of Mrs. Eddy's students in a simple ceremony ordained her pastor of the Church of Christ,

Scientist. A week later, in a meeting at the Choates' home in Boston, the Christian Scientist Association adopted a set of resolutions drawn up by Clara Choate, Putney Bancroft, and Abbie Whiting. These resolutions were marked by a new, bold, somewhat mystical tone which the events of the period seem to have evoked by way of reaction:

> *Resolved, That we the members of the Christian Scientist association, do herein express to our beloved teacher, and acknowledged leader, Mary B. Glover Eddy, our sincere and heartfelt thanks and gratitude for her earnest labours in behalf of this association, by her watchfulness of its interest and persistent efforts to maintain the highest rule of Christian love among its members.*

> *Resolved, That while she has had little or no help, except from God, in the introduction to this age of materiality of her book,* Science and Health, *and the carrying forward of the Christian principles it teaches and explains, she has been unremitting in her faithfulness to her God-appointed work, and we do understand her to be the chosen messenger of God to bear his truth to the nations, and unless we hear "Her Voice," we do not hear "His Voice."*

> *Resolved, That while many and continued attempts are made by the malpractise, as referred to in the book,* Science and Health, *to hinder and stop the advance of Christian science, it has with her leadership attained a success that calls out the truest gratitude of her students, and when understood, by all humanity.*

> *Resolved, That the charges made to her in a letter, signed by J. C. Howard, M. R. Rice, D. B. Rawson, and five others, of hypocrisy, ebullitions of temper, and love of money, are utterly false, and the cowardice of the signers in refusing to meet her and sustain or explain said charges, be treated with the righteous indignation it justly deserves. That while we deplore such wickedness and abuse of her who has befriended them in their need, and when wrong, met them with honest, open rebuke, we look with admiration and reverence upon her Christ-like example of meekness and charity, and will, in future, more faithfully follow and obey her divine instructions, knowing that in so doing we offer the highest testimonial of our appreciation of her Christian leadership.*[36]

Here was the evidence of one of those moments in religious history when a movement, emerging from its earliest formative stage, begins to view as a prophet chosen of God a leader whose guidance has hitherto been accepted in limited charismatic terms. Up until now Lynn had thought of Mrs. Eddy as the woman on Broad Street with queer ideas; Boston in the next decade would come to know her as author, lecturer, teacher, head of the flourishing Massachusetts Metaphysical College, publicist and polemicist for a burgeoning religious movement; but in the document of 1881 one can already catch a foreglimpse of the authoritative figure who would finally stand before the world as the almost legendary Discoverer and Founder of Christian Science.

She was through with Lynn, however. Quickly she and Gilbert Eddy drew up plans to go to Washington, D.C., for a few weeks, then find a new home in Boston. By Christmas Day, when a last church meeting was held at 8 Broad Street, their household goods were nearly all packed. As Julia Bartlett described the scene:

> *The floors were bare. There were a few chairs, a small writing desk, and a packing box in the room. There was a lamp on the packing box which stood on end, and Mrs. Eddy sat beside it. There were about ten church members to occupy the available seats. Mrs. Eddy read the 17th chapter of John, and her parting remarks to us on the event of her leaving the city and her admonitions in regard to the care of the Church and the Cause sank deeply in our hearts.*[37]

Miss Bartlett, who had decided to leave her Connecticut home and settle in Charlestown near Boston, was voted into the church at this same meeting. Mrs. Eddy wrote her later that after "the long night of struggle," her entrance into the church was like the stone for Jacob's pillow, and then burst out, "O! my darling girl, all I ask is that the ladder of light shall rest upon it and on this ladder you go up higher."[38]

For the time being, Julia Bartlett and Clara Choate, despite their mutual dislike, filled the places that Miss Rawson and Mrs. Rice had occupied in earlier years. Mrs. Eddy was seeking to stabilize the situation in the Boston area before she left and on January 13, 1882 (still at Broad Street), she wrote Mrs. Choate: "I don't know what to say or do from one day to another in such a chemical [*i.e.*, state of chemicalization] as this. The very plan that is best for today, the next will require to be changed."[39] Commenting many years later on this period, Clara Choate wrote: "If one plan did not work another must be adopted. I have seen her in these days, walk the floor with her Bible in hand asking for guidance, or direction."[40]

Within a week the Eddys had left Lynn. A farewell letter from

Mrs. Eddy to Julia Bartlett appointed her "a substitute for me to lead this people." Not, she hastened to add, that any of the students were ready to unloose the latchets of her shoes but that she considered Miss Bartlett "rather more fit" than anyone else. Then she added significantly:

> Now dear remember that Mrs. Choate is a sister in our church and doing much good for our cause in selling books and bearing testimony for Christ.
>
> This I beg that you "love one another even as I have loved you" that no root of bitterness springs up among you. That no pride comes up or vain inquiry "who shall be greatest" but remember I have made myself the servant that I might lead others to Christ. Farewell.[41]

And with that she made her farewell to Lynn.

3

As a young girl in the simple rural society of nineteenth-century New England, Mrs. Eddy had had a life replete with brothers, sisters, friends, beaux, all the normal appurtenances and interests of a young girl's world. In later years she often looked back a little nostalgically to those days. Both her sisters had subsequently had daughters, and she had seen them grow to womanhood; but she had no daughter of her own, nor had she ever seen the small granddaughter in the Black Hills of Dakota.

Somehow it left a gap. Through her middle and later years she always responded with warmth to the impulsive idealism and sheer high spirits of young girls. In return, many of them gave her an ardent devotion compounded of schoolgirl admiration for an accomplished older woman and simple affection for an understanding friend. The correspondence which she carried on with sixteen-year-old Alice Sibley through the grim events of 1881 illustrates this side of her character.

The acquaintance had begun back in the spring of 1879 when Alice was a plump fourteen, pretty, adoring, but lighthearted and nimble-witted. Living with her family in Roxbury, near Boston, she had met Mrs. Eddy through Lucretia Brown of Ipswich, a family friend, and over the next year developed a strong case of hero worship. When the Eddys had left Boston in the summer of 1880 for Concord, New Hampshire, Alice had written a letter pouring out her breathless homage. Mrs. Eddy replied with motherly affection, quietly pointing to the advantage of "a more moderate kind of calm, strong friendship" over this schoolgirl emotionalism. She had been too busy to think of Alice much, but "always with the same kindness and appreciation of your great goodness. . . . Busy your thoughts with noble plans and keep persons out of mind. Let your daily duties *interest* you, and the loving thoughts of a Mother cheer and satisfy your mind."[42]

By November, 1880, when Mrs. Eddy was back in Lynn, Alice was writing her in the best of spirits, bubbling along about the "grand and noble lecture by Mrs. Livermore" she had just heard and her activities as soloist in the school choral society.[43] Evidently Mrs. Eddy spared time for her whenever she could, for a letter two or three months later announced that she had resolved to give herself the great pleasure of going with Alice to a much-talked-of exhibition of paintings but was suddenly faced with a new influx of demands on her time. "I could not in that case pass another day in pleasure when God requires so much of me and I am doing so little."[44] Will Alice use the money enclosed for a ticket to see the paintings and tell her about them when they next meet?

Something of what the young girl brought into her life is suggested by a letter she wrote her three weeks later, expressing her pleasure at Alice's poetry:

> That word embraces to my mind all the graces. I wish O! I wish, but vainly, I had my fancy free to write you a little offering, but will some time. I have no broken wing only a folded one. Now dear Go forth into the fields, drink in the breeze, be happy and free. O the bliss of freedom! I would I were a child again, but you, dear one, are now both child and woman; you are, in other words when I descend to pet names, my naughty wild girl wayward in goodness impulsive as the March wind and sunny as the flowers. . . . I hope you will remain at your best all the time next Sabbath and not get impatient with me because I have passed the hay day of Life and have now no time for the sweet joys of friendship but must show my love for you all working at the treadmill of metaphysics.[45]

At the end of June, Alice, who had written Mrs. Eddy that she would be a "grave senior" next year, delivered a talk on zoology at the closing exercises of the Roxbury High School and a few days later reported that the dancing at the graduation exercises had been stopped early because of the "national calamity." The news had just come through that President Garfield had been shot by an assassin, and during the summer months the country waited anxiously while his life hung in the balance. This was the summer in which the concealed tensions among Mrs. Eddy's students in Lynn were growing toward the final breaking point, but Alice continued to dance with airy unconcern across the scene.

When she came to see Mrs. Eddy early in August and the visit had to be cut short because Mrs. Eddy was either too busy or too unwell to continue it, the girl wrote quickly to reassure her that she had enjoyed heartily the time she did have with her, adding that she arrived home

> . . . *safe and sound without even meeting with the adventure of having a man follow me. . . . So do not be discouraged but try to look on the brightest side of it. As I went to the station last night, I saw a cloud almost black it was so dense and it seemed to overspread the entire sky. But all its edges were tinged with a bright gold and presently they mastered the darkness and all was light and clear. . . . I trust you had a comfortable night and that you looked your handsomest this morning for your picture. Don't trouble yourself or* MR. SMITH *to answer this.*[46]

Hanover Smith, who by this time had moved into 8 Broad Street, had evidently become general factotum, and Alice scented a rival. A few days later she wrote Mrs. Eddy:

> *I should think, if you are anything of the nature of "common people" (which I strongly begin to doubt) that you might by this time have lost at least one button, which needed to be restored to its proper place. However I suppose Mr. Smith has learned by this time to sew them much better and stronger than your humble servant who is entirely out of practice. Do you not feel in duty bound to reward such an expression of extreme jealousy. . . .*[47]

And so the correspondence went, through days of increasing challenge to Mrs. Eddy. Toward the end of August she wrote that on September 1 the Massachusetts Metaphysical College was to open and there would then be no play, no pastime for her.[48] Alice bounced back with the information that the birthday of the college coincided with her own, and on September 1 "your naughty wayward child of 'sweet sixteen' is lost to you forever and the girl of 'charming seventeen' is ushered into existence." Her own school began in another week and then she must really *work*. "I am trying to get my wild oats sown in season, but I think it doubtful if I do."[49]

Only a few days after the defection of the eight students in October, Mrs. Eddy wrote, "My little friend is never forgotten by me, however many friends or *enemies* come between us." Is Alice busy? Never let a thought of the writer mar her peace—"but never forget me, will you? I am hanging yet, even as a monkey hangs from a branch, in all respects except the hinder appendage." Yet seriously she would say to Alice:

> Take care of the company you keep, be not deceived in any one. Attempt no more than is thy duty, teach people to be unselfish and bear their own burdens, at least, while you are willing to do more than they. Do not make my mistake, to take upon yourself all the baggage of this journey onward, but correct people's taste if not their conscience in that they think to make others their handy slaves. All this is a "new tongue," is it not, dear little one? but I mean it and you need it. The day is done; shadows fall, the curtain of night shuts out the light, and I must quit my seat at the window, light the gas and give up writing more at this time.[50]

In writing to Alice, Mrs. Eddy might almost have been writing to the young Mary Baker, impetuous and eager for life. There was always a hint of the wayward young girl about her, even when she was in her eighties, but now she was being disciplined in a very stringent school.

4

By the end of January, 1882, the Eddys were in Washington. A week later they had found two pleasant rooms, just across from the Capitol, into which they could settle for the next few weeks— much to the relief of Mrs. Eddy, who wrote James Ackland on February 6, "I fear I never shall make a good traveller."[51]

But on the same day she wrote Clara Choate with lively satisfaction, "I have awakened a *ripple* of interest in this *beautiful grand* old city,"[52] and in her letter to Ackland added with gratification, "An M.D. has endorsed me." Washington was no exception to the fact that Mrs. Eddy had only to arrive in a community for her presence to be immediately felt.

This was helped along by a printed card which she soon got into circulation:

> *You are respectfully invited to attend*
> *A Course of Lectures*
> *by Mrs. Eddy, Author of "Science and Health,"*
> *At 13 First Street, N.E.*
> *Commencing Feb. 10th   First Lecture Free*[53]

The lectures began at 8 P.M. in the front parlor of George Durfee's boardinghouse at 13 First Street, a site now occupied by the Supreme Court Building. "My front parlor," Mrs. Eddy wrote back to Massachusetts, "commands the most magnificent view of the entire Capitol and grounds,"[54] and she seemed to breathe a larger air in that ample setting. After two lectures she wrote Ackland that she had an audience of about fifty—editors, colonels, teachers, one clergyman, and so forth. Among the "colonels" was Eldridge J. Smith, formerly of Philadelphia, who, with his wife, had been corresponding with her since he had first read *Science and Health* in 1876.

Soon she had a visitor who rated a paragraph in the *Washington Post* of February 12:

> *Mrs. Judge [Chandler Eastman] Potter, of New Hampshire, or as she is better known to her new friends, Mrs. Fanny McNeil Potter, paid a visit to the Senate Chamber one day last week— something that of late years she rarely does. To those who know this estimable lady the circumstances must have recalled the days of "auld lang syne," when as the guest of her uncle, ex- President Pierce, she presided at the White House with so much graceful courtesy. She is of truly noble birth, being [descended from] Sir John McNeil. . . . During her sojourn at the Capitol, Mrs. Potter, who is at 1712 "L" Street, has been the recipient of many cordial greetings, and is always especially pleased to meet the sons and daughters of her own state.*[55]

One of the daughters she was delighted to meet was Mary Baker Eddy, whom she had known as a girl when Mary's brother Albert was Franklin Pierce's law partner. The two women apparently met at Colonel Smith's,[56] and afterward Mrs. Potter called on Mrs. Eddy several times and showed considerable interest in Christian Science. Together they drove to the Botanical Gardens, the Smithsonian Institution, and the Congressional Cemetery where they knelt at the grave of General John McNeil, Mrs. Potter's father and the cousin of Mrs. Eddy's grandmother, Maryann McNeil Moore.[57]

Mrs. Eddy at this time may also have been visited by her salty cousin Henry Moore Baker, who had been practicing law in Washington since 1874. Four years later he was to become judge advocate general of the National Guard of New Hampshire, afterward serving as a Republican member of Congress. Still later when the two cousins had become fast friends Mrs. Eddy described General Baker as one of the two "most genuine characters" she had ever known.[58]

"To-day I go into the Capitol by invitation," she wrote Clara Choate[59] on February 25, and the invitation may have come by way of either Mrs. Potter or General Baker. Either one of them may also have been responsible for getting her permission to visit Charles J. Guiteau, who on January 25 after a ten-week trial had been found guilty of assassinating President Garfield. Because of the press of curious sightseers, strict orders had been issued on February 6 that no visitors should thereafter be permitted to see the prisoner except his relatives, but on February 13 the *Washington Post* noted: "A number of people were granted the privilege yesterday of looking at Guiteau in his cell, but only a few were allowed to converse with him, and none on matters relating to his execution or the trial."

Mrs. Eddy's account of her visit with him was given in an address in 1895:

> *The mental stages of crime, which seem to belong to the latter days, are strictly classified in metaphysics as some of the many features and forms of what is properly denominated, in extreme cases, moral idiocy. I visited in his cell the assassin of President Garfield, and found him in the mental state called moral idiocy. He had no sense of his crime; but regarded his act as one of simple justice, and himself as the victim. My few words touched him; he sank back in his chair, limp and pale, his flippancy had fled. The jailer thanked me, and said, "Other visitors have brought him bouquets, but you have brought what will do him good."*[60]

While her own days were touched with occasional drama, Gilbert Eddy undertook a pedestrian but thorough study of copyright law in order to protect her writings from further depredations by Arens or other literary adventurers. It was a busy, serious month for both the Eddys.

"I have met with a better reception than my most sanguine expectations promised," Mrs. Eddy wrote Alice Sibley,[61] but to Clara Choate at the end of the month she revealed that the success had not been won without labor: "I have worked harder here than ever, 14 consecutive evenings I have lectured three hours . . . besides what else I am about. Get to bed at 12, rise at 6, and *work*."[62]

With the arrival of March, the Eddys moved on to Philadelphia, where James Ackland had made preparations for their coming. Soon more teaching was in progress, and on the first Sunday of March, Mrs. Eddy wrote back to Colonel and Mrs. Smith in Washington:

> *They are singing the same songs you sang at Washington in the parlor here, and I am writing you in the midst of music, very sweet. One song is my favorite . . . "We shall know each*

other better." O! I love it, my tears dim my eyes, as they sing, with joy, with a sense of the beauty and truth of the words of the song.[63]

A week or two later she wrote them in more purposeful vein:

The relation that Jesus sustains to the race is not primarily as a teacher but an inspirer of faith, understanding, immortal hopes and divine love. . . . There is a greater power than speech, the power of Being, yea of Life. Speech is of man; Life, Spirit, is of God. . . . Do not as you love me and love Truth omit your Sunday meetings. A real revival in Metaphysics is going on in Boston because my dear students there are carrying out my advice to keep up these meetings in my absence. . . . Heal the sick.[64]

During the two-month absence in Washington and Philadelphia, Mrs. Eddy was in constant touch with the Boston students. At the time she had left Boston, Julia Bartlett had been unanimously elected president of the church, and Miss Bartlett and Mrs. Whiting were now conducting services successfully in Charlestown, where they had taken joint lodgings.

A sign had been placed outside their house: "Meetings held here for the purpose of explaining Christian Science on Friday evenings of every week at 7.30 P. M. All cordially invited."[65] The sign immediately brought curiosity seekers, whereas their hawking of Mrs. Eddy's printed sermon *Christian Healing* from door to door had aroused expressions of interest from housewives but had attracted no visitors. Now the meetings flourished, and Julia Bartlett was kept busy with some thirty patients a day. She and Mrs. Whiting deserved all praise, Mrs. Eddy wrote her. No one could any longer say that Clara Choate was the only student who *did* anything. "She is doing gloriously," Mrs. Eddy added, "and so are you all I expect."[66]

It was Mrs. Choate who was having the really spectacular success. She was conducting large meetings in Boston and Lawrence, teaching small classes in both places, instituting readings of *Science and Health* to draw the students together for discussion, and selling copies of the textbook right and left. She showed great skill in leading the meetings, Hanover Smith wrote, and was the main speaker whether she led or not.

Mrs. Whiting, after conducting one of the services, wrote Mrs. Eddy:

I feel as though my ideas wanted stretching. I can't get out of a certain train of thought, and that is too small to attempt

to talk from, before people. But I suppose that is only belief
that is so small. Truth is large enough to talk from forever.[67]

Mrs. Choate had no such misgivings. There had been seventy-five
at the last Thursday meeting, she wrote Mrs. Eddy, and everyone
said it was the best lecture she had given yet. She was ready to start
a fourth class, was overwhelmed with practice, her rooms full of
patients every morning. Soon she was writing of overflow meetings—
eighty seated, forty standing—and describing how she stood "meekly"
while they poured out praises.

Whatever doubts Mrs. Eddy may have had of Mrs. Choate's
temperamental ability to withstand such success, her own praise
throughout this period was unstinted: "You are doing what God
knows, and I know, and everybody else ought to know is . . . a
greater blessing to the race than history has recorded before of one
but myself at this period."[68] Her letters were filled with a sort of
comradeship which seems to hint at her longing for someone to
share the burden with her.

One of the striking phenomena of this period was the way in
which women were coming to the fore in the movement. Heretofore,
the most prominent of Mrs. Eddy's followers had been men. But
with the apostasy of Kennedy, Spofford, Arens, and such second-string
figures as Barry and Howard, she was learning to appreciate the
capacity for vigorous apostleship as well as faithful discipleship on
the part of housewives and spinsters who were not afraid to face a
hostile world. To some extent this doubtless reflected the increasingly
militant feminism of the period, but its roots went deeper. Mrs.
Eddy did not ask for women half the world that men had made;
instead, she demanded an entirely new world for both of them.

At the moment, however, the balance was in favor of the women.
Clara Choate wrote that she had just one man patient.[69] Moreover,
her husband, George, who had gone to Providence, Rhode Island,
to practice, was getting into difficulties and borrowing from her again.
Mrs. Eddy had doubted the wisdom of his going and had written
Ackland from Washington:

> *His wife told me when I was there she should have to give
> up getting him patients he so neglected them and every time
> injured the cause. I pity him from the depths of my heart but
> can do no more than I have done for him. It is demonology
> and his old appetite for liquor that they bring back. He would
> do well but for them.*[70]

Now, when she heard that the situation was worsening, she wrote
Clara Choate in sympathy:

. . . when I see the great advantage or disadvantage a partner is, it seems hard, hard, that some women who are formed for love must be so awfully situated. . . . Where is God? is the constant question of this mortal discord. And this question He will answer in the whirlwind, until Job-like we put our finger to our lips and say be still I see Him and He is supreme.[71]

His answer, at the moment, seemed to be that the women should press on if the men were unable or unwilling to fight in the front ranks, and on March 15 Mrs. Eddy wrote Mrs. Choate from Philadelphia:

It is glorious to see what the women alone are doing here for temperance. More than ever man has done. This is the period of women, they are to move and carry all the great moral and Christian reforms. I know it. Now darling, let us work as the industrious Suffragists are at work who are getting a hearing all over the land. Let us work as they do in love "preferring one another." Let us work shoulder to shoulder each bearing their own part of the burdens and helping one another and then the puny kicks of mesmerism will give up the ghost before such union.[72]

Despite this passing word of approval for woman suffrage, Mrs. Eddy was in general no feminist.[73] Her femininity took a different form, as when she signed a letter to Julia Bartlett, "Lovingly my dear child, Mother Mary."[74] Mark Twain was later to take her occasional use of this last expression as an attempted inauguration of a new Mariolatry, but in its context it seems much more like an expression of Victorian sentiment than of thirteenth-century mysticism.

Years later Mrs. Eddy wrote in reply to the great humorist's animadversions on this subject, "I have not the inspiration nor the aspiration to be a first or second Virgin-mother—her duplicate, antecedent, or subsequent." To which she added the noncommittal statement: "What I am remains to be proved by the good I do."[75] For that proof, she now felt, Boston lay waiting.

5

Clara Choate, though no Boston Brahmin herself, had married into a distinguished Massachusetts family and knew how to put on style when she wanted to. Consequently her formal evening reception for Mrs. Eddy on April 5, 1882, in her spacious rooms at 590 Tremont Street, was conducted with considerable social éclat.

The Eddys, just returned from their travels, stood in the reception line for an hour, shaking hands with the fashionable and the faithful. There were speeches and music, a cross and a crown in flowers, a quiet hubbub of excitement. "This was my entry into Jerusalem," Mrs. Eddy wrote Ackland later. "Will it be followed with the cross?"[76]

A week before her return the *Boston Globe* had run a full-page article on Christian Science, replete with gratifying headlines: "Miracles?/ Phenomena of a Startling Nature/ All Manner of Diseases Cured/ Without Medicine or Ceremony/ What Is 'Religious Science?'/ The Lame Walk and the Blind See/ Infirmities of Every Description Dissipated/ 'Disease a Belief, Not a Reality'/ Startling Theory of God and the Bible."[77]

The following week a new set of headlines on a companion article recorded the inevitable reaction: "What They Think of It/ Opinions of Prominent Clergymen and Physicians/ In Regard to the 'Christian Scientists' and Their Work/ 'Arrant Nonsense,' 'Sublime Rubbish' and 'Psychic Force' as an Explanation/ 'Miracles Should be Left to the Ministers'/ 'Diseases Only Cured by Skillful Treatment.' "[78] To Colonel Smith, Mrs. Eddy wrote, "Boston is boiling with the ferment of this glorious 'leaven.' "[79]

Accounts of healing were flowing in to her not only from the Boston students but also from those farther afield. Among the latter was Arthur True Buswell, now executive head of the Associated Charities of Cincinnati but diligently practicing Christian Science in his free time. During a recent smallpox epidemic in Cincinnati he had been quickly healed, and he was meeting with much success in his private practice. On April 22 a colleague in the Associated Charities, one Otto Anderson, M.D., wrote Mrs. Eddy:

> *Having been together daily in the same office with your disciple, Mr. A. T. Buswell, for the past four months, I have learned to respect him professionally and love him individually. . . . I am an "old school" practitioner, have served as surgeon in two European navies and have practiced medicine for about ten years in New York and Brooklyn until my health compelled me to relinquish my profession. I became a victim of the Morphine habit and had to take as high as thirty grains, of the most diabolical drug that ever was manufactured, daily. My physicians who treated me declared me consumptive and banished all hope of recovery. In the month of December last year, I made the acquaintance of Mr. Buswell and commenced assisting him in the discharge of his noble duties. He being a metaphysician*

and I Allopathic we naturally often discussed the matter and as drugs did me no good, I stopped taking any whatever, save Morphine without which I thought it impossible [to] get along. I, to my great astonishment, commenced to gain in flesh and am by this time 20 lb. heavier in weight than I was on January 1st. Recuperating, my ambition and energy returned in proportion, I felt in my mind that I could stop my loathsome habit and I performed the wonderful feat in a week without any discomfiture worth mentioning (the case standing alone in our medical records). I have administered one quarter of a grain of Morphine (hypodermically) to Mr. Buswell without the slightest physiological effect, clearly proving the existence of metaphysical laws.[80]

About the time Mrs. Eddy received this letter, Gilbert Eddy noted in his diary that they had finally found a house in which they could establish the Massachusetts Metaphysical College for the study of metaphysical law. By May they were settled in a four-story dwelling at 569 Columbus Avenue, in the then dignified though less-than-fashionable South End of Boston.[81] A large silver plate on its gray stone front announced the presence of the college, and a prospectus announced its faculty:

Mary B. G. Eddy
Professor of Obstetrics, Metaphysics, and Christian Science

Rufus King Noyes, M.D.
(formerly Resident Surgeon of the Boston City Hospital)
Professor of Surgery and Accouchement

Charles J. Eastman, M.D.
Professor of Medical Jurisprudence[82]

The reference to obstetrics is ambiguous. Although Mr. and Mrs. Eddy had both taken a short course in obstetrics from Dr. Noyes in January before leaving for Washington and had been certified by him as "possessing a requisite knowledge of accouchement," Mrs. Eddy never attempted to teach obstetrics from a medical or physiological point of view. In fact, the subject was not offered at the college until five years later when it appeared in a wholly different context from the semi-medical one suggested by the 1882 prospectus.[83]

Certainly there was something anomalous in the use of the names of Noyes and Eastman. The two men sympathized with Mrs. Eddy's aims, and she in turn doubtless felt a lingering need for the conventional sort of respectability their names theoretically might add to her undertaking. But the experiment in collaboration was unsuccessful, and the connection was severed a few months later.[84]

In actual fact, Eastman probably lectured at the college only once (to the small class which began about May 12) and Noyes not at all. Seen by hindsight, the attempted coalition was bound to prove unproductive. Whatever Mrs. Eddy was to accomplish, she could do only by following her own unique bent and by exercising her own radical leadership. Conventional props had a way of simply collapsing under the pressure of her purpose.

And now she was to lose her strongest moral support. Through six years of trial in Lynn, Gilbert Eddy had stood by her devotedly. His sole concern seemed always to be for her welfare. In the preface to the third edition of *Science and Health* he had stepped before the world as her champion against Arens, and in Washington he had devoted himself to gathering the information that would enable him to stop that same Arens from continued infringement of her copyright.

But he was tired, and perhaps discouraged. The failure in Lynn had hit him harder than it had Mrs. Eddy, and he faced the new challenge of educated Boston with less resilience. If it is difficult to imagine his wife's weathering the concentrated storms of the preceding few years without his support, it is even more difficult to imagine his grappling with the problems of a movement which, within the next decade or two, would have developed global dimensions.

Already, despite her reluctance to go to law once again, Mrs. Eddy felt that, in order to assure the future of *Science and Health,* the matter of Arens' plagiarism must be settled legally once and for all. Gilbert Eddy undoubtedly shrank from the ordeal of fighting a court action against the pugnacious man who had once urged him to so many lawsuits. By this time the Eddys had begun to suspect that Arens' hands were not entirely clean in the 1878 conspiracy-to-murder case,[85] and it was not pleasant to think that he was now the enemy.

Even so, Gilbert Eddy would never have hesitated, had his strength not been failing for a month or two. A woman in Philadelphia, who fifty years later recalled the vivid impression made on her by one meeting with Mrs. Eddy in March, added, "Mr. Eddy . . . actually, as well as figuratively . . . was in the shadowy background."[86] There is little mention of him in letters during this period, and he appears to have remained in the background of the new college. In May he showed increasing evidence of illness. Severe attacks of abdominal and chest pain confined him to bed at times. At other times he sat in on his wife's class sessions, apparently quite bright and cheerful, and went out for occasional rides.[87]

Absorbed in her mounting duties, Mrs. Eddy would go to his rescue when he experienced an attack, but when the suffering was relieved, she would accept his assurance that he could carry on by himself and would return to her work.[88] Sometimes she would ask one or another of the students to help him, instructing them that he needed to be awakened by handling malicious mesmerism more vigorously. "Nobody wants to harm me," he would insist, and Mrs. Eddy would reply that nobody wanted to harm Jesus, either, "but they did!" And, she would add, "they will try to put us out of the way too."[89]

On one occasion a student in her May class, Mrs. Delia S. Manley, told her how, as a little girl, she had seen a snake watching a bird, the bird circling nearer and nearer and calling out louder and louder until, when it was almost close enough for the snake to strike, her brother had thrown a stone between the two creatures, thus liberating the bird. Mrs. Eddy quickly asked her to tell the story to Gilbert Eddy to help him understand better the nature of animal magnetism and the means of breaking its delusion. "Mr. Eddy," wrote Mrs. Manley later, "was a dear, courteous, gentle character, and it seemed as though he couldn't conceive of anyone doing him an injury."[90]

Mrs. Eddy, however, was sure not only that his illness was the effect of mesmerism but also that Arens was the mesmerist. Her husband's symptoms seemed to her similar to the gastric pains she had experienced the preceding summer and had got rid of by defending herself from the "poison" of Arens' hatred.[91] Arens himself, whose teachings show that he believed implicitly in the power of directed suggestion to injure and even to kill, was fascinated by the idea of arsenic. His writings in the next two or three years returned to the subject compulsively, as in his 1884 volume, *Old Theology in Its Application to the Healing of the Sick:* "It is said that arsenic kills; but it would be very difficult for anyone to prove how it kills, since persons have had all the symptoms of arsenic poisoning without having taken any arsenic."[92] This is exactly the condition which Mrs. Eddy believed to be manifesting itself in the case of her husband. In view of Arens' obsession with the subject, it is not surprising that she linked his mental influence with the appearing of the symptoms that seemed to indicate poison.

To verify her conviction she asked Dr. Noyes to examine Gilbert. Noyes came up with a diagnosis of organic heart disease, dangerously advanced. Unconvinced, Mrs. Eddy called in Eastman, who obligingly concurred with her own opinion. Medically, Noyes was right, as events were to prove. Metaphorically, there was more than enough mental poison in the situation to disturb anyone as sensitive to undercurrents of thought as Mrs. Eddy.[93] Later Arens would expostulate that he actually liked Gilbert Eddy and that "if he were going to poison anybody, he would have poisoned Mrs. Eddy first, rather than Dr. Eddy."[94] The assertion is not reassuring as to his own mental equilibrium, and within a few years Arens did in fact become violently insane, ending his days in a state institution.[95]

On June 2, 1882, Gilbert Eddy went out with Julia Bartlett for a ride on the horse cars in the afternoon sunshine and came back saying he felt much better. That night, however, while Miss Bartlett and Hanover Smith watched by his side, he slipped quietly away. When Mrs. Eddy was called, he had been dead for some time. They had thought he was sleeping.[96]

6

For Mrs. Eddy it was an almost stunning shock. For the past six years she had been trying to understand the nature of evil as suggestion—or, in the term she borrowed from her own century, as animal magnetism. Now the suggestion of defeat, or irreparable loss, almost overwhelmed her. Her basic conviction remained unshaken that man's God-derived spiritual life is indestructible, but her heart cried out at the human loss and waste. Her writings show the comfort she drew from the fact that Jesus himself had had to taste the full bitterness of suggested defeat before he rose to ultimate victory, but for a few days the note of near-desperation sounded in her words. In a dozen ways she echoed the Psalmist's cry, "I am come into deep waters, where the floods overflow me."

Her personal grief was mixed with a sense of deep injustice at what seemed to her the world's implacable opposition to Christian Science—an enmity now concentrated into what she described as the "mental murder" of Gilbert Eddy.

Mrs. Eddy's critics have often asked how someone who taught the ontological unreality of evil could have so sharp a sense of the criminal possibilities of the human mind as to believe that thoughts could kill. To be sure, Jesus had defined the devil as "a murderer from the beginning," and there is a certain sense in which death is always murder. Regarded simply as a biological unit in the natural order, every newborn child is doomed to be killed off eventually —if not by man's inhumanity to man then by nature's ultimate indifference to humanity. But Mrs. Eddy meant more than this.

In her teaching, the only devil (and the quintessential criminal) was the belief in a life apart from God. This belief, she held, fought for its own existence like the unclean spirit crying out in Mark's

Gospel, "Let us alone; what have we to do with thee, thou Jesus of Nazareth? art thou come to destroy us?" Increasingly she was to define this kind of hostility as basically impersonal—the resistance of error to truth, or in Pauline terms, the working of the "carnal mind" which is "enmity against God." But always she insisted that it might come to its sharpest focus in those persons who consciously lent themselves as tools to the hate that kills, the envy that poisons, the pride and ambition that stab and lie and steal. If thoughts were more tangible than material things, then it was logical that they might prove quite as lethal, unless recognized and repelled from a superior mental standpoint. It was to her a simple fact of psychology that the unwary person is constantly thinking other people's thoughts which he mistakenly regards as his own.

The crisis precipitated by her husband's death marks the climax of Mrs. Eddy's six-year effort to deal with this problem on the level of persons. His death, she held, was clearly the result of malicious mental malpractice. Many years later she recalled:

> *After the death of my husband, Dr. Eddy, I sent for one of the mental malpractitioners to come and look on his calm, dear face. The messenger, who stood at the door and delivered my request, said that on hearing it, he grew deadly pale and clutched at the door to stand. He never came.*[97]

This was on the morning of June 3, and the individual so described was Arens. Later that day she wrote his father-in-law, her old student Benjamin F. Atkinson, an anguished letter:

> *With the cold form of [my] beloved husband lying on his bier in my desolated home I appeal to you once more, and if you are not darkened to the sense of the awful crimes [of Arens] I know you will stop them by every influence in your power.*
>
> *I have power to discern the cause of his death . . . and what I say the future will declare, namely: that Edward J. Arens has caused the death of my husband in connection with his co-operators so far as I can clearly discern in my diagnosis of the case.*[98]

She also sent for a reporter from the *Boston Globe,* and his story the next day made unusual reading. The charge she had made to Atkinson was repeated, though without naming Arens, and the reporter noted that she appeared "much overcome" throughout the interview. "She had formerly had the same symptoms of arsenical poison herself," he wrote without comment, "and it was some time before she discovered it to be the mesmeric work of an enemy."[99]

At her request Noyes and Eastman performed a joint autopsy.

The death certificate issued by Noyes gave heart disease as the primary and secondary cause of death, and Noyes even showed Mrs. Eddy the evidence of physical deterioration in the heart.[100] Instead of accepting his explanation she called another press conference. As the *Boston Post* reported her words the next day:

> I know it was poison that killed him, not material poison, but mesmeric poison. My husband was in uniform health, and but seldom complained of any kind of ailment. During his brief illness, just preceding his death, his continual cry was "Only relieve me of this continual suggestion, through the mind, of poison, and I will recover." It is well known that by constantly dwelling upon any subject in thought finally comes the poison of the belief through the whole system. I have seen mesmerists, merely by a glance or a motion, make an arm or a leg of a subject stiff, and then relax it again or give pain and relieve it again. I never saw a more self-possessed man than dear Dr. Eddy was. He said to Dr. Eastman when he was finally called to attend him: "My case is nothing that I cannot attend to myself, although to me it acts the same as poison and seems to pervade my whole system just as that would."
>
> . . . Circumstances debarred me from taking hold of my husband's case. He declared himself perfectly capable of carrying himself through, and I was so entirely absorbed in business that I permitted him to try, and when I awakened to the danger it was too late. . . .
>
> After a certain amount of the mesmeric poison has been administered it cannot be averted. No power of mind can resist it. It must be met with resistive action of the mind at the start, which will counteract it. . . . I do believe in God's supremacy over error, and this gives me peace.[101]

The peace was not yet visible, and the *Post* reporter commented that she "seemed much affected by her recent grief, her voice trembling at times so that she could scarcely proceed with her narrative." That same day her new student Delia Manley was standing alone in the hallway when Mrs. Eddy came downstairs, put her head on Mrs. Manley's shoulder, and wept. "I feel that there is something in your heart," she confided, "that will understand what is in mine."[102] Most of the students, Mrs. Manley wrote, expected their teacher to stand up against any calamity without a tremor.

The next day, June 5, a funeral service was held. A Unitarian minister conducted it and the group sang "Nearer my God to Thee." Mrs. Eddy, according to the same Mrs. Manley, "sang with us and her voice was clear and sweet; she seemed uplifted above the sense of death."[103] The following day George Choate took Gilbert Eddy's body to Tilton, New Hampshire, where it was interred in the Baker family lot, next to the graves of Mrs. Eddy's mother and father.

In the first shock of loss Mrs. Eddy wrote to George Glover in South Dakota asking him to come and stay with her. Very much immersed in his mining ventures, he replied simply that his wife was unwilling for him to leave. Still feeling the need for masculine support, Mrs. Eddy then wired Arthur Buswell in Cincinnati, and he came immediately. On June 27 she wrote Colonel Smith that she felt almost as though she never could be comforted while separated from her beloved Gilbert: ". . . he was *strong, noble,* and [with] the sweetest disposition and the most benevolent charitable nature I ever recognized in any person."[104]

It was clear that Mrs. Eddy must get away from Boston for a short period of quiet. Leaving the college in the hands of Julia Bartlett, she journeyed up to Buswell's old home in Barton, Vermont, which he had offered her as a refuge. And there, with only Buswell and Alice Sibley for companions, she fought a battle that seemed to be the climax of all her struggles of the past six years. A woman who talked to Buswell almost forty years later wrote:

> *Although she had exhibited heroic qualities of energy and fortitude, neglecting nothing of direction and command before leaving Boston, she showed on the journey traces of nervous exhaustion and at times the hysteria of grief threatened to overwhelm her. . . Mr. Buswell relates that her great struggle was known to his household, but that she carried it through alone, though they often watched outside her door. After a night of agony, she would emerge from her struggle with a radiant face and luminous eyes, and they would hesitate to speak to her for fear of disturbing the peace that enveloped her.*[105]

Her letters of that period reflect something of this. On July 16, she wrote to Clara Choate:

> *I am up among the towering heights of this verdant state, green with the leaves of earth and fresh with the fragrance of good will and human kindness. I never found a kindlier people. I am situated as pleasantly as I can be in the absence of the* one true heart *that has been so much to me. O, darling, I never shall master this point of missing him all the time I do believe, but I can try, and am trying as I must—to sever all the chords that bind me to person or things material.*[106]

In the same letter she added that Alice Sibley "has hovered round me like a flower of light." They would all be ready for work when they returned to Boston, and she concluded: "I long to return and the time will soon pass. I dread to return but the days glide by."

To Julia Bartlett she wrote:

> *I cant yet feel much interest in anything . . . of earth. I shall try and eventually succeed in rising from the gloom of my irreparable loss, but it must take* time. . . . *I think of you at the fort and always as little, or rather great heroes and pray that my coming shall be a joy and not a sorrow to you. . . . It is beautiful here the hills vales and lakes are lovely but this was his native state and* he is not here.[107]

On July 27 she wrote Clara Choate with a new note of decision: "Hold the Fort for I am coming. . . . I hope my forty days in the wilderness is about over."[108]

A letter to Ackland the next day shows her reaching forward for new assurance:

> *I thought to while away a weary hour I would write you a few lines telling you in brief how I am* changed. *I see it in the mirror and my heart tells me it every hour. I would like more than ever to be myself again if only for one short year that I might establish myself on a firmer foothold than ever yet it has been. But I question my ability to walk over all, only as God gives me aid that I never have had before.*[109]

A week later she was on the way home, and on the day of her arrival she wrote in her Bible: "Aug. 6th 1882 returned Boston opened to Isaiah 54."[110] To her it must have seemed like a welcome written for the occasion.

Chapter V

The Faces of Janus

Two months after her return Mrs. Eddy, commenting in a letter to Colonel Smith on her pleasure in the "soft Indian summer days," went on to remark: "Like an innocent child I am looking again on society, and feeling almost afraid since my dear one left me to take the forward steps to do good that I could take so firmly with my husband by my side."[1]

The words reveal little of the energy that had fired her almost from the moment of her arrival. On August 16 she had started a small class with George and Clara Choate (who had studied in 1878 with Gilbert Eddy but never with her), Alice Sibley, a Mrs. Sarah J. Crosse, and the Reverend Charles D. Barbour, an Episcopal clergyman who was the first of a number of gentlemen of the cloth to go through her classes during the next seven years. The Christian Scientist Association sprang to renewed activity and soon public services were being held at the college, with Mrs. Eddy giving weekday talks and Sunday sermons.

By the end of October she was teaching another class of eight and writing to a student:

> I have on hand the largest class I ever had, and our Sunday services fill all our rooms with interested hearers. I think in the Spring we shall graduate about fifty. The ship of science is again walking the wave, rising above the billows, bidding defiance to the flood-gates of error, for God is at the helm.[2]

Now, at the age of sixty-two, she was to demonstrate new energies, new confidence, a new outreach. Although the crisis she had passed through recently might have been expected to slow her progress, it seems instead to have shot her forward. Mrs. Eddy was always one for whom the uses of adversity were—if not sweet, then kinetic.

At a meeting of the Christian Scientist Association on October 11, 1882, she told the students that she wished an "element of energy" to steal away any "consciousness of lethargy" they might have. The minutes read in part:

The subject of nothingness, commonly called mesmerism, was approached but was thought to be unworthy of considera- tion. The president, Mrs. Eddy, thought there was a great excess of talk about the error, she said "all there is to mesmerism is what we make of it."[3]

There would, nevertheless, continue to be a great excess of talk through the 1880's, much of it stimulated by Mrs. Eddy's renewed warnings on the subject as she discovered, like Bunyan's Christian, that there were trapdoors to hell outside the very gates of heaven. But a definite stage had been reached in her emergence from the standpoint represented by the chapter on demonology. The minutes of a meeting three months later record her as saying: "I want to tell you the blessed fact of discovery in this hour: it is to make nothing [of error]. . . . When we start from the basis of Being, error must fade as we grow."[4]

It was probably in this period that she paid a visit to a menagerie, taking Hanover Smith with her, and planted herself in front of the lion's cage shortly before feeding time. As the animal paced up and down, roaring loudly, she "worked" quietly until it lay down peace- fully with its head between its paws. One account states that she then put her own hand between the bars and confidently patted the creature. While that particular detail may be a bit of later em- broidery, the incident as a whole seems to represent an experiment which she consciously related to the overcoming of animal magnetism —a demonstration to herself of the power of Spirit over brute in- stinct.[5]

Yet mesmerism or animal magnetism, as she saw it, was mani- fested in a continued falling away of her students from the Lynn days. It was almost as though the earlier period were being systematically wiped out.[6] At the annual meeting of the church on December 11, Mrs. Eddy announced that the numbers of the faithful had de- creased by fifty in the past year. Undismayed, she might have been a female Gideon deliberately paring down her army to a hard core of tested reliables.

By the end of 1883 she had taught close to fifty more students, but there was a new emphasis on training the more promising ones for larger responsibilities. Some of them she encouraged to hold meetings of their own in their suburban communities. On occasion she would turn up unannounced at one or another of these parlor gatherings, taking a seat in the background to observe how the stu- dent made out. Meanwhile, at the regular meetings of the Christian Scientist Association she gave the members concrete advice on handling their more difficult cases.

It was a trying task. A woman who attended the services at 569 Columbus Avenue at that time but never became a member of the church wrote half a century later, "It always seemed to me in those days that Mrs. Eddy's pupils had a way of floating off in a sort of ecstatic rapture and that Mrs. Eddy had her hands full keeping them down to earth."[7] She was getting better material now to work with than she had had in Lynn, but by later standards the whole enterprise was still exceedingly ramshackle. As the same attendant at the 1883 services wrote, "Back in the early days as I rehearse what we listened to [it] seems so crude & the Science of today [1934] stands out to be almost a different language so much has developed in thought."

The theory has been advanced that after her husband's death Mrs. Eddy steeled herself against her own softer emotions and imposed an increasingly ruthless leadership on her followers.[8] Putney Bancroft, who became inactive in the movement after she moved her headquarters to Boston, wrote forty years later:

> *Did she change? I think not. Some have stated that she became harsh and arbitrary. No doubt she was denunciatory towards error, or those who were evil-minded, but her nature was gentle and affectionate. I do not believe it could be changed. Mrs. Eddy showed to her early pupils the loving-kindness of a mother, or the faithful devotion of a sister, and many of her later students have given testimony to the same effect.*[9]

Many, but not all. Bancroft's conjecture is interesting mostly for its mellow evaluation of the earlier period. The fact is that the last three decades of Mrs. Eddy's life, like the 1870's, produced two conflicting sets of evidence. In her later years, as in the earlier ones, there were students who ended in rebellion against what they considered to be "harsh and arbitrary" demands and who subsequently wrote and spoke of her as a dictator. On the other hand, there were an increasing number who saw even her rebukes as expressions of loving concern and who were much more impressed by her solicitude for their progress than by her exercise of authority.[10]

Because of the divergent testimony on this crucial point the evidence of Mrs. Eddy's own letters is of special importance. Into these letters she poured her uncensored feelings. Julia Bartlett, who lived with her at the college for a time, has written of the remarkable energy she expended on her correspondence, dashing off incredible numbers of letters to students and inquirers and sometimes dictating them to Miss Bartlett when the latter was so tired she could hardly push her pen across the paper.

That Mrs. Eddy herself did not always keep on top of the demands on her time is evidenced in a letter she wrote to Colonel and Mrs. Smith on January 3, 1883. Her manifold duties, she wrote, "make me too perplexed too mindworn often to think—so I would give up writing and at a late hour would crawl into bed to toss all night and half asleep give directions on business *cares* that concern the good cause."[11]

Among those cares were her plans for a periodical of her own. Such a journal would allow her to do several things: reach a wider audience, educate the neophyte, strengthen the committed, and comment on the passing scene. All through the early months of 1883 she was busy on this project, and on April 14 the first issue of *The Journal of Christian Science* appeared, with the subtitle, "An Independent Family Paper to Promote Health and Morals."[12]

Mrs. Eddy herself was editor, and most of the material in the first issue was by her, although it is not always easy to tell exactly what is from her own pen. Used as fillers were such gratifying statements as Turgot's "He that never doubted the existence of matter may be assured he has no aptitude for metaphysics," and Emerson's "Intellectual science invariably begets a doubt of the existence of matter." Subsequent issues drew appropriate nuggets or "gems" from Aesop and Sydney Smith, Darwin and Josh Billings. Jokes, mostly at the expense of the medical and ministerial professions ("Ah!" said the pastor, "your father is dead, then; did he have a doctor?" "No sir," said the boy; "he died himself"),[13] nestled frivolously among more weighty matter. Modest in appearance and at first issued only bimonthly, the new publication was to prove a considerable asset to the young movement.

This was the year in which the diphtheria germ was identified by Edwin Klebs, one in a series of widely publicized discoveries which were making people increasingly conscious of unsuspected dangers in everyday living. It was also the year in which the French psychologist Bernheim was writing his classic *Hypnosis and Suggestion in Psychotherapy*, which recorded the fact that pathological symptoms might be obtained by suggestion even without inducing the hypnotic trance. Although Bernheim's insights were subsequently lost sight of by psychology for a time—largely through Freud's espousal of Charcôt's physiological explanations—his description of hypnosis as heightened suggestibility opened the way for a new clinical understanding of many disease phenomena.

An editorial from the first issue of the *Journal* entitled "A Timely Issue" bears witness to the atmosphere of thought in 1883:

> *An organ for the Christian Scientists has become a necessity. After looking over the newspapers of the day, very naturally*

comes the reflection that it is dangerous to live, so loaded seems the very air with disease. These descriptions carry fears to many minds, to be depicted in some future time upon the body. This error we shall be able in a great measure to counteract, for at the price we issue our paper we shall be able to reach many homes. A great work has already been done, and a great work yet remains to be done.[14]

But before it could be done, there was a major piece of unfinished and almost forgotten business to be confronted. As usual, the door that led to the future had one face looking toward the past.

2

Probably few if any of the twelve students in Mrs. Eddy's January, 1883, class had ever heard of Phineas Parkhurst Quimby.

In October, 1862, Mrs. Eddy—then Mrs. Daniel Patterson—had gone to Portland, Maine, to seek help from Quimby for the invalidism which then dogged her. She found him a keen-minded though self-taught man who had formerly been a traveling mesmerist and gradually had discovered that he could heal people by the force of suggestion without throwing them into the mesmeric trance. Although he retained many of the stock practices of the popular animal magnetism of the period, he had evolved some interesting and original theories to explain his cures.

Mrs. Eddy was not only benefited immediately (if temporarily) by Quimby's treatment but was also swept off her feet by his theory. His characterization of disease as the result of false "opinion," to be destroyed by a mental process involving clairvoyance, telepathy, and what he called the "truth" about the origin of the trouble, confirmed her own embryonic conviction that all disease was at bottom mental. Quimby identified his healing with that of Jesus, and Mrs. Eddy enthusiastically read into his pronouncements a degree of Christian faith and philosophical idealism which it is hard to find in them objectively.

For instance, she was deeply impressed by his reiterated statement that "there is no intelligence in matter,"[15] but she seems to have brushed aside that part of his theory which related intelligence to a spiritual body emanating like a mist or odor from the material body. Again, she was greatly struck by his distinction between Jesus the man and Christ the "science" or truth practiced by Jesus in his healing; but while Quimby himself portrayed that science as an empirical technique, she kept groping for the metaphysical understanding of ultimate being which she felt must constitute its real essence.

Stimulated by his ideas and trying to relate them to her own biblical faith, Mrs. Eddy made some successful experiments in healing in 1864 which caused that year to stand out for her as a landmark in her development.[16] Two years later, shortly after Quimby's death, came a healing which led her to a very much more important discovery. This she later described as a glimpse of "the great fact that I have since tried to make plain to others, namely, Life in and of Spirit, this Life being the sole reality of existence."[17]

At first she tried to relate to Quimby's theories the new vistas of thought opened up to her by this basic insight. In formulating her ideas, parts of his vocabulary did prove genuinely helpful to her, though she gave such terms as she borrowed a very different content from his.[18] By the time Kennedy broke with her in 1872, she had discovered the radical incompatibility of her vision and Quimby's, as well as the impossibility of combining the spiritual method of Christian Science healing with the physical manipulation she had allowed her early students to take over from the Portland healer.

Long before 1883 she had come to the conclusion that, despite Quimby's humanitarian purpose, his method was essentially a variant of animal magnetism. A similar judgment, though from a different standpoint, was made in 1872 by another of his patients, Warren F. Evans, in his widely read book *Mental Medicine*.[19] Apart from a few lines of explanation and tribute to Quimby in that volume and a paragraph in the first edition of *Science and Health*, which lauded his character but disavowed his influence, there was virtually no public mention of Quimby for seventeen years after his death in January, 1866.

Yet he was not wholly forgotten. His widow and his son George, though they laid no claim to understanding his ideas, revered his memory and hung on to the jumble of manuscript he had left behind. The Misses Sarah and Emma Ware of Portland, who had induced him to write out his observations and speculations and had then acted as copyists, putting his chaotic papers into better form, also looked back on him with awe but made no pretense of understanding his technique of healing. Julius Dresser, who with his wife had been an ardent admirer of Quimby, might have been expected, as a successful newspaperman, to do some writing about the Portland healer and his theories, but instead he had maintained complete silence on the subject through the intervening years.

Interestingly enough, however, Mrs. Eddy's successive breaks with Kennedy, Spofford, and Arens had each stirred the ghost of Quimby.

On August 19, 1872, one Peter Sim, in whose house Mrs. Eddy

lived during the months of her final jousts with Kennedy, wrote Quimby's widow asking whether any of her husband's manuscripts were in Mrs. Eddy's possession. Kennedy, who had first known Mrs. Eddy in 1868 before she had completely discarded the use of a short manuscript of Quimby's called "Questions and Answers," had apparently sown a doubt of her originality in the new student's mind, and Sim wrote Mrs. Quimby, "The fact that a stranger [Mrs. Eddy] should represent a principle discovered by another and be reaping the fruits of such discovery when the real Hairs of the discoverer seem to be lost sight off or left out Move me to write you."[20]

So far as is known, the letter was never answered, and nothing came of the inquiry. Six years later Daniel Spofford, at the height of his disaffection, was moved also to ask about Quimby's literary remains, though without mentioning Mrs. Eddy. George Quimby, the son, replied on August 21, 1878: "My father did not leave any published book, although he had a good deal of manuscript, which had he lived, he undoubtedly would have published."[21]

On December 13, 1878, George Quimby again wrote Spofford, after reading a newspaper account of the bizarre conspiracy-to-murder case, asking whether the Mrs. Eddy mentioned in the story was the Mrs. Patterson he had known. The letter went on to speak about his father. "By some he was called a humbug, by others a mesmeric doctor, by others a Spiritualist, and by others a man endued with a peculiar power." But, wrote George, in his own estimate he was none of these, and "treated the sick in a common sense way and in a way that he could teach to others." George himself "was about 20 at that time and took no interest whatever in his ideas," but not so Mrs. Patterson, whom he remembered as "very intelligent and smart." She seemed, he wrote, "to take a great interest in his ideas and could see into them, and father talked with her a good deal."[22] Would Spofford be willing to lend him her book?

Spofford evidently would, and on May 12, 1879, George Quimby returned *Science and Health* with the comment:

> *I recognized a great many ideas and even full sentences as "children" of my father's ideas and then there were other parts that were entirely at variance with his ideas. . . . if she had never met Dr. Quimby she would never have written that book nor would she have written it if he had lived.*
>
> *If it has been the means of doing any good, I am very glad she has published it, but I should imagine that there was not enough of the practical about it, and too much of the ideal to attach itself to the common mind.*[23]

The letter was obviously written without guile or rancor. In examining the first edition of *Science and Health,* which was the one that Spofford would necessarily have sent him,[24] George Quimby would have read Mrs. Eddy's statement in the preface, "We made our first discovery that science mentally applied would heal the sick, in 1864"—clear evidence that at the time she wrote those words she had not yet made a complete separation between her own thinking and Quimby's. In a section of the last chapter that was written almost a year after the rest of the book she explicitly commented on Quimby:

> *He never studied this science* [Christian Science], *but reached his own high standpoint and grew to it through his own, and not another's progress. He was a good man, a law to himself; when we knew him he was growing out of mesmerism; contrasted with a student that falls into it by forsaking the good rules of science for a mal-practice that has the power and opportunity to do evil.*[25]

It was through her experience with Kennedy, Spofford, and Arens that Mrs. Eddy came to draw a line of absolute distinction between Christian Science and all forms of "mental science" based on suggestion. If she herself was not entirely clear about the distinction when she first wrote *Science and Health,* it is hardly surprising that the practical George Quimby regarded her adoption and adaptation of some of his father's basic language as evidence of the derivative nature of her ideas. At the same time he seems to have recognized the different mental *atmosphere* of her book—what he described as its lack of the practical. The elder Quimby, whatever one may think of him, moved in a world of intense practicality, a world of thought and value where tangible results were all-important. It was these results which had made young George fiercely proud of his father, even though he took "no interest whatever" in his ideas. That Mrs. Eddy's book seemed impractical to him was a measure of the distance between *Science and Health* as a total religious view of life and his father's empirical "science of health."

And so began the comedy of errors that was to develop into the long-drawn-out Quimby controversy. At the moment George Quimby seemed undisturbed by his assumption that Christian Science was the illegitimate offspring of his father's theory, and the wry equanimity of his letter betrays none of the rankling sense of injustice that possessed him after the issue heated up.

Spofford at this point drops out of the narrative, as he soon dropped out of Mrs. Eddy's serious consideration.[26] But Kennedy reappears in an enigmatic reference in a letter written by Mrs. Eddy to George Choate on March 3, 1880, linking him with Quimby's devoted amanuensis, Emma Ware. Choate was at that time practicing Christian Science in Portland, and Mrs. Eddy wrote him to "get her that was E. W. (now in Scotland) word to look out for K's mesmeric control that he will try on her to make her yield to his wishes; and another measure that he will take, and that is to get it through a third party into his hands."[27] Actually it was Emma's sister Sarah who had married and gone to Scotland to live, although Emma may conceivably have been visiting her just then. In any case, the letter suggests a connection which may go back to the summer of 1871 when Kennedy, already beginning to rebel against Mrs. Eddy, suddenly "took a fit to go to Portland."[28] At that time he may have become acquainted with either or both of the Ware sisters, and Mrs. Eddy's reference to an unexplained "it" which he is trying to get into his hands may denote manuscript material—Quimby's? her own?—which was temporarily in their possession.

No further light is thrown on the subject until October 2, 1882, when Emma Ware wrote Edward J. Arens from Portland that she had received his letter inquiring about Quimby's methods, George Quimby having already informed her that Arens was seeking information. "I remember Mrs. Patterson," she wrote, "as a patient of Dr. Quimby and as a bright clever lady who took an interest in his 'theory.' . . . I devoted myself to his instruction as long as he lived, but I never learned the art of healing." His writings, she added, were in her "care," though evidently not in her possession. She wished she could talk with Arens but could not be present "at the discussion to which you extend me an invitation."[29]

The discussion may have been in the nature of a council of war and the chief participants, other than Arens, were almost certainly Julius Dresser and his wife. Sometime in 1882 the Dressers, who were then living in the West, had heard what was going on in Boston, as they put it, and decided that the time was ripe for the resurrection of Quimby. Accordingly they moved to Boston, got in touch with Arens (perhaps because his name had figured in the press as an "enemy" of Mrs. Eddy), took a course of instruction with him, moved into the house in Chester Square where he carried on his healing and teaching, and opened offices of their own there as healers.

The war was to be against Mrs. Eddy and the rallying cry was to be "Quimby." Early in 1883 Dresser wrote George Quimby of Arens' hostility to Mrs. Eddy: "He fought her, he says, day and night. Finally he left her and would have nothing more to do with her, nor her husband . . . who died last June. She now proclaims Dr. Arens her enemy."[30]

He hoped to see a book of Quimby's manuscripts published within 1883, he added, but the campaign would not wait on that. An article would appear in a Boston daily in a few days—"the Traveller first, I think"—stating that Quimby "founded the science." It would not mention Dresser's name, he explained, but the clear implication was that he had written it. Actually the article appeared in the *Boston Post,* on February 8, in the form of a long letter signed "A.O."

After presenting Quimby as a successful practitioner of mental healing, Dresser went on to say:

> *He always claimed that it was a science which could be taught and demonstrated, and that the demonstration was as clear and sure as that of mathematics. The writings are all preserved, and will soon be published, those having them in charge have only been waiting for the general thought to progress before placing them before the public. Some parties healing through a mental method, which they claim to have discovered, did, in reality, obtain their first thoughts of this truth from Dr. Quimby, and have added their own opinions to the grain of vision thus obtained, presenting to the people a small amount of wheat mixed with a great quantity of chaff.*[31]

Eleven days later, on February 19, a letter, signed "E.G." but almost certainly written by Mrs. Eddy, appeared in the same paper, with a description of Quimby's healing as selective in its way as A.O.'s had been in his:

> *Dr. Quimby's method of healing the sick was manipulation; after immersing his hands in water he rubbed the head, etc. He never called his practice a mental method of treating diseases to our knowledge, and we knew him and his history. He was very successful in many cases of lameness. We asked him several times if he had any system, aside from manipulation and mesmerism of treating disease, and he always avoided the subject. We were his patient, but he never gave us any further information relating to his practice, but always said it is a secret of mine, and I have thought best not to divulge it. After treating the sick he would retire to a side room and note with pen the especial case with such other paraphrase as he thought best. This copy he gave to certain individuals to bring out, or, as he said, "put into shape." His scribblings were fragmentary, but sometimes very interesting. He requested us to transform them frequently and to give them different meanings, which we did.*[32]

Five days later Dresser was back in the *Post* with a rebuttal, this time over his own signature:

> The undersigned is a quiet, humble citizen of Boston, who seeks no controversy with anybody. . . . Now Mrs. Patterson-Eddy knows positively that the assertions of "E.G." in last Monday's POST are a tissue of falsehoods. . . . Mrs. Patterson-Eddy knows, or has reason to believe, that Dr. Quimby was a mesmerist in his young days, but that he ceased to be such when he became a healer of diseases by the application of truth, and that at the time she knew him he never used mesmerism at all in healing the sick. . . . Dr. Quimby never had regular students, but to such of his patients as could understand him he freely explained his life-giving doctrine, for it was no secret, and such ones had access also to a portion of his writings, and copied them, as did Mrs. Patterson-Eddy. Such persons as herself and others of an enquiring mind were therefore in a sense students of the doctor, and they made the most of their opportunities.[33]

This spurred Mrs. Eddy into replying under her own name in the *Boston Post* of March 9:

> We never were a student of Dr. Quimby's and Mr. Dresser knows that. . . . We were one of his patients. He manipulated his patients, but possibly back of his practice he had a theory in advance of his method and, as we now understand it, and have since discovered, he mingled that theory with mesmerism. . . . We defended Dr. Q. from unmerited scorn, asserted in public that his practice was not mesmerism, for we so believed it then, being truly ignorant of the nature, theory or practice of mesmerism. Since then the sin and subtlety of a student, who departed from our teachings and became a malpractitioner, caused us to investigate the subject of mesmerism, when we learned that manipulation includes animal magnetism; and if one manipulates the sick no matter what his theory is, it precludes the possibility of his practice being mental science.[34]

This can hardly be called Mrs. Eddy's happiest effort in historical reconstruction, but it pointed to the misunderstanding at the heart of the controversy. Quimby had been a mesmerist for many years. In his own view, he ceased to be one when he started healing by suggestion without inducing the mesmeric trance, although he saw the healing as a natural development from the earlier mesmerism. The general public continued to think of him as a mesmerist, but the few people who became seriously interested in his theory, including the then Mrs.

Patterson, followed his lead in disclaiming the term as applicable to him any longer. On the other hand, when she later became convinced that all mental suggestion was mesmeric in nature, it was logical for Mrs. Eddy to classify his palpably suggestive therapy under the generic name of mesmerism or animal magnetism. It is not necessary to assume bad faith on either side in order to understand the cause and nature of the controversy.

The exchange in the *Post* closed with Mrs. Eddy's second letter, but the echoes of battle were to sound thinly though persistently down the next century.

3

In two books which she acquired during 1883 Mrs. Eddy marked passages that bore on her life at this period. The first passage was from Plato:

> *And at his side let us place the just man. . . . Let him be the best of men, and be esteemed to be the worst; then let us see whether his virtue is proof against infamy and its consequences. And let him continue thus to the hour of death; being just, and seeming to be unjust.*

The second was from a contemporary Boston minister:

> *There is, to a high-souled man, no wrong more hurtful or more difficult to pardon than to have mean motives falsely ascribed to him, to be placed by misinterpretation on a lower plane than that where he belongs. Every such experience stabs the moral scource of life, and draws blood from the soul itself.*[35]

Opposite the first passage Mrs. Eddy wrote the single word "Glorious," opposite the second the stark phrase, "There was I murdered." To have what she saw as a life-and-death struggle between Christianity and mesmerism reduced in public opinion to the level of a sordid squabble for personal prestige was sometimes a matter for anguish, but it was never a reason for scuttling from the battle.

"We tread on forces," she would write later. "Human knowledge calls them forces of matter; but divine Science declares that they belong wholly to divine Mind, are inherent in this Mind, and so restores them to their rightful home and classification."[36] In other places she referred to the counterfeit forces of the human mind and indicated that the action of the divine Mind would uncover their most hidden operations. In her own experience she frequently showed remarkable intuitive perception of the psychological undercurrents in a given situation even when many of the leading factors were unknown to her.[37] An interesting example occurs in connection with the activities of Edward J. Arens.

On January 9, 1883, Emma Ware, Quimby's amanuensis in the 1860's, wrote Arens from Washington, D.C., that she was sorry she could not come to his lectures, but honored the ardor with which he pursued his work and knew him to be honestly and earnestly seeking the truth. Since honesty, by any reckoning, was not a conspicuous virtue of the enterprising Arens, it is not clear how Miss Ware, the daughter of a Supreme Court Justice, arrived at her charitable conclusion.

Although Mrs. Eddy could hardly have known of the correspondence between the two and had had little occasion to think of Miss Ware for the past seventeen years,[38] she dictated the following words to her secretary on February 7:

> *Vision: Wednesday morning 3 o'clock   Emma Ware. Saw woman in a crowd whispering and when she came near me seemed to be friendly but was two-faced. Seemed to be influencing the people against me. . . .*[39]

The vision had continued symbolically with a gorilla (identified by Mrs. Eddy with Arens) attempting to hold her down and "when I tried to speak he would put his huge paw over my mouth and stopped me." Interestingly enough, it was the next day that the Dresser-Arens campaign to launch Quimby as the founder of Christian Science was opened by Dresser's first letter in the *Boston Post*.

A few days later Mrs. Eddy told the Christian Scientist Association:

> *There is a tidal wave coming. It is to be an attempt to wrest from me the fact of the origin of Christian Science and place it upon a mesmeric basis, giving to a former noted mesmerist the honor, thus endeavoring to get onto a Christian platform. But this tidal wave need not harm us, although it is an awful responsibility to me. I give a great deal of time in the long hours of the night to study my duty, and how to carry it out.*[40]

The ensuing controversy with Dresser in the *Post*, together with her study of the sixteenth chapter of Jeremiah, seems to have crystallized Mrs. Eddy's decision to bring suit against Arens for infringement of her copyrights. Accordingly on April 6 she entered a bill of complaint in the Circuit Court of the United States, asking for an injunction restraining him from printing and circulating the offending pamphlet, *The Understanding of Christianity, or God,* with its whole-sale plagiarisms from *The Science of Man* and *Science and Health.*

Arens immediately rushed out a new version of his pamphlet, with a slightly changed title and a revised preface which read in part:

> *In a former pamphlet similar in some respects to this one, which I used in teaching, I gave the credit of authorship of some thoughts which I took from another work to the wrong party. Having been informed, since that time, by those who furnished proofs, that Dr. P. P. Quimby, of Portland, Me., was the author and originator of those thoughts, I transfer the credit to him.*[41]

Two months later he filed his answer to Mrs. Eddy's bill of complaint in the Circuit Court. Mrs. Eddy's two works, he alleged in defense, had themselves been copied from Quimby's manuscripts, and, in any case, he had not circulated his pamphlet for more than a year.

When the hearing opened on July 3, it was a simple matter to disprove the latter claim. A number of witnesses, including some of his own recent students, testified that Arens dispensed his pamphlet freely to anyone who expressed an interest in it. Nor was he in any better case as regards the Quimby manuscripts. Although George Quimby showed himself eager to help Arens in any way he could and wrote him that "I don't consider you a thief, or a rascal,"[42] he had quickly made it apparent that he was in no position to furnish his father's manuscripts (*i.e.,* the copies of them by himself and/or the Misses Ware[43]) to back up the Arens claim.

"The package of Mss," he wrote Arens on June 6, "I have sent to Miss Ware at Washington and they have either been forwarded by a friend or will be in a few days to her sister in Europe who was father's copiest."[44] To have them safely on another continent put them effectively beyond the reach of legal process, which otherwise could have compelled him to produce them as evidence essential to the case. His remarkable action in sending them abroad underlines his further statement in the same letter to Arens: "I will be honest with you and say that were they in my possession I would not allow them to go out of my hands into a strangers under any circumstances where there would be the barest possibility of their being copied."

It may have been this situation that caused the case to be carried over to the next court term, but it was obvious that without the arbitrarily withheld manuscripts Arens had no case at all. On October 4 an injunction was issued against the continued existence or circulation of his pamphlet, and on the following day the 3,800 remaining copies of the pamphlet were put to the knife. With the peculiar ineptitude that marked his ventures both as litigant and as publicist, Arens wrote the *Boston Globe* the day before the injunction was served on him, explaining that the court had not "decided in favor of the plaintiff."[45]

While the suit hung fire in August, 1883, Mrs. Eddy had written Colonel Smith in Washington:

> *I flee to you, but my poor tired womanhood shuns the pity of it all. If only the warfare was open, and I had one strong nature like dear Gilbert's or your own to share my cares and burdens I could endure it better. As it is, I have all this superstructure of Christian Science resting on my shoulders and no moments yet of rest. I hope it all will not again go crashing down over my head and ears if I let go for a brief space, for if it does I shall not rebuild again at the awful cost of the past two years.*[46]

The "cost" included moments of nightmare disorientation. Mrs. Eddy had launched a powerful attack on the human mind's conventional structure of assumptions, and in her own life she felt the shock of the demolition. The psychosomatic struggles that beset her at times were a sign of this, as were the occasional strange "visions" she had in the early morning hours.[47] Kennedy and Arens stalked through these visions as symbols of conspiratorial evil, the source of even her daytime ills. But with the winning of the court case there came a lightening of the burdens. Six days after the injunction was served on Arens, a vision of a different kind is recorded: "In a house in which there was a large number of my books stored and was a great smoke and cry of fire but I had no fear."[48]

About that time the sixth edition of *Science and Health* was published with the addition of the long-planned *Key to the Scriptures*.[49] This addition was composed of the chapter now called "Glossary" and consisted of Mrs. Eddy's definition of various biblical terms in their metaphysical dimension.[50] Of special interest is the fact that the chapter on demonology was slashed from forty-six pages to thirteen and all personal references to Kennedy, Spofford, and Arens eliminated.[51] Gilbert Eddy's foreword, with its denunciation of Arens' plagiarisms, had been removed; instead, Mrs. Eddy simply made passing reference in the preface to the fact that in the writings of "E.J.A.," adapted almost exclusively from her own, were "thirteen paragraphs, without credit, taken verbatim from our books."[52]

Of Quimby she wrote in the December issue of the *Journal of Christian Science:*

> *He commenced miscellaneous writings after we saw him; had no school education, but had a sound mind, and many advanced views on healing. We caught some of his thoughts, and*

135

*he caught some of ours; and both of us were pleased to say this
to each other. He never claimed what others claim for him.*[53]

On the whole, one could say that Mrs. Eddy had emerged victor
from the struggles of 1883. In the next issue of the *Journal* was a
quotation from Newton: "Trials are medicines which the great Physician prescribes because we need them." She herself expressed a similar
idea in *Science and Health:* "Trials are proofs of God's care."[54]

4

Life at 569 Columbus Avenue—or at 571 after the spring of 1884,
when the college moved to a slightly larger house next door—was
carefully regulated.

In addition to the austerely furnished rooms where classes were
taught and meetings held, there were living quarters for Mrs. Eddy
and several of the students who assisted her. These students also
carried on their private healing practice, and the back parlor was set
aside as an office where each of them could see his patients at certain
assigned hours. Meals were punctual and simple, expenses minimal
and shared. It was a life of much work and little play, but in the
evenings the household sometimes gathered to read aloud and discuss
books of general interest or to have "recitations and music."[55] On
musical evenings Mrs. Eddy herself would occasionally sing for them
in a clear, light soprano, with her secretary Calvin Frye at the piano.
"We had a pleasant little number in last evening to sing and play
the piano," she wrote a student on one occasion, "and the hours
passed swiftly."[56]

Frye, who had studied with her in the fall of 1881, was major
domo as well as private secretary. Picked as a likely prospect for the
position by Gilbert Eddy in the spring of 1882, he had finally been
summoned by telegram to join Mrs. Eddy on her way down from
Vermont the following August and had come at once. From that
moment till the end of her life twenty-eight years later, he never left
her side for a day. Faithful, meticulous, dogged, he occupies a unique
place in the history of Christian Science as the secretary, steward, aide,
coachman, spokesman, and confidant of its remarkable leader. At
that time he was also bookkeeper and secretary of the college.

The diaries which he sedulously kept are for the most part a
tedious compendium of household and organizational expenses, appointments, chores, with here and there a dry little note of one of
Mrs. Eddy's visions, of a physical "problem" that beset her, of her
directions for handling the latest arguments of the malpractitioners.[57]

Occasionally, when detailing a moment of dramatic struggle or suffering she was going through, he would change over to shorthand, to ensure privacy. Occasionally, too, he would use the diary as a safety valve for a sudden flash of rebellion or spurt of fantasy, but these moments were rare. The outstanding fact about Calvin Frye was his unquestioning acceptance of Mrs. Eddy's spiritual and temporal leadership.

His own background was a little bleak. Formerly a machinist in Lawrence, Massachusetts, he came of a good family which had seen better days, his father having been a classmate of Emerson's at Harvard. He himself had only a public-school education. After a marriage that ended with the death of his wife a year later, he returned, childless, to live with his crippled father, his psychotic mother, and a widowed sister. It was hardly a stimulating existence.

All this changed suddenly in 1881 when Clara Choate, then lecturing in Lawrence, restored his mother to sanity.[58] Both Frye and his sister immediately began the study of Christian Science and, shortly afterwards, its public practice. Then for Calvin came the call to Boston. For a while his sister was also at the college, serving as housekeeper, but soon she returned to her work as a Christian Science practitioner at Lawrence.

In appearance Frye was mild, neat, plumpish. Contrary to later legends about his taciturnity, he was not without a certain cheerfulness and dry Yankee humor. He watched over the expenditure of Mrs. Eddy's funds with a thrift that was also Yankee and sometimes approached parsimony, but in everything he did his whole concern seemed to be for the welfare of the woman whom he saw as the modern spokesman for God.

For some of Mrs. Eddy's men followers there was a basic problem involved in following a woman's leadership.[59] Her sudden reversals of decision, her intuitive leaps ahead of what they considered to be common sense, her unexpected sallies and demands, her apparent defiance of conventional logic, her combination of reason and sentiment, of girlishness and authority, of the practical and the visionary —all this was a challenge to the masculine mind. Yet for all his unimaginativeness, Frye seemed to understand these things, or at least to find them natural.

His attitude contrasts interestingly with that of Arthur Buswell, who also lived in the college and acted as clerk of the church and association. On the face of it, Buswell should have been the more useful of the two. He had a kind of intellectual flair, a touch of sophistication, lacking in Frye. Back in Cincinnati he had written Mrs. Eddy urging her to read *Walden* and a just published life of Thoreau; he had sent her other books that might be useful to her; he had proposed that she and Gilbert Eddy come out to Cincinnati as delegates to the Annual Convention of the Society for the Advancement of Science (in the department of anthropology, he suggested), and he had commented before the publication of the third edition of *Science and Health:* "Trust the grammatical construction may suit the most fastidious intellect."[60]

After coming to Boston, it was natural that it should be he who interviewed Dr. Charles Cullis, a devoted physician who had become a leading exponent and practitioner of "faith healing," and compared notes with him on their respective methods of cure. Buswell expressed a good deal of admiration for this cultivated Christian gentleman and in turn won Cullis' sympathetic interest. Where Frye's concern was focused single-mindedly on 571 Columbus Avenue, Buswell's extended to the social and intellectual framework in which the college existed.

Mrs. Eddy apparently recognized and appreciated this, while also acutely aware of the dangers of dilettantism. The work of grounding Christian Science in individual character had to be carried on at any cost before romping off to neighboring intellectual pastures, and she valued Buswell's potentialities only to the extent that he accepted the basic discipline the task demanded.

Although he had written her at the end of 1881, "I have explicit faith in our leader and consider her love and labor as divine,"[61] Buswell found it harder in the close quarters of the college to be always sure of the divine inspiration behind her demands. For instance, in April, 1883, he noted in his diary that she had asked him to preach for the Church of Christ on Sunday, then burst out, ". . . how she can ask a liar and thief (as she recently in a fearful rebuke called me) to take the stand as a christian teacher is more than I can tell at present."[62] Asked to speak again a Sunday or two later, he added that although he considered her accusations against him to be "unjust not to say unladylike," he hesitated to speak because of them, for "how can a morally degraded person as I have been recently represented appear before an audience as a teacher of this high form of Christianity even if innocent."[63]

To accuse Mrs. Eddy in such circumstances of being unladylike was a little like complaining that the thunderings of Jeremiah against the respectable citizens of Jerusalem were not what one would expect of a perfect gentleman. Frye, but not Buswell, seemed to understand instinctively that Mrs. Eddy's rebukes were directed to the "error," not to the person, and that they arose from her overriding sense of what was at stake in the spiritual enterprise on which they were all launched. There was a world in question—a world which scientific materialism was ready to drain of all spiritual meaning—and whatever would rob her lieutenants of their full spiritual integrity was a liar and a thief. The purpose of her denunciations, Mrs. Eddy insisted, was to cause her students to recognize and abandon the errors that were crippling them, thus freeing them to perform their God-given tasks.

Frye received many such rebukes from her, but his resulting struggles were less those of rebellion than of self-deprecation. An early notation in his diary records the struggle, with a dash of unexpected mysticism:

> *I was sad and sobing at the thought of how imperfectly I was demonstrating this science in my own life and struggling to find my way when there came a voice saying "You don't need to struggle but simply to waken and see you are there."*[64]

Nevertheless, he was not always charitable in his judgment of others, particularly of Buswell. Early in March, 1883, he had written in his diary, "Buswell is staying here to get the coll. into his own hands."[65] A month later Julia Bartlett moved into the already crowded house, and as a result the two men had to double up in the same bedroom. This could hardly have made matters easier.

On one occasion, according to a story related more than twenty years later, Frye roused Buswell from sleep in the early night and told him he was wanted in the parlor. Upon dressing and going downstairs, Buswell found Mrs. Eddy there with half a dozen resident students. They sat down, and after a few moments of silence Frye rose and said, "Mr. Buswell, I charge you with having worked upon my mind last Sunday, so that I could not introduce the speaker." (The guest preacher had been a distinguished Cambridge clergyman, who had ended by introducing himself when Frye failed to rise to the occasion.) The story concludes cryptically: "Mrs. Eddy listened while Mr. Buswell defended himself. Several other students spoke, and then everybody went off to bed."[66]

Despite its incompleteness, the anecdote hints at some of the internal strains within the household and helps to explain Buswell's eventual defection.[67] More significantly it illustrates the continued drag of the small-minded rivalries that would have kept Christian Science a quarrelsome sect instead of the revolutionary force Mrs. Eddy saw it as being.

To catch even a glimpse of the proportions of the challenge she proposed to offer the world one must go back to her concept of healing as evidence of the scientific validity of Spirit. Beneath the false confidence of the age, beneath the surface bloom of materialism, she saw a mortal illness which demanded radical measures. The spiritual healing of physical disease was both an instance and a test of the healing of all trust in matter. The miraculous was not an exception to universal law, but an illustration of it.

Young Ellen Brown, a student who lived at the college through the summer of 1883, has recorded an incident which illustrates the sense of miracle that constantly broke through the dailiness of life there.

Sent down to tell a visitor that Mrs. Eddy was too busy to see her, Miss Brown found in the reception room a quiet, dignified woman, earnest in manner, whose face clouded with disappointment at the message. She was passing through Boston, she told Miss Brown, and had hoped very much to see Mrs. Eddy, who had healed her in one treatment several years before when she was dying of cancer. "Did the cancer disappear all at once while Mrs. Eddy was treating you?" Miss Brown asked, and the reply was no, but the pain had stopped and the cancer had at once begun to heal, so that in "a very short time" all traces of it had disappeared.

"When she said this," Miss Brown wrote, "her voice had dropped to a very low tone and her eyes were filled with tears. . . . She left the college keenly disappointed at not seeing Mrs. Eddy." Similarly, the latter, when she heard who her visitor had been, expressed great regret at not having seen her. The woman's cancer, she told Miss Brown as she recalled the incident, had eaten its way to the jugular vein, and the sight was "so awful" that "I turned away and knew in the most positive way that God knew nothing of such a thing. That was all the treatment I gave her."[68]

Later she would write:

> *Healing physical sickness is the smallest part of Christian Science. It is only the bugle-call to thought and action, in the higher range of infinite goodness. The emphatic purpose of Christian Science is the healing of sin; and this task, sometimes, may be harder than the cure of disease; because while mortals love to sin, they do not love to be sick.*[69]

Few of them, she found, loved the discipline that she saw as a requisite for establishing Christian Science.

5

In the brash young Chicago which had risen less like a phoenix than a turkey cock from the ashes of its great fire, Christian Science had found a hearing, but was running a little wild. By the middle of 1883 a father and son, Bradford and Roger Sherman, were practicing and teaching it as they understood it, selling copies of *Science and Health* right and left but using methods that were closer to the frank mental suggestion of Arens than to Mrs. Eddy's system of healing.

George B. Charles, who returned to Chicago in the fall of that year after studying with Arens in Boston, busily spread stories against Mrs. Eddy, to further confusion of the metaphysical scene.[70] Some eager neophytes like Mrs. Fannie Silsbee, who had studied with the Shermans, attempted to combine whatever version of Christian Science they had learned with the bizarre Arens technique of sitting back to back with the patient they were treating. Mrs. Caroline D. Noyes, who had heard Mrs. Eddy lecture once in Boston, had her own unorthodox method of mental treatment, but when she sent for young Ellen Brown to come to Chicago and assist her, she discovered to her dismay that her own method was "all wrong."

Another Sherman student, Dr. Silas J. Sawyer, who was now making his lucrative dental practice in Milwaukee secondary to his struggling practice of Christian Science, came by himself to the conclusion that none of them was following the pure teachings of *Science and Health* and that they all needed to go to Boston to study at the fountainhead. Meanwhile, however, a Miss Harvey of Milwaukee, whose cousin had studied with Clara Choate, announced that Mrs. Choate was coming out to the Middle West to teach—and who could be a better authority than Mrs. Eddy's "favorite student"?

This characterization of the volatile Clara, with her undeniable capacities and her unfortunate penchant for antagonizing Mrs. Eddy's other students, was a little less than accurate. In August, 1883, when she asked Mrs. Eddy whether she might hold classes in Christian Science, the latter told her to examine her motives closely and arrive at her own decision. With lightning speed she concluded that her motives were of the highest and began to teach. Two months later Mrs. Eddy asked her to take no more classes and instead to send prospective students to the Massachusetts Metaphysical College. She complied, but announced in various quarters that the reversed decision showed clearly Mrs. Eddy's jealousy of her success.

Later Mrs. Eddy wrote her:

> *I asked you to try teaching, but when I took your pupils I found your mental influence, not your words, had done them an injury that I could not repair at once. Your sensuality and untruthfulness have their effect, although you think them out of*

*sight. That was the only reason I asked you to stop teaching—
and never have told this before to a mortal.*[71]

Mrs. Eddy had indeed for some time tried to shield Mrs. Choate
from censure. In the October *Journal* she published a glowing account
of one of the young woman's more outstanding healings. She poured
oil on her constant differences with the other Boston students: "About
Mr. Frye he is a better friend to you than he appears to your face
perhaps, he defends you to others. . . . He is *honest*."[72] And of the
joint failure of Mrs. Choate and the other students to resist the influences that turned them against each other she wrote her, "I cant
make one more than another see how it is, they all *will* take their
own way."[73]

When the situation in Chicago and Milwaukee called for someone to go there and get things straightened out, Mrs. Eddy chose
Mrs. Choate, despite her shortcomings, as the one with the requisite
healing and speaking ability. The lady, however, blew hot and cold
on the proposition. At one point, she was all eagerness; at another
she refused on the ground that she had not a proper wardrobe. Mrs.
Eddy replied with a touch of asperity that the lack of a wardrobe
had never hindered *her* from doing Christ's work and that Clara's
vacillations had let the Arens faction take over the Chicago scene.
"Now do not sell your tickets," she added decisively, "[but] *wait* until
I say *again* go."[74]

Mrs. Eddy was entering on a new stage of action in which she
would dispatch her leading students on emergency missions with the
expectation that they shared enough of her vision to subordinate their
personal convenience to "Christ's work." The Chicago assignment
was a test of Clara Choate's fitness to take a position of trust in a
movement that aimed at what might be called the total Christification
of the natural order. More than a contest of wills or a clash of feminine temperaments, it was a trial of moral intensity and spiritual
mettle. The "bugle call" of physical healing might be a thrilling
sound, as Mrs. Choate had found it, but the "higher range" of total
commitment to which it called might well prove both lonely and risky,
as the great spiritual pioneers of Christian history had found it. However inadequate the verbal-conceptual wardrobe in which Mrs. Eddy's
vision for her movement was then clothed, the magnitude of the end
at which it aimed was clearly visible. Clara Choate herself had recognized this on many occasions, even while she shrank from its
ultimate demands.

And so a struggle to "save" the young woman began. While the
Boston students, like the earlier ones in Lynn, accused Mrs. Choate

of duplicity and malpractice, Mrs. Eddy saw her more as the unresisting victim of the mental forces arrayed against Christ's work. Mrs. Choate meanwhile was convinced that the students were working against her welfare and trying to force her mentally to go to Chicago. Mrs. Eddy brushed aside this charge impatiently in a letter on December 11, hinting at a far deeper problem Clara must face:

> *You are laboring under the same delusion now that you were years ago and caused by the same malpractice. . . . I have learned* unmistakably *that no one here in this house has taken you up mentally or has any care one way or another about your going West. . . . I see what your fits and starts will end in. Christianity is fixed. Before you ever heard of Christian Science I had been commissioned of God to lead his children out of the darkness of today. You never can do this until your life is changed as you well know.*[75]

That night Mrs. Choate went through a fierce struggle. At three o'clock in the morning she wrote Mrs. Eddy that she definitely would not go to Chicago, though she could feel the mental pressure from the students trying to force her out of Boston. Why, she asked, should she leave her home and her work? "My *practice* may seem of little account to you but to *me* it is as great as your Church or college."[76] The letter reached Mrs. Eddy later in the day, and she wrote back immediately in a last effort to rouse Clara to resist her own particular devils:

> *The battle of the demons, they think, has been fought and you are* conquered, *because you rose up from their night's campaign resolved to do just what they told you. Now listen to me, the best friend you have on Earth, take back the resolve they made you form and go to* Chicago and Milwaukee. *Say as Luther said "if there were as many devils between here and Worms as tiles on my house I would go."*
>
> *Will you do it? If you will not hear God's voice speaking through me they will conquer you and kill you just as they did Gilbert. I* know it.[77]

That Mrs. Choate's "demons" were doing their best to destroy her as a Christian healer became apparent five days later when an incident came to light that showed her personal morals and professional ethics to be in considerable disarray. On that date one of her male patients confided to Arthur Buswell that, while treating him, she had made sexual advances to him which he found highly disconcerting. Later the charge was seconded by Mrs. Sarah Crosse, who had treated the same man subsequently.[78]

In the correspondence between Mrs. Eddy and Clara Choate over the years there are many references to the latter's "sensuality." Animal magnetism has been defined as simply the pull of the flesh—the will of the flesh, or the carnal mind, in Pauline terms. In the deepest Christian sense, the antidote to this was not a repressive psychological mechanism but a liberating spiritual grace. The carnal mind, as Paul described it, covered considerably more territory than the Freudian libido, and for Mrs. Eddy it denoted the all-encompassing claim that life is so much animate matter. This was the "enemy." In the chapter on demonology in the third edition of *Science and Health,* she had written, "In the warfare with error we attack with intent to kill, and the wounded or cornered beast turns on its assailant."[79] On this ground Clara's weakness of the flesh might be understood as a measure of the young woman's failure to understand the spiritual enterprise in which she was engaged.

Mrs. Eddy, however, did not reproach her student's moral weakness but drew attention to her mental dishonesty in not facing up to the claims of animal magnetism—and even this she did with considerable tenderness. That she herself really loved Clara Choate is evident from her letters, and never more so than when she is pointing out to her the dangers that beset her. "I would not for the world give you a single unnecessary pain," she wrote her about this time, "but I am the surgeon of mind and must probe and cut before I can heal. That is the most cross-bearing part of my mission. May God help me to do it and you to be blessed by it."[80]

At some point Buswell suggested to her that she call a private meeting of several of her best students to do concerted work about the situation. In a letter to Ellen Brown, Mrs. Eddy described how they worked together on the theme, "There is no animal magnetism, no hatred, malice, no will power, no power in evil, etc."[81] The subject for consideration at a second meeting held within the week was described by her in one place as "God is all and God is Love," in another as "God is All; there is none beside Him."[82] Only two meetings were held. While the intent was to help free Mrs. Choate and one or two other rebellious students from the influence of malicious mesmerism, a few of those present apparently fell into the trap of working "against" these recalcitrant students.[83] Mrs. Eddy never repeated the experiment, and later she wrote that one had no more right to treat a person without his knowledge and consent "than one has to enter a house, unlock the desk, displace the furniture, and suit one's self in the arrangement and management of another man's property."[84]

In any case, Clara Choate remained eminently unhealed and un-repentant. The moral issue was only one element contributing to the almost solid opposition of the other students, who were convinced that she was trying to control mentally both her patients and her opponents. After lying awake most of the night for one week and praying day and night,[85] Mrs. Eddy came to the conclusion that there was only one way to save the situation, and on January 5, 1884, she wrote Mrs. Choate:

> This is my candid conclusion—that because the people are believing you the cause of pretty much all their disasters, you had better withdraw from the Church and Association, and not attend our meetings of the students. I have fought in your defense seven years on this very question, and at the end of all this fidelity I hear of your accusing me publicly of working against you because I am envious of your popularity.[86]

Mrs. Choate sent in her resignation the same day. Two days later she wrote Mrs. Eddy in one of those spasms of humility which had marked her conduct for years, "I feel I have been ungrateful . . . will you forgive me all or any sin I may have committed, and bear with me patiently in the future?" She hoped to prove that "a true repentance and reformation" had already begun, and asked her "fellow associates to forgive me all transgressions."[87]

It was too late, however. At the next meetings of the church and association her resignation was refused and she was then expelled from membership, with Mrs. Eddy abstaining from the vote. The minutes of the association meeting for February 5 read:

> With great regret for the need of such action the Association, upon motion of Mrs. Emma Hopkins, seconded by Mr. Buswell, voted almost unanimously that Mrs. Clara E. Choate be expelled from this Association. Mrs. Eddy . . . was deeply moved because of her student's failure, after her many years of counsel and forgiveness, to maintain a Christian character. Mrs. Eddy advised that this action should not be made public unless it became necessary.[88]

So Mrs. Choate departed into a kind of metaphysical limbo, and Emma Hopkins, a young woman of even more brilliant potentialities, stepped onto the scene. A pupil in the class Mrs. Eddy had just concluded, Mrs. Hopkins would be editor of the *Journal* in little more than six months, then off on a meteoric career of her own fourteen months later.

Students in the same class were Silas Sawyer of Milwaukee and his wife Jennie. Returning to the Middle West, Sawyer quickly called on the Shermans in Chicago to "strike a blow for Science there" and "place the Truth before them, and the *facts* in relation to E. J. Arens,"[89] whose mental methods they had unconsciously absorbed. After his visit he wrote Mrs. Eddy on February 6:

> *Previous to my telling them of Mrs. C_____ [Choate] they expressed doubts of you, and had shown no signs of yielding. Afterward Mr. B. Sherman said to Mrs. Silsbee, "Well we have had our foundation knocked out from under us, but of course, we want to know and practice the best, and only that."*[90]

The result was that Bradford Sherman, his wife Mattie, his son Roger, his pupil Mrs. Silsbee, and his sister-in-law Miss Platt, all went to Boston to go through Mrs. Eddy's next class at the end of February. While there, they attended a meeting of the Christian Scientist Association at which, among other things, Mrs. Melissa J. Smith of Allston, a suburb of Boston, reported "that her parlor lecture had recently been invaded by Mr. Edward J. Arens and his party and that they used means calculated to disturb and break up her meetings." Mrs. Smith, the minutes of the association recorded with quiet satisfaction, "held her position and was continuing the meetings with renewed interest."[91] It was a nice little object lesson for the Shermans on the tactics of Arens, which they had previously doubted.

Another member of the same class was Mrs. Caroline D. Noyes, who represented a further element in the Chicago picture and who at the next association meeting "spoke very encouragingly of the Science in that part of the country."[92] The class marked a decisive turning point for her as for the Shermans in terms of spiritual discipline, and she subsequently became one of Mrs. Eddy's most trusted lieutenants in that area.

Chicago, it appeared, was getting along satisfactorily without benefit of Clara Choate.

6

If Mrs. Choate represented the unstable past, Julia Bartlett represented the increasingly disciplined future.

As treasurer of the church and a resident at 571 Columbus Avenue, Miss Bartlett often found incoming funds insufficient to meet current church expenses. From time to time she made up the difference from her own pocket. Then suddenly a small personal crisis emptied her pocket even more drastically. As she later told the story:

> *I took a few patients and had good success in healing, and this supplied me with necessary funds, until all at once not one*

came to be healed. I understood the cause of this and worked assiduously to overcome the error in realizing God's government and that He is the source of supply and in actively doing my part to start my practice again, yet with no apparent result. To be sure I had all I could do with work for the Cause, but my little practice which had met my daily expenses, was taken from me. To reduce expenses I then began to take meals out and to reduce the supply as well, and for the first time I knew what it was to suffer from hunger day after day. I did not trouble dear Mrs. Eddy or any one with the extreme conditions, so far as I could hide them. It was my problem to solve. I finally thought relief must come soon if I was to remain in the College, and taking my Bible for my guidance, I opened to these words: "Thou shalt remain in this house." It was no longer a question with me. I must and could work it out. Then one day patients began to come. The attempt to take me away and deprive Mrs. Eddy of the help she needed had failed and I had no more trouble that way, and she said I never would.

I remarked to Mrs. Eddy, "We are commanded to take up our cross daily, but I am not doing so, for I do not see any to take up." Her answer was, "It is because it has ceased to be a cross."[93]

Two patients who came to her in March, 1884, were a father and daughter from Littleton, New Hampshire, whose quick healings aroused a clamor of interest in that town. Miss Bartlett was besieged with requests to go there, but felt herself too busy at the college. Finally Mrs. Eddy told her, "Write them you will go for one week."[94]

By her own decision Miss Bartlett stipulated that her sponsors should hire a hall where she could give a talk the first and second evenings after her arrival, and that they should get sixty subscriptions to the *Journal* for one year. "My object in doing this," she wrote later, "was first for the aid the *Journal* would be to them after I left them as they were starting in a new and untried way. Then, the *Journal* itself was in its first year of growth and needed our best efforts to support it."[95] The mixture of care and shrewdness was typical.

The talks were a success and almost immediately she was seeing and treating some seventy patients a day. "There is a perfect *rush* of patients," she wrote Mrs. Eddy on April 9, and most of them were being healed. Three doctors were sending her patients, and she had to turn away many from surrounding towns for simple lack of time. At one point she telegraphed to Boston for help, but no one could come. "It is God that is doing this work," she wrote Mrs. Eddy, "but when it is done I shall be so glad to go home. It is late in the night. I have no time to eat drink or sleep."[96]

A number of the people who became interested in Christian Science during her eleven-day stay in Littleton later became teachers, healers, and prominent workers in the movement. Recalling this almost pentecostal experience years later, Miss Bartlett in her rather spinsterish prose noted the obvious fact that not everyone was pleased by what was happening there:

> *Christian Science was the one topic of conversation in town and on the outbound trains, and much antagonism was expressed by certain clergymen and M.D.'s when their people and patients rejoiced in the proof of the great healing power of Truth and trusted in it for their help. On one occasion a gentleman whose wife and daughter were being benefited by the treatment, was met by his minister who bitterly denounced Christian Science and among other things said it was the work of the devil. The gentleman replied, "If it is the work of the devil, then I only wish there were more devils and less ministers." The minister much amused by his quick wit took it good naturedly.*[97]

Some of the good nature drained away later as entrenched theological and medical positions were further challenged, and professional opposition stiffened. The Littleton experience was a phenomenon to be repeated in many places: large-scale healing at the first fresh impact of Christian Science, followed by increasing demands on the faith and understanding of those who held to it in the face of intensified opposition. Miss Bartlett found her own answer in what she had heard from Mrs. Eddy's earliest students:

> *They had wonderful cases of healing and their work was easily done until all at once they were not successful and it was said the Scientists had lost their power to heal. Then our great Leader discovered that evil minds were at work to hinder the progress of Truth in its healing power and that the students must be taught how to meet and overcome this evil. As this was done, their patients began to improve and their work went on as before.*[98]

Shortly after the Littleton episode Miss Bartlett had a somewhat similar experience in Vermont.[99] Then at the beginning of May she was needed back at the college to take charge of affairs while Mrs. Eddy, accompanied by Calvin Frye and Sarah Crosse, went off to teach a class in Chicago.

Quickened to new determination by their recent study in Boston, the Sawyers,[100] the Shermans, and Mrs. Noyes, together with Ellen Brown, at almost a moment's notice had gathered some twenty-five people together to take a course of instruction that would really set Christian Science in the Middle West on a straight course. It was not a brilliant assemblage, or even a promising one, but it marked a significant step forward in a wide-open, brand-new field. At the end, on May 25, Mrs. Eddy delivered a lecture to a couple of hundred people in Hershey Hall on the text, "Whom do men say that I am?"

She returned to Boston with the vision of a great preparatory work still to be done. A week or two later she wrote Clara Choate:

> *This lovely morning I wish I could see you and put my arms round your neck and tell you how much I love you. I never feel so happy as when thinking of you in the old way and asking God to bless my child. . . .*
>
> *I have forgiven you in years past, and can and do again, because I love you and cannot hold any enmity against one who has done the good that you have done; or even if they had done much that was wrong.*[101]

Even so, she could not linger over the Clara Choates, and she turned with decision toward the future.

Chapter VI

Pulpit and Podium

New England culture was enjoying what Van Wyck Brooks would later call its Indian summer. In Boston's Copley Square each Sunday the genial eloquence of Phillips Brooks poured through beautiful Trinity Church (a splendor of Richardson Romanesque, with Saint-Gaudens carving and Burne-Jones windows) while on nearby Exeter Street the more utilitarian auditorium of a great new temple of spiritism buzzed with spectral intimations from Beyond.

It was a scene rich with contrasts. On Good Friday the socially formidable, ostentatiously penitential Mrs. Jack Gardner could be seen scrubbing the altar steps of the Church of the Advent, Beacon Hill beachhead of fashionable Anglo-Catholicism. On a midsummer afternoon Miss Elizabeth Peabody, the veteran virgin of American Transcendentalism, could be found addressing assorted Platonists and Hegelians at Bronson Alcott's Concord School of Philosophy on women's rights, or dozing peacefully on the platform while William James made vigorous forays into the alluring wilds of psychology.

While the Sunday afternoon meetings of the new Spiritual Temple drew large crowds to hear excellent organ music, violins, singers, followed by titillating exhibitions of mediumship, the Sunday afternoon meetings of the Christian Scientists at Hawthorne Hall on Park Street drew more modest numbers to its more confined space for its far more audacious revelations. For while the paranormal world of spiritism offered a temporary escape from the boredoms of daily life, Christian Science offered and demanded a new view of reality itself. Spirit, instead of being a word of ghostly ambiguity, became quite simply the substance of whatever was real and permanent in experience.

On the days when Mrs. Eddy herself preached, an expectant congregation overflowed the attractive little hall whose windows overlooked Boston Common, with the handsome gilded dome of Charles Bulfinch's State House just up the street to the right and the lovely white spire of the Park Street Congregational Church just below to the left. On the surface it was all decorous enough—flowers on the platform, singing from the Unitarian hymnal, a quiet-spoken sermon, an attentive congregation. But the message that was breaking through was challenging the age-old conviction that, in the last analysis, man is both wombed and tombed in matter.

Conventional Christianity, in Mrs. Eddy's view, had simply ignored the logical implications of the birth and resurrection of Jesus, with their smashing of accepted physical law at each end of human life. Her own Christmas and Easter sermons brought those distant events to bear with startling relevance on the individual auditor's mind and being. One young man who frequently went to hear Phillips Brooks preach at Trinity Church on Sunday morning and Mrs. Eddy preach at Hawthorne Hall in the afternoon, suggests something of the difference in his reminiscences.[1] Brooks, the great-hearted Episcopalian who regarded preaching as "the bringing of truth through personality," delivered an Easter sermon which the young man found eloquently "uplifting." But Mrs. Eddy, he wrote, seemed with less eloquence to carry him right to the sepulcher where Jesus stepped forth in spiritual triumph. Resurrection, as she presented it, was more than history or symbol; it was present fact.

That was the way it looked also to those sick and crippled people who came to the services and walked out well and sound.[2] In healing, Mrs. Eddy made clear, apostolic and scientific Christianity were one. Healing was both sacrament and validation.

Like all preachers, of course, she had her off days. On one occasion she wrote to Ellen Brown: "My last Sunday sermon has called out much praise. It was extempore and I thought but a feeble effort."[3] Inevitably, too, her sermons were variously estimated by those who heard them. A critical clergyman who attended a communion service wrote afterward, "The congregation appeared intelligent and devout, and the service, conducted by Mrs. Eddy, was free from cant," but he complained of the absence of visible sacraments and went on to describe the sermon as "a spiritual balloon, with texts of Scripture enough to keep it from floating out of sight."[4]

On days when she could not preach, the pulpit would be filled sometimes by a student, sometimes by a liberal minister from one of the other churches, such as Andrew P. Peabody, for many years Plummer Professor of Christian Morals and Preacher to Harvard University.[5] A few of the clergy were beginning to express open sympathy for her, coming to visit her, even attending her classes. Among the first to talk with her was Cyrus A. Bartol, venerable Transcendentalist of the old breed, luminously hospitable to all that validated the power of spirit.[6] In May and again in October of 1884 he preached to his own congregation at the West Church in support of the new system of healing.[7] Only a few days later a young Baptist minister, O. P. Gifford, took public issue with his fellow pastors who "would rather see their friends die than subject them to this system,"[8] and before long the press was brimming with discussions of the new "mind cure," as it was often called.

In the autumn a Boston University professor, Luther T. Townsend, addressed the Boston Methodist Preachers' Meeting on the topic "Prayer and Healing." It proved to be the opening gun in an outraged clerical attack on Christian Science.[9] Describing Mrs. Eddy as an example of infidelity of the rankest type, Townsend contemptuously offered her one thousand dollars if she could put into place a dislocated hip or ankle bone by purely mental means, and two thousand dollars if she could restore sight to someone born blind. Later the address was printed and the challenge repeated in the Methodist weekly, *Zion's Herald*. Replying in the *Journal* of February, 1885, Mrs. Eddy declined being drawn into a "prayer gauge test," cited her healing record, invited her challenger to match it, and concluded unexpectedly: "I agree with Prof. Townsend, that every system of medicine claims more than it practices. If the system is science, it includes of necessity a principle which the learner can demonstrate only in the proportion that he understands it."[10]

Next in the lists was the Reverend A. J. Gordon, a conservative Christian of abundant faith and narrow understanding, who granted freely that Mrs. Eddy healed the sick, but who then confounded her teaching with spiritism, theosophy, and all manner of heathen abominations. In a letter read aloud by the Reverend Joseph Cook at one of his immensely popular and influential Monday lectures at Tremont Temple, Gordon wrote of Christian Science, "One has only to open the published volumes of its lady apostle in this city to find such a creed of pantheism and blasphemy as has been rarely compounded."[11]

In a spirited "Defence of Christian Science" published in the March *Journal* and then in a separate pamphlet, Mrs. Eddy quoted this statement among others and remarked dryly that to open her books was all that Gordon and Cook could have done, judging by their description of what she believed. Cook had, in fact, borrowed a copy of *Science and Health* only a day or two before the attack and had declined an interview with her at that time. Now she demanded an opportunity to reply at one of the Monday Morning Lectures to so cavalier a misrepresentation, and Cook grudgingly conceded her ten minutes on March 16.

If Mrs. Eddy's appearance there can be taken as a symbol of her confrontation of the Protestant orthodoxy of her own day, it illustrated at a deeper level the timeless encounter of the prophetic spirit with proscriptive orthodoxies of every kind. To act directly on experience from new sources of spiritual insight and authority has always been to threaten both the conceptual framework and the power structure of the religious establishment. In such matters, of course, it is hard to distinguish the true prophet from the false, whose fire may be snatched from some other source than heaven.[12] The easiest form of defense, as Cook and Gordon found, is to assume the worst and throw up a semantic smoke screen to blur the issues. For the pious Christian of Mrs. Eddy's day, her teaching could be damned as dangerous pantheistic heterodoxy—as, for the secular Christian of the next century, it could be discredited as old-fashioned philosophical idealism.

In simple human terms, Mrs. Eddy felt acutely the burden of the world's incomprehension. Under such circumstances, it took all her courage to appear at Tremont Temple. Looked upon as the representative of "evil," the tool of Satan, she was to stand before the high priests of a Boston over which the ancient shadow of theocratic intolerance still lay. "The star of Bethlehem is the star of Boston," she had said in her last Christmas sermon,[13] and in her view the central purpose of Christian Science was to bring the good news that Christianity still had untapped resources of spiritual energy with which to confront the all-devouring claims of secular science. "Jesus of Nazareth," she wrote, "was the most scientific man that ever trod the globe. He plunged beneath the material surface of things, and found the spiritual cause."[14] Her reward for taking this advance position was the cry of heresy from a Christianity already scuttling ignominiously before Darwin and the scientific materialists. More than once Mrs. Eddy found a kind of sad comfort in the biblical words, "He came unto his own, and his own received him not."

On the Sunday before her reply to Cook and Gordon she preached "a powerful and awakening sermon" at Hawthorne Hall, as the *Journal* put it, going on to describe perfervidly how the "deep abiding interest of all was strengthened by the reassuring words of the faithful messenger of the Second Coming."[15] But this very attitude was enough to cause a gnashing of clerical teeth among the two thousand grim Christians who awaited her at Tremont Temple the next morning.

Cook's brief introduction was icy. Her extemporaneous speech, taken down by a reporter and found today in her *Miscellaneous Writings,* was cool and pointed, ending exactly as her ten minutes were up. Without wasting a word, she spoke in question-and-answer form to the chief issues raised by Gordon. At the end there was silence, except for a scatter of defiant applause from one or two pockets of sympathizers. She left immediately and rode home in her carriage with Julia Bartlett, sunk in thought. In Miss Bartlett's words:

> I saw she must be left to herself and her help came from a higher than a human source, and when we reached home she went to her room where she remained alone. I thought if I could only have shared some of the burdens how gladly I would have done it, and if the world only understood, these trials would not have been put upon her. No one but herself could know the burdens of that hour.[16]

The text of her address was published in the April *Journal*, together with an open letter from her to Professor Townsend, who had just referred to her again in *Zion's Herald* as "the pantheistic and prayerless Mrs. Eddy." The same issue of the *Journal* contained a more general comment by her on the mounting onslaught of pulpit and press. In an article entitled "Veritas Odium Parit," she wrote:

> I have loved the Church and followed it, thinking it was following Christ; but if the pulpit will allow the people to go no further in this direction and rejects Apostolic Christianity, seeking to stereotype infinite Truth, it is a thing to be thankful for that we can walk alone the straight and narrow way. . . .
>
> It was the Southern pulpit and press that influenced the people to wrench from man both human and divine rights to subserve the interests of wealth, religious caste, civil and political power. And the pulpit had to be purged of that sin by human gore, when the blood of Christ would have washed it away in Christian Science.[17]

Before the end of the month, the Boston press was reporting that the last session of the Baptist Ministers' Meeting had been greatly disturbed over the issue of Christian Science, A. J. Gordon leading the attack against it and O. P. Gifford speaking in its defense. A week later the Congregational ministers were treated to a paper by the Reverend Stacy Fowler (subsequently published in the *Homiletic Review*) in which he took issue with everyone. It was ridiculous, he said, to call Christian Science pantheism, as both Townsend and Cook did:

> The pantheist holds that God is in everything, and that the All is God. Mrs. Eddy eliminates God from everything but spirit. All else she calls shadows and reflections. She places the "mortal mind," a whole hemisphere of thought, outside of God and over against Him. Her language is often pantheistic but her thought

is not. In a note to me she writes: "*I am the only anti-pantheist, for I see that God, spirit, is not in His reflection, any more than the sun is in the light that comes to this earth through reflection. Can you understand this? No: and no one can fully until I educate the spiritual sense to perceive the* substance *of spirit, and the* substancelessness *of matter.*"

Fowler then pointed out the errors of those who confused Christian Science with spiritism and faith cure, described it himself as "the forth-putting of a mind of quick perceptions, but wholly unable to classify and construct," and reduced the whole issue to the question of whether Christian Science healed. Gordon, he declared,

> . . . *gives* [Christian Scientists] *the credit of healing, and then turns round and fiercely attacks their theology as dangerous, and calls them by harsh names. If, however, they cure the sick, people will not hesitate and turn away from them at the call of a halt from theologians. Not much. If the scientist can snatch you from the jaws of disease and death you will not boggle over a question of theology. Besides, it is by their theology, by their peculiar views of God and of man that they assume to work the cures. If they can heal, as they claim they do, they will carry the day, and they ought.*

But, he concluded magisterially, he had found no evidence that they healed "in the strict sense of the term," and was convinced that "the science is waning" and would soon disappear.[18]

Not all his colleagues shared this last conviction. Three weeks later a Boston correspondent of *The Times* of London reported in that august journal that

> . . . *clergymen of all denominations are seriously considering how to deal with what they regard as the most dangerous innovation that has threatened the Christian Church in this region for many years. Scores of the most valued church members are joining the Christian Scientist branch of the metaphysical organization, and it has thus far been impossible to check the defection.*[19]

The "Boston Craze," as Townsend had called it, was continuing to spread.

2

On the face of it, the Massachusetts Metaphysical College invited amusement. Here was a college with one faculty member (who was also its president) and one course (which lasted less than three weeks) and one textbook. Yet if it bore little relationship to the luxuriant scholarship of Harvard College across the Charles River, it perhaps came closer to the familiar definition of the ideal college as consisting of Mark Hopkins at one end of a log and a student at the other.

Mrs. Eddy was the college and the college was Mrs. Eddy. If a prospective student called at 571 Columbus Avenue to inquire about joining the next class, the front door was likely to be opened by the president herself. In fact, when one of the many successive rumors that she was ill, unable to speak, or even dead was being widely circulated, she inserted a sociable notice in the *Journal* of September, 1884, according her enemies "due credit" for their desires but inviting her readers to "call at the Mass. Metaphysical College, and judge for yourself whether I can talk, and laugh too." To which she added flatly, "I was never in better health."[20]

Because her time was now given up to teaching others how to heal, Mrs. Eddy seldom took patients. When Joseph S. Eastaman, a simple sea captain of Spanish or Portuguese extraction,[21] returned from a long voyage to Peru to find his bedridden wife in worse condition than ever, he came to Mrs. Eddy, of whom he had just heard, to ask her to take the poor woman's apparently hopeless case. To his utter astonishment, she asked him earnestly, "Captain, why don't you heal your wife yourself?" In some bewilderment Eastaman enrolled in her next class, and by the end of the brief term his wife had recovered sufficiently to accompany him to the final session. "That one lesson," he wrote later, "dispelled her every doubt as to whether Christian Science had any kinship with Mesmerism or Spiritualism—for which she had strong antipathies."[22] With the resolution of this doubt, she was soon entirely well and, like her husband, became a practitioner and in time a Christian Science teacher.

A somewhat similar healing had taken place when Dr. Silas Sawyer of Milwaukee came to study with Mrs. Eddy a year earlier, bringing his invalid wife Jennie with him. While it seemed impossible at first that Mrs. Sawyer would be able to sit up through the daily classes, she not only succeeded in doing so but came out of the course healed. At the end, Mrs. Eddy asked her what she was going to do with what she had learned. As Mrs. Sawyer recounted it later, "I answered, 'I am filled with wonderful Truth. I do not know what I am to do with it.' Then she said in the most convincing way, 'You are going to heal with it.' "[23]

Shortly after her return to Milwaukee, Mrs. Sawyer wrote back:

> *Now! as to my work. I took a patient with curvature of spine, deafness in one ear, and her arm perfectly useless, could*

not open her hand, arm in a sling, caused from inflammatory rheumatism (in belief). After two treatments she used her arm & hand freely. . . . After one week's treatment her back seemed to straighten so that she is now able to wear a straight corset instead of one fitted to a curvature as before. . . . I feel to thank God day & night *that* through even me *such things can come to pass. I am treating a sister who has a belief of insanity, her reports are very favorable; also a man who has stammered. . . . I am treating four regular patients besides many friends. I have nothing unfavorable to report.*[24]

Silas Sawyer, on the other hand, had a failure as well as successes to report. Soon afterward Mrs. Eddy authorized him to commence teaching, although he had written her on his return, with a kind of awe, "Oh! Mrs. Eddy—when I look at what I am undertaking, I am almost dismayed, and were it not that you advised, and are helping me, I would not dare try it."[25]

Some of the other students felt less humility. Among these was A. J. Swarts who, with his wife, had sat in on the last five days of Mrs. Eddy's Chicago class. A former Methodist minister of doubtful standing, he had become a lecturer on spiritism, with his young wife serving as a successful medium, but he fastened on Christian Science as a "good thing" with a promising future.

After Mrs. Eddy had returned to Boston, Swarts wrote her a letter of thanks for "granting us admission to the pure and high teachings in your class," and added that he felt impelled to "identify in some public or traveling method with your system." Before long he was traveling from one "fine Spiritualist Camp Meeting" to another, holding classes on "mind cure," which he identified vaguely with the Massachusetts Metaphysical College, writing Mrs. Eddy proudly that in one class he had three M.D.'s and several mediums, all "in lovely harmony and beauty of spirit," and finally announcing in printed circulars that he had had a course of instruction from Mrs. Eddy and followed her teachings "to a fair extent, yet I cannot ignore Mediumship, Clairvoyance, or Magnetism, in their proper offices."[26]

One thing was clear to Mrs. Eddy. If the purity of Christian Science was to be maintained, she must train qualified students to become teachers and not leave its propagation to the mercies of every cheerful rascal who chose to appropriate its name. As a result, the first Normal class at the college was opened on August 8, 1884, with ten students, including such local figures as Frye, Buswell, and Julia Bartlett. The next one, held in February, 1885, brought a contingent from Chicago—Mrs. Noyes, Miss Brown, Bradford and Roger Sherman—as well as Janet Colman, a Bostonian who only recently had moved with her husband to the Middle West and was sowing Christian Science through that fertile region like Johnny Appleseed scattering orchards.

Authorized teachers were now encouraged to start Christian Science "institutes" of their own in various localities and to form their students into associations comparable to the Christian Scientist Association, which was made up of Mrs. Eddy's own students. But the Massachusetts Metaphysical College remained the fountainhead of authentic Christian Science, and its graduates in the Christian Scientist Association formed the reservoir of experienced workers from which Mrs. Eddy drew the future teachers of the movement.

The charge for Normal classes was $100. Primary instruction was still $300, though clergymen were admitted free, a husband and wife were taught for the price of one, a large percentage of the students entered at a reduced fee, and some were taught without charge. Mrs. Eddy felt it necessary to put a high valuation on her teaching; but her frequent refusal to accept wealthy applicants who would have been happy to pay her the full fee—because, as she wrote them, she did not feel they were spiritually ready or otherwise qualified for instruction—hardly seems the action of a grasping money-maker, as she was sometimes pictured.

Swarts, for instance, in his printed circular compared his bargain price of twelve dollars for twelve lessons with the Boston price, which, he piously noted, "seems much like extortion and speculation in truth."[27] The ironic fact, however, is that it was Swarts's students who were apt to conclude eventually that they had been swindled, whereas Mrs. Eddy's students almost uniformly felt that what they paid was a small return for what they got. A characteristic reaction was that of Mrs. Emma A. McDonald, who entered the Chicago class with some misgivings but wrote her lawyer husband in Green Bay, Wisconsin, at the end of the sixth day:

> *This grows more glorious every day. . . . It seems to me now as though I was blind before, when I used to sit down and read the Bible. . . . This Science makes God and the Bible a reality. . . . The more I read the more I want to. . . . In all the preaching I have ever listened to I have never gained as clear a light as these six lessons have given me. . . . If I went back home today I should feel as if I was repaid for all time and money. I would not give up the little light I have for twice three hundred. . . . I cannot write half I want to, perhaps I cannot say it all when I get home, I must live it.*[28]

For the most part the students were not, at this time, wealthy or prominent or brilliant people. They were preponderantly in the middle range of the middle class, Protestant in background; but, contrary to the assumptions of many social historians, they were not overwhelmingly products of the larger cities suffering from the increasing tensions of industrialized urban living. Some of them, to be sure, were healed of what today would be readily recognized as neurotic ailments, and there were two or three women to every man in the movement, so to that extent they conformed to the popular stereotype. But more than half of Mrs. Eddy's students came from rural districts and small towns, and the pattern of country visits to patients on lonely farms was a prominent part of the total Christian Science picture.[29]

The daughter of the Mrs. McDonald quoted above later recalled the days of her mother's practice:

> *I remember many times that my mother received calls from different places in the country, eight or ten miles out of Green Bay, which was a long way in the day of horses. My father would have to walk about five blocks to where the horse was stabled, harness the horse and take mother where she was called. Often they would be gone the rest of the night. Sometimes she would get a dollar for a week's treatment, sometimes five dollars, but more frequently nothing. Often she had to go to homes and stay overnight. Many times she would have to sleep in the spare-room that had been closed all winter and had no heat in it; it would be so cold that she would have to go to bed with all her clothes on, and then not be warm.[30]*

Many students faced severe financial crises after they took up the practice of Christian Science. This was the case with William B. Johnson, a man of modest means who lived with his wife and thirteen-year-old son in South Boston, at that time a conservative, churchgoing, residential district unfriendly to new ideas. A sign in his window in an elm-shaded street brought him few inquirers or patients during the summer of 1884. The result was that when his son was about to enter high school in the fall, with the hope of going on to Harvard afterward, Johnson came to the boy with tears in his eyes and asked him whether he would be willing to forego school for a while and continue working in order to bring in a little income.

Out of his love for his father rather than for Christian Science the youngster agreed, and for a year or so the three dollars a week he earned provided most of the income for the family. Their small store of books, engravings, and jewelry was sold in order to pay the rent, and in after years the son recalled that he had "known what it was to have only a bowl of stewed tomatoes and a few crackers for supper, after a hard day's work, and for weeks we did not know the taste of butter."[31]

Yet through all this time the father he admired was gaining in his understanding of Christian Science, slowly gathering new recruits in South Boston, and successfully carrying out innumerable small tasks for Mrs. Eddy. The result was that after another year or two he was made Clerk of the Church and later a member of its first Board of Directors.

As the upward trend in the family fortunes began, the young Johnson was able to complete his education and finally was graduated from Harvard, but his reminiscences of the early struggles have a bittersweet quality that helps to recreate the atmosphere of the time. Especially vivid was his recollection of a period after the Sunday services had outgrown the Hawthorne Rooms and been moved to Chickering Hall on Tremont Street, where they were later augmented by Friday evening testimony meetings. Often before these Friday meetings a little group of the early workers would have supper at a small nearby restaurant, among them Miss Bartlett, Captain and Mrs. Eastaman, and Mr. and Mrs. Johnson, with young William. As he later recorded it:

> Here, over a simple meal, the work that was laid out for the coming week and the experiences of each since they had last met would be talked over. . . . This hour of the evening meal was filled with a wonderful sweetness. There was a free and generous exchange of thought, a simple association which bore the fruits of faithfulness and unity, while there was always a pervading perfume, since some one had seen Mrs. Eddy yesterday or today, and the few words which she had spoken opened new vistas of the truth that they must seek for and find.
>
> There was no idolatry among these early Scientists. They were not sentimentalists for they had been tried in the fires of struggle and the battles for right. They were middle-aged people who had learned much of the world before coming into Science, and the quiet and reverent way in which they referred to the Teacher, their gentleness, and their ever-present love, spoke the impress which the spirit of Mrs. Eddy had made.[32]

In their own way this bourgeois little group of people had a calculated recklessness in their commitment to "truth." If what Mrs. Eddy told them was true, it was worth risking everything for. It must be tested on sick bodies, empty larders, twisted desires, broken lives. It was not merely a subject for the classroom.

3

"Supposing that Truth is a woman—what then?" The question was Nietzsche's in 1885, and with it he led philosophy to the open grave where the traditional Christian God already lay with his faithful dogmas stretched across his feet. Is there not ground, Nietzsche continued,

> . . . *for suspecting that all philosophers, in so far as they have been dogmatists, have failed to understand women—that the terrible seriousness and clumsy importunity with which they have usually paid their addresses to Truth, have been unskilled and unseemly methods for winning a woman? Certainly she has never allowed herself to be won; and at present every kind of dogma stands with sad and discouraged mien—if, indeed, it stands at all.*[33]

Despite his contempt for women as thinkers—for the "eternally tedious in woman"—Nietzsche paid them the ironic compliment of recognizing that Truth might need to be wooed by means inaccessible to Aristotelian logic and Hegelian dialectic, to the enraptured intellectualism of a Spinoza, the tidy empiricism of a Locke, the structures and systems and formulations of a thousand gifted masculine aspirants to total consistency. One might as easily argue a woman into a reasoned position against her will as pin down with syllogism and theorem the knowing that is creating, the creating that is law-giving, the consistency that is transformation, the logic that is action.

Boston was a long way from the Upper Engadine where the preface to *Beyond Good and Evil* was written, and Mrs. Eddy was a long way from the perverse genius who felt that the one sure thing about woman was that she does not *want* truth. Yet in the atmosphere of her classroom many of his paradoxes might have seemed like platitudes. No more than Nietzsche could she stomach the slave morality that poured a sickly "Christian sympathy" on weakness, mediocrity, and passive suffering. No more than Marx[34] could she accept a religion of submission which was in very truth an opiate of the people. But neither the rule of Nietzschean supermen nor the dictatorship of a Marxist proletariat would have seemed to her more than a rearrangement of the terms of slavery under which the human race generally lived. To accept human life as defined by the physical senses was itself the primal slavery. The scientist confidently marshaling the forces of brute nature was no less in need of rescue than the child frozen with terror in the dark. And the rescue demanded a revolt.

As in the biblical parable that compared the kingdom of God to leaven, which a woman took and hid in three measures of meal till the whole was leavened, Mrs. Eddy started her revolution at a single point in her students' thinking: their concept of God.

Many of her students had an evangelical background. Some were narrowly fundamentalist; some, devout ritualists; some, liberals and agnostics; some, chronic delvers into strange faiths. But all of them had their thought tinged, consciously or unconsciously and to a greater or lesser degree, by the anthropomorphism (or anthropopsychism) that pictured God, if He existed at all, as a magnified personality— whether one thought of Him as an Oriental potentate doling out rewards and punishments or as a kind of super-Euclid running the universe as a problem in celestial geometry. They had not yet learned what Mrs. Eddy and Nietzsche in their respective ways both knew— that *that* God was dead.

At the beginning of the class she would ask each student in turn to explain his idea of God. Then for three days she would proceed to open up to them a view of divinity which seemed to shake the whole world as they had known it. Instead of a Providence busily attending to the affairs of a material universe prolific in havoc, suffering, and general derangement, they were presented with a divine Principle which knew no pain or death, no evil or disorder, no finity or material- ity—a God whose providence lay in the inviolable innocence of His creation. Some of them would "chemicalize" at first, ready to echo Mary Magdalene's cry: "They have taken away my Lord, and I know not where they have laid him." Others would stand so in awe of the dazzling glimpses they were catching that an almost unbearable sorrow would descend on them as they felt their human distance from so great a good—as though centuries of spiritual growth on their part would be necessary to grasp the vision. Yet the curious fact is that by the end of the third lesson such a basic transformation would have taken place in their thinking that Mrs. Eddy would sometimes send them back to their lodging places with the demand that before they met again each one should have found and healed a sick person through his newly developed consciousness of God.

She did not commence her teaching, as masculine logic would demand, by attempting to prove the existence of God in the manner of an Anselm or a Descartes. It was rather as though she simply let her students see at the heart of existence a divine Love that was the very Principle of man's being, an infinite Mind whose universe was all light, all loveliness, an inherent order awaiting their recognition.

It was, as they afterward put it in one way or another, as though reality were breaking through to them for the first time.

The remarkable thing is that it broke through not as theory but as fact, not as promise but as capacity, not as ideal but as demand. Many a college education of four years' length has produced less fundamental change in a person's thought processes and life attitudes than did Mrs. Eddy's twelve lessons. Here was proof that the dry bones of metaphysical abstraction could clothe themselves in living flesh and leap to vigorous action, as in Ezekiel's vision.

Emerson who had found even liberal Unitarianism too confining a creed for him, and whose hubristic individualism had won Nietzsche's admiration, had predicted that the religion of the future would not waste time in trying to reanimate a defunct historical faith. To Mrs. Eddy, however, the discovery of reality was one with the resurrection of a truth which had been clothed in flesh and lived in practice some eighteen hundred years before but had moldered away in a great desert of creed and dogma through the intervening centuries. The Christian "scandal of particularity" was swallowed up for her in a concept of the Christ as universally operative Truth, antecedent to all historic particulars though supremely embodied in one historic figure.

In her metaphysical terminology she drew a distinction between Divine Science, as God's understanding of His own nature and creation, and Christian Science, as the application of that divine understanding to human needs. Yet the two could not be severed, she emphasized. Like the universal Christ and the personal Jesus, like any timeless truth and its temporal discovery, the dualism was only apparent. "The divinity of the Christ was made manifest in the humanity of Jesus,"[35] she wrote, and the absolute must be made manifest in the transformation of the relative.

O. P. Gifford, the Baptist minister who had defended Mrs. Eddy before his Boston confreres and who studied with her in November, 1885, gives a hint of this in an article which he wrote shortly afterward for the *Journal:*

> *The Christian Scientist takes his place in thought, by God's side, attempts to get the Divine point of view, judges all things from the spiritual side. "The far-off divine event, to which the whole creation moves," is a present accomplished fact. . . . The tree reaches the height of its power when it fruits. The individual reaches the height of his power when he* knows. *The fruit is in the sap. The tree evolves what is involved in its sap. . . . The Christian Scientist takes his stand in the fruit-stage of man, sees*

in hope the "promise and potency" of fruit, sees in faith a nearer state of fruit, thinks fruit, talks fruit, realizes fruit, and of course is misunderstood by those who think and talk sap and flowers. . . . The fig-tree, that had no fruit in its sap, was not a tree, but a lie.[36]

Arthur Buswell late in life noted that Mrs. Eddy, in her class teaching—as distinct from her published writings and public sermons on the one hand and her private letters and intimate conversation on the other—did not talk of regeneration in the usual Christian terms of repentance, humility, and petitionary prayer. Regeneration of thought, life, and character was rather the natural sequence of a metaphysical change in one's essential view of himself and the universe. The change, as Gifford indicated, was absolute: from matter to Spirit, from sense to Soul. Released from the downward and selfward pull of the biological past, one discovered what it meant to be the son of God, endowed with dominion over human circumstance.

Instead of offering pietistic exhortations, wrote Buswell, instead of "serving Christianity on ice and bringing on the chills," Mrs. Eddy made it appear "a thing of daily love and devotion to suffering humanity."[37] Out of the classroom she frequently and fervently exhorted her students to accept the disciplines of Christian life, but in her actual teaching she attempted to lift them to the very fountainhead of Christianity, to the spontaneous and inexhaustible delight at the center of being.

4

It was in teaching rather than in preaching that Mrs. Eddy's greatest gifts lay. "She never seemed quite at home in the Sunday service," Buswell wrote:

. . . the set sermon did not suit her revolutionary ideas—there was not the opportunity for handling the individual mind at close range which was her chief delight. She excelled as a conversationalist, foresaw one's question with a seeming clairaudiant ear and asked and answered one's waiting thought before he formed it into words.[38]

Although students sometimes received healings during their course of instruction,[39] Mrs. Eddy as a rule did not welcome into her classes those with bodily ailments, sometimes advising them to wait for instruction until they had been healed. She explained this later in her book *Rudimental Divine Science:*

It is seldom that a student, if healed in a class, has left it understanding sufficiently the Science of healing to immediately enter upon its practice. Why? Because the glad surprise of suddenly regained health is a shock to the mind; and this holds and satisfies the thought with exuberant joy.

This renders the mind less inquisitive, plastic, and tractable; and deep systematic thinking is impracticable until this impulse subsides.[40]

So far as Mrs. Eddy was concerned, her classes were for *thinking*. She sometimes told prospective students that she could easily spend an hour or two amplifying, analyzing, and developing a single sentence from *Science and Health*. Hanover P. Smith in a fervent little booklet published in 1886 with the title *Writings and Genius of the Founder of Christian Science* described how she presented to her classes each subject "in all its aspects, developed to the greatest conceivable extent, and pointed with the most penetrating dialectical subtleties."[41] But other reports make clear that this was not done without reference to the students' individual states of mind. A Universalist minister who was in her Chicago class reported back to his congregation afterward, "She asked nobody to cater to her thought, or to concede anything to her faster than they understood it." But, he added, she showed "contempt for all ninnys, whom she never failed to score with her piercing logic."[42]

Her greatest power, wrote Smith in his booklet, lay not in rhetoric or in excitement of the imagination but in reasoned dialogue—"in gentle repartee"—then he added surprisingly, "Her greatest weakness, as well as her strength, lies in her great love and charity." This may refer to her willingness to suffer some obvious troublemakers to remain in her classes while she labored long and hard to rouse them to the "spiritual sense" of her teaching.

Sometimes she succeeded. After one class she wrote Ellen Brown:

Miss Blackman you had described to me briefly in a letter but I had forgotten your words until in the class I found myself beating furiously against certain traits, and in an instant recognized that they were the ones you alluded to with the hope that I should exterminate them. Well dear she went out very much advanced from what she came in.[43]

Interestingly enough, that particular student has left a revealing illustration of her development during the class term. At the end of the first three days it seemed to her that Mrs. Eddy's understanding of God as the only reality had "obliterated everything I had deemed substantial and actual."[44] The word "God"—"God"—"God" repeated itself over and over to her, yet she had lost her familiar sense of God and had not yet found the God she was looking for. When Mrs. Eddy told the members of the class to go home that night and take their first patient, Miss Blackman felt relieved to remember that, as a stranger to Boston, she could hardly be called upon to find a patient. When she got back to her rooming place, however, she found to her dismay that a member of the household was ill with erysipelas. As she hurried to escape to her room, the sick man called out to her, "If you can do anything for me, why don't you do it?"

According to her later account of the incident, a short but sharp struggle with herself followed on the spot. The suggestion came to her that she did not know enough of Christian Science to heal by its method, but that there was a power in her own mind which she could use instead. As she afterward explained it, she had been precipitated into a mental arena where she had to make a clear decision between the power of the human mind and the power of God. She realized that there was a question here greater than that of the physical healing itself, and she determined that whatever happened she would not resort to will power. Almost immediately a verse from the Bible flashed into her thought: "Put off thy shoes from off thy feet, for the place whereon thou standest is holy ground." She had forgotten the patient during those few moments of struggle, but when she turned to him again she saw that he was sleeping peacefully. The healing, she later wrote, was immediate and complete.[45]

Several days later when Mrs. Eddy turned to the subject of animal magnetism in the class, Miss Blackman began to sense something of what had been involved in her own struggle. In some small measure this had been her "temptation in the wilderness"—the satanic suggestion to arrogate divine power to herself. It was easy to see how such a suggestion would necessarily be the adversary of the Christ-spirit that said, "I can of mine own self do nothing."

As Mrs. Eddy, in Miss Blackman's words, "shared the hemlock cup with her half-comprehending students," the young woman felt she was catching a glimpse of the price her teacher had paid for making this distinction, and she was reminded of a passage from *Science and Health:*

> *Remembering the sweat of agony which fell in holy benediction on the grass of Gethsemane, shall the humblest or mightiest disciple murmur when he drinks from the same cup, and think, or even wish to escape the exalting ordeal of sin's revenge on its destroyer?*[46]

Other students have written of a phenomenon that occurred when Mrs. Eddy turned from the subject of Truth's invincible power to the question of animal magnetism. In a moment her erect, sprightly, almost youthful figure would seem to be bowed with the weight of ages and her face would be that of a very old woman—until the light broke through again as she emphasized that the terrible force of a lie rested solely on the acceptance of its claim to place and power within the ordered structure of reality. Confronted by Truth it must shrivel into nonentity. The tragedy of human life was that so many people clung to their self-deceived sense of evil when the truth was at hand that could free them.

This was a side of her that was best known to the students who lived and worked with her day by day and who saw the struggles leading to her victories. On one occasion Emma Hopkins wrote her, "I want to see you *only just* when I am cheerful for I know you are one 'of sorrows and acquainted with grief' like your Master and we must not add one care or anxious thought as your students."[47] A few months later Mrs. Hopkins wrote again: "You seem so often like a tired sobbing body to me. Then again you are like the archangel Gabriel as you peal forth doom to error. But no mood moves me to other than a sheltering tenderness for one whose life has been so stormy."[48]

Both statements would have seemed surprising to some of the students in her classes who saw her as an angel of light undimmed by even a passing cloud. This is illustrated by the experience of Mrs. Janette E. Robinson (later Weller) from Littleton, New Hampshire, one of several people who studied with Mrs. Eddy as a result of Julia Bartlett's remarkable healing work in that town.

During one of the class sessions Mrs. Robinson told of bringing about a healing which startled her, so instantaneous was the patient's recovery and so slight her own understanding of Christian Science. She mentioned in passing that the patient was Dr. Patterson. Mrs. Eddy asked at once whether he happened to be Dr. *Daniel* Patterson. He was not, Mrs. Robinson replied, but she knew a Dr. Daniel Patterson, a dentist, who had lived for several years in Littleton.

Two weeks later, when the class was over Mrs. Eddy drew Mrs. Robinson aside for a private conversation about the Littleton Patterson. "You know he was my husband?" she asked her astounded student, who actually had known nothing of Mrs. Eddy's unhappy second marriage. To Mrs. Robinson her teacher was the revelator of Truth, the recipient of divine inspiration, unbound by human ties of any kind. It was profoundly disquieting to her to be drawn into the revelator's personal life in this way and to connect her with the rather dandified though kind-hearted dentist she had known. But Mrs. Eddy proceeded to talk of her past life, including Dr. Patterson's repeated infidelities, as the necessary discipline which had brought her to the feet of Science.

There was no bitterness in her account. Of Patterson she said, "Never was man more tender to a woman," and even his unfaithfulness she characterized as weakness rather than viciousness. She was obviously quite unembarrassed in owning to the deep affection she had felt for him, and Mrs. Robinson presumably got the point that the deepest revelations of life are not won without full commitment to living.[49]

Mrs. Eddy, in fact, had her feet very firmly on the ground. When students gave abstruse metaphysical answers to questions which demanded simple common sense, she soon brought them down to earth. If a young couple had no place to leave a child while they were studying, she would tell them cheerfully to bring the child along, and in at least one case she taught an entire class with a delighted little girl sitting on her lap. When the summer heat caused a certain amount of restiveness in one of her classes, Mrs. Eddy asked dryly, "Shall we move to some cooler part of the city, or shall we remain and make our own atmosphere?" The restiveness stopped.[50]

On another occasion she wrote Colonel Smith lightly: "I have a class of twenty sinners on hand; by that do not think them sinners above all others, but rather one of the very promising classes."[51] With all her emphasis on the infinite capacities of spiritual man, she had few illusions about unregenerate human nature. Her theology and her psychology both embraced the Christian demand: "Ye must be born again."

5

In an article entitled "The New Birth," Mrs. Eddy wrote: "The new birth is not the work of a moment. It begins with moments, and goes on with years."[52] The same may be said of her teaching. It began with twelve lessons but might continue through twenty-five years of correspondence, visits, personal messages, and general care.[53]

Her mail brought constant appeals from her students to help them with difficult cases, to answer their questions, encourage them, advise them, settle their disputes, approve their schemes, forgive their mistakes, rejoice in their triumphs. The thousands of letters she poured out to them over the years constitute a spirited exhibition of devotion, each one directed to the particular need of the individual—scolding, inspiring, analyzing, comforting, educating.[54] When she described herself as a mother watching over the first footsteps of her children, it was more than a sentimental figure of speech.

Take her relations with Albert B. Dorman who lived in the city of Worcester not far from Boston. This young man, converted to Christian Science by *Science and Health,* wrote Mrs. Eddy at the end of 1883 that he would like to study with her and was confident that Christian Science healing would be easy for him. "I should *push* it," he wrote. "I have (as I have been told) valuable ideas of advertising."[55] But after going through her class and returning to Worcester, his letters for some months record discouragement: he is not making the progress he should in his practice, he is having some healings but not doing well financially, he is upset because Mrs. Eddy does not like the circulars he has issued. Then, as his healing work improved, he wrote with considerable self-satisfaction that he was sure he was developing into an instantaneous healer and his parlors were crowded with the élite of Worcester:

> *A second cousin of yours Dr. Chamberlain one of our lead-*
> *ing Homeopathists came in and placed himself under treatment,*
> *and has also brought S. & H. I cured one of his patients in one*
> *week that he has tried to cure for some years.*[56]

Dorman still had some difficulties, he acknowledged, but not from malicious mesmerism, as Mrs. Eddy suggested. He was completely free from *that!* Eager but unstable, he would cry for help at one time—"I am determined not to be overcome by error and evil again"[57]—and overflow with assurance at another. Upset by his teacher's occasional sharp rebukes, he could nevertheless write her after one of these, "You *remind* me that I am getting out of the path again, and you are right, and I almost at times seem to be stupid to the *Truth."* Will she not write him again? "Write *right to the point* and talk to me as you would your own Boy."[58]

Eventually he would join the ranks of those who found her discipline too strict, but he never turned against her with the sharp hostility some of the defectors showed. Indeed quite a few of those who left her for one reason or another continued to feel grateful for the care she had expended on them and looked back with a kind of qualified nostalgia to their period of association with her.

One of these was Alzire Chevaillier, a young woman who might have stood in for Henry James's Olive Chancellor in *The Bostonians.* Educated, ardent, devoted to radical causes, combining an obsessive Puritan conscience with a sharp Yankee intellect, Miss Chevaillier suffered the neural disabilities of her kind. She had taken the enlightened but highly unpopular side in the public controversy as to whether the assassin Guiteau should be considered insane, had served on a United States commission appointed by President Arthur to visit European institutions "for the dependent, defective, and delinquent classes,"[59] was an officer in various embattled social organizations, and longed to be able to heal all the world's ills.

When she took class instruction with Mrs. Eddy early in 1885, the latter at once recognized both her potentialities and her high-strung nature but was very gentle in handling the young woman and quickly won her affectionate gratitude. Even so, Miss Chevaillier found her bodily ills increasing rather than lessening during the next few months, seemed unable to bring healing to anyone else, and quarreled with what she felt to be the arbitary and undemocratic rules of the Christian Scientist Association. As a result, she resigned from the organization in November, detailing a list of rational objections with which it would be hard for most liberals today to disagree. Recognizing her evident honesty, Mrs. Eddy let her go without reproach or attempt to hold her.

Later Miss Chevaillier studied with Mrs. Anna Newman, then had a brief flirtation with some of the other disaffected Christian Scientists and mind-curers who were proliferating like metaphysical rabbits, but in the very midst of this she wrote Mrs. Eddy in 1889: "I wonder if you have forgotten me? I *know* you have not misjudged me —for I have never heard of an unkindly word said of me." This had been a surprise to her, for friends had warned her when she left that the Christian Science leader would spread malicious slanders about her. Referring to the many mind-curers who pictured Mrs. Eddy as an unscrupulous woman avid for total control, she concluded:

> *I do feel that the world is indebted to you for the recrystallizing of this Truth into a practical Science which you taught to those unripe for it, & [who] even lost it, and that those who condemn you are indebted to you, indirectly at least, for their health & power to heal.*[60]

Still looking for an absolute panacea, she was drawn a few years later to that extraordinary mystic and poet, Thomas Lake Harris, who founded his Brotherhood of the New Life in northern New York, holding his disciples in abject slavery. In considerably less than the seventeen years it took the brilliant English milord, Laurence Oliphant, and his wife Alice to break free from Harris' incredible tyranny, Miss Chevaillier was writing Judge Septimus J. Hanna, then editor of *The Christian Science Journal:*

> *One thing I know Mrs. Eddy was right about and I wrong and it would have saved me great suffering, viz. malicious mesmerism. I felt she was creating thousands of devils in place of the one the church worships. Years afterward I longed so for truth I went to study with Thomas Lake Harris, a most wonderful*

man of high culture. When I learned of the poisonous asp in his teachings and practice, I gave my lecture on True and False Mysticism. I left him, however, because he claimed divine leadership, and then it was, he told me it would mean death to me, and that he killed Lord Oliphant and Alice at Haifa, Syria. Tho I replied, "I do not fear you, my hand is in my Father's Hand, and you cannot come within my circle of His protection," thus partially arming myself with fearlessness and purity, I was not armed with the knowledge which if I had accepted what Mrs. Eddy taught, would have made me invulnerable. The result is I have been laid on the shelf of uselessness, tho longing for service, ever since I was there.

Headstrong and self-willed, a little comic and a little pathetic, Miss Chevaillier now looked back wistfully at her earlier brush with radical Christian Science:

I wish now that I had gone to Mrs. Eddy and had a talk with her when Phillips Brooks and some of her students and others led me into channels of thought that carried conscientious conviction. . . . There is one thing about Mrs. Eddy, no immorality of any kind can attach itself to her teachings, and unless the feet are planted in the ten commandments, no search for truth is safe. . . . I only wanted to say that tho a "disaffected student" I love Mrs. Eddy, wish to be just to her, and above all to do right and to do good.[61]

By 1885, however, there were coming to Mrs. Eddy increasing numbers of students who would remain pillars of the movement through the years to follow. Among them was Ira O. Knapp of Lisbon, New Hampshire, a farmer with the flowing beard, blazing eyes, and invincible rectitude of an Old Testament prophet. When his serious, calm-faced wife Flavia was healed by Christian Science after years of invalidism, she walked to the next farm and back with her four children dancing around her for sheer joy at seeing their mother able to go out again.

In a letter to Mrs. Eddy written three years later, Knapp, who was much given to Ezekiel-like visions, described the background of his own wholehearted acceptance of the new teaching:

Some years ago, before I knew Christian Science, I had a vision in a dream. Heaven, with all its splendor of light . . . seemed to open to me; but this was only for a moment; for I awoke in this dream, and wept and prayed, because I could not abide there forever.

Time passed on, until one day Christian Science dropped

down at our door, to speak a word of peace; and in my glad moments I exclaimed: "It brings a message of Love." To my surprise a voice—nothing like a human voice—answered and said "Where shall I abide? Your house is occupied. Turn out your old tenants, and put on one measure of humility, and another measure, and yet another measure; and then I will abide with you, and Charity will abide with you."

I pondered this a few days and applied to you for instruction. Early one morning I was again surprised, with what seemed a mighty rushing wind, which no man could stay. It made the earth as a desert, and left me bare and naked; but before me was a great rock, square and upright; and on its sides the word Truth appeared. On this rock I saw that I must build.[62]

Upon returning to New Hampshire at the conclusion of their class in Boston, the Knapps, like quite a few other students, at first found the healing work hard. Commenting on this, Mrs. Eddy wrote them:

God is perhaps trying you as He has tried all his own, and if you stand the test, all at once you will come into the kingdom of our Lord, a clear and abiding sense of your power to heal. Only be faithful over a few things and He will make you ruler over many, and then you will enter into the joy of your work.[63]

Ira Knapp, reporting back "a little progress and much tribulation," showed where his heart really was: "I am hungering and thirsting for more of the Spirit of Love. . . . And we will not mind the tears and trials if only we can be counted among the least of His faithful servants."[64] Seven years later Mrs. Eddy would choose him as one of the first Directors of her reconstituted church.

A "faithful servant" was the last thing that anyone would ever call a fashionable, undisciplined woman who studied with Mrs. Eddy in the same class as the Knapps and who was to attain a unique notoriety in the annals of Christian Science. Josephine Curtis Woodbury was the wife of E. Frank Woodbury, one of the original trustees of the Massachusetts Metaphysical College. Attracted to Christian Science by Clara Choate in 1880, Mrs. Woodbury had written Mrs. Eddy that she and her husband would work "to introduce you into the best circle of minds we have in Boston."[65] She did, in fact, introduce her to Edward Everett Hale and possibly to James Freeman Clarke, but under the influence of Mrs. Choate she held off from going through Primary class in the college until December, 1884.[66] Fourteen months later she took the Normal course.

Gifted with literary facility, a glamour which some people described as being a little serpentine,[67] and complete freedom from a New England conscience, Mrs. Woodbury gathered around her at her "Massachusetts Academy of Christian Science" on Dartmouth Street a group of spellbound disciples. She did not advertise the fact that some time before taking up Christian Science she had studied hypnotism with the famous "Professor Carpenter."[68]

Mrs. Eddy's letters to her show that Mrs. Woodbury was a troublemaker from the beginning, stirring up quarrels with the other students. An 1885 letter reads:

> *Will you not take my advice once and abide by your word with me. I asked for the sake of Christianity that this picking quarrels cease. Now you promised me you would write no more, and the next thing is this late attack upon those unattacking.*
>
> *I do not approve of it and it is against my will. . . . Stop, stop, stop! and let love and peace do the work of Christian Science for nothing else can do it.*[69]

Mrs. Woodbury, whose remorse flowed out as easily as her irresponsibilities, and who was at that time angling to get into the next Normal class, replied a little later:

> *I am sure now that animal magnetism claims the power to make me do and say things the exact opposite of my desires and intentions. At first this frightened me, as the poison of sickness did two years ago. Now I am calmer again, and I will battle with the enemy on this question of sin as faithfully as I did the old fear of sickness.*[70]

Sometime afterward Mrs. Woodbury visited her old classmates, the Knapps, on their New Hampshire farm, and they were horrified as she poured into their ears what they felt to be, in the language of the book of Revelation, the poison of the Babylonish woman. In more commonplace terms, this seems to have been a liberal admixture of hypnoidal techniques with Christian Science metaphysics. When Ira Knapp wrote Mrs. Eddy of the perversion of truth he felt in the woman's teaching, Mrs. Eddy at once sent for him, and their conversation was followed by Mrs. Woodbury's being recalled to Boston and sternly rebuked. The climax of the struggle to "save Mrs. Woodbury" was not reached, however, for several more years.

Another woman of commanding presence and unusual potential for good or ill was Augusta E. Stetson, who swam into Mrs. Eddy's view at a parlor lecture in 1884 and immediately arrested her attention. Reared in Maine but living for some years in India, Burma, and London after her marriage, Mrs. Stetson was training in Boston at that time for a career as an elocutionist in order to support her now invalid husband. Reluctant at first to abandon this new career, she finally accepted Mrs. Eddy's invitation to study without charge at the college and before long was doing outstanding work in both healing and public speaking.

Mrs. Eddy early put her to a remarkable test, which she passed with éclat. It had been arranged for the Christian Science leader to address a large audience in the neighboring town of Reading. Mrs. Stetson had made the preliminary arrangements and was on hand to see that all went well. But on the appointed day the speaker failed to appear. After meeting three successive trains from Boston, Mrs. Stetson hurried to the crowded hall and in a last-minute decision stepped before the audience, made a vague excuse for Mrs. Eddy's absence, then launched into an extemporaneous speech for an hour and a half, with gratifying success. The next morning she went straight to the college and reproached Mrs. Eddy for not coming. "I was there," the latter replied softly, adding, as her face lighted up, "But you stood, Augusta. You stood, you did not run."[71]

The incident symbolizes the whole relationship between the two women. Through the twenty-five years of their association, Mrs. Eddy was deliberately and consciously taking a risk and conducting a test. On no one did she lavish more care and affection than on this brilliant, wilful, ambitious woman whom, she explained, she loved for the incalculable good of which she was capable. In the Christian Science scheme of things everyone, including Mrs. Eddy herself, was on trial before the ultimate judgment seat of Principle.

6

A more immediate crisis was the breakaway of Emma Hopkins. With greater intellectual power than either Mrs. Woodbury or Mrs. Stetson and greater concentration of purpose than Alzire Chevaillier, this wife of an Andover professor wrote Mrs. Eddy after studying with her in 1884, "I lay my whole life and all my talents, little or great, to this work."[72]

In September of the same year Mrs. Eddy made her acting editor of the *Journal*, which at that time became a monthly instead of a bimonthly publication. One of Mrs. Hopkins' first editorials paid tribute to Mrs. Eddy's founding of the *Journal* "single handed and alone, to lead its untried footsteps upon Puritan, conservative soil, alongside haughty contemporaries"[73]—phraseology which suggests an unconscious hankering for lusher intellectual fields and more modish company. In an article preceding her editorship, she drew analogies between Christian Science and Buddhism, the Upanishads, Moslem philosophy, Spinoza, and the Zend-Avesta—a list suggesting her tendency toward an indiscriminate eclecticism.[74] And in other ways she showed a responsiveness to the fashionable cultural climate somewhat at variance with the metaphysical rigors of pioneer Christian Science.

Significantly, Mrs. Eddy never made her a teacher. Nonetheless Mrs. Hopkins gave good service as an editor,[75] and in the *Journal* of September, 1885, she took to task those students who thought they could impart metaphysics quite as effectively as Mrs. Eddy herself. In an editorial entitled "Teachers of Metaphysics" she wrote:

> *No student (I speak from knowledge of facts) has ever yet been qualified to teach Christian Science, except rudimentarily. . . . To me . . . the words of my teacher on the theme of Spiritual Being were first as the gentle touch of a mother lifting the world-weary form of her wayward child to her bosom. . . . I was made to know Him face to face of whom I had heard by the hearing of the ear as a name only. . . . I know that every single student that has ever studied under "this teacher sent from God" has realized it all. How great, then, the folly of falling back to earthly ambitions and earthly ends by claiming to work the same miracle—for the pottage reward of a little publicity and a few hundred dollars.*

There is a wry coincidence in the fact that the very month in which these words were published brought to Mrs. Hopkins the irresistible temptation to set herself up in rivalry to the teacher she had so eulogized.

Among the members of Mrs. Eddy's September Primary class was a Mrs. Mary Plunkett, a caustic, flamboyant Victoria Woodhull of a woman, who freely admitted that both her children had different fathers, neither of whom was Mr. Plunkett. Mrs. Eddy was ignorant of this, however, when she admitted her to the class, as she also was of the fact that Mr. Plunkett was a cousin of Richard Kennedy and that Mrs. Plunkett, following her dramatic healing in Christian Science, had studied first with the opportunistic A. J. Swarts of Chicago.

Once in the class, Mrs. Plunkett, a born promoter, seems to have looked around to find someone she could use in carrying out her already half-formed purpose to set up and stage-manage a rival leader to Mrs. Eddy. First she assiduously cultivated a classmate, Mrs. Laura Lathrop from Freeport, Illinois. The latter was a well-educated, intellectually able woman who for a time was flattered by Mrs. Plunkett's attentions and befuddled by her arguments. Mrs. Lathrop's good sense, however, prevailed over Mrs. Plunkett's appeals to her spiritual pride and ambition.[76]

Emma Hopkins, who was not a member of the class but was living at the college at that time, now became the object of Mrs. Plunkett's full attention. By the end of the class term they were close friends, and a few days afterward Mrs. Plunkett wrote her a letter pouring out her scorn for Mrs. Eddy and clearly confident that such sentiments would be acceptable to her dear friend Emma. According to later statements, she was at once convinced that Mrs. Hopkins was a natural-born teacher, a true prophet and seer, but she added that it took some months to persuade the "modest" but charismatic young woman to join forces with her.

Mrs. Eddy, who had had some sharp tussles with Mrs. Plunkett in the class, seems to have recognized fairly early the influence that determined lady was gaining over Mrs. Hopkins. The result was that after a few weeks the latter was relieved of the strategic *Journal* editorship by Sarah Crosse and was asked by Calvin Frye to vacate her room in the college. In a letter to Mrs. Eddy following this action, the ousted editor continued to protest her devotion, but on November 4 the Christian Scientist Association accepted her resignation. That same day she wrote a letter to Julia Bartlett which reveals the ambivalence of her feelings:

> *I was very glad to receive a letter from you. Rest your loving heart in peace. I know you too well to think for a moment that you are any other than my friend, whatever you may be called upon to express to the contrary in appearance. . . . I agree with you that our experiences in C. S. are helpful. Mine have been greatly so. I shall never serve a cause or a person without sharp business arrangements again, and shall hold strong guard over personal reverence and worshipful feeling at every point. I see that all my self-abnegation and self-effacement ended in an appearance of discredit to myself which I do not merit.*
>
> *You remember that it was said the article on* Teachers of Metaphysics *would get me into trouble. Everything I said and did after that was watched and exaggerated and reported. I really was under heavy fire mentally. If I were to report what the students said to me I could get them into trouble, but I never did, for deep under all sudden resentments, I heard the sweet chord strike in every student—worshipful, reverent love for their teacher. But they could not understand my complex way of expressing myself, nor know that I was digging for facts. I have much to say of assurance for you. I saw all the letters said to be written by Mrs. E. to Dresser and Quimby and not one of them could be held as argument against her supreme originality. I was always ferreting out things to their basis in fact back of the*

179

statements made—I do not care who by, and I know this, that with my critical, cynical gaze I found her true to her own original marvellous inspiration.[77]

With all its air of frank sincerity, the letter is carefully silent on the subject of Mrs. Plunkett's influence. However, that even more cynical lady had been quick to accept the Dresser charge that Quimby was the real originator of Christian Science, and Mrs. Hopkins' just completed findings on this subject may have awakened in herself a temporary doubt as to whether she was making a good bargain in exchanging Mrs. Eddy's leadership for Mrs. Plunkett's management. There was no doubt in Julia Bartlett's mind that it was not only a bad bargain but also a gross betrayal, and she wrote Mrs. Hopkins a reply which left the latter very unhappy indeed.

During her editorship of the *Journal,* Mrs. Hopkins had taken A. J. Swarts to task for plagiarizing and perverting Christian Science in his monthly publication, *Mind-Cure Journal,* subsequently renamed *Mental Science Magazine.* Now—probably through the instrumentality of Mrs. Plunkett, who had defended Swarts militantly while in Mrs. Eddy's class—she became editor of his magazine until, in May, 1886, she left to go into full-time partnership with Mrs. Plunkett. With the latter as business manager and herself as teacher, "Christian Science" institutes[78] were formed in Chicago, Detroit, Minneapolis, and other Midwestern cities.

In a letter written on October 24, Mrs. Plunkett remarked that God had shown her how people could be taught without paying exorbitant fees. "Although I was taught by Mrs. Eddy," she added, "I can say truly that I had but barely touched the hem of truth, until I heard it in the inimitable way Mrs. Hopkins gives it."[79]

Two months later, on Christmas Day, Mrs. Hopkins wrote Mrs. Eddy about her current success, assuring her that she always promoted *Science and Health* and spoke highly of its author in her classes, that she had been taken up by the "literary ladies" of Chicago, that she had considered Miss Bartlett's reply to her "malicious"—then suddenly burst out, "Oh, if you could only have been mental enough to see what I might be and do—and given me time to work past and out of the era through which I was passing when Mrs. Crosse suddenly ordered me to leave."[80]

The letter marked the "mental" distance that Mrs. Hopkins had traveled in one year from Christian Science. It is significant that the Plunkett-Hopkins students were told that the one section of *Science and Health* they could safely skip was the chapter called "Prayer and Atonement."

Chapter
VII

Culture
and
Probity

Culture and Probity

Back in January, 1885, Emma Hopkins had written in the *Journal:*

> *An impression obtains in the mind of outsiders that Chris-*
> *tian Scientists take no interest in the live questions of the day,—*
> *political issues, public schools, the Woman movement, labor*
> *questions, etc. But this is a mistake. While it is true that they*
> *do not enter into discussion of such subjects, their views, upon*
> *investigation, will be found sound and decided. They have*
> *learned to look such problems squarely in the face, and by under-*
> *standing the drift and tendency and ultimate of mortal mind,*
> *their solutions are clear, matter of fact, and incontrovertible.*

The statement itself was far from incontrovertible. At best, it expressed a possibility rather than a fact.

In her early years Mrs. Eddy had always had a lively if spotty interest in public affairs; in the last two decades of her life she would devote a considerable amount of thought to the problems of the world community. But during the 1880's she was almost entirely absorbed by the task in hand. Alzire Chevaillier, committed to a dozen varieties of social reform, has left an illuminating reminiscence:

> *Mrs. Eddy was very appreciative of my voluntary welfare*
> *work and in a serious talk I had with her one of the many*
> *evenings she invited me to speak with her, she admitted when I*
> *said the other half of Christian Science would demand human*
> *brotherhood practically applied in every relation of life. But she*
> *said the first thing is to implant firmly in human consciousness*
> *the Power of God to heal sickness, sorrow, etc. When that has*
> *taken hold of mankind, the other will in time follow as a neces-*
> *sary sequence.*[1]

During its early years *The Christian Science Journal*—this was the new name of the *Journal of Christian Science* received in April, 1885—reflected little awareness of public affairs. If Chicago was mentioned, it was more likely to be in connection with the activities of

A. J. Swarts than with the history-making Haymarket Riot, and Grover Cleveland's mild but commendable campaign for tariff reduction was of decidedly less interest than the annual picnic of the Boston Christian Scientists at Point of Pines.

At this latter event in 1885 Augusta Stetson gave two "recitations"; a friendly physician, Addison D. Crabtree, made a speech congratulating the one hundred Christian Scientists present on their tranquil conviviality unspoiled by anyone's inflicting on his companions a gossipy recital of bodily ills; one of Mrs. Eddy's students, Edward N. Harris, who was a dentist by profession, was singled out for special honor because he had recently presented a paper on Christian Science to the American Academy of Dental Science[2]; and Mrs. Eddy herself gave a "spiritual interpretation" of the sea. Newspaper accounts of the festivities were proudly reprinted in the *Journal*.

A year or two before, Matthew Arnold had lectured in Boston on one of those tours on which he brought to the presumptive wilderness of the New World not only a little of the sweetness and light of Hellenic-Hebraic culture, but also a little of the acerbity of Oxford *snobisme*. Had he read the account of the picnic at Point of Pines, it might have furnished him further matter to illustrate the provincialism he had so fastidiously pilloried in his earlier *Culture and Anarchy*. America itself, he wrote in that book, had so far been "hardly more than a province of England," and its religious pluralism—proliferating in Mormonism, Shakerism, and such-like curiosa—elicited from him something between a shudder and a smile. Quoting in all its egalitarian anarchy the praise given by an American writer to one home-grown cult as "a theory which has been accepted by men like Judge Edmonds, Dr. Hare, Elder Frederick, and Professor Bush," and to other doctrines supported by equally obscure names, Arnold comments:

> If he was summing up an account of the teaching of Plato or St. Paul, Mr. Hepworth Dixon could not be more earnestly reverential. But the question is, have personages like Judge Edmonds, and Newman Weeks, and Elderess Polly, and Elderess Antoinette, and the rest of Mr. Hepworth Dixon's heroes and heroines, anything of the weight and significance for the best reason and spirit of man that Plato and St. Paul have?[3]

It could be answered that they might, theoretically at least, have as much weight as a group of unknown and unlettered Jewish fishermen of the first century—who, however, were knitted by the theologically sophisticated Paul into the cultural fabric of the world. Perhaps the test of a new religion would be its ability to produce a Paul, and there were critics of Mrs. Eddy who held that she needed just such a

Paul to acculturate Christian Science. There were also defectors who aspired to the role.

But Mrs. Eddy was destined to be her own Paul. Through the theological controversies of 1885 it became clear to her that the movement's lines of communication with the educated world needed strengthening. In the course of that year she threw off her powerful *Defence of Christian Science* (nucleus of her later book *No and Yes*) and another pamphlet, *Historical Sketch of Metaphysical Healing* (nucleus of her later *Retrospection and Introspection*), but both showed the signs of hasty composition and stylistic indiscipline. There was a shaping and polishing process necessary if she was to reach the intellectually exacting audience she hoped for.

Through the columns of the *Journal* she poured out a constant stream of instruction and explanation. In the flow of articles, poems, notices, answers to questions, and miscellaneous fillers which she furnished both as editor[4] and as chief contributor, she drew not only on the inspiration of the moment but also on her cultural capital. For some years now she had had little time for outside reading to augment that capital. When in need of extra material to fill the earliest issues of the *Journal,* she sometimes turned to the books she had known in her young womanhood, and especially to the scrapbook she had kept and treasured through her years of invalidism in the 1850's. Aphorisms and anecdotes from this scrapbook studded the pages of the *Journal* and found their way into her own writings, sometimes undergoing minor surgery *en route*. Verbal echoes from Pope's "Essay on Man" and Young's "Night Thoughts" rubbed elbows with phrases from the yellowed pages of forgotten New Hampshire newspapers in a style which ended up being unmistakably Mrs. Eddy's own.

Some of the ephemeral articles and poems which she herself had written before discovering Christian Science were revised and refurbished to do metaphysical service in the *Journal*. Stray paragraphs were used as fillers without attribution to any author, so that it is often difficult today to say for sure whether they are by Mrs. Eddy or not. One anonymous article from an old number of *Godey's Lady's Book* was reprinted without credit to any source, was then reprinted (in part) a second time by a later *Journal* editor, who introduced it with the phrase, "Somebody has written these wise words," and ten years later was gathered, with minor verbal changes, into the corpus of Mrs. Eddy's *Miscellaneous Writings,* though differing markedly from her own work in style and content.[5]

In her several revisions of *Science and Health*, Mrs. Eddy's aim had always been to state Christian Science more clearly and relevantly, but she was still far from satisfied with the result. By 1885 she was embarked on a major new revision. In April of that year she had a letter from one Edward E. Allen, who had applied to her for class instruction the preceding August and had offered to pay by rendering her literary assistance. Now, belatedly, he wrote her: "Please find a few of the errors [presumably grammatical] I have noted in reading Science and Health. I send them to you as promised and as samples of others noted."[6] Mrs. Eddy replied that she had taken the matter of revision into her own hands and had already corrected the first volume. But after another two months had passed, she was ready for expert help, and she turned, not to Allen, but to a redoubtable gentleman by the name of James Henry Wiggin.

Wiggin, an ex-Unitarian minister, was recommended to her as index-maker and literary aide by her old friend John Wilson of the University Press. Since retiring from the ministry ten years before, the Reverend but irreverent Mr. Wiggin had been doing proofreading and general editorial work for Wilson. A cultivated man, a *bon viveur*, amateur playwright and ardent playgoer, scholarly dilettante and theologian *manqué*, he was thoroughly at home in a Boston that preened itself on being the Athens of America. He has been variously described by those who knew him as "a man of enormous bulk and . . . immense geniality . . . courtly and polished in manner," and as "a vainglorious, pompous man with a very high opinion of his own ability."[7] The two descriptions are not necessarily incompatible, and in any case he represented the world of "culture"—even if it was the rather selective culture of Brahmin Boston—with which Christian Science must increasingly come to grips.

2

In later years Mrs. Eddy insisted that she had not employed Wiggin to correct her *diction*,[8] and the voluminous correspondence between the two bears this out. On matters of vocabulary, she withstood him firmly and repeatedly. On matters of "punctuation, capitalization and general smoothing out as to construction of sentences"— the words with which the head clerk of the University Press described Wiggin's services to her[9]—she consistently deferred to him.

"I engaged Mr. Wiggin," she wrote later, "so as to avail myself of his criticisms of my statement of Christian Science, which criticisms would enable me to explain more clearly the points that might seem ambiguous to the reader."[10] In general, the ambiguities lay in the area of syntax rather than diction—in a dangling participle, a misplaced subjunctive, a pronoun without visible antecedent, an unwieldy sentence or overloaded paragraph. Occasionally Wiggin's criticisms were more substantive, and Mrs. Eddy considered them carefully before accepting or rejecting them.

At first she had approached him only in regard to indexing the new version of *Science and Health* on which she was working, but a month later she sent him the manuscript with all her changes and wrote:

> *I can see no end to its improvement, but I am so weary of the task I have not looked over all the pages or punctuated them. I leave this for you.*
>
> *If anything is a muddle and you so see it indicate it on a slip of paper page and par. or make it correct yourself, but never* change *my meaning, only* bring it out.[11]

In the months that followed, she sent him repeated instructions and commendations.

> *Whatever is irrelative in the Chaps. had better be grouped into a chapter by itself. . . .*
>
> *I always admire and preserve your changes unless they interfere with my meaning. . . . I told you I did not notice the grammar left that to you. . . .*
>
> *I always have yielded and shall yield to you on punctuation when you have my meaning clear. . . .*
>
> *I thank you for the wise, kind suggestions in your note, and especially I thank you for the learned and convenient treasures laid up for my use by your thoughtful care. I will try to improve by them.[12]*

When the new edition—the sixteenth—finally came out in the spring of 1886, Wiggin's influence was perceptible in more than the smoother flow of the sentences. He had persuaded Mrs. Eddy to introduce each chapter with epigraphs not only from the Bible but also from the Bhagavad-Gita, *Paradise Lost,* Shakespeare, Longfellow, Mrs. Gaskell, and such Boston worthies as William Ellery Channing, James Freeman Clarke, and Julia Ward Howe. Scattered through the text itself were tags of verse from minor nineteenth-century poets, giving it a "contemporary" flavor which would soon have dated the book if Mrs. Eddy's good judgment had not removed them from a later edition, along with the epigraphs.[13] She had reason for very real gratitude to Wiggin, but the "learned treasures" he provided were a little too much like costume jewelry on a sky diver.

In the last analysis, Mrs. Eddy's bold concern with a cosmos in which the astronomer "will no longer look up to the stars,—he will look out from them upon the universe,"[14] related her to the scientific culture of the next century far more significantly than could the genteel refinements of Boston's literati in the 1880's. Pascal[15] had described reality as a circle whose center is everywhere and its circumference nowhere. Wiggin did his best to domesticate Mrs. Eddy within the urbanely circumscribed culture of Beacon Hill, but her thought found its natural reference points in issues that would have more relevance to the exploration of outer space.[16]

To Wiggin it was a matter of some wonderment that, with no knowledge of Graf-Wellhausen or the whole *Formgeschichte* development in biblical criticism, Mrs. Eddy had arrived at a clear perception of the separateness and disparity of the two creation accounts in Genesis.[17] What he failed to notice was the fact that by her striking reinterpretation of these accounts she had vaulted over the whole dismal quarrel between biblicism and Darwinism. In the sixteenth edition her treatment of the creation stories was for the first time incorporated in a separate chapter entitled "Genesis." This, together with "Prayer and Atonement" and a new chapter, "The Apocalypse," was added to the "Glossary" to enlarge the section called *Key to the Scriptures*.

For many years Mrs. Eddy had quoted the twelfth chapter of Revelation in her letters and conversation. Now, in her new chapter, she wrote of its symbols as having a special suggestiveness for the nineteenth century. As Wiggin explained it to a critic of Christian Science a little later, she found a "parallelism" between herself and the woman clothed with the sun who was persecuted by the great red dragon; but, he added, "it is not her personality that she supposes to be persecuted, but the Truth that speaks through her."[18] The woman, she herself wrote, stood for "the spiritual idea"—a phrase amplified in a later edition to "generic man, the spiritual idea of God."[19]

A discussion of another part of the book of Revelation found its way into *Science and Health* through a curiously complex series of events. Because of a renewed attack on her by Arens, Mrs. Eddy decided to restore in the sixteenth edition the kind of personal indictment which, in the sixth edition, she had excised from the chapter "Demonology," now named "Animal Magnetism."[20] However, early in 1886 when the book was almost ready for publication she had second thoughts.

At the time she was engaged in extensive last-minute revisions. A little later Wiggin, using the pseudonym Phare Pleigh, commented on this:

> *Whatever is to be Mrs. Eddy's future reputation, time will show. . . . Within a few months she had made sacrifices, from*

which most authors would have shrunk, to ensure the moral rightness of her book. . . . Day after day flew by, and weeks lengthened into months; from every quarter came importunate missives of inquiry and mercantile reproach; hundreds of dollars were sunk in a bottomless sea of corrections; yet not till the authoress was satisfied that her duty was wholly done, would she allow printer and binder to send forth her book to the world.[21]

The most outstanding example of this was the fact that, as Wiggin wrote a friend several years later, "after the work was not only in type, but cast . . . she wished to take out some twenty [actually ten] pages of diatribe on her dissenters."[22] The great question then was how to fill up the pages left blank by the deletions from the chapter "Animal Magnetism." Wiggin quickly came up with a recommendation.

Back on December 29 he had written her about her preaching. For some months she had been too busy to take the pulpit, and he proposed that he should occasionally prepare an outline to help her, enclosing one as an example:

Of course I cd write it out in full, but that is not my idea, & I understand that you preach best from notes simply, without a full manuscript. Besides I cd not fill in the Christian Science properly. That you can readily do—enlarging upon the illustrations &c. in yr own way, only keeping intact the main divisions.

She had tried out the idea on January 24, and although she decided not to do it again, the occasion had gone reasonably well.[23] When the urgent need for the extra pages of copy for *Science and Health* occurred, Wiggin at once bethought himself of this sermon and suggested to Mrs. Eddy that he write out the substance of her remarks in order to fill the space. She agreed, and a new chapter was included, with the enigmatic title "Wayside Hints (*Supplementary*)" intimating its ambiguous origin. A rather labored development of Revelation 22:16 in terms of the history of Christian culture, it was dropped by Mrs. Eddy at the next major revision of her book and a more metaphysical interpretation of "the city foursquare" introduced into the chapter on the Apocalypse.[24]

Wiggin, in retrospect, seems to have been a mixed blessing. From his general literary advice Mrs. Eddy profited greatly, but most of the learned allusions he persuaded her to include in her work she later threw out. In the long run she assimilated what was useful to her purpose and sloughed off the rest. The evidence of her books and letters shows that Wiggin "toned up" her sense of style, but affected her basic thinking not at all.

He in turn remained skeptical of both the Bible and Christian Science but on several occasions came to Mrs. Eddy's defense in a kind of gallant appreciation of her intellectual and spiritual courage. After a particularly savage attack by a clergyman in California, Wiggin responded with a pamphlet entitled *Christian Science and the Bible.* "As nineteen hundred years ago," he wrote, "opposition came less from populace and rabble than from priest and rabbi, so now the strongest antagonists of Christian Science are in the learned professions." He took pleasure in showing up the logical inconsistencies of Mrs. Eddy's California critic and thereby increased her gratitude to him.

By the beginning of 1886 she had asked him to take over the editorship of the *Journal* from Mrs. Crosse, who remained as business manager and publisher. Writing again as Phare Pleigh, he contributed lengthy leading articles on books such as John Fiske's *The Idea of God as Affected by Modern Knowledge,* Francis E. Abbott's *Scientific Theism,* and Sarah E. Titcomb's *Mind-Cure on a Material Basis,* comparing them with Christian Science. Commendatory references to the *Methodist Review* and other religious publications began to pepper the *Journal* pages. An article on Ritschl's theology was reprinted from the *Unitarian Review,* with comment by Wiggin. Zeno's theories were contrasted with Mrs. Eddy's, to the undoubted puzzlement of the simpler *Journal* readers, and erudite squibs on the etymology of Christian Science terms vied for place with heartfelt testimonies of Christian Science healing. The new sophistication was evident in the tone of the editor's comment on Madame Blavatsky, the founder of Theosophy, when that spectacular lady was accused of arranging fraudulent miracles:

> *Some years ago I knew Madame quite well, and found her an exceedingly clever woman, who smoked cigarettes in true Oriental style, and told wonderful stories of her peregrinating experiences. . . . Madame was always a delightful woman to meet, though she impressed me not only with a sense of her strength, but of doubt whether she herself believed the occult theories of which she spoke so warmly.*[25]

Wiggin's articles and letters at this time show that he had no doubt of Mrs. Eddy's sincerity, and he himself tried sincerely to serve the needs of the new movement.[26] Yet the metaphysical gaffes he made in the *Journal* from time to time—for which Mrs. Eddy took him to task with unhesitating though kindly authority—suggest the disorientation of a parent trained in conventional mathematics who finds his children moving at ease among mathematical concepts and processes that persistently elude his grasp. The trouble was that Wiggin found it hard to take these new concepts seriously and this put inevitable limits on the sincerity of his efforts. Like a non-Euclidean geometry which has its own internal logic but no apparent applicability to the practical tasks of the construction engineer, Christian Science demanded a leap forward into a different *kind* of universe to which its logic did apply. To Wiggin, happy in the small certainties of Boston's Unitarian culture, such a leap was unthinkable.

At the end of March, at Mrs. Eddy's invitation, he sat in a class she was just starting, with the agreement that she should ask him no questions and he would start no debate. It was a wise provision, she decided after a few days, but in a note to him she confided wistfully that it was her "heart's desire and prayer to God"[27] that He would reveal to Wiggin the truth of Christian Science. What *was* revealed was noted by Wiggin in the May *Journal:*

> *From hearing Mrs. Eddy preach, from reading her book (however carefully), from talking with her, you do not get an adequate idea of her mental powers, unless you hear her also in her classes. Not only is she glowingly earnest in presenting her convictions, but her language and illustrations are remarkably well chosen. She is quick in repartee, and keenly turns a jest upon her questioner, but not offensively or unkindly. She reads faces rapidly. A brief exposition of the Book of Job, which one day entered incidentally into her statement of how God is to be found, would have done honor to any ecclesiastic. Critical listeners are often astonished at the strong hold she has upon her thought, and at the clearness of her statements, even when they cannot agree with her. While she is sharp to detect variations from her own view, and to expose the difference, she governs herself in the midst of discussion. In fact, Rev. M. B. G. Eddy is a natural class-leader, and three hours pass away in her lessons before you know it.*

Although he remained a stubborn disbeliever in what he persisted in calling "miracles," one of the minor miracles of Christian Science is the fact that two such disparate personalities as Mary Baker Eddy and James Henry Wiggin should have been able to work together as long, as closely, and as good-naturedly as they did.

3

The more alert members of the Christian ministry felt the future crowding them. Must they sell out completely to the self-confident sciences, or was there demonstrably solid ground to stand on in a more sharply perceived Christianity? Among the restless seekers was the Reverend William I. Gill of Lawrence, Massachusetts.

One of three clergymen (in addition to Wiggin) who were members of the class of April, 1886, Gill was a strong-minded Yorkshireman, turned fifty, with a heavy North Country accent and a somewhat rustic appearance. Since coming to America he had written for *The Christian Register, Zion's Herald,* and other journals, and was also the author of three books: *Evolution and Progress, Analytical Processes,* and *Christian Conception and Experience.* A fourth on the verge of publication, was entitled *Philosophical Realism* but oddly enough was an exposition of philosophical idealism. At one time a Baptist, he was now a Methodist, while the Unitarian ideas he expounded to his Lawrence congregation had brought him under suspicion by his orthodox brethren. Immediately following his class with Mrs. Eddy he parted company with the Methodist Episcopal Conference and wrote her that he was now free from all ecclesiastical relations:

> *I . . . find myself developing a strange intellectual affinity with you and your work. . . . I now see that you are and will be one of the greatest benefactors of our times. You are contributing to the elevation of the average intellectual level, and to put a new glory in Christianity by restoring its primitive power.*[28]

A few days later he was in Boston discussing with her and with Wiggin the possibility of his becoming assistant pastor of the Church of Christ, Scientist, now meeting in the greater amplitude of Chickering Hall on Tremont Street. Mrs. Eddy, of course, would remain the pastor. Gill proposed also to carry on his church at Lawrence as an independent society, with the hope that it would become in time a Christian Science church.

In a long talk with Wiggin on April 21, he brought up the one theological point on which he seriously differed with Mrs. Eddy. This had to do with her teaching that God could not know evil, since for Him to know it would be to give it a place in the eternal spiritual order. Wiggin assured Gill—mistakenly, as it happened—that Mrs. Eddy meant this only in the sense that God does not admit the claims of evil. His explanation of the point in a letter to her afterward suggests that he felt that this was what she *ought* to mean:

> *As God is omniscient . . . He of course knows that His children do not always obey his commands, & in that sense he sees their disobedience; as the Bible says in many places, such as*

"the thing was evil in the eyes of the Lord," & "the eyes of the Lord are on the evil kingdom. . . ." I think you & Mr. Gill wd practically agree.[29]

The explanation shows that Wiggin himself failed to understand the logical consistency of her position or to realize that "practical" agreement would ultimately not be enough in regard to a system in which every metaphysical postulate had practical consequences—and requirements.

Gill himself at times sensed his need of a power that was more than intellectual or theoretical, as his letters over the next month or two indicate:

> *How singular that after my interview with you today I felt a conviction of healing power such as I never had before. . . .*
>
> *I grow ever more to see that you have a loving heart as well as a strong and subtle intellect. . . . But that [Christian Science] is your own child; and I can only help the mother as a dry nurse in bringing it up. . . .*
>
> *[In regard to the divisions which have always sprung up between the disciples of great teachers] I foresee that this will in some degree be inevitable among your followers. I wonder whether you cannot say something clear and strong and striking which shall unfang this serpent. . . .*
>
> *I do not think there is one other man in all the world so thoroughly prepared [as I am] to take up this work. . . . Here is your great and precious work, and it consists in the very subtle and original exposition which you give of Mind in relation to the illusions of mortal thought and all the phenomena of sense as temporal or absolutely subject to the spiritual and eternal.*[30]

In July, Gill was formally invited by the Church of Christ, Scientist, to become its assistant pastor, and the following month Mrs. Eddy made him editor of the *Journal*. On August 17, in a momentary and unusual spasm of humility, he wrote her in regard to the latter appointment, "Now, Dear Woman, let me have your help in prayer, in kind word and suggestion and charitable construction and patient forebearance, and give me all you can from your own pen."

Only the month before, she had contributed an article, "True Philosophy and Communion," in which she gently but firmly gave a lesson to Gill and Wiggin. In it she took issue with the Pythagorean concept that the study of geometry and astronomy was necessary to disengage the soul from objects of sense. What good, she asked, would geometry be to a poor sinner struggling with temptation or to a man with the smallpox? Was it through astronomy that Jesus pointed the way to heaven, the reign of harmony?[31]

Gill had an example of what she meant when he injured his ankle in jumping from the train by which he commuted daily between Lawrence and Boston. For several days he suffered intensely but managed to hobble to the *Journal* office each day. Finally he sent a telegram to Mrs. Eddy that the condition was so much worse he would be unable to come to work that day. She wired him in return that his duty was in Boston and that he should report at once to her. He arrived, as he later told a Lawrence friend, in such acute pain that he was totally unfit for work. When Mrs. Eddy came into the room, she spoke to him briefly, then turned and gazed out the window silently. Suddenly the ankle snapped back into place with a loud crack. When Gill returned home that night, the Lawrence friend who had been greatly disturbed by the situation in the morning met him walking easily and naturally.[32]

But while Gill might marvel a little at the way Mrs. Eddy combined "a strong and subtle intellect" with the "primitive power" of early Christianity, he failed to find in her simpler followers the charm of the earliest Christians. After a session with several of them one night he wrote her:

> *Oh! Mrs. Eddy, Oh! Mrs. Eddy! how insufferable is the shallow conceit which prevails extensively among your followers . . . and through delusion they will do their utmost to drive me off from you. . . . Dear Teacher and friend, if your system is not better expounded, if brains are not allowed among your followers, your personal life will be the limit of your influence. . . . Oh! dear Mrs. Eddy, I thought I had found my great work as your disciple! Was it all a dream or is there a sphere for intelligence among your disciples?*[33]

Mrs. Eddy herself shared some of his feeling. To Hannah Larminie in Chicago she wrote that the movement required "teachers who are educated by the schools of learning first, next by me," and to Ellen Brown, "I want a *learned* Teacher, and a *firm, honest* character to take the head of a Chicago Institute."[34] But the honesty was essential. While she brushed aside her students' complaints that Gill was egotistical and intellectually arrogant in his dealings with them, she was not able to dismiss so easily his double dealing in the matter of his book *Philosophical Realism*.

The book had been written before he knew anything of Christian Science, and by no stretch of the imagination could it be considered a presentation of that subject. When Gill took advantage of his editorship of the *Journal* to publicize the book, deliberately creating the impression that it was a work on Christian Science, it was hard to escape the conclusion that he was using his position to promote himself rather than the new faith he professed. At one point he had agreed to add a chapter on Christian Science to the next edition, but when the edition appeared there was no new chapter—and Gill explained that the material to be added had been "lost" by the printer. Finally it came to light that in conducting a class ostensibly on Christian Science in Lawrence he was teaching entirely from *Philosophical Realism*, an odd procedure for someone who pronounced himself a spokesman for Christian Science and a "disciple" of Mrs. Eddy.

Even before this last-named fact was known, dissatisfaction had been growing among the church members. They complained that he cut the service short at Chickering Hall in order to get to his flourishing congregation in Lawrence, that there was more Gill than Christ in his sermons, that he increasingly threw his weight around in the Christian Scientist Association, that he could not brook the slightest degree of opposition. Mrs. Eddy was troubled, watchful—and patient.[35]

The underlying problem came to the surface on Thanksgiving Day, 1886. Mrs. Eddy had invited Gill and his wife and their small daughter to dinner. Mrs. Gill through the past months had remained basically unreconciled to Christian Science. In her eyes her husband was a great man who ought to be second to no one; moreover he should properly be a great Methodist preacher, not attached to an outlandish little group which her friends in the old church eyed askance. The dinner was jolly enough, however, and afterward the company went into the parlor, where the discussion eventually turned on the point about God's not knowing evil, which had troubled Gill from the outset. Another student who was included in the party wrote later:

> *He was constantly plying her with questions from a theological standpoint, but he never seemed to grasp her metaphysical statements. Suddenly she turned to him, as they were sitting on the sofa, and said: "Brother Gill, you will* never *understand these things until you heal the sick."*[36]

As usual in her presence, Gill seemed anxious to learn, but later that night in great turbulence of mind he wrote her about the subject they had discussed:

> *This is the awful shadow, and really the only serious one, that has hovered [over] me ever since I knew you. . . . I fear*

I can never be as positive as you on the subject, and I dont see that any healing proves anything on the question.

[Immortal Mind, she teaches, is all good, mortal mind all evil, and therefore unreal.] But to this I have a psychological difficulty. I seem to be the same one self conscious individual who feels and knows both good and evil. How is that? Am I both mortal and immortal mind?

[Also, the Bible speaks of God's pity and mercy and redeeming work; does that not imply His knowledge of evil?] If you are not too rigid and exacting here, if, as in all the other points, I can feel at home with you here, then I shall feel that I have a free and happy scope to serve you in the Cause.

The next morning he continued the letter, telling her that he felt the doctrine in question laid Christian Science open to ridicule:

It is clear that God cannot know *(by experience, impression, acquisition) evil, but He must be able to* understand *it as the logically contrasted opposite of himself, as a falsity, a claim to be what it is not. I have all along thought that this must be what you mean. If it is not, I am in deep distress.*[37]

Mrs. Eddy received and answered his letter the same day, plunging directly to elements in the situation that lay beyond the question as mere theory:

I trace a strong element of malicious mind acting on your morning thoughts. This to me is so very discouraging, for my morning thoughts always come clearer and are nearer His. . . . There may be such a thing as discouraging me. It looks like it now. You regard this grandest point of Science as once religionists regarded Foreordination. . . . You are a shining mark, you are in the open field, your bosom companion is dark as most all are on this question, the enemy are talking audibly and inaudibly to lead you astray.

You see for a moment, in my atmosphere, the glimpse of this God-summit, then go away and the fowls of the air pick up this good *seed. . . . It is only a spiritual not an intellectual darkness that causes the human reason to reject this highest revelation of God.*

Your wife seeks to still the storm in your breast just when I should bid it rage, then it would vent itself and the sunshine of the above Truth would appear. I stand forever here. God put my feet on this Rock. . . . It was what I saw, felt and knew, that first saved my life; but the conviction of its truth that raised me up from a helpless injury was not the understanding of it. That I gained afterwards. Now the person convinced or convicted of this great Truth is the best healer for their faith in its Truth saves themselves and others until they can understand it. This is the case with my best practitioners. . . .

You are not both mortal and immortal mind or body. The Ego, you, is immortal only. The mortal is the suggestive lie calling itself you when it is not. . . . You are not two opposites but are one. entity and individuality. The lying "you" is likened by Paul to that which was not him, "no longer I but sin."[38]

Another letter from Gill the next day expressed his bafflement:

I can discern a profound argument for your doctrine, but if that doctrine is carried to the extent to which I suppose you do carry it, I am spiritually paralysed, because it seems to oppose all practical action and effort for spiritual good. This convinces me that I have not thoroughly understood you yet, because it does not hamper your practical action in any good direction.[39]

In this interchange lay the genesis of Mrs. Eddy's later book *Unity of Good,* sometimes described as her most "philosophical" work. More immediately, an article entitled "Science and Philosophy" which she had already sent in for the December edition of the *Journal* summed up the issue at stake—without any mention of Gill.[40]

Mrs. Eddy was still loath to see him go, but her students were losing patience as his sermons bore less and less relation to genuine Christian Science. The last straw was the discovery that he had substituted *Philosophical Realism* for *Science and Health* in his teaching. At a special church meeting on January 13, 1887, it was voted that he was "not in any particular fulfilling the terms of our engagement with him." Gill in a rage took the controversy to the pulpit in both Boston and Lawrence and six days later resigned as assistant pastor. On February 2, evidence was brought in that he was attacking Christian Science and Mrs. Eddy in the most opprobrious terms, and he was expelled from the Christian Scientist Association.

When the notice of expulsion reached his home, Mrs. Gill, almost beside herself, released her long pent-up feelings in a letter to Mrs. Eddy, whom she addressed as "you poor foolish old woman." Gill, she wrote, had already sent in his withdrawal "from your Jesuit Club"—not that he cared "what your dupes and slaves would do." She felt disgraced that "we ever had any connection with Mrs. Glover Patterson Eddy. . . . I know what you would *do if* you *could!* . . .

Poor woman, I pitty you, tottering so near your grave, and yet so full of malice."[41] It was not a very amiable letter.

Gill, too, with outraged intellectual pride, turned furiously on Mrs. Eddy. He went at once to Edward J. Arens to gather all the ammunition he could, then let loose an article against her in the *Religio-Philosophical Journal,* a mind-cure publication in Chicago. The article defeated itself by its own violence and elicited a wave of sympathy for Mrs. Eddy. She herself wrote Ellen Brown, "It is the midnight of sin in Boston [;] the last Judas I hope has appeared."[42]

4

An editorial note in the *Journal* of February, 1887, mentioned that Mrs. Eddy had admitted no clergymen to her last class, though eight had applied. The announcement brought forth an immediate letter from her student M. C. Spaulding of Chicago, congratulating her on her attempt to "shake off the ministerial incubus which has rested upon you & your work." The letter went on to say:

> *Your love of the church of your childhood has followed you into C. S. and can be distinctly traced through your wonderful book & later writings—and your partiality towards the Clergy & Church has been one of the weak props of your cause— a cause which needed no such artificial supports.*
>
> *You fondly hoped that men with "Rev" prefixed to their names would be the glittering bulwarks of your cause—forgetting that the very worst foes Christ had to contend with were the Clergy of his day. . . .*
>
> *I have just read Mr. Gill's "article" in the Religio Philosophical Journal of Chicago. Do not reply to it—he cannot hurt you or your cause by any such disjointed articles—the weak pleas and protestations of a discharged clerk who feels bad because he has lost his place. His articles in the C. S. Journal were well written—though full of I—I—I—and Gill Gill Gill, but that in the R-P Journal is the work of one partially insane. You are fortunate in losing Mr. Gill.*[43]

Steeped as Mrs. Eddy was in the religious and largely evangelical culture of New England, she found it hard to believe that the clergy could not be won over to a faith that grounded Christianity, as she saw it, in demonstrable spiritual law rather than outworn superstition. Gill had gone wrong in one way; his classmate, the Reverend Joseph Adams of Oakland, California, went wrong in another. Between them they raised a doubt as to whether the Protestant ministry even yet recognized the seriousness of its quandary. Religion in the United States, she would note a few years later, had passed "from stern Protestantism to doubtful liberalism,"[44] and Adams was for her an education in the ease with which liberalism could lose itself in a genial fog of good intentions.

Like Gill, he was an Englishman about fifty years old, head-strong and self-willed, but otherwise quite different in character. Where Gill was intellectual and argumentative, Adams was evangelical and exuberant, yet he trod constantly on people's toes from the sheer ineptitude of his determined benignity. It was a failing that would become increasingly evident in the flabbier aspects of ecumenism in the next century.

As a boy of sixteen in England, Adams had been converted by the famous revivalist Charles G. Finney of Oberlin, Ohio.[45] Two years later he came to America to live in the Finney household as protégé and pupil. Returning later to England, he became a Wesleyan evangelist, until a final return to America (and to Finney's Congregationalism) took him out to California. There his second wife, a woman physician, became interested in one of the many varieties of mind-cure-*cum*-spiritism floating around in that atmosphere, and soon Adams and she were happily challenging their respective establishments, medical and ecclesiastical.

Early in 1886 he read to the Bay Association of Congregational Ministers a "statement of my present beliefs," which resulted in his separation from that body. Happening on *Science and Health* in the meantime and finding that it contained "the ripe kernel, the rich wheat"[46] of spiritual healing, he got in touch with Mrs. Eddy and before long was on his way to the Massachusetts Metaphysical College.

At the conclusion of the April class, he preached in Chickering Hall for several Sundays. At that time Gill had not yet been appointed assistant pastor, and Mrs. Eddy wished to try out Adams for the position. But the latter's revivalist techniques were ill adapted for the purpose. George H. Bradford, a proper Bostonian and fellow student in the late class, wrote Mrs. Eddy:

> *He is an unfit man—and unfit in too many different ways ever to be made over—(and be, at least, useful to the present generation—) He lacks painfully in dignity—and reverence— and overflows on the side of gush, empty declamation and egotism. Say nothing of unsound doctrine—a man may be cured there. . . .*
>
> *And in the presence of the glorious solemn truths considered so lately in the class, if he could not feel some degree*

199

*of dignity and reverence, he never can or will. When he finished
his shouting . . . your calm voice came to lift us into an atmosphere of peace—I couldn't take in the sense of what you
said—it was enough to feel the up-lift—and Holmes' couplet
came irreverently to my mind—*

> *"And silence like a poultice came,*
> *To heal the blows of sound."*[47]

After another try or two, Mrs. Eddy tactfully called Adams off,
and on May 14 he wrote her:

> *I cannot forbear to comfort you with the information that
> the Truth has already healed the error you have so kindly tried
> to correct in me. Within one hour from the time I left you last
> evening I had the assurance that the work was done, and from
> that time . . . I have had . . . a "restless calm," but I know that
> Christ has stilled the storm of my mortal nature. . . . If the
> Church would give me my railway fare home and you think it
> best, I will close my labors here at the end of this month, for
> I do not feel comfortable in knowing that some of the leading
> members purposely absent themselves from Church because of
> my boisterous preaching. . . . [In conclusion] your faithfulness
> to me has not only secured my highest esteem but undying
> Christian love for you. And I would assure you that you may
> count on one (at least) who will stand by you as a practical
> Christian Scientist.*[48]

The church did pay his way back to Oakland, though he took
his time in making the journey, stopping off with leisurely gusto
to lecture and preach on Christian Science wherever possible. In
September his wife—Mrs. J. A. D. Adams, M. D., as she signed herself
—studied enthusiastically with Mrs. Eddy at the latter's invitation.
The following month Adams himself returned to Boston, at Mrs.
Eddy's expense, to take the Normal class, preparatory to going to
Chicago to help Ellen Brown with her Christian Science Institute.
Soon he was established (with a certain appropriateness) in the Windy
City, while his wife carried on the work in Oakland.

Miss Brown before long wrote Mrs. Eddy that the Plunkett-
Hopkins faction in Chicago was making great efforts to capture
Adams. He had, she observed, no wisdom or discernment but took
the defectors at face value, "being so simple and good himself he
thinks everyone is what they *seem* to be."[49] Mrs. Eddy replied:

> *Have written Mr. Adams in my strongest terms. If this
> does not change him I can do no more at present and time will
> have to ripen him for my instruction. . . . Teach him by every*

word look and act of your own the great difference between seeming and being.[50]

It was a tough assignment. The lack of sharp realism that has dogged liberal Protestant thought was very evident in Adams. The traditional doctrine of original sin had at least kept alive an astringent sense of the capacity for self-deception in the human mind and heart, and Mrs. Eddy quoted with approbation even some of the more direful words of Jonathan Edwards on that subject.[51] Yet it was the sense of Christian *agape* that she had loved most in the clergy she had known in her youth, and it was this that she appears to have valued in Adams. She may have hoped to see realized in him the faith she expressed in a later comment on the old-time ministers of her New England girlhood:

> *I believe, if those venerable Christians were here to-day, their souls would take in the spirit and understanding of Christian Science through the flood-gates of Love; with them Love was the governing impulse of every action; their piety was the all-important consideration of their being, the original beauty of holiness that to-day seems to be fading so sensibly from our sight.*[52]

Unfortunately Adams lacked the stern integrity of those earlier men, not to mention their common sense. Mrs. Eddy's disillusionment in him was inevitable, and it came in February, 1887.

Ostensibly the issue was one of plagiarism.

For some time Mrs. Eddy had been disturbed at the way many of her students tended simply to parrot her words and thoughts in their writing. Eighteen months before, she had written Ellen Brown, "Bravo! young lady, your wit at the close of the article was just the thing"—but had gone on to say that the young lady in question borrowed too much from her teacher without quotation. "*You* are capable of writing from out your own throughts," she wrote, and in another letter enlarged on the point: "You can originate. I have filled you with glorious thoughts of *your own* [;] use them."[53] But the tendency to trot out Mrs. Eddy's statements in an inferior imitation of her language continued, reaching its *reductio ad absurdum* later in 1887 when one article in the *Journal* included more than twenty lines verbatim from *Science and Health,* given as the author's own, while the rest of the article was plainly borrowed in content and style.[54]

Adams, though garrulous, was in no wise an original thinker. When he sent Mrs. Eddy a lengthy article of his which the *Chicago Inter-Ocean* had just published and which he intended to have reprinted in pamphlet form, she found it to be one more example of a student's rewriting portions of *Science and Health* and presenting the result as his own. Ordinarily she might have taken him to task gently, but the article arrived just as the Gills had let loose their private and public blasts against her, and Julius Dresser had fired the opening shot in a major new campaign to establish Quimby as the originator of Christian Science. With evident intent to shock Adams to an awareness of the need for self-discipline, Mrs. Eddy wrote him a stiff reprimand for his "plagiarism" and told her she would have to take legal proceedings if he followed his plan of reprinting the article.

It was a kill-or-cure tactic. She had a movement to establish which required sharp, clear thinking, the unreserved assumption of intellectual and spiritual responsibilities. If this fuzzy-minded clergyman was unwilling to grow up to his new responsibilities, it might be better for him to clear out. And he promptly did. When Miss Brown, who had been absent in Boston, returned to Chicago and found that he had cut loose from their jointly run institute, she wrote Mrs. Eddy, "Could you not have smitten him less severely?"[55] Yet probably Adams welcomed the excuse to set up on his own, and he bore Mrs. Eddy no malice.

Her letter, he wrote, had "caused for the time being a sorrow that no language [can] describe, but it has done me incalculable good."[56] It had opened his eyes, he told her, to the fact that he was "depending as much for my inspiration and joy upon the personal approbation of Mrs. Eddy as upon My Blessed Master," In setting up independently, he concluded, he was not leaving Christian Science and would continue to teach from *Science and Health* alone.

He continued also to carry on a friendly correspondence with Mrs. Eddy, who bore patiently with his indiscriminate hospitality to every variety of *soi-disant* Christian Scientist. His own reason for not wanting to be identified with any particular school of Christian Science, he wrote her, was that it was God's Truth, not man's. Citing I Corinthians 3:4, he piously deplored anyone's saying, I am of Mrs. Eddy, I of Hopkins, I of Swarts, I of Arens, and so forth, although he was presumably not averse to Paul's warnings against the perversions of Christianity in the primitive church.

When Adams asked for a renewal of his certificate from the Metaphysical College, Mrs. Eddy commented on the inconsistency of his request with his repudiation of organization, then added:

> *You have tried teaching Christian Science. Did ever you find a student who after taking 12 lessons was better able than*

you were to pioneer this cause? Then can you, only one year old in this knowledge know better than I who have worked it and earned my knowledge of it 21 years how to carry it on? After over ten years of experience and success far beyond yours, I learned that nothing but organization would save this cause for mankind and protect it from the devouring disorganizers. The apostle likens the church to the body of Christ. I liken the blood of Christ to the life of Truth. Then if you would break up His church, are you not breaking His body and spilling His blood? You are commanded to go to the lost sheep *and gather them in: but you go to the* goats *to gather them in.*[57]

Shortly afterward Adams started a monthly periodical of his own, *The Chicago Christian Scientist,* which announced in its first issue (June, 1887) that the truth taught him at the Massachusetts Metaphysical College and in *Science and Health* was still basic to his thinking and that all he claimed was the privilege of propagating that truth in his own way. A few months later he protested the widespread use of the words Christian Science to describe systems departing radically from Mrs. Eddy's. She had chosen the name, he wrote,

> *. . . after much patient, persevering, and self-denying labor to the public. . . . Any impartial person who has no axe to grind must admit that the name is her exclusive right. Will some one please explain, why those very same persons [who say that she and her system are in error] cling with such tenacity to her name and palm themselves off as Christian Scientists while they disclaim against it . . . ?*[58]

Consistency, however, was not the strong point in Joseph Adams' character, as illustrated in his sacerdotal flirtations with Mrs. Plunkett and Mrs. Hopkins. When these two ladies were not busy holding classes and starting institutes all over the Middle and Far West, they devoted themselves to the Emma Hopkins College of Christian Science in Chicago and held Sunday services in close imitation of Mrs. Eddy's. Since they paid lip service to *Science and Health* as the source of their inspiration, this certified them sufficiently in the eyes of Adams and inevitably he turned up as a guest preacher in their pulpit, assuming a community of outlook which even they found a little disconcerting.[59]

It was this failure of discrimination that made the Reverend George B. Day describe Adams to Mrs. Eddy as "irreclaimable," a "marvel of self-deception."[60] Day had studied along with Gill and Adams in her class of April, 1886. Of the three clergymen, he was the least vivid but the most able. Reticent and quietly intelligent, he became pastor of the Christian Science Church formed in Chicago that summer, preaching his opening sermon on the text, "They were first called Christians in Antioch." Later he wrote Mrs. Eddy that while the attempts of Adams to attach the students of Mrs. Hopkins and all others to himself had proved abortive, the Chicago church —which at its founding had been designed to be "in all respects in accord with the Mother Church in Boston"[61]—was flourishing. The irrepressible Adams, on the other hand, wrote her that "Brother Day" was growing and preaching in splendid style.

Many of Mrs. Eddy's students were highly condemnatory of Adams, but she herself took a tolerant view. "He teaches and acknowledges my writings," she explained to one student, "beyond some who call themselves loyal; for this I cannot [and] will not come out against him."[62] There was a residual probity in his position, she believed, and it was related to his being a genuine if foolish Christian.

5

In 1887 the religious malaise of the age found popular expression in Mrs. Humphrey Ward's novel *Robert Elsmere,* which soon swept the English and American reading publics off their feet. Mrs. Ward was no Dostoevsky; but as the outstanding example of a genre that included Margaret Deland's *John Ward, Preacher* and Harold Frederic's *The Damnation of Theron Ware,* her book presented in bourgeois-liberal terms the torment of a religious soul wrestling with its loss of faith in Christianity's miraculous origin.

Hundreds of sermons were preached about it, including several by George Day in Chicago, but Day had a counterargument denied to most of the others. By the logic of Mrs. Eddy's teaching, the Christian miracles were capable of being "scientifically" understood and reproduced as instances of universal law rather than arbitrary interventions of Deity. In her own words, "The miracle introduces no disorder, but unfolds the primal order, establishing the Science of God's unchangeable law."[63]

Christian Science, in a sense, bypassed the burning question of the historicity of the New Testament narratives by its emphasis on a continuing revelation and incarnation of the Christ in human experience. When the skeptical Wiggin grew restive in Mrs. Eddy's class under her attack on agnosticism and finally burst out, "How do you know that there ever was such a man as Christ Jesus?" she replied crisply, "I do not find my authority for Christian Science in history, but in revelation."[64] Truth would be no less true even if it had never been lived by Jesus. Later she would write, "Christianity and Science, being contingent on nothing written and based on the divine Principle of being, must be, are, irrefutable and eternal."[65]

Nevertheless, historically the revelation had come to her through the Bible; concretely it was coming to her students through the Bible and *Science and Health*. In the final edition of the latter book, the second sentence of the opening chapter on prayer would read, "Regardless of what another may say or think on this subject, I speak from experience"[66]—and regardless of what biblical scholarship might say or surmise about the historicity of the gospel narratives, her experience confirmed their essential truth. Hence without any sense of inconsistency she could write in the *Journal:*

> *My students need to search the Scriptures and "Science and Health with Key to the Scriptures," to understand the personal Jesus' labor in the flesh for their salvation: they need to do this even to understand my works, their motives, aims, and tendency.*[67]

In a booklet entitled *Christian Science: No and Yes*, which went through several editions in 1887, Mrs. Eddy returned to the theological points that her various ministerial critics had raised in their concerted assault two years before.[68] Written that same year out of the same urgencies that had confronted her in her dealings with Wiggin, Gill, Adams, and Day, were two other small books, *Rudiments and Rules of Divine Science* and *Unity of Good and Unreality of Evil*,[69] which gave less attention to traditional theology and more to the metaphysical implications of biblical Christianity. Yet in all three there was not a trace of the syncretizing tendency which made Emma Hopkins, for instance, feel more at home with the Hindu Upanishads than with the Christian Gospels.[70]

Under Wiggin's urging, Mrs. Eddy had inserted into the sixteenth edition of *Science and Health* several excerpts from the Hindu scriptures, introducing one of them with the words: "The ancient Hindoo philosophers understood something of this Principle, when they said in their Celestial Song. . . ."[71] But later she withdrew all such references. The analogy that might seem satisfactory enough as a vaguely suggestive cultural adornment failed to stand up in a textbook for rigorous daily study and application.

Eastern thought might deny the reality of matter in terms that suggested Christian Science, but the latter insisted, along with traditional Christianity, that the Word must become flesh—the absolute must be experienced humanly as redemption and transformation, not merely as nonattachment and abstraction. Moreover, the self-denial or surrender of will at the heart of Christianity meant commitment to active living, not ascetic withdrawal from the world. Neither the mystic's ecstasies nor the adept's mental techniques were an adequate substitute for the ethical imperatives and healing outreach of practical Christianity.

"All that is needed to make my students a power that would put to flight the aliens," Mrs. Eddy wrote in a letter, "is the whole substance of Science, viz. Christianity; seen in unselfishness *love* cross-bearing."[72] The same note is struck again and again in her correspondence, and one can trace in her students the deepening awareness of what she meant. On one occasion Caroline Noyes wrote her with disarming frankness that she had come to recognize an element of selfish ambition in her own Christian Science work, and with that she had realized with a shock that "if one has any selfish thoughts of advantage to be gained by following the Truth . . . our work is corrupted thereby, and is more or less will power, or mind cure, for it certainly partakes of the material."[73] Janet Colman, too, concluded that the mind-curers who professed Science uniformly left out the Christianity, and "if you leave out that you have left out the whole of it."[74]

In contrast, A. J. Swarts, who had no qualms about possible corrupting influences, wrote Mrs. Eddy that he saw the value of the term *Christian* Science to *start* the work but regretted to see a "failing" adjective associated with a permanent Science well in advance of Christian civilization. Mrs. Plunkett with equal cynicism disparaged Christianity in private while giving it occasional lip service in public. Emma Hopkins was frankly enchanted by all varieties of mysticism and was eclectically hospitable to a number of incompatible theories; but the dominating influence on her, in Mrs. Eddy's opinion, was the "esoteric magic" of theosophy.

With the formation of the Theosophical Society in New York in 1875, two weeks after the publication of *Science and Health,* a movement came into existence which was sometimes confounded with Christian Science. Dedicated to the occult, the theurgic, the "hidden" lore of the East, it moved in the half-world of the mythic imagination, drawing on what Jung would later call the collective unconscious, uniting the interests of the primitive necromancer with those of the contemporary hypnotist, interlacing the revelations of ancient mystery cults with piecemeal borrowings from modern anthropology and astronomy.

To Mrs. Eddy—as to many traditional Christians and, for that matter, to hard-bitten rationalists—these teachings represented an intellectual corruption equally repugnant to religion and to science. Where she exalted both the light of revelation and the light of reason, Madame Blavatsky lauded primeval "DARKNESS" as the one true actuality, the Great Mother, the source and womb of light.

It was bad enough to have critics of Christian Science carelessly lump it together with theosophy, spiritism, and mesmerism; it was even worse to have people who called themselves Christian Scientists try to combine it with one or more of these psychic novelties. Mrs. Eddy felt a little as might an astrophysicist who had discovered a new principle of celestial mechanics, only to find his discovery being hailed, appropriated, and misused by astrologers, flying-saucer enthusiasts, Velikovskyites, and assorted stargazers.

In her new pamphlet *Rudiments and Rules of Divine Science* she wrote:

> *A slight divergence is fatal in Science. Like certain Jews whom St. Paul had hoped to convert from mere motives of self-aggrandizement to the love of Christ, these so-called schools are clogging the wheels of progress by blinding the people to the true character of Christian Science,—its moral power, and its divine efficacy to heal.*
>
> *The true understanding of Christian Science Mind-healing, never originated in pride, rivalry, or the deification of self. The Discoverer of this Science could tell you of timidity, of self-distrust, of friendlessness, toil, agonies, and victories under which she needed miraculous vision to sustain her, when taking the first footsteps in this Science.*[75]

When her *Unity of Good* appeared several months later, she was still concerned with drawing the lines of definition more conclusively:

> *Sometimes it is said, by those who fail to understand me, that I* monopolize; *and this is said because ideas akin to mine have been held by a few spiritual thinkers in all ages. So they have, but in a far different form. Healing has gone on continually; yet healing, as I teach it, has not been practised since the days of Christ.*
>
> *What is the cardinal point of the difference in my metaphysical system? This: that* by knowing the unreality of disease, sin, and death, *you demonstrate the allness of God. This difference wholly separates my system from all others. The reality of these so-called existences I deny, because they are not to be found in God, and this system is built on Him as the sole cause.*

It would be difficult to name any previous teachers, save Jesus and his apostles, who have thus taught.[76]

And that is the very point at which claims were once more being advanced for Phineas Parkhurst Quimby.

6

On February 8, 1887, Julius Dresser delivered a lecture at the Church of the Divine Unity in Boston on "The True History of Mental Science." In it he quoted for the first time in public from Quimby's own writings to show that it was the Portland healer who made the psychological discovery that disease is a "belief."[77]

The discovery, he noted, "was not made from the Bible" but came from Quimby's "experiments in mesmerism," which served as "a stepping-stone to a higher knowledge." Then he quoted Quimby's words regarding those mesmeric experiments: "Here was where I first discovered that mind was matter, and capable of being changed."[78]

In this speech of Dresser's, published afterward as a pamphlet,[79] the process of reinterpreting Quimby as a sort of Ur-Christian Scientist really began. The sentence from Quimby quoted above provided a foundation for the attempt—not very prepossessing, perhaps, but at least having a serviceable ambivalence that was missing from the statement later quoted from the Quimby manuscripts by Dresser's wife, Annetta: "My foundataion is animal matter, or life. This, set in action by wisdom, produces thought."[80] Yet with the subsequent help of their brilliant son, Horatio,[81] the Dressers so succeeded in "spiritualizing" the terms which Quimby took from animal magnetism as to befuddle several generations of critics.

The interesting thing is that Julius Dresser, by placing the origin of Quimby's ideas in mesmerism, provided the key to the latter's terminology but never used it. The whole vast literature of animal magnetism, including the efforts of several writers to give mesmerism a biblical basis, formed the context of Quimby's thinking. Far from emphasizing this fact, the Dressers did their best to conceal it,[82] attributing Christian and metaphysical meanings to terms which Quimby actually used in a wholly empirical and psychological sense. In Horatio Dresser's detailed interpretations in later years, for instance, he pointedly ignored Quimby's crucial conception of "the Christ" as a clairvoyant power by which the healer was able to perceive a person's mental atmosphere or identity and feel his sickness; instead he wrote as though this pragmatic concept were roughly equivalent to Mrs. Eddy's theistic definition of Christ as "the true idea voicing good, the divine message from God to men speaking to the human consciousness."[83]

This trick of reading quasi-Christian Science meanings back into Quimby may not have been conscious on the elder Dressers' part. They had been exposed for a number of years to Mrs. Eddy's ideas and could hardly afford to admit, even to themselves, how far the idolized figure of their youth had been from the Christian theism which undergirded her teachings.

It was left to Horatio Dresser at the end of the century, however, to do the real job of making over Quimby's working philosophy into a full-blown system of Christological metaphysics.[84] Neither the two older Dressers nor George Quimby, who wrote an article on his father for the *New England Magazine* in March, 1888, proved very skillful in disguising the basic materialism of the theory and practice they were describing. In fact, George Quimby, who frankly admitted his lack of interest in metaphysical questions, made no real effort to do so. With refreshing frankness he would let small cats out of bags, then throw damaging admissions at them like old boots. His father, he noted casually in his article, had not even begun to set down his ideas in writing until the Misses Ware persuaded him to do this about 1860—a fact which adds fresh doubt to the dating of the Quimby manuscripts as they exist today.[85]

Despite this renewed flurry of propaganda, surprisingly few people in the 1880's, even among the mind-curers, expressed any real interest in Quimby. If they did, it was likely to be less in the man and his philosophy than in the Dresser *claim* as a convenient weapon with which to attack Mrs. Eddy's primacy in the field. She, for her part, offered to publish the Quimby manuscripts at her own expense if she could examine them first and determine that they were not manuscripts she had left with him during the period when they were sharing ideas. Rather naturally, this suggestion did not appeal to George Quimby, since it would have meant his releasing the manuscripts to her, and the shrewdness of the move hardly increased his love for her.

In reply to Dresser's speech and pamphlet, on the other hand, Mrs. Eddy wrote of Quimby in the *Journal:*

> *I would touch tenderly his memory, speak reverently of his humane purpose, and name only his virtues, did not this man Dresser drive me, for conscience-sake, to sketch the facts. . . . It has always been my misfortune to think people better and bigger than they really are. My mistake is, to endow another person with my ideal, and then make him think it his own. . . .*

> *If ever Mr. Quimby's ominous manuscripts are brought to light,*
> *it will be when my copyrights have expired, and the dear-bought*
> *treasures of Truth are appropriated by both the evil and the*
> *good. Then arm-in-arm, Mr. Dresser and his skeleton (like*
> *Dorcasina and her hero in* Female Quixotism) *may enter the*
> *drawing-rooms of Mind-healing Science. Stumbling up my stairs,*
> *they may fall unexpectedly into good company.*[86]

The company into which Dresser *had* fallen was that of Warren F. Evans. At least, Evans was the name he invoked to support his case. The slightly bewildering fact is that, on the evidence of the six influential books on mental healing written by Evans, the latter actually demolishes Dresser's chief assumption.[87]

In only one of these books does the author refer to Quimby, whom he had visited twice in 1863. The reference consists of a few sentences which praise the Portland healer not as the originator of mental healing but as an example of it.[88] More crucially, the passage identified Quimby as a practitioner of animal magnetism, the very point which Dresser strenuously denied.[89] Since Evans himself frankly combined the techniques and concepts of animal magnetism with ideas somewhat closer to those of the psychiatrically-oriented pastoral counselor of today,[90] he felt thoroughly at home with those elements in Quimby, which Dresser felt compelled to ignore, conceal, spiritualize, or explain away.

Where the Dressers determinedly downplayed the importance of Quimby's physical manipulation of his patients, Evans consistently hailed the magnetic power of the hands as an important element in healing and endorsed all the stock mesmeric practices which Quimby retained to the last. In his book *The Primitive Mind-Cure,* published in 1885, Evans wrote, "In treating a patient by the transcendental method, we must learn to talk to him in *thought,* in *words,* and with the *hand.* When a person is in the magnetic state, what you suggest to him becomes the law of his being."[91]

This, of course, was exactly what Mrs. Eddy deplored in Quimby, in Evans himself, and in the fifty-seven varieties of mind-cure around her. Her intellectual and spiritual austerity on this subject stood in strong contrast to the enthusiastic eclecticism of Evans. The latter, with his immense if superficial, learning, had responded even to her own writings sufficiently to show a marked trend toward philosophical idealism in his 1881 book, *The Divine Law of Cure.*[92] Later the more congenial influence of Madame Blavatsky became evident, and in 1886 his book *Esoteric Christianity*—obviously suggested by A. P. Sinnett's popular theosophical work *Esoteric Buddhism*—came loaded down with hermetic and gnostic elaborations of its Quimbyesque system of suggestion. As for the "Christianity" in it, this was so Orientalized as to be undiluted pantheism.

Back in 1885 when A. J. Gordon, writing in *The Congregationalist,* had attacked Christian Science as "pantheism of the most revolting kind," he had quoted in support of this not *Science and Health* but *The Primitive Mind-Cure,* especially a passage in which Evans described how a stream of nervous energy could be made to flow upon an ailing organ. The passage read:

> *This nervous energy I prefer to call the universal, divine life-principle in nature, the akasa of the Hindu metaphysics, an all-pervading, omnipresent, vivific principle of life and action identical in its higher aspects with the Holy Spirit of the Gospels.*[93]

It was the casual equation of Christian Science with the lucubrations of Evans or anyone else who happened to be handy that almost drove Mrs. Eddy to despair at times. It was even worse when some of her own students, hankering after a broadened culture, fell into the same error. A. J. Swarts, who could always be trusted to act like a scruffy parody of a Christian Scientist, wrote her in tones of injured innocence that he was thoroughly faithful to her teaching and used only two textbooks in his classes—*Science and Health* and *The Divine Law of Cure* by Evans. Somehow their incompatibility had escaped his notice.

Quimbyism, the psychological or transcendental medicine of Evans, the self-styled Christian Science of Swarts and Hopkins, all could be described by a chapter title from *The Primitive Mind-Cure:* "Psychological Telegraphy, or the Transference of Thought and Idea from one Mind to Another." The phrase, descriptive of animal magnetism, summed up what Mrs. Eddy rejected as having any part in Christian healing.

Chapter VIII

Acclaim and Dissent

Generally speaking, a prophet is better off without family ties. To his brothers and sisters and cousins and aunts he is likely to be an acute embarrassment. How preposterous to those who once heard young Jasper tell his piano teacher to go to blazes that he should now set up to be the voice of God. What supernally bestowed commission can justify his leaving home just when the pantry roof needs fixing?

Mrs. Eddy, to whom family ties had once seemed the chief assurance of human good, had been stripped of them one by one. Her favorite brother was the first to go, then her adored and adoring mother. Later came the deaths of her father, her two remaining brothers, the stepmother she had learned to love—and in those same years the estrangement of her two sisters. That the youngest and frailest of the family—the darling of their early years—should launch forth as a prophet was altogether too much for those two strong-minded women. And now they also were gone. Martha had died in 1884, and Abigail, the eldest, two years later.

That shrewd, proud lady of Tilton, New Hampshire, had been torn for years between angry disapproval and bewildered incomprehension of her once-favorite sister.[1] On at least one occasion when she was seriously ill she had been on the point of sending for Mrs. Eddy to come and heal her but had been dissuaded by others.[2] In 1885, outraged by the increasing press references to the Reverend Mary B. G. Eddy and by more personal considerations,[3] she let the frustration of years explode in a savage little note which began with the mocking salutation, "My Dear Rev. &c, &c, &c,"[4] and ended with a chilling reminder that she knew sister Mary through and through —a claim which there is more than a little reason to doubt in view of the lack of correspondence between them for almost twenty years.

In her will she made no mention of her sister but left ten thousand dollars to her nephew George Glover. To her sister-in-law Martha Rand Baker, who was leading a life of tranquil if somewhat penurious widowhood in Tilton, she left "the note I hold against her."[5] Martha

Rand and Mary Baker had been enthusiastic friends at the time George Sullivan Baker was courting Martha, but their paths had diverged hopelessly since then. In the middle 1880's Mrs. Eddy invited Mrs. Baker to come to Boston as her guest and take one of her courses, but Mrs. Baker had more important domestic tasks in Tilton, it appeared. Her sharp-eyed and sharp-tongued son, George W. Baker, had a sneaking admiration for his aunt Mary—"I want you to know that personally I *loved* her," he wrote George Glover's daughter in 1924[6]—but he had faded off into Maine and kept up no correspondence with her.

In fact, the only remaining link with her vanished family was another sister-in-law, Mary Ann Cook Baker, widow of her eldest brother, Samuel.[7] This deeply religious woman, who had served for some years as a missionary and was now prominent in the Park Street Congregational Church in Boston, remained to the end of her days a warm friend and admirer of Mrs. Eddy, but she never became a Christian Scientist nor did Mrs. Eddy try to make her into one.[8] The two women corresponded affectionately and had occasional visits. Mrs. Baker, for instance, was a guest at the 1886 Thanksgiving dinner at which the argumentative Gill opted for God's knowledge of sin, and without accepting Mrs. Eddy's views on the subject she apparently found them more spiritually digestible than did Gill.[9] But pleasant as the relationship was, it merely underlined Mrs. Eddy's basic isolation from the intimacies and responsibilities of traditional family life.

The isolation was probably inevitable, and perhaps even salutary. A religion that would survive in the modern world must speak to the increasing rootlessness of industrialized society. It must find a larger sense of family than nineteenth-century tribal mores encouraged. Mrs. Eddy, who had placed home and family at the apex of her scale of human values, was forced into the sort of loneliness that was really freedom to embrace, as she saw it, the "whole human family."[10] At this point of her development, she especially liked to compare her own followers to a family whose common loyalties would, hopefully, prevail over their internal squabbles. The incipient tendency among her followers to call her "Mother" and her own inclination to think and write of them as her "children" was an obvious if rudimentary example of this extension of the family concept beyond its common social and biological significations.

It remained a fact, however, that she had an actual son with an actual family. Mrs. Eddy wrote him, sent him money which he promptly lost in wildcat mining ventures, gave him advice regarding the education of his children, which he seldom took, and—since things had turned out as they had—was grateful on the whole that she could love him at a distance.

216

Late in October, 1887, she received word from him that he had decided to bring his wife and three children to stay with her for the winter. Consternation descended on 571 Columbus Avenue. The household was already overflowing its limited quarters. Seven classes were held there that year, with a total of 167 students—much the largest number Mrs. Eddy had ever taught in a twelve-month period. Students and visitors were constantly pouring in to consult her. The "enemy" was besieging her. Across the country the movement was growing. Her writing, editing, and publishing activities had never been greater. Her correspondence was oceanic. About this time she wrote a student, "Was so full of calls and perplexing questions last week I about lost my head and am sound this week, at least sound as usual."[11] And to another student she wrote three weeks later, "I am *daft* with business. . . . I am not doing for my church a tithe of what is needed."[12]

In the circumstances it is not surprising that she answered George Glover that Boston was the last place on earth for him and his family. She had asked him to come after Gilbert Eddy's death, when she needed him, and he had been too wrapped up in his mining ventures. Now it would be a positive disservice for him to arrive on her doorstep with plaintive wife and wailing children in tow. "I want quiet and a Christian life alone with God, when I can find intervals for a little rest," she wrote him, then added:

> *You are not what I had hoped to find you, and I am wholly changed. . . . When I retire from business and into private life then I can receive you if you are* reformed, *but not otherwise. I say this to* you *not to* any one else. *I would not injure* you *any more than myself.*[13]

Undismayed and undeterred, the Glovers came anyway. Mrs. Eddy was in the midst of a class, with another one to follow shortly, but she installed George and his family in a house in Chelsea across Boston Harbor and gave them what time she could. As always, her love of children came immediately to the rescue, and shortly afterward she took her grandchildren with her onto the platform of Chickering Hall at a Sunday service and introduced them to a somewhat surprised congregation. The family was invited to spend Thanksgiving Day with her, and once again Mrs. Mary Ann Baker was probably present at the festivities—as an indulgent member of the family this time rather than as a foil to a difficult guest.

But George and Nellie Glover simply failed to fit into Boston. Attracted there in the first place by Mrs. Eddy's growing fame and prosperity, they had no real interest in the purpose that gave meaning to her life. George, to be sure, thought it would be nice for Nellie to go through his mother's next class and learn about Christian Science, but Mrs. Eddy was more concerned with the whole family's learning to read and write. While he roamed aimlessly around Chelsea, booted and bearded like a character out of Bret Harte, Mrs. Eddy wrote him on March 1, 1888:

> *I want your children* educated. *No greater disgrace rests on my family name than the ignorance of the parents of these darling children.*
>
> *You could read in the Bible very well when you left your Mother long ago. It should be a shame to any one at any age not to be able to read. If I were 50 years old and could not read I would learn to do it then, even if I knew I should not live a year longer. . . .*
>
> *If [your wife] will read to me a page of Science and Health* wherever I open to it, *I will then talk with you about her joining my next class.*[14]

The attempt of the Glovers to find a reason for staying on in Boston was obviously doomed. After another three months, they trooped back to South Dakota and George's prospecting. Mrs. Eddy continued to send money and directions for the children's schooling and later built the family a "mansion" which became something of a showplace in Lead City. But apart from a few short visits to the East by George in later years, both mother and son accepted the futility of trying to combine their modes of living.

Mrs. Eddy herself had moved into a handsome new residence during the Christmas season of 1887. Weary of living in a schoolhouse, as she put it to George, she sought a little more quiet, space, and even elegance in which to carry on her daily labors. Classes were still held at 571 Columbus Avenue, but the bulk of her work was now tackled in the new house at 385 Commonwealth Avenue.

A notice in the January *Journal,* probably written by Wiggin in an excess of Bostonianism, described this "Material Change of Base" with a certain grandiloquence. Commonwealth Avenue was "the most fashionable in the city." Mrs. Eddy had as her neighbors "scores of Boston's wealthy and influential men." On nearby Beacon Street were "more families of note . . . the blue blood of Boston." There were murmurings among some of the more democratically-minded Scientists, but it was soon clear that the "material change of base" had altered nothing. Mrs. Eddy worked harder than ever, if that was possible, and showed no inclination to adopt the interests and pursuits of her blue-blooded neighbors.

In an article entitled "The Man for the Hour" in the *Journal* of February, 1887, Hanover P. Smith wrote with a certain orotund zeal:

> *I tell you, there must be struggles and victories; birth-throes of new thoughts; a strong, sturdy grapple with error; a laborious search, an irrepressible conflict for light and Truth. . . . We want men of rigid, steady purpose; men who are full of grim earnestness, tact and industry; who ingeniously toil toward a noble end with spontaneous fervor; with unwavering devotion to the Cause, even when the hope of reward may be relentlessly withholden.*

Young Smith himself, for all his faithfulness, was far from having the force of character described. But men of superior ability, men who would serve the church in important executive positions, were increasingly turning up. In that very year Mrs. Eddy taught three male students who would later be members of the Board of Directors of her reorganized church. One of these, Stephen A. Chase, a quiet little Quaker manufacturer from Fall River, Massachusetts, would also serve for many years as Treasurer of the church. Another, Joseph Armstrong, a husky lumberman and banker from Kansas, would be publisher of Mrs. Eddy's works. The third, Edward P. Bates, a businessman of Syracuse, New York, would first serve as a Trustee of the yet-to-be-established Christian Science Publishing Society.

Two men who, by the turn of the century, would stand before the general public as Christian Scientists more prominently than anyone save Mrs. Eddy herself were Alfred Farlow and Edward A. Kimball.

Young Farlow had first written her back in 1886 announcing that he, his brother, and two sisters desired intensely to study with her. They had previously had instruction from Mrs. Colman in Beatrice, Nebraska, and were now at work in Illinois. "We have left our yoke of oxen at home and have gone out empty handed," he wrote, and then went on to say:

> *We are only boys and girls. People hear of the faith doctors (as M.A.M. calls us) and expect to see an old gray bearded man with a crooked back and hooked nose . . . but when they find only a boy they are taken aback.*[15]

Later he wrote Mrs. Eddy that he was the eldest of eight children. His father, an affluent farmer, had met with reverses, and Alfred, then in college, had had to go home to help the family. "I have since acted as clerk, school master, traveling salesman, mechanic, anything to earn an honest living." Meanwhile, he had taken night courses in mathematics, Latin, the sciences, with the ultimate aim of entering the legal profession. But Christian Science had changed all that and "has placed me in my proper sphere."[16]

His proper sphere would eventually turn out to be that of chief publicist for Christian Science and official spokesman for Mrs. Eddy in his office of Manager of the Christian Science Committees on Publication. But as the May, 1887, Primary class started with Alfred and his brother William in attendance, the former's special proclivity emerged in an account which he wrote for the *Gage County* (Illinois) *Democrat* of the first impact of the teacher and the class on him. He was astonished to find that Mrs. Eddy, then in her mid-sixties, had "the bloom of youth" and could easily be taken for forty. Her class now in session, he continued, was composed of sixteen ladies and sixteen gentlemen:

> *Some are ministers, some lawyers, some doctors, merchants, mechanics, farmers, etc., who are as a rule people of sense and ability. We make this statement simply to show that the followers of Mrs. Eddy are those who will push the work, and to one who understands Christian Science it is plain that the little leaven will leaven the whole lump.*[17]

Certainly he would push the work and help to leaven the lump. A few months after the class had ended, both his parents in Nebraska became Christian Science practitioners. In a short time Mrs. Eddy was writing him, "By all means *lecture* and do all in your power for the prevention of error and the support of Truth."[18] Nine months later, in writing her about his lecturing in the Middle West, he told of the effort of pulpit and press to damn Christian Science by misstating it:

> *This effort I have endeavored to meet by holding up the Christianity of Science, the true idea of it. I try to show the difference between Christian Science and mind cure. . . . I try to be kind in my address and above all to practice and bring out in my life what I preach. I know my inability, in belief, my fallibility.*[19]

Farlow shared with Edward A. Kimball, who studied with her in March, 1888, the qualities of humility, common sense, and breadth of outlook, but Kimball brought to Christian Science a large clarity of mind which made his service to the growing movement almost unique. At last Mrs. Eddy had found a student who answered to the demands of her statement, "The time for thinkers has come."[20] It was not a matter of intellectual brilliance or wide-ranging scholarship, but of calm, penetrating insight into the very structure and substance of her thought.

As Kimball in later years expounded Christian Science to an audience, its abstractions became live, vertebrate, and warmly relevant to the human situation. In time, Mrs. Eddy would put many of the most promising students of Christian Science into his hands for preparation as practitioners and teachers. Many Christian Scientists today would rate his metaphysical contributions only below those of Mrs. Eddy herself. With no more than public-school education, augmented by a successful business career and European travel, he was able by the spiritual power and logical persuasiveness of his lectures to draw overflow audiences to the Queen's Hall in London and Emerson Hall at Harvard University, as well as to coliseums, opera houses, concert halls in New York, Chicago, San Francisco, and a host of lesser cities. To sophisticated Europeans he may well have seemed an example of Henry James's self-made American nobleman, a Christopher Newman "born again" into the lucid life of the spirit.

Not that Kimball emerged at once into prominence after going through Mrs. Eddy's class with his wife Kate. Returning to their home in Chicago, the two chose to study and practice Christian Science quietly until they felt thoroughly grounded in it. Four years later, when the Chicago church asked Kimball to become its pastor, he wrote Mrs. Eddy that his thoughts on the invitation could be summed up in two words: unprepared and unworthy.

This slow ripening process contrasts favorably with the more rapid but short-lived emergence of two other men in 1888: Frank E. Mason and Ebenezer J. Foster.

Little is known of Mason's background. He was a bluff, hearty, jovial man, physically robust and mentally vigorous. Although irreligious before embracing Christian Science, he was quick to respond to Mrs. Eddy's teaching and became a prolific writer for the *Journal*, contributing especially a series of lengthy biblical expositions. Soon he was assistant pastor of the Church of Christ, Scientist, in Boston, preaching most of the time except when Mrs. Eddy herself took the pulpit. She encouraged him to embark on English studies that would help him to improve his literary style and devoted time and care to his spiritual education, with the hope that he might succeed her as head of the Metaphysical College.[21] But the energy of character which so appealed to her was coupled with a certain hotheadedness, and after three or four years Mason rocketed off into historical oblivion.

Ebenezer J. Foster, M.D., was a different kind of person—a quiet-spoken man, kindly, undistinguished, with a love of music and flowers, his greatest faults a personal vanity that ran toward dandyism and a susceptibility to flattery. After graduating from the Hahnemann Medical College in Philadelphia, he settled down to a comfortable homeopathic practice in Waterbury, Vermont, until he was forty. In that year, 1887, he was attracted to Christian Science by healings he had witnessed, and before the end of the year he had entered one of Mrs. Eddy's classes.

This was the class she was teaching just as George Glover and his family turned up in Boston. The two men were almost the same age—Glover was forty-three—but in all other respects they stood in striking contrast: the one roughhewn, bumbling, hopefully trying to cash in on his mother's prosperity; the other a little too smooth, but affectionate, genuinely devoted, eager to do whatever would lighten his teacher's load. Foster seems to have adopted the term "Mother" for Mrs. Eddy almost immediately, and in his letters to her after leaving the class he referred to himself as "your child." In the year that followed she relied on him more and more for help, and toward the end of 1888 she legally adopted him as her son.

The adoption reveals Mrs. Eddy's continued hunger for intimacy, for the kind of service that only a son could give. With all his faithfulness, Calvin Frye did not fill the bill; there was something a little dry and unnourishing about his devotion. In Foster, on the other hand, there seemed to be not only some of Gilbert Eddy's Vermont simplicity, but also a touch of that opulence of nature which had won her heart in Daniel Patterson. In time the rigors of her leadership would expose this strain of emotional extravagance as weakness. Eventually Foster would vanish from the scene, showing that ideal sons are not made any more than they are born, but for the first few years his position as Mrs. Eddy's personal spokesman gave him immense prestige among her followers.

At times the Christian Science leader longed to be merely a woman. While Edward and Kate Kimball were studying with her, they paid a visit to her at 385 Commonwealth Avenue, and Mrs. Kimball later described the incident:

> We were taken up to her private sitting room which was on the second floor, and she looked so different from her first appearance before us as a teacher when she rather loomed as a tall woman and a manifestation of power. On this occasion she sat curled up in an easy rocking chair, and looked rather small and delicate, and she said she deeply wished sometimes that she could be a little old lady in a cap with nothing much to do.[22]

More characteristically Mrs. Eddy wrote to another student about this time:

Your trials are many. God is testing you and you are being found faithful. . . . *He scourgeth every son whom he receiveth. This is the first time for 21 years that I have not been* flooded *with* all sorts. *And now I can bear the floods for there are intervals between them and God has given me more strength in Spirit to* wait *on* Him.[23]

In her renewed encounters with the floods, some of her strongest support continued to come from women. Most of the pioneer work in far-off areas was still done by women. Men might increasingly fill executive positions, but a large part of the healing work was done by women

There was, for instance, Annie Macmillan Knott, a Scots-Canadian housewife and mother who was now carrying on a large healing practice in Detroit. Mrs. Knott—a tiny, feminine figure with a voice deep as a man's and a heart stout as a lion's—would serve the cause with distinction as practitioner, teacher, lecturer, writer, and editor. When the public showed itself loath to invite her to lecture because she was a woman, Mrs. Eddy informed her energetically that she must "rise to the altitude of true womanhood" and then the whole world would want her.[24] As a result, the invitations began to flow in, and Mrs. Knott welcomed the opportunity to prove that she could "declare the truth" as well as a man. Fittingly enough, she became in 1919 the first woman member of the church's Board of Directors.

There was a whole constellation of talented women in Chicago who would give service as Christian Science teachers and church builders, as well as healers—Mrs. Mary Adams, Mrs. Elizabeth Webster, Mrs. Ruth Ewing, Mrs. Hannah Larminie, and others. There were in Denver two socially prominent girls just out of their teens, Minnie and Nettie Hall, who, along with their mother, would often treat a hundred patients a day and have to turn others away from the door. There was Sue Ella Bradshaw in San Francisco and Lou Aldrich in Arkansas and Clara Shannon in Montreal and Marjorie Colles in Northern Ireland and Annie Dodge, the teen-age daughter of an American general, who would open services in London in 1889 with the counsel of Mrs. Colles.

Meanwhile, in New York, Laura Lathrop was finding the demand on her for healing so great that she could hardly get time to teach. But she did find time to run down to Washington and conduct a class which included Susan B. Anthony, Phoebe Cozzens, and Mrs. Mark Hopkins. Following each daily session she would hurry over to the palatial residence of Senator Leland Stanford to give private instruction to the senator's wife.

Back in New York, she had to come to terms with Augusta

Stetson, who had been sent there by Mrs. Eddy in 1886 to use her conspicuous preaching talents to help advance the work. Mrs. Stetson was greatly distrusted by the other Christian Scientists in the area, and Silas Sawyer (whom Mrs. Eddy used as a kind of troubleshooter) was sent to pacify the waters. When Mrs. Lathrop and Mrs. Stetson, under Sawyer's guidance, joined forces to hold a first church service in January, 1888, Mrs. Lathrop was completely won over by Mrs. Stetson's sermon. "I never loved her so much as when I heard her preach," she wrote Mrs. Eddy afterwards.[25] But two months later she amended her report to add that Sawyer looked old and worn, trying to steer between the Scylla and Charybdis of the New York Scientists, while she herself had gone back to her first opinion of Mrs. Stetson as underhanded, hypocritical, and supremely selfish.

In scores of situations across the country Mrs. Eddy had now to chide and guide, encourage and mediate, in addition to her immediate labors in Boston. At her instigation a National Christian Scientist Association had been formed in 1886. It was open not only to those of her own Christian Scientist Association who chose to join, but also to the members of all other teachers' associations to which she had granted charters. The annual meeting of the new organization in 1887 had brought together about one hundred and fifty representatives from fifteen states. Mrs. Eddy had sent an urgent invitation to attend:

> I have gotten up this N.C.S.A. for you and the life of the cause. I have something important to say to you, a message from God.
>
> Will you not meet this one request of your teacher and let nothing hinder it? If you do not I shall never make another to you and give up the struggle.[26]

Her address to the convention was not recorded, but in a subsequent letter to a student who had not been able to attend she gave a brief outline of it:

> The "message" was an appeal to my students to look over their minds and examine their desires and see what they are. I find the desires not as consecrated as their words and works, that they need purging and purifying. That selfishness weighs too much in the scale of action, and this self-love must be rooted out or our Cause will drift into the wrong direction.
>
> To accomplish this I counseled them to pray mentally for a great uplifting and spiritualization of their desire. This must be done by daily prayer and watchfulness. It must be done by careful self-examination and separating the right from the wrong

motives and being governed in our actions only by the purely unselfish motive.

I know this growth in grace is what my students need at this present time to give them more power in healing and teaching. The time has come for them to wax stronger and more valiant in the Truth.[27]

The urgency of her message can be understood only in the light of what was happening outside the ranks of her committted followers.

3

A year earlier A. J. Swarts had held a convention of assorted mind-curers in Chicago. Among those present was Luther M. Marston, M.D., from Boston, a disaffected student of Mrs. Eddy's, whom the *Chicago Tribune* described laconically as "a man with an immense amount of black whisker and very little voice."[28]

Marston was a slightly more respectable Swarts, and his *Mental Healing Monthly* was a more staid Bostonian version of Swarts's *Mental Science Magazine*. After his return from Chicago, he incorporated a "Boston College of Metaphysical Science," with himself as president, and published a book, *Essentials of Mental Healing*. Although in his advertising he was careful to borrow what prestige he could from being a "Normal Graduate of the Massachusetts Metaphysical College" he made no acknowledgments to Mrs. Eddy, and the one mention of Christian Science was in the preface to his book, which simply stated that he recognized and explained "the principles of 'Christian Science,' 'prayer-and-faith cure,' and 'other methods of metaphysical and psychical treatment of disease, which have a common basis in truth."[29]

The book and the magazine were products of a rational, educated, but commonplace mind, "intellectual" in a mild, unoriginal way. If Emerson complained of the pale negatives of Boston Unitarianism, a similar complaint might be brought against the pale positives of Boston mind-cure. "The great question is, what is it that heals?" wrote Marston." The power that heals is . . . eclectic, is catholic in the broadest meaning of the term. It is the spiritual part of modern Christianity, of Paganism, Brahmanism, Buddhism, Mohammedanism, and all other isms."[30]

This amorphous eclecticism found expression also in the Church of the Divine Unity (Scientist) founded by Marston and his friends late in 1886 and "catholic in the broadest meaning of the term." Soon it became the focal (or at least vocal) point for most of the dissidents in Boston—disaffected Christian Scientists, mind-curers, faith healers, magnetic doctors, amalgamators with spiritism and theosophy, and it enjoyed as a patron that perennial Transcendentalist, Cyrus Bartol, who found its vague inspirationalism more congenial to his anti-nomian soul than Mrs. Eddy's rigorous metaphysics.

What was missing in all these sanguine systems was Mrs. Eddy's acute sense of the difference between wishful thinking and exacting fact, her insistence on the inexorable demands of scientific truth. "Truth is the rock of ages," she wrote, "the headstone of the corner, 'but on whomsoever it shall fall, it will grind him to powder.' "[31] Christian Science was not just a way to get well or achieve peace of mind, certainly not a sentimental posture or a psychological technique prettied up with a little Christian terminology. It was, as she saw it, the "law of God,"[32] a law which demanded fearful surrenders—of her quite as much as of any other person who aspired to the rewards of obedience. In this respect scientific and Christian disciplines were strangely alike. In *Science and Health* she wrote:

> *Wisdom and Love may require many sacrifices of self to save us from sin. One sacrifice, however great, is insufficient to pay the debt of sin. The atonement requires constant self-immolation on the sinner's part.*[33]

This was more than a theological argument. The way of science was quite as strait and narrow as the way of salvation. An easy eclecti-cism, shaped by personal preference, was no more a virtue for the scientist than a rigid dogmatism would be. The first requirement of scientific integrity was a willingness to put the demands of fact before any other convenience or commitment. This remained true at what-ever level of fact one penetrated to. Though the scientist himself might avoid the words "truth" and "reality," the metaphysician was necessarily committeed to that ultimate factuality which is properly denominated truth—to a structure of reality shaped not by his prefer-ences but by being itself.

Some of Mrs. Eddy's severest struggles came from the necessity of surrendering deeply entrenched personal inclinations to the logic of truth as it confronted her. God was the ultimate power before which one said, in agony and in ecstasy, "Not my will, but thine, be done." The mind-curers who all held in one way or another to the theory of the "God within,"[34] were troubled by no such necessity. It was a simple matter to deify one's own inclinations. As a result, the Church of the Divine Unity was rather more of a polyglot pantheon than a temple dedicated to the single-minded pursuit of truth.

It was here, in February, 1887, that Julius Dresser gave his address, "The True History of Mental Science," which was afterward printed in the *Mental Healing Monthly*. Six months later the editorship of that journal passed to the religiously peripatetic William Gill, and at the same time Marston announced, "We have for some time seen the necessity of confining the Monthly more strictly to the teachings of Christian or Divine Science." While almost the only thing that really united the members of the Church of the Divine Unity was their opposition to the Founder of Christian Science, they, like dissidents elsewhere, were increasingly feeling a need for the name if not the substance of her discovery.

Even Swarts, who had once had the cockiness to send Mrs. Plunkett to Mrs. Eddy to propose a merger of *The Christian Science Journal* with his *Mental Science Magazine* provided the word Christian could be dropped, now found it expedient on occasion to use the term "Christian Science" to describe his own teachings. Mrs. Plunkett and Mrs. Hopkins had never ceased to call themselves Christian Scientists, and when they started a monthly journal in November, 1887, they named it *Truth, A Magazine of Christian Science*. Joseph Adams, who was far closer to genuine Christian Science, called his monthly publication *The Chicago Christian Scientist*. Young Albert Dorman, who was still a member of the Christian Scientist Association and on precariously good terms with Mrs. Eddy,[35] described his popular little paper, the *Messenger of Truth,* as "Devoted to Metaphysical, Mental, or Divine Healing in Strict Accordance with Christian Science."

It was a chaotic situation, in which people who had never so much as read *Science and Health* tried to pass themselves off as Christian Scientists and graduates of the Massachusetts Metaphysical College. Mrs. Eddy, in order to protect the public from this sort of imposture, advised anyone seeking help from a healer who claimed to be a student of hers to ask to see his annually renewed certificate to that effect, and her action was at once hailed by her critics as an attempt to monopolize the field. Mrs. Plunkett, on the other hand, paid her a special visit to propose with casual effrontery that they should divide the Christian Science field between them, she taking everything west of the Mississippi and Mrs. Eddy everything east of it. Mrs. Eddy rejected the proposal with contempt and Mrs. Plunkett departed in rage.[36]

Book after book appeared, borrowing Mrs. Eddy's terminology, her ideas, often her very words, but losing the whole structure and character of her thought. Writers and lecturers who insisted that they were Christian Scientists railed against her exclusivism, her claim to a divine mission, her exercise of authority, her teaching about animal magnetism, her style, her metaphysics, and in effect called her a liar, a thief, a fraud, a tyrant, a fanatic, and a fool. Others praised her to the skies and claimed her sanction for ideas and practices which she had explicitly disapproved.[37]

The public was totally bewildered and Mrs. Eddy at times almost desperate. "There are 20 false lecturers and teachers to one that is true," she wrote Ellen Brown on one occasion; and on another, "All you say of the great lack of [those who falsely claim to practice Christian Science healing] is known to me and that is why like the lioness robbed of her young I am more savage over the symptoms of their taking others [to teach]."[38] A male student in Chicago wrote her in amazement, "They all look like a company of school children, playing truant and keeping school for themselves."[39]

On October 19, 1887, these "truant" healers met for a two-day convention at the Parker Memorial Hall in Boston, where Mrs. Eddy had preached eight years before. They were all there: Marston, Gill, Swarts, Dresser, the Mesdames Plunkett, Hopkins, Choate, Stuart, and a host of others. No one agreed with anyone else, but everyone got a hearing. A Hopkins fan reported in the first issue of *Truth* that her idol was introduced to the convention as "the star that rose in the East and has spread its glory through the West,"[40] but there were plenty of other stars to dispute her primacy. Mrs. Plunkett, who in the same issue of *Truth* poured adulation on "our beloved leader [Emma Hopkins]," had, in a burst of candor or perhaps in a calculated policy move, told the conference, "People have tried to get truth in various ways, but the world never knew how to get it until it came through 'Science and Health.' "[41]

Mrs. Eddy, in her very absence, loomed over the gathering as an almost palpable challenge. With a kind of bitter weariness she read of their veiled attacks on her and of their assurance of easy success to all and sundry. "Today," she wrote in the next issue of the *Journal*, "Christian Science is sold in the shambles. Many are bidding for it, but are not willing to pay the price."[42] Eighteen months earlier, writing a student about those who felt that with the appearance of the sixteenth edition of *Science and Health* they could now "see the meaning of Christian Science," she had burst out suddenly: "O! do they see it? How little they dream of the awfulness of its heights and depths."[43]

After almost a century it would be easy to dismiss the Boston conference of mental healers as a comic-opera affair, a somewhat desiccated replica of the Chardon Street Convention described so wittily by Emerson, but to Mrs. Eddy it was something quite different. If Christian Science was to become a term that would mean whatever any ambitious claimant wanted it to mean, then truth would again be lost through dismemberment, perversion, fraud, and sheer trivialization. There were more ways than one of killing a new idea.

4

During the years 1887 and 1888 a renewed emphasis on animal magnetism grew up in the Christian Science movement. The earlier term "malicious mesmerism" was gradually replaced by the phrase "malicious animal magnetism," often referred to familiarly by Christian Scientists of that period as M. A. M.[44] A monthly column in the *Journal* entitled "Animal Magnetism" reprinted items on hypnotism from other publications (including comments on the work of Charcôt and Bernheim) and ran original articles (including Mrs. Eddy's highly charged "Ways That Are Vain")[45] on recognizing and handling the sort of suggestions imposed on thought by outside circumstance or agency.

The new department was greeted with derision by the mind-curers, who almost to a man scoffed at the thought that they were influenced by anything but their own freely arrived at opinions. With the brashness of a psychologically naive age, they sniped at Mrs. Eddy in full ignorance of both the oedipal conflicts involved in their hostility and the powerful environmental influences driving them toward spiritual anarchy.

To them she represented the figure of matriarchal authority whom they must escape even while they sought to appropriate what they supposed to be the substance of her discovery—not to mention the prestige of her name. The result was a love-hate relationship which frequently revealed itself in the ambivalence of their references to her.[46]

In Mrs. Eddy's vocabulary, this was clear evidence of animal magnetism, the attempt of material-mindedness to separate spiritual truth from its human mouthpiece. Her denunciation of the attempt was actually a definition of the problem. A good example of this was her reply to Dresser's lecture on Quimby after it had been printed in the *Mental Healing Monthly* with an additional scatter of bird shot from Marston.

Dresser, she wrote caustically, had again let loose the dogs of war. "In other words, he has loosed from the leash his pet poodle, to alternately bark and whine at my heels." In his lecture he had exaggerated and fabricated in Quimby's behalf, but that at least was kind:

> I commend gratitude, even in the child who hates his mother; and this gratitude should be a lesson to that suckling

229

littérateur, Mr. Marston, whom I taught, and whose life I saved three years ago, but who now squeaks out an echo of Mr. Dresser's abuse.[47]

One is reminded by such a passage of Franklin Pierce's comment about her brother Albert in a letter in 1841: "I have rarely noticed a more easy, off-hand facility for saying very provoking things that it were difficult to gainsay and mighty hard to bear."[48] Quite understandably, those whom Mrs. Eddy castigated were frequently enraged, and she herself came to feel more and more the uselessness of such sallies.

In the first edition of *No and Yes* she pointed sharply to abuses in the practice of mental science and named names; in the second, the names disappeared; and in the third, the whole section on animal magnetism was dropped—all within a few months of the book's first publication. As one of her students wrote her when the third edition came out, "It is more like what I think of you as being *in fact— no acidity.*"[49] Ten years later when she gathered the *Journal* articles of this period into a new book, *Miscellaneous Writings,* she wrote in the preface, "In compiling this work, I have tried to remove the pioneer signs and ensigns of war, and to retain at this date the privileged armaments of peace."[50]

Yet the war while it lasted was a war to the death. Mrs. Eddy saw it as a struggle with "error"; her critics and even some of her students saw it as a conflict with persons. Her own development during these years marked a steady growth toward "impersonalizing error," and she had to bring her older students along with her in this process.[51]

In one way, the whole of Christian Science was an effort to lift the individual out of a limited, personal sense of things into a realm of thought where perfect freedom was the unhampered operation of universal and impersonal law.[52] In this effort the real enemy was the concept of life as finite, contingent, self-devouring. As Mrs. Eddy wrote one student:

> *Was* sorry, sorry *to learn of the discord among the students who are acquiring the* Science *of harmony. . . . Why can they not learn when these tares spring up among the wheat that, as the Scripture says, "an enemy has done this." If only they knew the cause and did not conclude it sprang from legitimate sources they would master the error.*[53]

Probably no part of her teaching was less understood. The students were constantly seeing the source of their troubles in other *persons*. They tended at times to idolize Mrs. Eddy personally, then again to resent as a personal affront the sharp rebukes she sometimes gave them. She, on the other hand, felt such rebukes to be part of the healing process—the shock tactics of spiritual therapy, directed at the "error" rather than the person. It required a kind of heroic humility, sometimes, to accept a rebuke in that spirit, but many accounts have come down of healings, physical and otherwise, which resulted from learning to make the discrimination.[54]

Some of Mrs. Eddy's clashes with gifted but maverick students are susceptible of two different interpretations, depending on whether they are seen as merely personal rivalries or in terms of relative commitment to an impersonal value system—a commitment, in her words, to "truth."

This is the key issue which arises in the case of Ursula N. Gestefeld.

Mrs. Gestefeld had studied with Mrs. Eddy in Chicago in 1884. A month later the new student had written her teacher in regard to the deplorable lack of intellectual and social standing that Christian Science had on Chicago's North Side: "I *will* make people respect and believe it sometime. I want to make money, I admit, but that shall be with me a secondary consideration."[55]

It was a less than winning start for an equivocal career. Soon extremely well-written articles on Christian Science by Mrs. Gestefeld began to appear in various newspapers and journals, including mind-cure publications. Seldom did they mention or quote Mrs. Eddy, but they presented her ideas as though they were Mrs. Gestefeld's own. Mrs. Eddy watched with wary appreciation of her student's literary and forensic skills. When a Chicago speaker complained that Christian Scientists charged for treatment whereas Christianity was free to all, Mrs. Gestefeld wrote with characteristic coolness:

> *I have never been able, with but few exceptions, to hear what is called the word of God preached regularly, without pay-ing for it. He who proclaimed it was in duty bound to pay the butcher and grocer, just as did those who listened to him.*[56]

Mrs. Eddy at one point asked Mrs. Gestefeld to become a special contributor to *The Christian Science Journal,* but the continued reservation in her mind even while she made the request is apparent from her comment: "I have not been able to learn from your lips what your feelings are on the *Christian* side of this Cause." Yet that, she added, "is the only side."[57]

It was not the only side for Mrs. Gestefeld, whose catholicity permitted her to be a member of the Theosophical Society of Chicago and also to pay her calm respects to the current gods of material success. There was little Christianity apparent in her writings, though a good deal of self-possessed rationality, and it is not surprising that her relations with Mrs. Eddy became somewhat tangential.

Finally appeared a book which was announced as Ursula N. Gestefeld's *Statement of Christian Science, Comprised in Eighteen Lessons and Twelve Sections.* A circular sent out on June 9, 1888, read in part:

> *This work is not intended to supplant* Science and Health, *but is offered as a key for those who are unable to discern its meaning. The book* Science and Health, *first published in 1875, was the first statement of Christian Science given to the public. Though many publications of the same nature are in wide circulation to-day, it still stands pre-eminent among them as the text-book of the Science, because its statements are positive, exact, and unmixed with theory. It is yea, yea; nay, nay. At the same time it is a book difficult of comprehension, and much patient study of it, for many, does not suffice for an understanding of its meaning.*[58]

Despite this advertisement, Mrs. Gestefeld's *Statement of Christian Science* did not burden itself with references to Mrs. Eddy and *Science and Health* but borrowed vastly without acknowledgment. The general impression it left with the uninitiated reader was that Mrs. Gestefeld had cleverly thought this up all by herself. On the first page she established the tone of simple clarity that she sought:

> *To you who say that there is no evidence of the existence of God this question is put:*
> *Have you any evidence of your own existence?*
> *"Surely," you answer.*
> *How?*
> *"Because we are conscious of existence; we are conscious of a power to think."*
> *Descartes' statement in another form:*
> *"I think, therefore I am!"*
> *Just so. We are conscious of a power of thought. Then consider for a moment this possibility. If we think up to God shall we not find Him, become conscious of Him as we become conscious of all things?*[59]

The only trouble was that the author was building on sand. The semantic hurricanes of the next century would thoroughly demolish Descartes' great axiom, and Mrs. Gestefeld's surface intellectuality would look oddly outmoded beside the opening sentence with which the first chapter of *Science and Health* plunges *in medias res*:

The prayer that reforms the sinner and heals the sick is an absolute faith that all things are possible to God,—a spiritual understanding of Him, an unselfed love.[60]

Mrs. Gestefeld, for all the reasonableness of her tone, could drop crucial elements of Mrs. Eddy's logic without realizing that she thereby undercut her whole argument. This is particularly clear in her treatment of the origin of evil.

The only metaphysically valid explanation, according to Mrs. Eddy, was that evil, being a lie, was non-entity and therefore had no origin. So regarded, it could be wiped out as false supposition or pretension, whereas any attempt to find a logical explanation for it would be, in effect, an attempt to legitimize it—to give it a logical place in the eternal scheme of things. The answer to the problem of evil's origin must therefore be not a rationalization but a rescue, a practical *healing* of false appearances.

It seems probable that Mrs. Gestefeld had not so much rejected this approach as not grasped it. In her chapter on the origin of evil, she wrote of evil as coming from "nowhere" and as being not even an "it," and in that respect she was in agreement with Mrs. Eddy's fundamental position. The question which confronted them both was where and how the capacity to *believe* in evil arose, and at that point Mrs. Gestefeld fell back on a variant form of the traditional "fall of man":

Man conceives, because of his power to think which is his from God. . . . His conceptions are either his cognition of all that is . . . or they are his own creations; conceptions which are a departure from truth which, expressed or externalized, are real to him because he sees them; and they shut out the perception of what really is, or what God's creations are.[61]

Quite evidently she has not even noticed that in giving this explanation she has abandoned the basic logical structure of Christian Science. Mrs. Eddy had insisted that an all-wise, all-loving, all-powerful God could not create a man *capable* of falling into error; therefore a sinful mortal was not God's man gone wrong but a lie about man, and the lie was to be systematically rejected as ontologically unreal.

Mrs. Eddy knew as well as anyone that such a view stood philosophy on its head, but she had arrived at it not as a feat of abstract intellection but by deduction from a thrust of concrete insight. In her earliest teaching she had simply dismissed evil as a logical impossibility in a perfect spiritual universe and had felt, in her later words, as strong "as a little giant" in her conviction of the allness of good. But suddenly one day, when George Barry asked her how she accounted for human error, the magnitude of the question rushed in on her and she saw the whole issue of truth and error as literally a matter of life-and-death struggle.[62]

This kind of struggle was obviously well beyond the comprehension of the self-assured Mrs. Gestefeld—or, for that matter, the rapturous Mrs. Hopkins, who could dismiss the problem of evil by appeal to the "vivific Life-Principle" which "thrills and shivers through me."[63] But to Mrs. Eddy the answer to Barry's question had to be beaten out by day-to-day demonstration of the supremacy of good, not by retreat to shopworn theodicies and second-rate ecstasies.

In view of all this, her first response to Mrs. Gestefeld's *Statement of Christian Science* was surprisingly mild. She simply forwarded to the letter column of the *Journal* a missive from a correspondent who wrote: "I recognize the same difference between Mrs. Gestefeld's Lectures and your book, that I do between the zeal of Saul and the zeal of Paul. Her Lectures lack regeneration. She has not yet been to Damascus."[64]

This was enough to sting Mrs. Gestefeld into an immediate counteroffensive, delivered in her usual tone of cool and slightly exasperated reasonableness. A pamphlet by her entitled *Jesuitism in Christian Science* appeared with lightning speed. In it she argued plausibly that Mrs. Eddy had no more monopoly on Christian Science than the first writer of a textbook on mathematics has a monopoly on that subject. Like any science, Divine Science existed independent of a particular discoverer:

> *Mrs. Eddy claims that her only text-book was the Bible. Then Christian Science as a whole, from premise to conclusions is in the Bible; and that book is common property. What is to prevent any one from finding in it what she had found and giving it in their turn? . . .*
>
> *And if Christian Science is Divine Science and one found it in the Bible and re-stated it, would he not, of necessity, say what Mrs. Eddy has said? Would he be blinded by "mad ambition" because he did so? Would it be arrogant presumption on his part?*[65]

A captious critic might reply that theoretically any number of people could deduce Newton's theory of gravitation from the same facts which led Newton to it, but that a "restatement" of it by a high-school boy who had been studying it in an elementary physics course might justly be considered a trifle redundant, not to say questionable. The fact was that Mrs. Gestefeld had not "found [Christian Science] in the Bible and then re-stated it" in words necessarily like Mrs. Eddy's. She had found it in *Science and Health* and had consciously paraphrased Mrs. Eddy's statement of it in so far as she grasped its meaning.

The urbanity of Mrs. Gestefeld's attack could not altogether conceal its lethal intent, and Mrs. Eddy at last replied directly in the *Journal*. In teaching this student, she wrote, she had found that her mind "presented a compilation of other minds"and that it possessed, to a remarkable degree, the qualities of vanity, intellectual dash, and courage without conviction. Her present criticism of her teacher's works was "at least, silly," and the picture she drew of Mrs. Eddy in her pamphlet was the subjective state of her own mind.

The members of the Chicago church had wanted, for many months, to expel Mrs. Gestefeld from membership for reasons connected with her local behavior, but Mrs. Eddy had urged them not to, in order to give her a chance to reform. Now it became evident to the members that she actually hoped to be expelled, so that she might gain the advantage of being a martyr to free speech, and some of them hesitated to give her that satisfaction.[66] But as her animosity increased, the step became inevitable. Mrs. Eddy finally advised the Chicago church to drop her with dispatch. It did, and Mrs. Gestefeld thereupon joined in uneasy alliance with the Hopkins-Plunkett forces and their mind-cure cohorts.

But the villain, from Mrs. Eddy's point of view, was none of these intellectually dashing ladies. It was the human mind's resistance to the impersonal demands of truth, in whatever terms conceived.

5

To an age in which molecular biology is opening the door to genetic engineering, Wordsworth's "Ode on Intimations of Immortality from Recollections of Early Childhood" speaks with a kind of faraway innocence:

> Our birth is but a sleep and a forgetting:
> The Soul that rises with us, our life's Star,
> Hath had elsewhere its setting,
> And cometh from afar:
> Not in entire forgetfulness,
> And not in utter nakedness,
> But trailing clouds of glory do we come
> From God, who is our home.

Mrs. Eddy was no Wordsworthian romantic. However much she might differ with the Calvinist of her youth who saw the newborn child as a little bundle of iniquity, predestined for damnation, or the scientific materialist of today who sees it as a small chaos of self-centered appetencies, predestined for eventual extinction, she nevertheless recognized the cosmic judgment under which all flesh stands. She did, however, find intimations of immortality in childhood's visionary grasp of a reality beyond the senses. And linking this with her New Testament faith, she held that of such is the kingdom of heaven.

Beyond the wonder and absurdity of human birth lay the metaphysical fact of man's pre-existent being. Man not as homunculus, but as idea. The child of flesh must be born again, born of Spirit, discovered in Mind. What was most to be loved in the child was what Jesus loved—that hint of a selfhood rooted in original innocence rather than in original sin. But the child no less than the man required a rescue that was also a revelation. He needed, like the Prodigal Son, to "come to himself."

On February 26, 1888, Mrs. Eddy presided at the first and last christening service ever held in a Christian Science church. Her three grandchildren, still in Chelsea at that time, were among the twenty-nine children on whom she pronounced a simple blessing, without any use of water. It was an experimental concession to orthodoxy that was really anomalous in view of her definition of baptism: "Purification by Spirit; submergence in Spirit."[67] But it signified her recognition that even the "innocent" child needed to be rescued from the web of mortality, to find its true, immortal being as the sinless child of God.

Two days later Mrs. Eddy wrote J. Henry Wiggin in connection with a change of wording to which he had objected:

> *Where you said the meaning was obscure I had to make the change to preserve the* scientific *statement. Mortals do not develop into immortals. A man no more starts a mortal, conceived and born through false process and material—and comes out a babe or man born of Spirit—than the eternal idea of Truth starts [as] a lie or develops into truth, and is truth born of a lie!*[68]

In the Christian Science scheme of things, this had a practical bearing on the birth as well as the upbringing of children. A good deal of Mrs. Eddy's correspondence with her students had to do with these two subjects.

Among her students were Francis J. Fluno, M.D., of Lexington, Kentucky, and his wife Ella. Both wrote ably for the *Journal*, and Mrs. Fluno described on one occasion the experience of painless childbirth that she, in common with many other Christian Scientists, had had.[69] She had been able to get up the day following the delivery and do her housework, which included carrying water from the well.

When the young parents sent a picture of the baby to Mrs. Eddy, she replied with a burst of feminine delight, "It looks like a cherub, the image of an artist's thought," but added:

> You must not love it too much, remember it is a thing of mortal as well as immortal Mind, and transfer your love from the little sweet personality to the idea you would embody in this lovely child. Then you can build for time and eternity a child that is God's pure and undying thought.[70]

Quite apart from the existential questions involved, human birth offered the Christian Science practitioner a problem somewhat different from the healing of disease. During 1887 Mrs. Eddy held two one-week classes on the subject of obstetrics, attended by a number of her most experienced students. The object was not to fit them to act as doctors or midwives, but to prepare them to cope spiritually with the various phases of "false belief" connected with childbirth.

This necessarily meant getting rather deeply into the nature of mortal existence, and some of her students found these the most challenging classes they ever had with her. Mrs. Eddy herself, at the end of the first course, wrote a student that it was "the hardest and the best class I ever taught," the one "best suited to the propulsion of the student."[71] Socrates had compared himself to a midwife helping to bring forth the true ideas already latent in his pupils' thinking, and a letter from Laura Lathrop to Mrs. Eddy at the end of the second course draws a similar analogy. She had never suffered more in bearing her two children, wrote Mrs. Lathrop, than in admitting to herself the truth that would enable her to lift this burden for others.[72]

Among the accounts of healing which flowed in constantly to Mrs. Eddy were numerous incidents of painless childbirth,[73] but the case that was to achieve historic notoriety was of a different character. It arose in connection with one of Mrs. Eddy's students, Mrs. Abby H. Corner, of West Medford, a suburb of Boston. In the spring of 1888 Mrs. Corner acted as practitioner for her daughter at the time of the latter's confinement. There were complications when the delivery took place, and both the daughter and her child were lost. Sensational stories appeared in the press. Mrs. Corner was hastily indicted for manslaughter, and the Boston Christian Scientists seethed with indignation and alarm.

Mrs. Eddy's attitude was one of thoughtful concern. She assured her students that there was no legal case against Mrs. Corner and turned out to be right. The defendant was, in fact, promptly acquitted by a jury on the ground that medical science could not have prevented the hemorrhage that was the cause of death.[74] But there were human and policy aspects of the situation which went beyond the legal question.

It would be easy, Mrs. Eddy saw, for the public to assume that Christian Science might be helpful in cases of normal childbirth but useless where there were complications. The years that followed were to bring forth repeated instances where abnormal conditions were rectified and safe deliveries brought about through Christian Science treatment,[75] but a single failure could revive the old bugaboo—if a qualified obstetrician were not present to perform the ordinary physical services. A Christian Science practitioner was neither trained nor entitled to act as a midwife, except in those rare cases where he or she had a previous medical degree or in those emergency situations where any willing bystander has to do the best he can. There was an obvious distinction between the mechanics of delivery and the practitioner's spiritual work in healing, protecting, and normalizing the situation.

This was illustrated in a much-less-publicized case in New Bedford, Massachusetts, which occurred while the Corner failure was still echoing in the press.

Mr. and Mrs. James E. Brierly were plain-folks Yankees who had studied with Mrs. Eddy several years earlier, and Brierly was now a full-time practitioner. Just before his wife's confinement, she was taken critically ill. The doctor who was called in for the delivery announced that she had only one chance in a thousand of coming through safely and the local newspaper announced that she was expected to die. Some years previously she had been told that it would be impossible for her to have a child.

The child was born naturally but turned out to be a four-and-a-half pound "blue" baby, who was given even less chance of survival than the mother. The next day both were still alive, but the baby could take no food. After considering the matter, Brierly dismissed the deeply concerned doctor and medical nurse and put the baby in bed with its mother. Quietly cherishing both of them spiritually and caring for them humanly, he soon had them in a normal, healthy state. Writing of the episode thirty-one years later, he observed with Yankee dryness that while the two medical attendants had since died, his wife and son continued to flourish. The son, who had never tasted medicine in his life, now had two boys of his own. It was not an unusual story in the annals of Christian Science; but, Brierly noted laconically, it had never made the newspapers.[76]

Over the years simple necessity would lead to increasingly harmonious co-operation and mutual respect between medical men and Christian Scientists in cases of childbirth.[77] But in 1888 much remained to be worked out in terms of church policy on the subject.

The Corner case, including the adverse publicity it received, had the good result of clarifying Mrs. Eddy's own thinking on the issues involved.

The situation, however, greatly disturbed the local Scientists. They were disconcerted by the fact that Mrs. Eddy appeared to feel that from the outset Mrs. Corner had acted with more human zeal than spiritual wisdom. The deceased woman's husband, who was not a Christian Scientist, had absolved his mother-in-law of all blame and had predicted in a *Boston Herald* interview that when the full facts came out in court "it would be plainly seen that Christian Science had nothing to do with the sad death of his wife."[78] Why, then, could Mrs. Eddy not have rushed to Mrs. Corner's defense with a brave flourish of trumpets and launched a counterattack against the critical press?

Instead, a cautious letter had gone to the *Herald,* written by Mrs. Eddy but signed by the Committee on Publication of the Christian Scientist Association, a committee which at that time consisted of Frank Mason, Josephine Curtis Woodbury, and Sarah Crosse.[79] The letter pointed out that Mrs. Corner had not taken the obstetrics course at the college, that only one side of the case had been presented by the newspapers, and that it was to be hoped "that extenuating circumstances will be brought to light." An ambiguous reference to "quackery" could be interpreted as applying to Mrs. Corner's handling of the case, but evidently was aimed at iatrogenic failures in regular medical practice, since the letter went on to say:

> *The West Medford case, so far as is known, is the first instance of death at childbirth in the practice of Christian Science. This fact is of vital importance when compared with the daily statistics of death on such occasions caused by the use of drugs and instruments. Does medical malpractice and the mortality that ensues, go unnoticed because of their frequency?*[80]

This went to the heart of the matter. Then, as now, a single Christian Science failure was hot news, whereas quantities of medical failures could pass without public comment.[81] But to some of the Boston students the defense seemed insufficiently heroic. They looked at Mrs. Corner's immediate plight, aghast at the threat of conviction that hung over her. Mrs. Eddy, who never doubted that she would be acquitted, looked at the future of the movement. What could she learn from this new trial to strengthen and safeguard the practice of Christian Science?

The difference in emphasis was more basically a dichotomy of outlook.

As far back as 1885 members of the Church of Christ, Scientist, began raising funds to put up a church building in Boston. In 1886 they bought a strip of land in the Back Bay for that purpose, making a down payment of two thousand dollars and accepting a three-year mortgage for $8,763. A year later they reduced this by $3,000, then came up with a plan to hold a fair to raise money to pay off the remainder.

Mrs. Eddy disagreed with this last scheme, which smacked to her of the endless fund-raising busyness of the older churches, but gave way finally to the urging of the students. When a fair was held in Horticultural Hall in December, 1887, she accepted the fact with grace and put in an appearance at the decorous festivities, accompanied by her son and his family.

The fair brought in five thousand dollars, and the students were jubilant. But Mrs. Eddy's warnings against reliance on "material methods" were somberly underlined a month or two later by the treasurer's running off with all the money. The members were back where they had started. They were all for pursuing the absconded treasurer, but Mrs. Eddy, who saw him as the victim of animal magnetism, assured them that his own sense of guilt was punishment enough.

Among those who were pushing for vigorous "material" action in every direction was a group of men headed by two of her trusted lieutenants, J. M. C. Murphy and W. H. Bertram. On the ground that they wished to fit themselves to act as qualified obstetricians as well as Christian Science practitioners in cases of childbirth, they had signed up at a medical college for a three-year course of study leading to the M.D. degree. Mrs. Eddy, with a mixture of skepticism and charity, gave them a provisional blessing and awaited results.

When the Corner case broke, the group was up in arms. The Christian Scientist Association should spring to Mrs. Corner's defense, pay her expenses, fight back in the newspapers. They were incensed at the coolness of Mrs. Eddy's letter in the *Boston Herald*. In this they were joined by Sarah Crosse, who was related to Mrs. Corner and had been a member of the Committee on Publication in whose name the letter in question had been sent to the *Herald*. She had sharply objected to it before it was sent, but the other committee members, Frank Mason and Mrs. Woodbury, had neglected to tell Mrs. Eddy of her objections.[82]

At this late date Mrs. Crosse's character seems curiously featureless and colorless. The few extant letters from her to "My darling Teacher" give no clue to her character. Until the spring of 1888 one might have supposed her chief characteristic to be an industrious though pedestrian faithfulness. At that time she rather surprisingly maneuvered William H. Bradford out of his position as manager of the *Journal* and herself into the position. Bradford was also treasurer of the association, and this bit of skulduggery practiced against him was presumably one of the factors contributing to his astonishing decampment a short time after.

At a stormy meeting on June 2, Murphy moved that the Christian Scientist Association should give two hundred dollars toward Mrs. Corner's legal defense. Although Mrs. Eddy was not present, it was known that she favored private contributions by Christian Scientists acting as individuals.[83] As a result, Murphy's motion was voted down and one hundred and seventy dollars was pledged by those present to aid Mrs. Corner.[84] The whole "medical" group, together with Mrs. Crosse and her husband, were incensed. The secretary of the association resigned, the dissidents tried to elect Murphy and failed, and Mrs. Eddy's loyal aide William B. Johnson was voted into office instead.

After a similar special meeting four days later, Alfred Lang, one of Mrs. Eddy's older students, wrote Calvin Frye, "I don't want to believe that those seven men [Murphy, Bertram *et al.*] whom I have loved and respected so long have it in their heart to break down our Association."[85] But at the next meeting, on June 12, at which Mrs. Crosse suddenly emerged to lead an all-out attack on Mrs. Eddy, it became clear that that was exactly what was in their hearts. The atmosphere of resentment grew more and more intense as the meeting proceeded, bewilderment among the neophytes mounted, and thirty-six members resigned on the spot. One man, who along with several others withdrew his resignation after he had thought the matter over in a calmer atmosphere, reported that under the mental pressure of the occasion it seemed to be a life-and-death matter that he should resign. Then, with the meeting in a shambles, Mrs. Crosse walked out triumphantly at the head of the seceders.[86]

At that very moment, Mrs. Eddy and several of her leading students were on their way to Chicago to meet with her most spectacular triumph to date.

The annual convention of the National Christian Scientist Association had been called to meet in that city on June 13 and 14. Mrs. Eddy had put a notice in the May *Journal* urging members across the country to attend it but adding that she would not personally be present. She wished "those who are halting or getting blind," the notice explained a trifle cryptically, neither to rest on her personality nor to abuse it.

As the situation in Boston heated up, however, she inserted a more urgent appeal at the last moment in the June *Journal:*

Christian Scientists: For Christ's sake and humanity's sake gather together; meet en *masse, at the annual session of the National Christian Scientist Association. Be "of one mind in one place," and God will pour you out a blessing such as you never before received. . . .*

Let no consideration bend or outweigh your purpose to be in Chicago on June 13. Firm in your allegiance to the reign of universal harmony, go to its rescue. In God's hour the powers of earth and hell are proven powerless.

At the end of the notice was the simple statement: "Mrs. Eddy will herself attend the convention."

Three or four days before leaving, she dispatched William B. Johnson, the new secretary of the association, to explain the Boston crisis to a few of her most trusted students in Chicago. Then, taking with her Calvin Frye, Captain and Mrs. Eastaman, and Dr. E. J. Foster, she returned to the city where, at her last visit four years before, she had been an almost unknown figure.

Not so now. The press was fascinated by the visit of the "Boston Prophetess." Eight hundred delegates turned up at the first day's meeting at the First Methodist Church, devoted to the business of the National Association. The second day's proceedings were held in the huge Central Music Hall, and the general public was invited as well as the delegates. Four thousand people crowded in, for Mrs. Eddy had been announced as the speaker of the morning.

This was contrary to her explicit instructions; she had stipulated that she would come to Chicago only if she did not have to make a speech. The pastor of the Chicago church and chairman of the convention, George B. Day, had, for reasons best known to himself, disregarded the stipulation. As she was about to step out on the stage with him to listen to whatever program had been prepared, he suddenly confided to her that she was the advertised speaker for the occasion. Stunned but trapped, she gathered herself together during the brief opening observances, then stepped forward and delivered an extempore address which brought the audience to its feet at the end in a wild burst of acclamation.

Her talk "depended largely upon its logic for its force," reported the *Chicago Tribune,* while the more critical *Chicago Times* conceded that she "spoke distinctly and with effect, though her talk was lacking in unity and coherence."[87] The *Inter-Ocean* noted the large number of middle-aged women in the audience, cheerful and serene in appearance, but the cynical *Times* account suggests that their serenity did not inhibit their enthusiasm:

When the speaker concluded the audience arose en masse and made a rush for the platform. There were no steps provided for getting on the rostrum, but that did not deter those who wanted to shake hands with the idolized expounder of their creed. They mounted the reporters' table and vaulted to the rostrum like acrobats. They crowded about the little woman and hugged and kissed her until she was exhausted and a man had to come to her rescue and lead her away.

According to other reports—some reverential, some tongue-in-cheek—numerous healings took place there and then, crutches were discarded, babies were held up to be blessed, strong men wept. But it was more than a charismatic triumph or the excitement of a Moody and Sankey revival; it was, in some degree, the triumph of metaphysics over philistinism. God, Mrs. Eddy had told them in her speech,

> *. . . is like Himself, and like nothing else. He is universal and primitive. His character admits of no degree of comparison. God is not part, but the whole. . . . His pity is expressed in modes above the human. His chastisements are the manifestations of Love. The sympathy of His eternal Mind is fully expressed in divine Science, which blots out all our iniquities and heals all our diseases.*[88]

To those who were more than curiosity seekers, the recognition that practical concerns could be implicated in theological definitions seems to have come with a certain startling impact. The concrete gratitude of those already indebted to Christian Science drove home the point.

That night, however, something else took over. A reception was held for Mrs. Eddy at the Palmer House, where she was staying. The reception rooms, the corridors, even the stairways were filled with an excited throng. "They pressed forward upon her regardless of each other," one later chronicler wrote, "Silks and laces were torn, flowers crushed, and jewels lost."[89] After the briefest of appearances, Mrs. Eddy withdrew. Despite her hungry longing to have the world recognize the importance of her mission, she was realist enough to know that this kind of emotionalism could easily turn to hostility once the uncompromising demands of Science were understood.

Upon returning to Boston, still filled with the glow of the genuine love and devotion that had been present in Chicago along with the hysteria, she found this painful truth all too evident. Things had gone from bad to worse. By a simple ruse on the unsuspecting wife of the absent secretary, the seceders had got the books of the

Christian Scientist Association into their hands. Holding them as a sort of paper hostage, they now demanded honorable dismissals from the association instead of the expulsions which, by the organization's own stringent rules, they were bound to receive. A few had already returned to the fold, but fresh withdrawals took place almost every day. Again and again William B. Johnson would come home and report to his wife and son, "Mr. and Mrs. So-and-so have resigned and gone off to Mrs. Crosse," and they would gaze at each other in bewildered dismay. No one could know then that some of these people would return to the church years later and give it good service. The one fact then visible was that a third of the church, including many of their staunchest workers, had left them.

Mrs. Eddy early made a supreme effort to heal the schism by inviting all the members of the association, including the dissidents, to meet with her at the college on June 27. The meeting was held at the building on Columbus Avenue in order that the familiar surroundings might help to reawaken old loyalties and love in those who attended. But as one student after another entered the lecture room on the evening of the twenty-seventh, the spirits of those already there sank lower and lower. Not one of the dissidents had come.

Rising to the occasion, Mrs. Eddy cheered and encouraged her depleted ranks and sent them off with renewed hope, but afterward she revealed her anguish to a few of her closest students who stayed to discuss with her the future of the movement.

Late that evening Johnson arrived home, pale and haggard. Refusing to eat anything, he lay down on the sofa and asked his son William to read to him from those Psalms in which David reached out to God from the depths of discouragement. Later he asked him to read from the New Testament, and turning to the first Epistle of John the boy wonderingly saw the heading of the page, "A warning against false teachers," and read aloud the words, "They went out from us, but they were not of us; for if they had been of us, they would no doubt have continued with us: but they went out, that they might be made manifest that they were not all of us."

"That is enough," Johnson told him. "I have my answer and I am strong now." Then at last he spoke of the failure of the schismatics to come to the meeting and of Mrs. Eddy's crushed hopes for reconciliation. He had been with her for three hours while she wrestled with the question of leaving them and moving out to Chicago. "I know that our prayers will be answered," he added with such assurance as he could muster, "and that she will obtain divine guidance before this terrible and heart-breaking day is finished."[90]

Actually, it took a little longer for the guidance to come clear.

Chapter IX

Exit from Boston

Exit from Boston

The next three years were to be pivotal ones in the history of Christian Science. They would bring Mrs. Eddy at the age of seventy to the brink of her greatest decision since 1866, to a new beginning for herself and her church.

Primitive Christianity, confronted by the great pagan world about it, had started as a total challenge to that world and had then begun building bridges to it, only to have paganism pour back across the bridges bringing with it the world's values, methods, rites, responses, so that Christianity ended up being paganized quite as much as paganism was Christianized. Was this the inevitable pattern for a new religious vision?

The small group led by Murphy and Bertram had embarked on a three-year course of medical study. John P. Filbert in Iowa wrote that he felt he should relax his Christian Science work sufficiently to take a three-year theological course to fit himself better for preaching. Ellen Brown, now married, wrote that she and her husband thought of taking a three-year recess from their healing and teaching in Chicago in order to go on a sort of pastoral hegira. As these instances mounted during the spring of 1888, Mrs. Eddy wrote sharply in a letter, "The devil has agreed on *three* years in which to get space to spoil God's work."[1]

Her counterattack began with an article "To Loyal Christian Scientists" in the July *Journal*, hinting at the direction which her own development would take in the transitional period ahead:

> *Falsehood is on the wings of the winds, but Truth will soar above it. Truth is speaking louder, clearer, and more imperatively than ever, Error is walking to and fro in the earth, trying to be heard above Truth, but its voice dies out in the distance. Whosoever proclaims Truth loudest becomes the mark for error's shafts. The archers aim at Truth's mouthpiece; but a heart loyal to God is patient and strong....*
>
> *Those only who are tried in the furnace reflect the image*

*of their Father. You, my beloved students, who are absent from
me, and have shared less of my labors than many others, seem
stronger to resist temptation than some of those who have had
line upon line and precept upon precept. This may be a serviceable hint, since necessities and God's providence are foreshadowed. I have felt for some time that perpetual instruction
of my students might substitute my own for their growth, and
so dwarf their experience. If they must learn by the things they
suffer, the sooner this lesson is gained the better.*

*For two years I have been gradually withdrawing from
active membership in the Christian Scientist Association. This
has developed higher energies on the part of true followers, and
led to some startling departures on the other hand. . . . My human affections would rejoice with those who rejoice, and weep
with those who weep; but over and above it all are eternal
sunshine and joy unspeakable.*[2]

It was soon evident to her that withdrawal to Chicago was not
the answer to her problem. The Chicago field could blow up as
easily as the Boston one if it felt the challenge of her constant, active
presence. The elements of disaffection were in fact already there.
Mrs. Gestefeld's *Statement of Christian Science* had been announced
only four days before the National Christian Scientist Association
meeting, and the Reverend George Day's curious behavior in the
matter of Mrs. Eddy's speech held out little promise for his future
reliability.

In August of 1888 she withdrew to the White Mountain House,
Fabyans, New Hampshire, in search of a little rest and perspective,
taking with her Frye, Foster, and a student named Anna Osgood.
While there she preached a sermon in the luxurious Fabyan House;
but on the whole her brief stay in the mountains failed to bring
her what she was looking for.[3]

On the way back to Boston, she stopped off for five days at the
farm of Ira and Flavia Knapp at Lyman, New Hampshire. These two
resolute figures were now carrying on a large healing practice with
such success that the hackles of their uptight rural community were
rising ominously. Only a short time before her arrival, Mrs. Eddy
had been hanged in effigy in the town square.[4] But she found solace
in the four Knapp children, in the simple farm life so familiar to
her from her own childhood, in the woods and fields through which
she went walking, in the ancient rustic types who dropped by—and
in the unbounded love of all the Knapps.

While there, she had one difficult night of physical and mental anguish. Early the next morning the family gathered around the melodeon in the parlor and sang with spirit the old gospel hymn, "Joy cometh in the morning." Mrs. Eddy heard the singing, listened, rose, dressed, and very quickly came down stairs with radiant face and renewed energy, to join the others at breakfast.[5]

This kind of instant recovery was a phenomenon repeated many times in her life. During her years in Boston, Mrs. Eddy sometimes found it necessary at periods of crisis to send for especially trusted students to help her spiritually through a night of struggle. One of these students was Captain Eastaman, with his combination of rugged faithfulness and simple affection. A letter of his to "My dear little teacher" suggests the kind of tender concern many of these students felt for her:

> *I have always consulted you before I undertook anything & for the past two years I have never left Boston for a night without asking you if I could go . . . and now little darling you know that I have been faithful in little things hence fear not to trust me in great things.*[6]

Some of Mrs. Eddy's students had been concerned for a year or two that she was working too hard and pleaded with her to take more time for herself. They noted with anxiety every sign of age or strain in her appearance and rejoiced in the continued and frequently astonishing evidences of her resilience. While the disaffected students complained that she was getting "too old" to head the Christian Science movement, the new students who were flocking to the college seemed almost uniformly struck by her vitality, the erectness of her figure, the freshness of her complexion—and, above all, by her eyes, which they described variously as blue, gray, violet, deep gentian, black, even as brown, and as flashing, sparkling, kindling, clouding, looking right into one, changing with every mood.[7]

Many of them spoke of the immense power and authority she conveyed in her teaching. This was even more evident in her healing. When she ran up the stairs one day as lightly as a young girl, Laura Lathrop, who was visiting her, tried valiantly to do likewise despite an unhealed heart condition which had not allowed her to perform such a feat for twenty-four years. Seized with a violent attack, Mrs. Lathrop collapsed in agony at the top of the staircase. As she described the incident eighteen years later, Mrs. Eddy "gave me one glance, then, without asking me a question . . . spoke aloud to the error . . . as one having authority." The healing was instant.[8]

When a correspondent in the *Journal* asked, "Has Mrs. Eddy lost her power to heal?" the latter replied with the question, "Has the sun forgotten to shine, and the planets to revolve around it?"[9] Whatever the physical struggles she might sometimes have to undergo, there is no evidence of any diminution of spiritual power and authority in her demonstration of Christian Science during these years. Although she held to her policy of taking no patients professionally, she continued to reach out in impulsive help in emergency situations.[10] The letters she received tell of healings that sometimes took place while she talked with a person, unconscious of his needing help.[11] And accounts of healing through the reading of *Science and Health* continued to pour in.[12]

Upon her return to Boston from New Hampshire, Mrs. Eddy launched out at once on a new Primary class of forty-five students. Her plans for withdrawal had not yet taken shape, though she wrote in a letter at this time, "I shall write less and less to my oldest children[;] they must take care of themselves now that I am having 45 born at once and must nurse them up to maturer years."[13]

In October she held another obstetrics class. This time—possibly in answer to the students who had left for medical school—she asked Dr. Foster to conduct the first five lessons and instruct the students in the physiological aspects of childbirth; then in the last four lessons she took up the subject metaphysically. Though the course was never repeated, there was general agreement that Foster acquitted himself well in a rather anomalous situation. On November 5, 1888, he became Mrs. Eddy's adopted son, and his name was legally changed to Ebenezer J. Foster Eddy.

A week later she took another large Primary class, with many more would-be students clamoring for admission. While she threw herself into the work wholeheartedly and on several occasions expanded the usual three-hour session to four hours without apparently noticing the fact, she announced to the class when they met for the eighth lesson that she had given them all she felt they could take in at that time. Since they had contracted for twelve lessons she would meet with them, if they wished, for the remaining days and answer their questions, but she frankly felt the class had accomplished its purpose. The students voted unanimously to accept her judgment and departed. After that, the regular number of lessons for the Primary class at the college was seven rather than twelve.[14]

To the November class she recounted a "vision" she had had the night before the session. She had been standing on a precipice with a high ledge before her, unable to turn back or move to the right or left. In her arms she held a baby which had been stripped naked. She knew that she must climb higher, but it seemed impossible to struggle upward with the child in her arms. So, as one student recalled her account, "she dropped the child at her feet and held it by one finger and took the step."[15]

The moral was as obvious as the feat was unusual.

2

On February 15, 1889, Mrs. Eddy gave an address in Steinway Hall, New York, which evoked some of the same enthusiasm as her Chicago speech nine months before. It was her only public appearance in that city and it drew from the newspapers the usual variety of responses. Whereas the *New York World* described her as "a pleasant little woman, with dark hair and dark eyes, [who] does not look more than forty years old," the *New York Times* gave a ferocious picture of her as she "stood for a moment surveying her audience, her keen and sunken black eyes peering weirdly from her colorless face, and her dark hair brushed severely down on her temples."[16]

It was to be her last public lecture of that kind. Ten days later, back in Boston, she opened a class of almost seventy, the largest number she had yet undertaken to teach at one time. Rather to her surprise, it turned out to be one of her most successful classes, but it was also her last at the college.[17]

On one occasion she wrote that she wished she could unteach all her students and start over again with the ten best.[18] A similar feeling has smitten most great teachers at one time or another. To envision a subject in all its scope and variety, its possibilities and urgencies, its depth and implication, and then to see all this cut down by the exigencies of classroom instruction and the limits of student comprehension—this is to long for a new language of communication, immediate, irresistible, suprapersonal.

Was there no higher way of teaching? Must experience always be the ultimate, clumsy teacher? To one of her most earnest students Mrs. Eddy wrote with quiet regret, "For you, my most honored student, have had to learn out of class what if you had accepted in it would have saved you much."[19] How long would it take the world to recognize what her own students were so slow to grasp in its larger meaning?

To the class of March, 1889, she said at the end of the last session:

> *We, to-day, in this class-room, are enough to convert the world if we are of one Mind; for then the whole world will feel the influence of this Mind; as when the earth was without form, and Mind spake and form appeared.*[20]

But four days later she wrote her student John Filbert of the human cost to her, the great lack in the field, and the need for a rethinking of the whole problem:

> *I do not want to teach, I am tired, tired, of teaching and being the slave of so many minds, but I had rather there would never be a teacher but the Bible and Science and Health than that such poor teaching should go on [in the field].*[21]

In May, Foster Eddy taught a Primary and a Normal class in the college, but Mrs. Eddy felt in her bones that the time had come to close it. Although applications for instruction were pouring in—more than she could possibly accept—the September *Journal* carried her decision. "Deeply regretting the disappointment this must occasion," she announced, "and with grateful acknowledgments to the public, I now close my college."

The effect on Christian Scientists everywhere is summed up in a letter to her from Frank Mason, who had just made a quick trip out to Iowa to conduct a class:

> *To say that I was surprised when I heard of the closing of the College is a mild statement. I was simply astounded. I supposed the College like the gate to Heaven would always be ajar. The West and in fact the whole country is dazed at the apparent sudden termination of the original source of Christian Science teaching.*[22]

The reaction was so sharp that, as a concession, Mrs. Eddy made one more attempt to keep the institution going. On September 14 she appointed General Erastus N. Bates, a student from Cleveland, Ohio, president of the college and sole teacher to succeed her. General Bates was a distinguished Civil War veteran, a classical scholar, and a man of exceptional courtesy, charm, and integrity. The one class he taught in Boston was very successful, but even before it began, Mrs. Eddy wrote him that she could not resist God's command: the college must close as soon as the class was over. On October 29, 1889, it was formally dissolved.

Right up to the last, some of her students could not accept the decision. Edward P. Bates, the Syracuse businessman (not related to General Bates), and two other male students journeyed up to New Hampshire, where she was then staying, to expostulate with her. In their eyes she was an inspired teacher who knew nothing about business. Evidently she simply failed to realize that it would be madness to shut down a flourishing and greatly needed institution at the height of its success.

When she entered the room where they were waiting for her, she began at once to share with them some of the vision that had led her to close the college. As they listened, they were filled with a kind of wonder and shame at their own attitude. Finally she turned to each of them and asked him kindly what he had come to see her about, and each in turn mumbled that he hadn't come about anything in particular. As one of them told Julia Bartlett afterward, he wished for a moment that the floor would open and the earth would swallow him up.[23]

The dissolution of the college was accompanied by that of the Christian Scientist Association, made up of students who had taken one or more courses there under Mrs. Eddy. Her relations with this body had been especially intimate; through it she had nurtured her students, consulted their needs, heard their grievances, talked over possible courses of action. It was democratic as a family conclave or even a family squabble is democratic, and in the schism of June, 1888, the Crosse-Murphy-Bertram faction had tried to take it clear out of her hands.

A year later the dissidents had finally been given the honorable dismissals they demanded, and they in turn gave up the association's records and funds which they had seized and held illegally. Once again the association was flourishing, but in a letter written on September 23 Mrs. Eddy "strongly recommended" that it should dissolve, and the members immediately voted to do so.[24] It was a striking evidence of their faith in her leadership.

That left the National Christian Scientist Association still in existence. It had held its fourth annual convention in Cleveland in June, but Mrs. Eddy had not attended. Instead, she was represented by her adopted son, who read a message from her in which she resigned as president of the association and turned over to it the ownership of *The Christian Science Journal*.[25] The process of withdrawal was going on.

Only two weeks before, she had resigned her pastorate of the Church of Christ, Scientist, in Boston. The letter of resignation came to the church from Barre, Vermont, where Foster Eddy had found her a pleasant house on the town square. There, with only Calvin Frye and her housekeeper, Martha Morgan, for company, Mrs. Eddy had several weeks of blessed quiet. A letter of hers in the July *Journal* gave a word of explanation:

> *These inquiries are coming from all "four quarters,"—For what purpose has Mrs. Eddy relinquished certain lines of labor in the field of Christian Science and called others to the work?*

Is she writing her history? or completing her works on the Scriptures? She is doing neither, but is taking a vacation, her first in twenty-five years. She is taking no direction of her own or others, but her desire is that God may permit her to continue to live apart from the world, free from the turmoil in which her days have been passed for more than a quarter century.

By the time these words were published, however, the quiet had been invaded. With the coming of summer, the town band settled down in the square outside her windows for almost daily concerts. To the thump of the bass drum and the braying of trombones, the household beat a dignified retreat to Concord, New Hampshire, which at least lived up to its name.

Mrs. Eddy had always loved Concord, peopled as it was with early memories and distant relatives. Some months before, she had sent her student Mrs. Ann Otis to get Christian Science started there. Mrs. Otis had taken rooms with the Morrill family, and Mrs. Eddy had written her that she would certainly enjoy "the great, kind heart of Dr. Ezekiel Morrill . . . as blunt as it is good."[26] Dr. Morrill, a second cousin, had been one of the first homeopaths to practice in that part of the country and his blunt, cousinly heart had room for Mrs. Eddy but not for Christian Science.

That was true of Concord itself in some ways, though Christian Science did gain a foothold there and gradually grew in spite of local conservatism. Mrs. Eddy meanwhile found a domestic foothold in a house at 62 North State Street which she leased for a year. It turned out to be far from satisfactory—was too close to the center of town, had insufficient privacy, needed repairs. Later in the summer she returned to Boston for some weeks to take care of numerous business matters. While there, she considered the possibility of settling in England or taking a house in Oconto, Wisconsin, where her students Laura and Victoria Sargent lived,[27] but ended by returning to the house in Concord.

Her one desire was to get away from society and the pressure of daily demands while she worked out the next steps for her movement. Even the neighborliness of Concord was a distraction, and the mountain of correspondence which she faced every day was a heavy burden. More and more she dictated her letters to Calvin Frye and Foster Eddy instead of pouring out personal replies in her own hand as she had done in the past.

Frye at all times was close by to take care of a thousand needs. Foster Eddy, on the other hand, nipped back and forth between Concord and Boston and points farther afield, on special missions for her.

Yet neither the letters nor the outward happenings of this period—not even the powerful directives she issued all through 1889—are an adequate index to the movement of Mrs. Eddy's thought. It is in her *Journal* articles that the deeper currents of her motivations come clear.

In an article called "The Way" in the December *Journal* she went to the heart of the problem facing the Christian Science movement as she saw it: the need for the spirit rather than the letter, for works more than words:

> *Less teaching and good healing is to-day the acme of "well done"; a healing that is not guesswork,—chronic recovery ebbing and flowing,—but instantaneous cure. . . . The student who heals by teaching and teaches by healing, will graduate under divine honors, which are the only appropriate seals for Christian Science. State honors perish, and their gain is loss to the Christian Scientist. They include for him at present naught but tardy justice, hounded footsteps, false laurels. . . . Human pride is human weakness. Self-knowledge, humility, and love are divine strength.*[28]

Although most of the article was devoted to the three last-named qualities, it went on to speak of the closing of the Massachusetts Metaphysical College "at the pinnacle of prosperity" and of the fact that Mrs. Eddy did not expect Christian Scientists in general to emulate this action, stop teaching and disorganize their associations:

> *When students have fulfilled all the good ends of organization, and are convinced that by leaving the material forms thereof a higher spiritual unity is won, then is the time to follow the example of the* Alma Mater. *Material organization is requisite in the beginning; but when it has done its work, the purely Christly method of teaching and preaching must be adopted. On the same principle, you continue the mental argument in the practice of Christian healing until you can cure without it instantaneously, and through Spirit alone.*

This careful delimiting of her strictures on "material" organization left the door open for more advanced forms of organization on a more "spiritual" basis. Until all Christian Scientists could heal instantaneously at all times, as Jesus did, and like him could walk on the water, they had better not try to do without organization:

> *Peter's impetuosity was rebuked. He had to learn from experience; so have we. The methods of our Master were in advance of the period in which he personally appeared; but his*

example was right, and is available at the right time. The way is absolute divine Science; walk ye in it; but remember that Science is demonstrated by degrees, and our demonstration rises only as we rise in the scale of being.

The emphasis, as always, was on step-by-step demonstration. It was evident that Mrs. Eddy herself could not see precisely the direction in which her actions were taking the church, but she could move with decision as soon as the next step was clear.

This was illustrated once more when, shortly after finishing "The Way," she wrote Julia Bartlett: "This morning has finished my halting between two opinions. This Mother Church must disorganize and now is the time to do it."[29] A few days later the church at her request dissolved its ten-year-old organization.[30] The ground at last was clear for whatever might come.

3

Oddly enough, Mrs. Eddy's leadership was never more evident than in her dismantling of the organizations she had built up through the 1880's. Many years later William B. Johnson's son wrote of the aftermath of the Boston "rebellion" of 1888:

> . . . *no previous upheaval in her Church and Association had brought forth such efforts as she made to save the remnants of her work in Boston, and no one who had not lived close to her at that time and knew the conditions could realize in any large measure the change that took place in her attitude toward her adherents. She had previously been the Teacher, but in the latter part of 1888 she became the General-in-chief, and the Leader.*[31]

Even as she "disorganized" the old church, Mrs. Eddy took decisive steps to build on a new basis. Specifically she gathered into her hands the parcel of land which the members had acquired for church-building purposes in Boston's Back Bay.

It was a complicated story. Back in December, 1888, she had purchased through her lawyer the $5,000 mortgage on the land. When the mortgage fell due the following summer and the members took no action to redeem it, Mrs. Eddy foreclosed. For three weeks the property was advertised for sale at public auction, but when the sale was held on August 3, 1889, there seems to have been little bidding, for George Perry—the son of Mrs. Eddy's lawyer—bought it for her at the remarkably low price of about $5,000.[32]

In her later account of the "circuitous, novel way"[33] in which the land was acquired and transferred, she invoked the words from II Corinthians: "For the weapons of our warfare are not carnal, but mighty through God to the pulling down of strong holds." The money already contributed by earnest Christian Scientists toward the purchase of the land had been given in confidence that it would be used to build a Church of Christ, Scientist, in full accord with Mrs. Eddy's teachings. More than human shrewdness or the wisdom of the carnal mind was necessary, she felt, to implement that purpose against the obduracy of human will. In explanation she wrote:

> As with all former efforts in the interest of Christian Science, I took care that the provisions for the land and building were such as error could not control. I knew that to God's gift, foundation and superstructure, no one could hold a wholly material title. The land, and the church standing on it, must be conveyed through a type representing the true nature of the gift; a type morally and spiritually inalienable, but materially questionable.[34]

One material question arose from the seceded faction, some of whom had been active in raising funds for the purchase of the land and who now felt that they had been maneuvered out of their interest in it. To satisfy them Mrs. Eddy, immediately following the formal dissolution of the church, wrote Mrs. Crosse and J. M. C. Murphy as leaders of the group and told them that they would have an opportunity to buy the lot if they acted quickly. On December 9, 1889, a notice appeared in the Boston Herald stating that any person who was a member of the Church of Christ, Scientist, Boston, at the time the lot of land was bargained for by the church could purchase the lot at any time within six days for $5,000. On December 10 Perry quitclaimed the property for the stated sum to Ira O. Knapp.[35]

Some time earlier, the Knapp family had moved down from New Hampshire to Roslindale, a suburb of Boston. Though Mrs. Eddy at that time considered Ira Knapp a little too "visionary,"[36] she also considered him to be a man of rocklike integrity and immovable faith in God's direction of her actions. At that juncture of affairs he provided the point of complete reliability she needed in order to secure the land for the building of a church that would rest, as she saw it, on Principle rather than persons.

After Peter's acknowledgment of the Messiah, Jesus had said to him, "On this rock I will build my church." He referred, Mrs. Eddy held, not to the personal Peter (petros) who might in fact prove a very unstable stone or pebble, but to Peter's acknowledgment of the Christ, Truth, made visible through Jesus. This was in truth the impersonal

Rock (*petra*), the mother-stone or bedrock on which all permanent building must rest.[37] Her own choice of Knapp to help her at this point seems to have been determined by his solid conviction that her motive was not to get personal possession of the land or to consolidate her personal power but to found her church on the Rock, on Truth itself. In the letter he had written her two years earlier describing the vision which had come to him before he went through his first class with her, he had told of being surprised by "a mighty rushing wind":

> *It made the earth as a desert, and left me bare and naked; but before me was a great rock, square and upright; and on its sides the word Truth appeared. On this rock I saw that I must build.*[38]

Knapp's actual role in conveying the land was brief and formal, though crucial. He paid Perry for the lot with a check furnished by Mrs. Eddy and Perry returned the check to her as soon as he had deeded the property to Knapp. Acting under her direction the latter then deeded the land to three trustees: two older local students, Alfred Lang and Marcellus Munroe, and an up-and-coming young businessman from South Dakota, William G. Nixon. They were to hold title to the lot on the condition that they would begin building a church on it as soon as $20,000 had been received in subscriptions.

It was several years and several controversies later that the building was actually started, but by January, 1890, the ground was metaphorically as well as literally cleared for a new kind of church to be built.

The one now dissolved had been modeled on the traditional Christian churches; it had been formed to "commemorate" the word and works of Jesus and to "reinstate" primitive Christianity.[39] It had reached out for ordained ministers to preach in its pulpits; it had sought to clothe itself in the respectability of an ecclesiastical tradition rooted in male dominance. It had been organized under a state charter; it had suffered from the rivalries and power struggles within and the social pressures and ideological infiltrations from without which are the normal lot of a temporal institution subject to variable human judgments. The vision of primitive Christianity had been swallowed up in just such ways in the first centuries. To recapture or even to purify the past was not enough, as the various periods of revival and reformation in Christian history had shown. A new *idea* of Church was necessary, Mrs. Eddy held.

In the Glossary of *Science and Health* she had defined Church as: "The structure of Truth and Love; whatever rests upon and proceeds from divine Principle."[40] Such a structure could rest on neither matter nor history, person nor dogma. It must inhere in the nature of things, but only as the true idea was perceived and established in human thought could it take visible form in improved organization. There was a good deal of growth to take place in both her own and her students' thinking before the militant little church which had fought its stormy way through the 1880's would be superseded by the institution of which she would write:

> The First Church of Christ, Scientist, in Boston, Mass., is designed to be built on the Rock, Christ; even the understanding and demonstration of divine Truth, Life, and Love, healing and saving the world from sin and death; thus to reflect in some degree the Church Universal and Triumphant.[41]

The vacant lot in Back Bay stood as mute testimony to the work still to be done.

4

While the calculated devolution of Mrs. Eddy's church was going on, a different sort of disorganization was taking place among the mind-curers.

Not to be outdone by the formation of the National Christian Scientist Association, Mrs. Plunkett, at the end of 1887, formed an International Christian Scientist Association. The only thing international about it was the name, which also illustrated Mrs. Plunkett's continued free use of the term Christian Scientist. Leaving Mrs. Hopkins to head their joint enterprises in the Middle West, she moved her headquarters to New York. There, in July, 1888, her magazine *Truth* and Marston's *Mental Healing Monthly* were merged in a new venture, *The International Magazine of Christian Science,* with Mrs. Plunkett as editor.

Marston, who brought his eighteen hundred subscribers along with him, soon discovered that he had become not so much allied with as absorbed by the enterprising editor. Unsatiated, the latter proceeded a month later to devour Albert Dorman and his *Messenger of Truth.* This second merger brought her an additional fifteen hundred subscribers, raising the total to almost five thousand. Emma Hopkins whose personal followers started a small magazine of their own called *Christian Science* in Chicago, appeared frequently and prominently in the *International,* but Marston and Dorman soon dwindled away to little more than the sickly grin of a cat who, contrary to the usual procedure, has been swallowed by a canary.

It was a constant source of concern to Mrs. Eddy to have her teaching confounded with the miscellaneous fare appearing in the *International.* Sometimes the magazine made caustic thrusts at her;[42] sometimes it claimed her in a kind of banal fellowship; mostly it ignored but imitated her.

Alzire Chevaillier, who had not yet departed for her sinister fling with the Brotherhood of the New Life, was all over the pages with happy tributes: "Mrs. Eddy most forcibly says . . ." "Mrs. Newman best explains . . ."[43] One Hector Vyr throws in a quick tribute to *Science and Health,* then adds with judicial gravity, "Mrs. Gestefeld's lectures I prefer to any statement of the Science that has yet been made, although Mrs. Hopkins' are very fine and helpful."[44] Albert Dorman, before disappearing from sight, paid tribute to Mrs. Plunkett herself as "an honest, earnest, untiring worker" and "a person of rare business ability."[45]

Through her skillful showmanship Mrs. Plunkett was so able to impress herself on New York as the "high priestess" of Christian Science that Mrs. Eddy's visit there in February, 1889, to speak at Steinway Hall was described by some of the local press as her invasion of a rival's territory. Although the address was in response to the urging of some of Mrs. Eddy's really serious students that she bring to New York a message that would provide spiritual underpinnings for the Christian Science work there, Mrs. Plunkett did her best to turn the occasion to her own advantage. At the conclusion of the address, as men and women crowded to the platform to clasp the speaker's hand, Mrs. Plunkett suddenly swept forward and dramatically embraced her "dear teacher," thus publicly identifying herself as a student of Mrs. Eddy's. It struck a strangely dissonant note. Many at the time were puzzled as to her motive, but a reason soon emerged.

First a signed statement by Mary and John Plunkett in the April issue of the *International* announced that they were dissolving their marriage—with mutual good will but without benefit of legal action. "The Truth has made us free," they concluded unctuously.

A spate of high-sounding articles on marriage and divorce in the next few issues prepared the way for a fifteen-page announcement in the July issue which shook the ranks of mind-cure. Mrs. Plunkett had taken to herself a "spiritual" husband. A. Bentley Worthington, a man who was associated with her in the business management of the *International.* Though still legally wed to poor Plunkett, she was to be known henceforth as Mary Bentley Worthington. A six-page open letter by her elaborated further on the subject of spiritual conjugality, an article by Alzire Chevaillier entitled "Judge Not" invited the readers to judge not, and the same readers were left to draw their own edifying analogy from a statement quoted from the Reverend Charles G. Ames:

260

George Eliot was not lawless, but more than most women she lived out of the reach of conventional influences and standards. She could not hold the traditional theories of marriage any more than of religion. . . .

But it was Mary Baker Eddy rather than George Eliot behind whom "Mrs. Worthington" really hoped to shelter herself.

Her long apologia quoted again and again from the highly moral chapter on marriage in *Science and Health,* turning the plain meaning of the words upside down. It was a flamboyant bit of legerdemain. No one but Mrs. Plunkett could have hoped to quote Mrs. Eddy's words, "Infidelity to the marriage covenant is the social scourge of all nations,"[46] and have them accepted as supporting her own variety of infidelity. Equally audacious was the cynical profession of faith by which she sought to establish the purity of her purpose:

> *The press, because of its slight knowledge of Christian Science, has persistently spoken of me as its "High Priestess." This is entirely unwarrantable and untrue. I am only the earnest and grateful student. Mary B. G. Eddy was my teacher, and the teacher either directly or indirectly of all who are teaching pure Christian Science. . . . While she may sometimes have seemed severe, with some of us, I am convinced that but for her determined and oft-repeated warnings, many, and I am not sure but all of us because of our belief in materiality, would have fallen back into mind-cure, or will-cure healing, instead of rising to the purely spiritual. I am only one of the many thousands who silently thank God every day for the truth revealed through Mary Baker Eddy.*[47]

Like her embrace at Steinway Hall, the passage attempted to identify Mrs. Plunkett with the teacher who, she obviously hoped, would serve to divert the fire of public criticism from herself. But events outpaced her tactics. Before the month was over, Worthington had been exposed as an embezzler wanted on an old charge and a bigamist with a child and several wives in other states. Quickly he melted away, not for the first time in his life, and with one of the few touches of dignity in her own career Mrs. Plunkett told the newspapers, "Mary Bentley Worthington is the name I have taken, and I shall carry it as long as I live."[48]

As it happened, that was not for long. Mrs. Hopkins dropped her colleague like an asp discovered in her breakfast cereal.[49] The various Plunkett enterprises folded up. The *International* labored along for a few more issues under the emergency editorship of Alzire Chevaillier, who seems to have been serenely unconscious of the meaning of what

261

was happening around her—and to have conceived of the magazine as an embryonic *Atlantic Monthly*.[50] But Mrs. Plunkett's career was over. Before long she moved to Australia and there she committed suicide.

Even before the spiritual marriage of the Worthingtons had been announced, Mrs. Eddy had come out in the *Journal* with an article on "Conjugal Rights." About 1875, she wrote, *Science and Health* had first crossed swords with free love and the latter had fallen *hors de combat*. She may have had in mind her public castigation of Victoria Woodhull at that date, but her next words pointed clearly in Mrs. Plunkett's direction:

> *In the present or future, some extra throe of error may conjure up a new-style conjugality, which, ad libitum, severs the marriage covenant, puts virtue in the shambles, and coolly notifies the public of broken vows. Springing up from the ashes of free-love, this nondescript phoenix, in the face and eyes of common law, common sense, and common honesty, may appear in the rôle of a superfine conjugality; but, having no Truth, it will have no past, present, or future.*[51]

The seriousness with which Mrs. Eddy regarded the marriage covenant is apparent not only from her published writings[52] but also from her letters.

When Ellen Brown, a highly independent soul, became engaged to Captain John F. Linscott, a former temperance lecturer whom Mrs. Eddy had sent to Chicago to help her in her Christian Science Institute, Mrs. Eddy wrote her with a gasp of surprise at finding herself an involuntary matchmaker:

> *O my student, be* wise *be* prudent *be* moderate *in what you do in such an awful casting of your life's die as this.*
>
> *You have my benediction, my prayer (but only as a* desire*) that you will be now and forever happier and better for this union. Capt. L. has a large heart*[;] *it* must be KEPT *if once possessed.*[53]

When Mrs. Woodbury offered advice to her students in regard to the sex relationship in marriage, Mrs. Eddy wrote that it was not for either of them to advise others on this most intimate of personal matters.[54] Such advice as she gave was always in the direction of seeking mutual compromises in order to preserve an otherwise crumbling relationship. To Fred A. Robinson, the non-Scientist husband of her student Janette Robinson, she wrote when she learned that their marriage had reached the breaking point:

> *My sympathies are with you both. I regret exceedingly that there should be this sad separation, but have written to your*

wife . . . recommending to her not to strive in any way against the wishes of her husband.

I hope God will reconcile this difficulty and make you both happy in following the path that He points out for you. Can I in any way help you by advising your wife? The happiness of you both I regard as very sacred.[55]

Marriage should not be dissolved, Mrs. Eddy held, except as an inescapable last necessity. It was a form of organization essential to a healthy society, and its disciplines—like the church's—needed to be refined and exalted rather than abandoned. As she saw it, the basic error of the mind-curers was their unwillingness to accept the moral disciplines of Christianity.

In the last issue of the *International,* an editorial by Alzire Chevaillier on "True Organization" quoted from a personal letter she had received from Phillips Brooks:

I feel constantly that unless the whole of the exterior part of religion is making itself unnecessary, it is not doing much. All the worship of all the Temples is making us ready for the world in which John says that he "saw no temple."[56]

Brooks, however, was not proposing an elimination of the church from society. Nor was the Founder of Christian Science, for all the radicalism of some of her statements, proposing an anarchic sweeping away of temporal institutions. The city of God in which John "saw no temple" was that wholly spiritual state in which, according to Jesus, men "neither marry, nor are given in marriage." In the human state, Mrs. Eddy made clear, marriage and family and church remained vital components of organized society.

5

The year 1889 saw other developments that affected the future of Christian Science.

In January of that year a new periodical, *The Boston Christian Scientist,* appeared under the editorship of Sarah Crosse. The title was obviously suggested by Joseph Adams' flourishing monthly, *The Chicago Christian Scientist.* Neither was to have a long life or lasting influence, but they were ably edited and they acted as spurs to *The Christian Science Journal*—which, despite Wiggin's efforts, had its decided literary shortcomings. At one point Mrs. Eddy wrote Ellen Linscott bleakly, "The enemy has captured my literati, and my loyal ones are not given to the pen."[57]

Except for the few months of Gill's editorship, Wiggin had, in effect, been acting editor since January, 1886. Now, three years later, he was replaced by Joshua P. Bailey, a recent student of Mrs. Eddy's from New York. At the same time, in order to meet the new competition from *The Boston Christian Scientist,* it was announced that Mrs. Eddy hoped to supply an article of her own for every issue.

Bailey, the new editor, was a man of extravagant contrasts. Starting life as a moral idealist with a strong attraction to Swedenborgianism and Quakerism, he had turned into a man of the world with expensive tastes and dissipated habits. At one time an obscure American schoolteacher, he had become Thomas A. Edison's personal representative in Europe, sallying forth from his home in Paris to organize companies and electric-light consortiums across the Continent. Later he had lost everything—his health, his fortune, his self-respect—and, back once more in the United States, had come across Christian Science and received an outstanding healing through Augusta Stetson.

On the second day of class with Mrs. Eddy in November, 1888, Bailey also lost what he himself described as a self-assertive intellectualism. At once he became an almost painfully humble disciple of the teacher who seemed to him the very incarnation of the spiritual purity he had worshiped from afar. His combination of childlike devotion with knowledge of the world endeared him to Mrs. Eddy, but what she had not counted on in his editing of the *Journal* was a certain headstrong impulsiveness which had failed to disappear with the "intellectualism."

For several years there had been a tendency among some of Mrs. Eddy's students to write about her in terms so adulatory that they almost suggested apotheosis. Bailey not only encouraged this but also became one of the worst offenders. The mind-curers and disaffected Christian Scienists made much of what they called the *Journal*'s "cult of personality," though in general it would be hard to find any group of people more personality-centered and more teeming with high-charged personalities than the mind-cure constellation itself.

Mrs. Eddy was torn two ways. On the one hand, she wrote the editor from time to time, asking that there be less mention of her personally. On the other hand, she felt deeply that a recognition of her special relationship to Christian Science as its "Discoverer and Founder" was an essential safeguard against the adulteration and perversion of her teaching. One of the efforts of animal magnetism, she was convinced, was to make every Tom, Dick, and Harry with a smattering of metaphysics feel that he was fully competent to expound and even improve what had unfolded to her through years of study, revelation, experience, hard work, and self-discipline. Such a one was likely to argue that his allegiance was to Truth, not to a person—and unexceptionable sentiment in the abstract, but usually combined with an inordinate regard for the aspirant's own person. It was frequently combined, also, with a high disdain of her warnings against animal magnetism.

The Reverend Joseph Adams offered a useful if complex example. In an article entitled "Common Honesty" in *The Chicago Christian Scientist* he pointed out that it was not fair for people to call themselves Christian Scientists yet omit Mrs. Eddy's teaching on animal magnetism. Not, he hastened to add, that he was asking anyone to deify or worship her, as some of her followers seemed to:

> *If there was one thing she impressed upon our mind, while passing through her classes more than another, it was this, not to look at Mrs. Eddy but the Truth which she declared.*
>
> *This eulogizing of personality*—pardon us if we seem vulgar —but we are sick of it.[58]

Mrs. Eddy wrote him a letter thanking him for the article and going on to say:

> *My personality asserted and aimed at by others has been under my feet twenty-two years; but the foes of Christ, marshalled under the signals of Christian Scientists seem to see my personality very vividly and are constantly firing at it. . . . True, I have troublesome friends who burden themselves with personality but I have scientific students who follow my teachings and leave my personality alone, more alone, than any others on the globe; for this I thank God and take courage.*[59]

Adams, however, when asked at a public lecture whether he had not learned whatever Christian Science he knew from Mrs. Eddy, answered no, he had learned it from Truth. Alfred Farlow, reporting the incident to Calvin Frye, commented that the answer showed "what a limited idea [Adams] has of Mrs. Eddy."[60] To Farlow, who was mercifully free from any tendency toward idolatry, it seemed simple common sense that Mrs. Eddy could not be separated from the truth she taught. As she had put it in her Chicago speech, "Christian Science is my only ideal; and the individual and his ideal can never be severed."[61]

What she faced was the old dilemma of the prophet who announces from the depths of conviction, "Thus saith the Lord," and by that very fact becomes an offence to all who question his message or his mission. To another student Mrs. Eddy wrote that she had put herself before the public "apparently egotistically" because of "the necessity that binds me to speak for Christ assured words."[62] Truth itself, in her view, determined the difference between authoritative and merely authoritarian claims.

Early in his editorship, Bailey wrote an article, "Christian Science and its Revelator," in which he undertook to answer the charge that Christian Scientists made Mrs. Eddy equal with Jesus. The mission of Jesus, he declared, was to show all men their true spiritual status as the sons of God—as heirs of God and joint heirs with Christ, in Paul's words. The mission of Christian Science was to show men how to claim that universal heritage and demonstrate step by step the freedom it involved:

> Christian Science proves that equality with Jesus is the spiritual estate that he showed us the way to enter into. The function of Jesus, his place in human consciousness, is his by acquisition and consummation; that of the Author of Science and Health, and every mortal who follows him, both in the spirit and letter of divine Science, is in the course of accomplishment.[63]

The distinction should have been clear, but it was lost in such a sea of highly emotive language that several generations of fundamentalist critics would refer to the article as proof that Christian Scientists *did* make Mrs. Eddy equal with Jesus. Nor were matters helped in the next issue of the *Journal* when the editor prepared the way for Mrs. Eddy's transfer of the magazine to the National Christian Scientist Association and her own temporary retreat to Barre, Vermont, with the words:

> As our dear Mother in God withdraws herself from our midst, and goes up into the Mount for higher communings, to show us and the generations that are to come the way to our true consciousness in God, let us honor Him and keep silence.

It would have been better if Bailey had. Mrs. Eddy immediately sent him a request that the next issue of the *Journal* should contain nothing of her personality.[64] The request was to be repeated several times during the next year or two, but Bailey found it easier to adore Mrs. Eddy than to obey her. The situation was complicated by the fact that public announcement already had been made that "Rev. Mary B. G. Eddy has entirely withdrawn from responsibility and control in the conduct of the Journal."[65] Her students must learn to take responsibility for their own statements, and to Mr. and Mrs. Colles in Ireland she wrote:

> I am weary of . . . so much responsibility that I cannot do justice to my calling, hence my retirement for young folks to take

their place in front and do some thinking for themselves and the cause without my aid.[66]

At the opposite extreme from Bailey, though equally unpredictable, was George Day of Chicago, who was now causing his hitherto admiring flock in that city to do some rather worried thinking for themselves. A year earlier, after Day had attended Mrs. Eddy's last class on obstetrics in October, 1888, she had written him:

> *My pain and disappointment at seeing your state of mind is better imagined than described. Old Theology and the Schools cling to you to such an extent . . . that I fear you will leave us eventually, and then you may be tempted to do as malicious mind prompts all to do, take with you many of my best students who are not watching. . . . To guard against this sadder result, this is my present petition, in all love and respect proferred to you. If you feel that Chris. Sci. as laid down in Science and Health is not what is genuine, you can not surely feel justified in promulgating it. Therefore I ask, yes, I beg you to resign your place now in this field to someone who is sound in this Science, and let us still be friends, and you a fair foe, if indeed you must be this to the truths of Christian Science.*
>
> *Please ponder this in your heart alone, and name it not. . . . Go to God alone for wisdom to enable you to deal with this subject justly, and as you would love to contemplate your action in time to come.*[67]

Day did not in fact take her advice, and for the next year and a half he wavered back and forth between faith and doubt. There were times when his presentation of Christian Science was clear and strong, his gratitude to Mrs. Eddy unreserved and outspoken. Then suddenly he would be full of questioning, darkness, resentment, criticizing the *Journal* bitterly for its emphasis on animal magnetism and its glorification of Mrs. Eddy. But when his relations with the Chicago church reached a crisis early in 1890, she refused to be drawn into it. Her whole effort at that time was to strengthen the bonds of love among her students, and to Ellen Linscott she wrote:

> *Darling if I could make all the Church love Mr. Day and agree to disagree with his views (if they must, for conscience sake) and then continue to live in love for one another as they once did I would sacrifice much to accomplish this.*[68]

Six months later, after Day had severed all connection with the church, she wrote another Chicago student who wanted to go and argue with him: "Brother Day or Brother Adams have a perfect right to their opinions and to express them the way we all have. I love them and feel interested in all that benefits them."[69] In a negative way, she had reason to be grateful to both men. They had driven home to her the uselessness of trying to structure into her church pastoral patterns derived from traditional Protestantism; her church of the future would be fully a church of laymen.

6

The year 1889 had meant formidable struggles for Mrs. Eddy as she demolished one familiar landmark after another.[70] She had had little time to sit down and write to her older students the long letters of counsel and encouragment to which they were accustomed.

Then, in the opening days of 1890, she suddenly sent out a flood of personal letters full of warm concern for each of them individually, full of hope, trust, and pride in them—above all, full of yearning to see them really live the love they professed. Where there were rivalries between them, she would say in effect: Go to Mrs. So-and-so. Tell her you love her and want to help her. Don't wait for her to change before you see her as the child of God.[71]

The letters were reassuring evidence that the new Leader was the same teacher and counselor they had known in the past. If anything, she seemed to be growing in patience.

On January 19 she wrote Clara Shannon in Montreal:

> *I will tell you some time . . . why my past and present seclusion has been and is kept up for an indefinite time. I have learned more of Christian Science the past year than I shall ever be able to communicate*
> *Mrs. Woodbury called on me on her return from Montreal. She was very pleasant and spoke of her experience with a kind of chastened joy. Be patient as you can with her shortcomings, she has her good points as well.*[72]

For years Josephine Woodbury had been a strong support to her at times, but more often a difficult burden. A year earlier Mrs. Woodbury had spent some months in Montreal, playing the sort of missionary role she greatly enjoyed, dominating the Christian Science scene, and leaving both healing and wreckage in her wake. At the time, Mrs. Eddy had written a male student there who had first studied with Mrs. Woodbury and then with Mrs. Eddy herself:

> *Dear Mrs. W. is not alone in the struggles of nature and grace. She is unfortunate in some things that hinder her prog-*

ress. I am stern and gentle by turns with her, but only to do her good—for I am not naturally mean in my mental states.[73]

Two months later, Mrs. Eddy wrote Joshua Bailey, who was planning a trip to Europe, that he should go first to Montreal and get in touch with Clara Shannon about the situation there. Then, referring to the male student to whom she had previously written, she added, "Poor, good Mr. _____ has been demoralized for a season by his first teacher, but is wholly blind to her effect on him."[74] Bailey was to "redeem the Cause" in Montreal, with Miss Shannon's help. As it happened, his trip to Europe was canceled and he never got to the Canadian city, whereas Mrs. Woodbury seems to have found an opportunity to complete the demoralization of poor, good Mr. _____. Later events suggest that the situation probably came to a climax in a clandestine meeting in September, 1889.

This, at least, is a plausible inference from certain startling events which occurred nine months later. Other happenings in the fall of 1889 also point to Mrs. Woodbury's having undergone an unsettling emotional experience in September. Later in that month she closed her "Academy of Christian Science." Then she and her husband withdrew from the National Christian Scientist Association and a little later resigned from the Boston church, just before its dissolution. The explanations which Mrs. Woodbury advanced in each case[75] were high-minded or at least high-flown espousals of Mrs. Eddy's strictures on material organization and were accompanied by ardent avowals of loyalty to Mrs. Eddy's leadership. Looked at realistically, however, they seem to have been acts either of remorse for what had happened in September or of alarm over what was going to happen before long.

This was the background of Mrs. Woodbury's January, 1890, visit to Mrs. Eddy.[76] The latter's charitable letter to Clara Shannon, already quoted, gives no hint of the deeper currents which may have run through the interview. Foster Eddy, who perhaps was privy to some of his mother's hidden misgivings on the subject, wrote to another student on the same day warning her to have nothing to do with Mrs. Woodbury.[77]

The next development is best described in that lady's own inimitable words:

> *On the morning of June 11, 1890, there was born to me a baby boy; though, till his sharp birth-cry saluted my ears, I had not realized that prospective maternity was the interpretation of preceding months of poignant physical discomfort, not unreasonably attributed to other physiological causes and changes,— growing out of my age, and former reliance upon medical opinion,—pointing in the direction of some fungoid formation.*[78]

It was no secret to those who knew Mrs. Woodbury that she had not had marital relations with her husband for several years, though he remained her devoted slave at all times. She had, in fact, urged some of her students to follow her example in this respect, and Mrs. Eddy had had to point out sharply the dangerous impropriety of such advice.[79] Now Mrs. Woodbury was faced with the embarrassing necessity of explaining—to her husband as well as to her students—the baby she had produced.

Since it could not be passed off as a fungoid formation, she devised the very dramatic solution of announcing it as the result of an "immaculate conception." Mr. Woodbury and the more bedazzled of her students found the explanation acceptable, if startling. In an audacious ceremony at Ocean Point, Maine, on July 4, Mrs. Woodbury immersed the child three times "in a singularly beautiful salt pool" and christened him "The Prince of Peace," while a crowd of her students who were "assembled on neighboring bluffs . . . joined in a spontaneously appropriate hymn."[80]

To Mrs. Eddy the birth of the baby was probably no surprise in itself, but Mrs. Woodbury's explanation of its conception came as a sickening shock. Knowing the struggle between "nature and grace" in her student, she was prepared to be charitable over even a serious moral lapse,[81] but this came close to being the sin against the Holy Ghost. The pious flummery with which Mrs. Woodbury had coated her deceit made it more than an embarrassing outbreak on the lunatic fringe of Christian Science; this was, as Clara Shannon had written her about Mrs. Woodbury's behavior in Montreal, "demonology in its highest forms."[82]

The full extent of the unexpectant mother's guile was apparent, however, only when she attempted to "father" the child on Mrs. Eddy herself by claiming that the latter had taught her students that mental conception was possible to the spiritually pure. Like Mrs. Plunkett's attempt to fasten her doctrine of spiritual conjugality on her teacher, the claim was a bald reversal of Mrs. Eddy's actual teaching on the subject.[83] The virgin birth occupied a place of considerable importance in that teaching, but always as a unique historical event bound up with the prophesied messiahship of Jesus.[84] At most, it was a *symbol* of all men's true origin in God, not a pattern for human generation. "Marriage," *Science and Health* declared plainly, "is the legal and moral provision for generation among human kind."[85]

Through the summer of 1890 word of Mrs. Woodbury's strange doings and stranger claims filtered back to Mrs. Eddy. What is perhaps most surprising of all is the latter's unwillingness to abandon this most difficult of students even under extreme provocation. For several more years she continued to work with Mrs. Woodbury patiently, trying to rescue the genuine good in her from the deceit which was all that most of the students could see. Mrs. Woodbury meanwhile vacillated between extreme contrition and increasing perversion of the Christianity she still professed.

When Mrs. Eddy asked her, on the occasion of a visit several years later, whether she still believed her child to have been immaculately conceived, Mrs. Woodbury answered bitterly, "It was incarnated with the devil."[86] Nevertheless, little "Prince," as she called him, remained an important part of the mystique through which she governed such students as still clung to her abjectly.[87] On the same occasion, when Mrs. Eddy asked her why she had resigned from the church in 1889, her shamefaced answer was: "What else could I do?" Reminding her of this two years later, Mrs. Eddy wrote:

> *During that visit you seemed deeply penitent and I pitied you sincerely. You referred to your past conduct and said, "If it will save others from doing as I did it is all that I ask." I forgave you then and there and told you I would try to have you admitted to our church if you so desired.*[88]

It was too late, however. The church would not have her, and before the end of the century Mrs. Woodbury was to launch an extraordinarily venomous public attack on Mrs. Eddy.[89] Not since Kennedy and Arens had the dissaffection of any student gone to such disastrous extremes.

Yet in an oblique way, Mrs. Woodbury throws a good deal of light on what had been happening to Mrs. Eddy since the days of Kennedy and Arens. The degree to which grace had triumphed over nature in the Founder of Christian Science is suggested in a letter written to her by Mrs. Woodbury in the early 1890's. Freely acknowledging her "sin," the latter wrote:

> *And you* never *speak of it*[;] you never seem to remind me of it or remember it *but always bless me so. I think I never suffered as I suffer now when I am beginning to understand you. Every time I see you it is harder to bear—this great chasm between your life and mine, and only because you are so gentle do I dare try to undo what I have helped to do in the past.*[90]

Mrs. Woodbury's tragedy was that of a passionately divided woman who could not, in the last analysis, accept the gift of grace.

Chapter
X

The Face
of
Autumn

The Face of Autumn

Mrs. Eddy's retirement from Boston was not a retirement from battle. To the end of her days the battles would continue, but they were increasingly private ones. With her church and with the world she shared the fruits of victory; with the members of her household she shared the labor and the struggle.

Like an autumn in which days of ripe serenity are interspersed with days of slashing rain and wind, her life illustrated that alternating "hush and stir" which in an earlier edition of *Science and Health* she had described as "the order of scientific evolution."[1] She spoke often of human life in terms of seasons. To her young student Frank Gale in California she wrote:

> *You are growing. The Father has sealed you, and the opening of these seals must not surprise you. The character of Christ is wrought out in our lives by just such processes. The tares and wheat appear to grow together until the harvest, then the tares are* first *gathered, that is, you have seasons of seeing your errors —and afterwards by reason of this very seeing, the tares are burned, the error is destroyed. Then you see Truth plainly and the wheat is "gathered into barns," it becomes permanent in the understanding.*[2]

To have truth become permanent in the understanding: This was the aim of all the pulling up and separating and discarding in this period of her life. So much was impermanent, human life most of all. In her letters she sometimes wondered aloud whether she would be spared to bring to fruition the task which, it seemed to her, she had barely begun. To the Linscotts in 1890 she wrote, "Silently, and *alone,* I contemplate the infinite peaks, and wait on God."[3]

Many trivial things fell into place. No longer did she feel it necessary to use artifice to conceal the fact that her hair had turned white.[4] Smartly turned out as always—in ruffled lilac silks and beaded black satins, with ermine trimmings on her coat and discreet little plumes on her bonnet, she nevertheless took on that delicate grandmotherly look familiar from her later portraits. Frailer in appearance than when she was in Boston, she seemed even more beautiful to some of her students. In one way or another many of them echoed John Donne's words:

> No spring nor summer beauty hath such grace
> As I have seen in one autumnal face.

As a Christmas present in 1890 George Glover sent her a ring containing a curious stone he had found in his mining. In a letter full of warm affection, Mrs. Eddy answered:

> *I shall keep it as long as I live on this earth in loving memory of my son. But it is too large for my fingers now. I am fifty pounds lighter than when you saw me last, but I am in divine health.*[5]

For years periodic rumors had been set afloat that Mrs. Eddy was ill, dying, or even dead. As long ago as 1885 she had dryly denied in the *Journal* a report, attributed to the *St. Louis Democrat,* that she had died of poison and left her property to Susan B. Anthony.[6] With the relative seclusion of her life at Concord, the rumors increased. Actually she had quite a number of visitors, went driving through the city daily, visited its shops, had dinner from time to time with her cousins, chatted with the children who played around her as she sat on a bench outside for long hours, writing.[7] But she was already becoming something of a legend and a figure of mystery. While her critics surmised the worst, many of her own followers saw her through a golden haze. At a time when she was under special stress, Foster Eddy wrote Knapp that she did not "want the students to talk [about] her too much in advance of where she has demonstrated as it may only impede her progress."[8] When Laura Lathrop proposed to make a special visit to Concord to consult her, Mrs. Eddy replied: "I hope you will understand me when I say you had better not see me. I am less personally than impersonally."[9]

On the other hand, she was more than delighted to have her student Laura Sargent of Oconto come to stay with her for several months in 1890. Mrs. Sargent had a special quality of intelligent devotion which made her an ideal helper and companion. Though she had to return to her husband in Wisconsin before the end of the year, much of her life for the next twenty years would be spent as a member of Mrs. Eddy's household. To Laura's sister Victoria at the beginning of the new year, Mrs. Eddy wrote:

> *What should I have done without your dear sister? . . . Oh! I wish it could be always so, and I could have her while I*

pilgrim here. She is the best, the kindest and dearest girl in all the world to me; and I have been so lonely with no female to be with me.[10]

It was out of this enforced loneliness, she felt, that her students' spiritual growth was nurtured. To Captain Eastaman, solicitous as ever of her welfare, she wrote:

If there is any change in me since my absence from Boston it has been an increasing estimate of what you were to me when I was there. You all are growing, and in three years I trust the pride that must be quenched, will be, and in its place will be found brotherly love preferring one another.[11]

To another student, Carrie Snider of New York, she wrote in fuller explanation:

Know this, that a Mother's love encourages self dependence and trust in God. It weans her child when it is old enough to be taken from her bosom. It would not be love that would keep her child a lifelong suckling! All these things, like Mary of old, I "ponder in my heart," and try to do by my students as I would have them do by me. Try to promote their happiness in ways that they do not see, for if they did they would not cry because I throw them, after long years, upon their own responsibility and leave them there with God to direct them.[12]

What she had done for the students in Boston she proceeded to do for students elsewhere when on May 27, 1890, the National Christian Scientist Association held its annual convention in New York City. In a written message to the members Mrs. Eddy, in the midst of praising their spiritual growth, quietly dropped a final bombshell. Let them disorganize the association, she suggested, "and each one return to his place of labor, to work out individually and alone, for himself and for others, the sublime ends of human life."[13] If they preferred not to disorganize, she recommended that they adjourn for three years; if they should disorganize, let them meet again in three years anyway. In point of fact, their action was ambiguous but they never did meet again as a deliberative body.[14] The Publication Committee appointed by the association still controlled the *Journal,* but local Christian Science associations and churches were now essentially on their own. Only the three-year proviso showed that Mrs. Eddy was keeping the door open for whatever higher forms of national or global organization might present themselves to her thought as she watched the developing situation.

For the moment she was fully occupied with what seemed to her a task of overriding importance: another major revision of *Science and Health*.

Since she had first started to write the book, Mrs. Eddy had never read it through consecutively. She had worked on it piecemeal, rewriting, rearranging, out of the inspiration of the moment and the lessons of experience.[15] Even the thoroughgoing revision for which she had enlisted Wiggin's help in 1885 had been more a matter of adding, deleting, and reconstructing sentences than of radically reorganizing subject matter. In any case, the book did not argue its way forward step by methodical step like a lawyer's brief or a dialectician's discouse. The structure of its logic was implicit in every part of it, but various aspects of the structure came to light in relation to different subjects or themes. These themes appeared and disappeared in the text in almost arbitrary fashion and sometimes in apparent disregard of the nominal chapter heading.

This thematic interweaving could be considered a source of strength in a work which was not intended to be a formal philosophical treatise but a textbook for living, directed to widely differing levels of thought and kinds of experience—to the heart as well as to the mind. Nevertheless, too many sudden switches of subject could spoil the total flow of the book and make more difficult its systematic study. Just about the time Mrs. Eddy was ready to start disorganizing the church structure that she had built up during the 1880's she was ready to undertake a radical restructuring of the Christian Science textbook. She did not yet foresee the day when the Bible and *Science and Health* would become the "pastor" of her reconstituted church, replacing all personal preaching, but she was aware of the intensive and exhaustive study to which her book would be put by increasing numbers of people of diverse backgrounds.[16] From her earliest teaching, when she had required her students to know her manuscripts inside out, Christian Science had been a *study*. With the cessation of her personal teaching, the book itself became the basic teacher. To systematize its arrangement at the same time that she enriched its content was the challenge she recognized even before she began the drastic disorganizing processes of 1889.

The same qualities in Joshua Bailey which led her to choose him as editor of the *Journal* caused Mrs. Eddy to turn to him for help in the new project. At the end of 1888 she asked him to go through the book sentence by sentence and suggest rearrangements of material that would bring together scattered passages dealing with a single topic. He was not to change, delete, or add to her words except for necessary transitions.[17] It was largely a scissors and paste job, and as it went on Mrs. Eddy questioned whether it was clarifying her presentation of Christian Science at all.[18] Shortly after the work had begun, she wrote

Bailey: "Your motives, aims, and transfiguration, are all known to me. I agree with your arrangement so far; perhaps our dear God will change it[;] if so amen."[19] Several times she had him stop work altogether, and eventually she wrote that she had had to throw aside all the work that he had done and start again.[20] But the experiment was instructive, and at least one major recommendation by Bailey bore permanent fruit. In September, 1889, Frye wrote him, "Mrs. Eddy consents to having you impersonalize [the chapter] 'Reply to a Critic,' but reminds you that it will involve changing the caption of the chapter."[21]

To Bailey himself the work was unutterably sacred—a task which, he felt, took him deeper into the heart of Christian Science than years of ordinary study might have done. In his own words, "As I weighed and compared and pondered and sought the subtle relations of the thought . . . it seemed to me that I was as one with a mass of threads of the most delicate and beautiful colors that were to be laid together by their shades." Sometimes, he went on, the thought of his own unworthiness for the task brought him to tears and he would ask, "What am I, O God, that thou shouldst serve thyself of me?"[22] To become associated with the composition or publication of Mrs. Eddy's book was to be drawn deeply into the atmosphere of her thought and so to become involved in a measure in her subjective experience, either by way of response or reaction.

Science and Health has been called fancifully an autobiography in cryptogram. To the question of a little Roman Catholic girl who was one of the Concord children who played around her as she wrote outside on fine days, Mrs. Eddy replied with a smile that she was working on the life of God.[23] Rooted though it was in her own experience, the book dealt almost wholly with universals. There were comparatively few references in it to the events of her life, yet even the generalized propositions of the "scientific statement of being" grew from and with her experience. The work combined, one might say, the maximum of personal involvement with the maximum of impersonal formulation. From the third edition on, each rewriting aimed at greater impersonality, wider applicability, a more timeless statement of what she called its "inexhaustible topics."[24] Centuries would pass, she wrote, before those topics were fully demonstrated, and she herself remained a close student of the book to the end of her days. Her own estimate of the way in which it grew into its final form was expressed in a statement which has never ceased to astound her critics: "I should blush to write of 'Science and Health with Key to the Scriptures' as I have, were it of human origin, and were I, apart from God, its author."[25]

The inner and outer turmoil that had accompanied each major

revision in the past was not to be escaped in this case, either. On April 10, 1890, she wrote to the young wife of William G. Nixon, who had now become her publisher, that the new book was "almost ready to go to press."[26] Then the situation took a sudden turn that plunged her into nine more months of work, struggle, and prayer. A letter arrived which convinced her that the revision was far from ready for the press and that her earlier doubts of the value of Bailey's transpositions were fully justified. The letter came from the still redoubtable Wiggin.

2

During the six years of their association,[27] Mary Baker Eddy and James Henry Wiggin wrote to each other with considerable frankness. As acting editor of the *Journal* until February, 1889, he sometimes pleaded with her to change or omit material which she submitted for publication. On one occasion soon after the defection of Sarah Crosse, Mrs. Eddy sent him an article highly critical of Mrs. Crosse, together with some of the latter's correspondence. Wiggin wrote back that he had heard her say that she wished people would advise her personally and he therefore offered the following blunt advice:

> *Don't allow yourself to be led into the printing of these articles. Your Cause cannot afford it. There is trouble enough in yr camp, & unwisdom shd not be allowed to aggravate it. Such documents will make outsiders laugh, while your judicious friends grieve. Pardon my plain speech.*[28]

The depth of his concern is evident from the fact that he rewrote the letter twice before sending it, trying to find the most persuasive way to put the matter. At first Mrs. Eddy remained unpersuaded and Wiggin again wrote, imploring her to reconsider the matter. At last she replied:

> *I yield to your advice knowing as I do your integrity of motive and respecting as I do your judgment. But not without a fervent prayer that the dear Father will guide me in it more than you can. Perhaps He is guiding me through you[;] with this sense I submit.*[29]

In his direct relations with her Wiggin seems always to have shown the best side of himself: a gallantry, sympathy, and genuine desire to help her in every way possible. But in the company of critical friends of his own intellectual circle who chaffed him on his connection with the "high priestess" of Christian Science, he quickly adopted their tone of supercilious amusement, became all man of the world, and laughed her off as "an awfully (I use the word advisedly) smart woman, acute, shrewd, but not well read, nor in any way learned."[30] There, in fact, was the rub. His sense of intellectual superiority was clearly affronted by something in her that refused to be patronized.

After Bailey replaced Wiggin as editor of the *Journal,* Mrs. Eddy had little occasion to see or write the latter for some months. Then, in September, 1889, she wrote him that in the edition of *Science and Health* she was now preparing she would like to acknowledge the work he had done on the chapter "Wayside Hints."[31] It hurt her conscience, she added, to take full credit for the authorship of that "supplementary" chapter. Wiggin replied that the Christian Science and the ideas in the chapter were wholly hers, while the illustrations, quotations, facts, outline, and most of the writing in it were his; that he saw no particular advantage in the use of his name with the chapter, but that if she did use it, he would like to see the proofsheets first.

That settled the question. Mrs. Eddy at once dropped the chapter.[32] She had already discarded the many quotations from other authors which Wiggin had persuaded her to include in the sixteenth edition and its successors. Bible verses alone were now to be used as epigraphs, except for Luther's "Here I stand. I can do no otherwise; so help me God! Amen!" The author was stripping the book down to basic Christian Science and eliminating the Victorian gingerbread. At the same time she was adding a good deal of new material of her own composing, not merely decorative but organically related to her main themes.

Sometime about the end of April, 1890, she sent Wiggin proofs of the first chapter of the revised edition with a request for his comments. He replied that as usual he would give her his unvarnished appraisal—"& then, as usual, you will do as you please."[33] It was the first he had seen of the text since Bailey's changes and he was appalled by them—perhaps also a little nettled at the way some of the "improvements" he had promoted for the sixteenth edition had now been done away with:

> *I marvel at the deterioration your book has undergone in these reprinted pages. I should suppose a cyclone had struck the leaves, and knocked them into unwonted corners. . . . Better let your volume stand as it is. Too much change looks like* vacillation.[34]

His letter confirmed Mrs. Eddy's already grave doubts about the Bailey changes and she promptly engaged Wiggin to work with her in setting the matter to rights. There was a new touch of asperity in some of his comments, but Mrs. Eddy wrote him good-naturedly, "Your interest in the work you are performing for me and mankind has the rare quality of King Lear's daughter's affection, it *never flatters.*"[35]

Wiggin urged her several times to leave *Science and Health* as it already was and make the material she was adding into another book. "By thus having a *new book*," he wrote, "you will *sell more copies*."[36] But the argument to the pocketbook carried little weight beside her vision of what the Christian Science textbook could and should be. One of the titles Wiggin advanced for the proposed new book was *Christian Science Restated;* he might as well have suggested with Solomon that a mother allow her child to be cut in two.

Science and Health itself must advance to a new stage of adulthood, and the process was painful in the extreme. Early along, Mrs. Eddy wrote Wiggin:

> *My faith in your criticism continues, but you know faith sometimes needs Mr. Wiggin's notes, and his notes, occasionally, need my metaphysics. . . .*
> *I have had to throw aside the work that [Bailey] did, and start again. And now, with your assistance, the book must come out right.*[37]

Then followed six months of almost indescribable confusion. Letters flew back and forth between Boston and Concord, between Mrs. Eddy as author, Wiggin as editor, Wilson as printer, Nixon as publisher. While Mrs. Eddy scolded and complained, copy was delayed and proofs were lost. Everyone and his brother seemed to be making unexplained and indecipherable changes on the proofs. At times Frye and Foster Eddy were in the thick of the action, sending out imperious and impossible orders in Mrs. Eddy's name. Both Wiggin and Nixon wrote her letters of barely controlled exasperation at what seemed to them unbusinesslike procedures and undue changeableness. Wiggin several times resigned in despair, only to be cajoled back by Mrs. Eddy. She herself expressed near-despair in a number of letters. And somehow, through it all, the new edition—the fiftieth—was beaten into shape.

Years before, she had written Wiggin that she could always measure the importance of her projects by the resistance she encountered in carrying them out. By that yardstick, the fiftieth edition should rank high. Mrs. Eddy saw the resistance in terms of the "red dragon" standing by to devour her child as soon as it was born. A more modern analogy might be the piling up of atmospheric resistance which for so long prevented aircraft from breaking through the sound barrier.

To push forward the constantly delayed work, she detailed especially trusted students to "work" mentally for the spiritual protection of key personnel engaged in the production of the book. Wiggin was assigned to Captain Eastaman, who wrote Frye in October that the thoughts Frye had given him to work with were not "strong enough Godward" for a worldly man like Wiggin to respond to. A week later he concluded that Mrs. Eddy should not employ such a man, who talked against her openly in large groups and announced that her only aim was to make money. Wiggin, he wrote Frye, spoke "damnable blasphemy against our darling," but "she is so good that maybe she has no idea of the badness of that or any man."[38]

A less *parti pris* opinion was that of a bright Harvard undergraduate, William Dana Orcutt, who had worked at the University Press as a proofreader in the summer of 1890. Young Orcutt regularly joined John Wilson, Wiggin, and the chief proofreader for biweekly evenings of whist, at which there was frequent conversation about Mrs. Eddy and the edition in progress. In Orcutt's later words:

> *Mr. Wiggin was a vainglorious, pompous man, with a very high opinion of his own ability. In his conversations with Mr. Wilson about the proof, he constantly spoke of the difficulty he had in trying to persuade Mrs. Eddy to accept his suggestions, and he seemed to be somewhat chagrined by that fact.*[39]

Not merely chagrined, sometimes, but outraged. Yet Eastaman's prayers may have had their effect, for Wiggin's good nature usually surmounted the outrage—at least when he was writing to Mrs. Eddy. In a letter of complaint which he signed "yrs resignedly," he added in a postscript that he enjoyed a recent chat with Nixon very much— "He is intelligent . . . & can reason for himself"—but that then Nixon had taken to Mrs. Eddy proofs that should have come to *him*, Wiggin. "Too many *Wigs & Nixies*," he concluded with unexpected mildness, "may spoil yr book, so prythee let the Wig quietly withdraw."[40]

Mrs. Eddy, for her part, always came back in the end to her appreciation of Wiggin. To Nixon she could write in regard to Wiggin's changes, "The second proofs have the most shocking flippancy in notations,"[41] and to Wiggin himself, "I am losing my patience. The nonfulfillment of your promises is unbusinesslike unjust and unbearable."[42] But when Wiggin wrote a dignified and reasonable rejoinder to this last charge, she sent him a winning apology. She had dictated the earlier note, ignorant of the true situation:

I humbly, tearfully, read it, now, and your noble business-like report—and wish it had not been written.

I have spoken of you always, as a model in promptness, up-rightness, executiveness, and have felt all I said.

Pardon me this once. . . . I felt pushed to make somebody move. . . . By all means go on with me to the end. You even will be proud of SCIENCE AND HEALTH *some day. . . .*[43]

There would be further work with Wiggin in 1891 after the fiftieth edition appeared and occasional friendly letters between them until his death in 1900, but it was clear that his usefulness to Mrs. Eddy was now essentially at an end. The genial relationship had been gradually corroded by Wiggin's acute sense of how Mrs. Eddy looked to the intellectual élite whose good opinion he valued so highly. In a half-shamefaced explanation of his earlier published defense of her logic and her Christianity, he wrote to a friend of his college days, "I did not know the old lady [then] as well as I do now."[44]

The "old lady," however, turned out to be more magnanimous in her final judgment than her erstwhile champion. When, several years after Wiggin's death, a friend of his published a stinging account of the relations between the two, Mrs. Eddy wrote in response, "I hold the late Mr. Wiggin in loving, grateful memory for his high-principled character and well-equipped scholarship."[45]

3

Among other changes in the fiftieth edition, Mrs. Eddy cut down by almost half the already short chapter "Animal Magnetism."[46] The act was symbolic as well as pragmatic.

In February, 1889, when Joshua Bailey had taken over from Wiggin the running of the *Journal,* the special department headed "Animal Magnetism" had disappeared from its pages—but not the subject itself. On the contrary, Bailey proceeded to give excessive emphasis to it, frightening some of the readers and irritating others by publishing sensational accounts of the dire effects of unresisted mental suggestion.[47]

Mrs. Eddy several times took him to task for this and ordered him to publish nothing more on the subject until the overheated readers should be prepared to look at it more rationally and positively. In the *Journal* of August, 1890, she wrote:

The discussion of malicious animal magnetism had better be dropped until Scientists understand clearly how to handle error,—until they are not in danger of dwarfing their growth in love, by falling into this lamentable practice in their attempts to meet it. Only patient, unceasing love for all mankind,—love that cannot mistake Love's aid,—can determine this question on the Principle of Christian Science.

This announcement did not mean that Mrs. Eddy's basic views on animal magnetism had changed. She frequently warned of the danger of making either too much or too little of error. It had to be recognized as a false claim, she held, before it could be denied as a reality. As she now expressed it in *Science and Health:*

> *A knowledge of error and of its operations must precede that understanding of Truth which destroys error, until the entire mortal, material error finally disappears, and the eternal verity, man created by and of Spirit, is understood and recognized as the true likeness of his Maker.*[48]

Malicious animal magnetism was only a more acute form of the general resistance of error to truth, she held, and it needed only to be recognized for what it was and rejected for what it was not. The individual mentality was constantly being bombarded with suggestions from all quarters. Unless properly alerted to the hypnotic nature of suggestion one was likely to accept many of these suggestions as products of one's own thinking. An earlier issue of the *Journal* had quoted from an article in the *Popular Science Monthly* on this subject:

> *Suggestibility is by no means peculiar to hypnotized persons. Almost everyone is sensitive to suggestion to a certain extent when awake. . . . There appears to be no serious reason why the term* hypnotism *should not be so far extended in meaning as to include those exceptional cases in which the phenomena characteristic of the hypnotic state can be produced without first inducing sleep.*[49]

Then, as now, psychologists made much of the fact that a person could not be hypnotized without giving his consent. In a very basic way this was Mrs. Eddy's own view, but she indicated that the consent might often be unconscious rather than conscious; the need was to root out the unrecognized tendencies that would open up one's thought to intruding suggestions. Few of her students, she complained, seemed able to grasp her instruction on this point, and so she came to the decision to say less about it and let them grow to an understanding of what she had already written.

In her own life and immediate circle, however, the high drama of the apocalyptic struggle with the "red dragon" went on. The incredible confusion which attended the printing of the fiftieth edition seemed to her to call for protective mental work to be done for John Wilson and the printers at the University Press. Foster Eddy was put in charge of the work for Wilson himself; several other trusted students were detailed to pray for the printers. But eventually Mrs. Eddy called them off. The typographical mistakes were actually getting worse, the delays were multiplying, and the students were clearly incapable of handling the situation.

Eastaman, who was one of those who was involved in this unsuccessful counteroffensive against error, illustrates both the strength and the limitations of what might be called the old Praetorian Guard. From his background of nautical adventure he brought to Mrs. Eddy's support a simple but quite unshakable faith and devotion. Toward the end of his life he wrote her:

> For more than sixty years my prayer, so simple and brief, has been, God help me, God help me, God help me! With this little prayer in my thought I have conquered attacks of pirates in the China seas, the mutinies of sailors on board the ship, hard gales, hurricanes, tempests on the high seas, disasters, shipwrecks, lee shores, lack of provisions and water, and worst of all, the enmity of men.[50]

At one point he wrote a series of articles for the *Journal* recounting these adventures. It was such a tale as Gilbert Eddy might have listened to with absorbed attention in the Godfreys' parlor at Chelsea. Of particular interest in connection with Eastaman's later career is one small but bizarre episode:

> An incident that occurred years ago, when I was ordinary seaman on shipboard, and before I had ever heard of such a thing as mesmerism, shows the cowardliness of these claims so clearly, that I venture to give it.
>
> A few days out on a trip from Havana to London, it was generally admitted by passengers and crew that our ship was haunted. Strange noises had been heard; and, though we had none on board, a large black dog had distinctly been seen running about the deck at a certain hour in the evening, frightening some very badly. I saw it, with the rest; and resolved to kill it, and so rid the ship of the disturbance. Two chums joined me in my watch, sitting in the passage where he was wont to pass before disappearing. After about four evenings fruitless waiting, the dog again appeared at the usual hour, and walked calmly over our legs; but, when we each grabbed him, there was nothing in our arms! After an evening or two the same thing was re-

peated, but this time I ran aft to catch it. The dog disappeared, as before, at the booby hatch; but one of the passengers, with elbows on the rail and face between his hands, stood laughing ready to burst. With no thought of the consequences or of what I was doing, I ran to him, put my large sailor's knife to his temple, and exclaimed: "If you don't stop these monkey tricks, I'll put this into you!" Astonished at the fearlessness of so young a lad, the man drew back and, without a word, entered the cabin, —but that was the last of the dog and the noises.

It afterwards proved that he was a mesmerist experimenting for his own amusement; being of the sort to have a good laugh at the fears of others, instead of saving them from their fears, as Christian Scientists are taught and have enlisted to do. Of all my early experiences, this one most clearly represents the nothingness of error's claims, whatever their seeming magnitude. I have seen cancers, tumors and insanity disappear before the sword of Truth, as effectually and permanently as both the dog and the man before the sailor-lad's knife.[51]

While the black dog carries a whiff of *Faust* and medieval demonology, Eastaman's impulsive action recalls George Glover's confrontation of Kennedy in 1880. It is hardly surprising that Mrs. Eddy had put her son and his family into Eastaman's special care when they came to Boston, hopeful that the bluff seaman and the rough miner would be able to understand each other. But Eastaman had progressed beyond the sailor's knife to "the sword of Truth" in his dealings with animal magnetism; in a very real sense the mariner had become a metaphysician.

Even so, he still lagged a good way behind his teacher. When he first studied with her, Mrs. Eddy had not advanced to her later position of "impersonalizing" evil, though she had emerged from the point of view represented by the Relief Committee of 1878. To that committee she had issued instructions about turning the evil arguments of the malpractitioners back on themselves. "This is reformatory," she had written, "designed to do good and not evil[;] the Bible says the measure you mete shall be measured out to you."[52] At a considerably later period she wrote of that stage of thought:

I have never countenanced any method in Christian Science which is not to be found in the Bible. For a short time I permitted students when attacked, to defend themselves with the Old Testament method, but this I very soon countermanded.[53]

By the time Eastaman studied with her, the position had been modified to that represented by the minutes of the Christian Scientist Association in May, 1883:

> *The law in Israel today is—what you have said or done to cause another to suffer shall cause you not them to suffer. Why we don't succeed is because we don't wake and enforce this law. Mrs. Eddy dealt very earnestly upon the necessity of the students' proper understanding of the Law of Love, in order that a spirit of revenge and mortal combat need not prevail.*[54]

The next step was reached in 1886 when she wrote a number of students along the lines of her letter to Minnie Hall of Denver:

> *I hasten to say the students are not treating the rule of sin just as I directed. As it is being done you had better drop it and take the argument that you do understand namely—God is All and He is* Love. *There is no* hate *hence no poison.*[55]

Three years later she wrote in the *Journal:*

> *This question is often proposed, How shall I treat malicious animal magnetism? The hour has passed for this evil to be treated personally, but it should have been so dealt with at the outset. Christian Scientists should have gone personally to the malpractitioner and told him his fault, and vindicated Truth and Love against human error and hate. This growing sin must now be dealt with as evil, and not as an evil-doer or personality. It must also be remembered that neither an evil claim nor an evil person is* real, *hence is neither to be* feared *nor honored.*[56]

The fact that Eastaman could see Wiggin only as a "bad" man showed that he had failed to draw the metaphysical distinction which Mrs. Eddy now saw as crucial. Wiggin, as she understood the matter, needed to be protected from the aggressive cynicism that would poison his mind against her if it could find a convenient foothold in his thinking. This cynicism might get to him by way of other people's thinking.[57] Wiggin was not to be condemned, but the mental aggression was. Later she made it a rule of her church that its members should defend themselves daily against aggressive mental suggestion.

It was an issue that went far beyond the stir attending the publication of a new edition of *Science and Health.* The mental influences which at all times aroused Mrs. Eddy's concern were not unrelated to later techniques of psychological persuasion, whether of the Madison Avenue or the Lubyanka Prison variety. "The present apathy as to the tendency of certain active yet unseen mental agencies," she wrote in the new edition, "will finally be shocked into another extreme mortal mood,—into human indignation; for one extreme follows another."[58]

On January 27, 1891, the Reverend Lanson P. Norcross, now pastor of the Christian Science congregation in Boston, wrote Mrs. Eddy, "You should have seen how all eyes glistened in Chickering Hall last Sunday morning when I picked the Book up & announced to them what I was about to read from."[59] The new edition had finally been launched.

The March *Journal* carried an unsigned article by Norcross in which he discussed the significance of this edition. Why was revision necessary? Was revision, in fact, compatible with the book's original inspiration? Certainly, he answered, if the truths presented remained the same, while the author's continued inspiration brought further verbal clarification, new illustrative material, the development of fresh applications and implications:

> *In the days of the Massachusetts Metaphysical College, when we sat at the feet of our teacher—days that we never shall forget —did that teacher ever instruct two classes precisely alike? Did she employ a stereotyped form of words by which to convey to us her rich, inspired thought? Far from it! and thus, the new volume seems to take us back to the College, to gather up its fresh methods and inspired sayings, so that little stretch of the imagination is required to convince us that the teacher herself again is before us, though this time in impersonal form. . . . Let the new volume be studied* in connection with earlier editions. *The very contrasts help to see how the thoughts have risen only as we have been able to receive them. This, again, will reveal why the new edition could now be written for us.*[60]

The final suggestion made by Norcross has a scholastic flavor not altogether in keeping with the spirit of *Science and Health.* More to the point, perhaps, was Alfred Farlow's comment to Mrs. Eddy a little later. He had had one of the latest of the old editions and felt that he wanted to keep it. "But I do not know for what purpose," he wrote her. "For I never read it and it seems to belong to a step left behind."[61]

He was right. The fiftieth edition marked a new era for Christian Science. It is the first edition of *Science and Health* with which the present-day Christian Scientist can feel really at home. It had moved out of the shadow of Wiggin's Boston[62] to confront a world and a decade that would witness the discovery of X rays, radium, the electron, wireless telegraphy. The opening chapter, "Science, Theology, Medicine,"[63] struck the new note in its account of the author's discovery of Christian Science. A single paragraph describing Mrs. Eddy's investigations in 1866–69 illustrates the book's general tone and its nearness to the final, definitive edition:

> *For three years I sought, day and night, the solution of this problem of Mind-healing; searched the Scriptures, and read nothing else; kept aloof from society, and devoted my time and energies to discovering a positive rule. The search was sweet, calm, and buoyant with hope, not selfish or depressing. I knew the Principle of all harmonious Mind-action to be God, and that cures were produced, in primitive Christian healing, by holy, uplifting faith; but I must know its Science, and I won my way to absolute conclusions, through divine revelation, reason, and experiment. I had no human aid. The revelation of Truth in the understanding came to me, through divine power. When a new spiritual idea is borne to earth, the prophetic Scripture of Isaiah is renewedly fulfilled: "Unto us a child is born . . . and his name shall be called Wonderful."*[64]

Subsequent revisions brought to the paragraph a few further changes which illustrate the author's continued search for absolute precision. The words "day and night" disappear from the first sentence. The phrase "and read nothing else" becomes "and read little else." The sentence "I had no human aid" is dropped altogether. The penultimate sentence is changed to read, "The revelation of Truth in the understanding came to me gradually and apparently through divine power."[65] So far as the scholarly investigator is concerned, Norcross was right in observing that there is much to be learned from Mrs. Eddy's verbal changes in successive editions.

For Christian Scientists of that period there was danger of falling into a new bibliolatry as well as a new mariolatry, and once again the well-intentioned Joshua Bailey led the way. In the *Journal* of September, 1890, Mrs. Eddy had announced in the strongest possible terms that she should not be consulted as to the matter to be published in that periodical. The very next month, taking advantage of the freedom thus accorded him, Bailey wrote editorially:

> *A beginner in Christian Science . . . progresses more rapidly, if the Bible is laid aside for a time. A student . . . who says to a Scientist "I take so much comfort in reading my Bible," if guided wisely, will be answered, "Let your Bible alone for three months or more. Don't open it even, nor think of it. But dig day and night at Science and Health."*

This ill-conceived statement sent shock tremors through the ranks of Christian Science and furnished ammunition to hostile critics for generations to come. It was followed by a second blockbuster the following month. Discussing the innumerable books and periodicals still borrowing the name "Christian Science" for their own miscellaneous wares, Bailey wrote in the "Editor's Note Book" for November:

> There is only one way out of this: it is to burn every scrap of "Christian Science Literature" so-called, except Science and Health, and the publications bearing the imprint of the Christian Science Publishing Society of Boston: return to the diligent study of Science and Health and the Bible; preach Christ as there unfolded: direct all inquirers to the same as the only sources of truth, and warn the public, at every opportuniy, against the refuge of lies.

While much of the trash describing itself as "Christian Science"[66] probably deserved to be consigned to the flames, the tone and tenor of the statement were so misguided as to be disastrous. The following month the Publication Committee responsible for the *Journal* issued a strong repudiation of the two pronouncements and Bailey was removed from the editorship, to be succeeded by a Miss Sarah J. Clarke, of mediocre ability but less impulsive temperament.

The mischief was done, however. Some literal-minded Scientists refused to read anything that did not come directly from Mrs. Eddy's pen, and even the *Journal* was held to be taboo.[67] Others both inside and outside the movement reacted vigorously to Bailey's dicta. Joseph Adams commented with his distinctive brand of sorrowing wrath in *The Chicago Christian Scientist*:

> Does our brother know that he has gone far beyond Mrs. Eddy, who in a letter to us, received during the present year says:
> "I have examined your sermons (published), have read your magazine, and am ready to certify publicly or privately that what you write presents the truth of Christian Science with much clearness and Christian fervor."
> What has come over the spirit of our brother that he should have fallen like Lucifer, the son of the morning?[68]

But Bailey was not the only one to fall into error through excessive zeal. Augusta Stetson, whose letters to Mrs. Eddy spilled over with adulation, was busy hatching a scheme for the distribution of *Science and Health* and such lesser Christian Science literature as she deemed to be pure and reliable. On December 18, 1890, Mrs. Eddy wrote Nixon:

> I never dreamed of such a platform as Stetson's being brought forward by a Christian Scientist! No man or woman has

*told me of this obnoxious feature but my Father has, and it shall
be stopped by His servant who has given His Word to the
WORLD—not to a privileged monopoly to tyranize over other
writers. . . . I only marval that you did not* tell me *of this
proscriptive tyranical clause on buying and selling other literature than mine.*[69]

Mrs. Stetson was duly slapped down, but with the publication of
the new edition she swung into action and revived the scheme on a
grander scale. The result was an announcement in the May *Journal*
of the formation of a General Association for Dispensing Christian
Science Literature, with an elaborate plan for sending out *Science and
Health* and certain approved tracts on a huge scale. Christian Scientists everywhere were invited to join, but the enterprise was under the
direction of a General Secretary appointed by Mrs. Stetson. At first
Mrs. Eddy was too preoccupied with other matters to pay close attention to what was happening. When she finally realized that the
organization was set up to prevent the circulation of unauthorized
literature among Christian Scientists quite as much as to distribute
authorized literature to non-Scientists, she was greatly distressed. To
Nixon, who had supported the scheme and published the announcement in the *Journal,* she wrote:

> *Can it be that one who has written to me as you have on
> oppressive measures used in our Cause could have done this?*
> *I will rip up all my business relations and take all into my
> hands before this most wicked, proscriptive, unchristlike measure
> shall be carried.*
> *I never read the May Journal and never knew till now the
> curse in this platform of Stetson's.*[70]

Her rebuke to Mrs. Stetson herself was modified by the strange
tenderness she persistently showed to that self-willed apostle. Patiently
she pointed out that such a system of censorship was an attempt to dig
up the tares before the harvest had come. Quoting Isaiah's messianic
prophecy that the bruised reed should not be broken or the smoking
flax quenched, she went on to speak with exceptional charity of the
false claimants to Christian Science:

> *The writers and teachers—all those who claim to be teach-
> ing Christian Science—are uttering some Truth and Christ did
> not break this reed that will be shaken by the winds until it
> grows stronger in Truth—then let these breezes of God deal with
> this broken reed—and let not human hands, opinions and meas-
> ures attempt to do His work.*[71]

The outcome of the matter was a notice by Mrs. Eddy in the *Journal* of July, 1891:

> Since my attention has been called to the article in the May Journal, I think it would have been wiser not to have organized the General Association for Dispensing Christian Science Literature.
>
> 1. Because I disbelieve in the utility of so widespread an organization. It tends to promote monopolies, class legislation and unchristian motives for Christian work.
>
> 2. I consider my students as capable, individually, of selecting their own reading matter and circulating it, as a committee would be which is chosen for this purpose.[72]

This was accompanied by another notice that the General Association had been disorganized in accordance with Mrs. Eddy's wishes. The whole episode showed her broadening outlook—but it did not signify any lessening of her conviction that Christian Science must be kept absolutely "pure."

In the very next issue of the *Journal* she sharply characterized Joseph Adams' *Truth Healing* as "a faulty detailed dialogue" which had few ideas that were not borrowed without credit from her own writings. Shaken by the wind, the bruised reed broke and Adams severed his tenuous connection with Christian Science. His magazine was rechristened *The Chicago Truth Gleaner*, his method was renamed Gospel Healing, and he announced editorially that neither the Bible nor *Science and Health* should be regarded as the standard. "The *only* authority," Adams wrote, "is God with me, and I recognize no other."[73] With a kind of inevitability he had landed in pure antinomianism. In successive issues of the magazine, he announced that he had abandoned belief in animal magnetism, in the unreality of matter, and finally in spiritual healing itself. But at Christmas in 1891 and again in 1892, he wrote Mrs. Eddy expressing continued love and gratitude—to disappear finally in a kind of benevolent blur.

Here was the other extreme from the censorious sectarian zeal manifested by some of Mrs. Eddy's followers. Both extremes were dangerous. Her final solution lay some years ahead in the *Manual of The Mother Church* which would provide the framework of government for her movement. In that book the Bible and her own writings are named clearly as the sole *textbooks* for the church member:

> The BIBLE, together with SCIENCE AND HEALTH and other works by Mrs. Eddy, shall be his only textbooks for self-instruction in Christian Science, and for teaching and practising metaphysical healing.[74]

A further bylaw proceeds to set forth the criteria for judging other literature which claims to be Christian Science, but leaves the application of these criteria and of the prohibitions named in the bylaw to the honesty and good sense of the individual church member. It makes no provision for the kind of official proscription that so shocked Mrs. Eddy in 1891, but neither does it countenance the kind of lax eclecticism that was ready to accept every self-announced expositor of Christian Science at his own valuation:

> A member of this Church shall neither buy, sell, nor circulate Christian Science literature which is not correct in its statement of the divine Principle and rules and the demonstration of Christian Science. Also the spirit in which the writer has written his literature shall be definitely considered. His writings must show strict adherence to the Golden Rule, or his literature shall not be adjudged Christian Science. A departure from the spirit or letter of this By-Law involves schisms in our Church and the possible loss, for a time, of Christian Science.[75]

The gravity of the warning shows that Mrs. Eddy considered the study and practice of Christian Science to be a very serious business indeed. As she was to write before the end of 1891, "The rare bequests of Christian Science are costly, and they have won fields of battle from which the dainty borrower would have fled."[76]

5

If an institution, as Emerson wrote, is the lengthened shadow of a man, Mrs. Eddy's shadow reached from Concord to Boston. The distance between the two cities symbolized the separation between her private trials and public triumphs, but in one sense Boston was never more conscious of her presence than when she took refuge in Concord.

Then it was that she stood out most clearly as the Discoverer and Founder of Christian Science. Almost fifteen years earlier she had described herself to Daniel Spofford as a tired and wounded fighter taken to the rear, whose wounds were enlivening her soldiers. If that was so, she had added, "God give me more . . . and make me more of a blessing; poor, weak and unworthy, on one hand, august and glorious on the other!"[77] Now she wrote to another student of what a reward it was for all her struggles to know that God had made her—"so poor, so nothing in my sight"—the means of telling His power and grace and glory,[78] while to Mrs. Stetson she wrote of the "marvel" of her life. "What would be thought of it, if it was known in a millionth of its detail?"[79] But it was not, and at the turn of the century she would write her Board of Lectureship: "Millions may know that I am the Founder of Christian Science. I alone know what that means."[80]

Among her most devoted students in Boston there was a yearning to have the world recognize something of the magnitude of sacrifice they glimpsed in her life. As contributions began to flow in for the church building which they hoped to erect within a year or two, a movement gained headway to make the church a "memorial" to her. The proposal finally got into the pages of the *Journal* in October, 1890:

> *Why not build this church the coming year? Why not make it strictly a Memorial Church, representing the voluntary offerings of Scientists from ocean to ocean, from Lake to Gulf? What people have greater cause for thanksgiving? And where so fitting a site for the erection of such a building, as in the heart of the very city where the Founder and Teacher of this Science has had the hardest battles to wage against error; where at its early inception she stood alone, sole advocate and defender of the Cause that is to bless the universal family?*

Mrs. Eddy was dumbfounded. Why had she not been told of this move? In stiff letters to Nixon and to Edward Bates of the *Journal*'s Publication Committee, she denounced the proposal as a "begging" scheme and supplied a corrective statement to be published in the next issue. Nixon, who looked at everything from a hardheaded business point of view and who was proving recalcitrant on almost every issue where genuine intuition was called for, strongly objected to publishing the statement. Forced by his stubbornness to break her own rule of noninterference with the *Journal*, Mrs. Eddy ordered him to run the statement, which consequently appeared in the November issue. Briefly but unequivocally it set forth her objection to being memorialized in a way that would bring "personal motives" into the building of "a house for the worship of God."

The scheme was dropped, and the danger of having a church that could be called Eddyite rather than Christian was avoided. Not long afterward Norcross preached a Christmas sermon on "Jesus, As He Appears to Christian Scientists," which cleared up some of the ambiguities of Bailey's earlier treatment of the subject. Mrs. Eddy, however, was her own most convincing witness to the central importance of Jesus, and each successive revision of *Science and Health* drove this point home in greater depth. In the fiftieth edition she divided the chapter "Prayer and Atonement" into two separate and enlarged chapters. They had not yet been placed at the beginning of the book, where they would later go as the best possible introduction to the metaphysical topics that followed, but they already showed Mrs. Eddy's deepening conviction that the letter of Christian Science could be understood only through the spirit of Christ.[81] In her *Journal* articles, too, her commitment to the Christian ethic of love found increasingly radical expression:

> *Who is thine enemy that thou shouldst love him? Is it a creature or a thing outside thine own creation?*
>
> *Can you see an enemy, except you first formulate this enemy and then look upon the object of your own conception? . . . Simply count your enemy to be that which defiles, defaces, and dethrones the Christ-image that you should reflect. . . .*
>
> *Even in belief you have but one (that, not in reality), and this one enemy is yourself—your erroneous belief that you have enemies; that evil is real; that aught but good exists in Science. . . . I used to think it sufficiently just to abide by our State statutes; that if a man should aim a ball at my heart, and I by firing first could kill him and save my own life, that this was right. . . . Love metes not out human justice, but divine mercy. If one's life were attacked, and one could save it only in accordance with common law, by taking another's, would one sooner give up his own? We must love our enemies in all the manifestations wherein and whereby we love our friends; must even try not to expose their faults, but to do them good whenever opportunity occurs. . . .*
>
> *The falsehood, ingratitude, misjudgment, and sharp return of evil for good—yea, the real wrongs (if wrong can be real) which I have long endured at the hands of others—have most happily wrought out for me the law of loving mine enemies. This law I now urge upon the solemn consideration of all Christian Scientists.[82]*

This carried the battle to higher ground than either Mrs. Eddy or her students had occupied in the 1880's, and it opened the way for her to advance to the prodigious tasks of the next two decades. Again and again she wrote to students at this period, "You are growing"— but she herself was growing most of all. That, at least, is the inference to be drawn from the dramatic accomplishments of the next two decades.

To the members of the Christian Scientist Association of the Massachusetts Metaphysical College, who continued to meet periodically despite the formal dissolution of the parent organizations, she sent a message in June, 1891:

> *You may be looking to see me in my accustomed place with you, but this you must no longer expect. When I retired from the field of labor, it was a departure, socially, publicly, and finally, from the routine of such material modes as society and our societies demand. Rumors are rumors,—nothing more. I am still with you on the field of battle, taking forward marches, broader and higher views, and with the hope that you will follow.*[83]

The problem that demanded her utmost thought was how to substitute government by law for government by persons. Her church must be built on Principle, not on personality—her own or another's —if it was to survive the shocks of the coming century. The centrifugal forces which already had sent the mind-cure cults spinning off toward oblivion would certainly tear Christian Science apart and scatter it to the winds if it were held together only by her personal presence.

To Mrs. Colles in Ireland she wrote late in 1891:

> *I have been hard at work 5 months pouring oil on the waves. . . . A tornado of inward pride and envy is tearing out the heart of Christian Science in many directions today. But God reigns, and I have noble, brave, selfsacrificing Students that are firm as the sea girt rock. And on this "Rock" Christ's Church must be built.*[84]

She had an object lesson before her of the dangers of leadership built on personality. Augusta Stetson's success was beginning to attract attention among Christian Scientists not only in New York but also throughout the country. Humanly, Mrs. Eddy enjoyed and even admired Mrs. Stetson's dash and sweep, and she appreciated the flood of affection which her "darling Augusta" poured on her. But she apparently recognized that such adulation could be a subtle form of self-exaltation.

To Mrs. Stetson's protégé, Carol Norton, a young man for whose honesty and idealism Mrs. Eddy had great respect, she wrote at one point:

> *Our basis in Science is IMPERSONALITY. . . . Here is where my dearest student Mrs. Stetson will make an awful mistake unless she heeds my oft repeated advice to drop my name out of her conversation, teaching, and lectures. . . . I hope Mrs. S. and yourself will be as saintly in yielding to my judgment on*

this as on the question just settled [the Association for Dispens-
ing Christian Science Literature]. You cannot build on person-
ality or you build on sand. . . . *I beg you will review sacred*
history and see this. . . . A St. Peter's or a St. Mary's religion is
far from Christian Science carried out Scientifically.[85]

The letter shows an astute recognition of the direction of Mrs.
Stetson's impulses. For the next eighteen years a struggle would go on
to tame her highly personal ambitions while encouraging her zeal,
and this is foreshadowed in further correspondence Mrs. Eddy had
with Carol Norton in October:

My heart is always touched by your pure goodness. But my
mission among men seems to be a corrective and alterative dose
administered to all with whom I come in contact. . . .

I am sensible of the zeal and good works of dear Mrs. Stet-
son and you. But none can know my necessity to reprove, *rebuke,*
exhort, but the loving Father and Mother of us all. You all are
babes in Truth and Love and the older you are the more the
Mother sees to love, and to reprove. *Why? because you* attempt
more, and each endeavor is an experiment with a student;
whereas it is an old and proven effort with me and I know just
how it will come out. . . . But darling Stetson is eager and will
mistake, and then recover her way on, on. . . .[86]

If her final comment was a little on the wishful side, it was nevertheless a tribute to potentialities which Mrs. Eddy saw as greatly
needed in her movement.

6

As early as 1866 Matthew Arnold had given classic expression in
his "Dover Beach" to a mood that would dominate much of the
world a century later:

> . . . The Sea of Faith
> Was once, too, at the full, and round earth's shore
> Lay like the folds of a bright girdle furled.
> But now I only hear
> Its melancholy, long, withdrawing roar. . . .
> Ah, love, let us be true
> To one another! for the world, which seems
> To lie before us like a land of dreams,
> So various, so beautiful, so new,
> Hath really neither joy, nor love, nor light,
> Nor certitude, nor peace, nor help for pain;

And we are here as on a darkling plain
Swept with confused alarms of struggle and flight,
Where ignorant armies clash by night.

The clash might seem far removed from the countrified hush and stir of Concord, New Hampshire, in 1891, but it was never far from Mrs. Eddy's concern. She had pitched her tent in Concord with a sense of impermanence, to snatch what time she could for rest and thought before moving on to the larger tasks ahead. So little accomplished, so much to be done—this was the constant spur to her gathering energies. A dream-burdened world to be wakened to the inextinguishable reality of joy and love and light, to the always fountaining possibility of certitude and peace and help for pain. The whole of humanity crying out to be rescued from its senseless and ceaseless struggles in the dark. Mrs. Eddy might need retirement from Boston to do her work, but she found no retirement from thinking.[87]

One advantage of the Concord seclusion was that she now had time for a little more general reading. For the first time she dipped into the Ante-Nicene Fathers, delighted to find in them "such close support" for some of her principal teachings.[88] She read a little biblical archaeology.[89] She read and recommended to others Henry Drummond's widely discussed *Natural Law in the Spiritual World,* writing Wiggin that she felt sure Drummond must have read *Science and Health* although his "spiritual protoplasm sometimes collapses into some nearness to a cataplasm."[90] She read with appreciation Edwin Arnold's *Light of the World,* companion piece to his influential *Light of Asia.*[91] She read and marked Tolstoy's *Work While Ye Have the Light* and *The Kreutzer Sonata.*[92]

As always, however, she found her chief inspiration in the Bible. Through the years she had kept up her habit of opening it at random in moments of need, but with a prayer for guidance. She continued also to make note afterward, in many cases, of the verse or passage that leaped to her eye with the answer to her problem. The notations reveal an interesting fact. In her more embattled earlier days she turned almost always to the Old Testament; now it was almost always to the New. The thunder of Sinai was being superseded by the Sermon on the Mount.

When Sue Ella Bradshaw of San Francisco wrote her that she had been passing through great trials, Mrs. Eddy replied that the letter showed that Miss Bradshaw was growing and had come at last to Mount Zion from the fiery ordeal of Sinai:

> . . . *the Mount that was awful to touch has frightened you a little, so that Zion beautiful to behold seems not so placid, so*

comforting, so homelike as it will when the scare of your foot-
steps thither has all passed.[93]

Mrs. Eddy knew from experience what she was talking about. The scare of her own footsteps still caused her sometimes to pause.

A literal example occurred in her search for the ideal home, where she could work in undisturbed peace and comfort. The house on North State Street continued unsatisfactory, and Concord itself had disadvantages. Ira Knapp and Foster Eddy were kept busy for months hunting around in likely spots for a property that would suit her needs. When Knapp came up with a beautiful house and grounds next to his own residence in Roslindale, just outside Boston, Mrs. Eddy wrote him:

> *If only I could be sure that my son and Mr. Frye would stand the fire upon them if I was there, I would go without another word. . . . If only I knew that Boston or the suburbs was the place that God wants me to go I would go without further counting the cost. . . . I always have this struggle if I am doing anything for myself. But for others I can generally see the best way at once.*[94]

The uncertainty lasted for some time, but finally she bought the house and on May 23, 1891, she moved into it. The experiment lasted only a month. Dogs barked, children shouted, visitors called, the heat was oppressive. By contrast, "dear, quaint old Concord"[95] seemed good. To escape the heat, she returned to the North State Street house, ostensibly for the summer only, but on July 8 she wrote Laura Sargent:

> *I have no desire to live in the place of beauty that the Roslindale home is—a beauty unavailing in Christian Science. There is no retirement, no solitude, no quiet in it.*
> *It is a hillside decked with flowers and ornamental shrubs and luxurious fruit and garden, but the walks are so steep that I cannot follow them, the arbor with call-bells from the house— tells of lager! The whole site is surrounded with streets . . . from every side you are saluted with noise.*[96]

The venture made clear to her, however, just what she wanted— stillness and nature and God, as she wrote to Knapp.[97] He was commanded to sell the Roslindale house and search elsewhere, but meanwhile her letters to others showed a growing appreciation of Concord. To Laura Lathrop in New York she wrote:

> *I am now giving students opportunity to call on me and thankful that God gives me time to do this. Come and see me while I have a few, few weeks of more leisure than usual. I want*

to talk *with you. . . . Concord in summer is one of the sweetest places of earth.*[98]

A letter to Eastaman about the same time showed less enthusiasm but a kind of cheerful resignation. "The summer is cool, and the shade trees friendly," she assured him," [but] that is about all I can say of dear, kind, old Concord. Wherever we are, *God is,* and that is all I can hope for here."[99]

To her student Robert Wickersham of Denver she wrote with a lift of the spirit akin to that light and springy step on which so many visitors commented: "I am well and younger than ever before. The foam of earth's billows have left their white waves on my hair but what of that if the heart is hopeful, and not tired of the strife?"[100]

Late in the autumn she found the place she was looking for, less than a mile outside Concord. While taking one of her daily drives, she passed a pleasantly situated farmhouse standing back from the appropriately named Pleasant Street. The land rose to a knoll, then sloped away to the south and east, with a sweeping but tranquil view over woods, fields, and a ribbon of river. By the first of December, Mrs. Eddy had bought the property. To Knapp she wrote that she had longed for a home by the seaside but now it seemed that God had prepared one on the hillside. There, with the farmhouse enlarged and remodeled, the estate augmented by additional land and renamed Pleasant View, she would live for the next sixteen years. There, surrounded by the quiet and beauty she had longed for, she was to become a world-known figure, taking masterful strides forward in the development of her church. Only in 1908 would she move back to the environs of Boston, to spend her last three years in consolidating her life work and launching *The Christian Science Monitor.*

That was a long way off, however, in 1891. As Mrs. Eddy, now seventy years old, stood on the site of the future Pleasant View and gazed across a wide valley to the distant Bow hills where she had been born, she might have been standing on a ridge between two eras. She had just said farewell to the past with the publication of her *Retrospection and Introspection* in November.[101] Actually, less than half that little autobiographical work was devoted to retrospection; much of it dealt with metaphysical issues that reached into the future. Even as the author wrote of her second marriage and her early separation from her son, she could break off—with a kind of indignation at the fraudulence of mortal life—to remind the reader that "material" history is a record of dreams, a play of shadows:

Mere historic incidents and personal events are frivolous and of no moment, unless they illustrate the ethics of Truth. To

*this end, but only to this end, such narrations may be admis-
sable and advisable; but if spiritual conclusions are separated
from their premises, the nexus is lost, and the argument, with
its rightful conclusions, becomes correspondingly obscure. It may
be that the mortal life-battle still wages, and must continue till
its involved errors are vanquished by victory-bringing Science;
but this triumph will come! God is over all. He alone is our
origin, aim, and Being.*

As she looked back over the years of trial that followed her discovery, she saw each period of testing as the prelude to a new advance,
like the "evening and morning" of Genesis and the Christian pattern
of cross and resurrection. In a later passage in the same little book
she wrote:

*A realization of the shifting scenes of human happiness, and
of the frailty of mortal anticipations,—such as first led me to the
feet of Christian Science,—seems to be requisite at every stage
of advancement. Though our first lessons are changed, modified,
broadened, yet their core is constantly renewed; as the law of the
chord remains unchanged, whether we are dealing with a simple
Latour exercise, or with the vast Wagner Trilogy.*

She was approaching the period in which she must reconstruct
her movement on a scale more than Wagnerian, but she ended her
Retrospection and Introspection on a note that suggests, rather, the
quality of a simple Latour exercise:

*I am persuaded that only by the modesty and distinguishing
affection illustrated in Jesus' career, can Christian Scientists aid
the establishment of Christ's Kingdom on earth. In the first
century of the Christian era Jesus' teachings bore much fruit,
and the Father was glorified therein. In this period and the forthcoming centuries, watered by dews of Divine Science, this Tree
of Life will blossom into greater freedom and its leaves will be
"for the healing of the nations."*

One thing is certain. The nations, in the upcoming century,
would find that they could *do* with healing.

Appendices

Notes

Index

1875	October 30	*Science and Health* (first edition) published.
1876	January 20	Bronson Alcott's first visit.
	February 14	*The Science of Man* published.
	March	Asa Gilbert Eddy studies with Mary Baker Glover.
	July 4	Christian Scientist Association organized.
1877	January 1	Mrs. Glover marries Gilbert Eddy.
	May 30	Spofford breaks with her.
1878	May 17	Trial at Salem.
	October	Second (Ark) edition of *Science and Health* published.
	October 29	Conspiracy charge brought against Arens and Gilbert Eddy.
	November 24	Weekly sermons begun at Baptist Tabernacle, Boston.
1879	January 31	Conspiracy case dismissed.
	April 12	Vote to form Church of Christ, Scientist.
	Autumn	Move to Boston for winter.
	November– February	George Glover visit.
1880	May 12	*Christian Healing* published.
	July–August	Research into "mystery of error" at Concord, New Hampshire.
1881	January 31	Massachusetts Metaphysical College chartered.

	August 17	Third edition of *Science and Health* published.
	October 26	Defection of Lynn students.
	November 9	Ordained pastor of church.
1882	February	Stay at Washington.
	March	Stay at Philadelphia.
	May	Opening of college at 569 Columbus Avenue, Boston.
	June 2	Death of Gilbert Eddy.
	July	Stay at Barton, Vermont.
	August 6	Calvin Frye joins household.
1883	February 8	Dresser opens Quimby campaign.
	April 14	First issue of *Journal of Christian Science* (bimonthly).
	May 19	*The People's God* published.
	September 21	*Science and Health* (sixth edition) has *Key to the Scriptures* added to text and title.
	October 4	Injunction issued against Arens pamphlet.
1884	March 3	Move to 571 Columbus Avenue.
	May	Class held in Chicago.
	August	First Normal class held
	September	Emma Hopkins becomes editor of *Journal* (now monthly).
1885	February	*Historical Sketch of Metaphysical Healing* published.
	March 16	Address at Tremont Temple.
	March	*Defence of Christian Science* published.
	July 30	Engages J. H. Wiggin as literary aide.
	November 4	Resignation of Emma Hopkins.
1886	January	Wiggin becomes editor of *Journal*.
	February	National Christian Scientist Association formed. Sixteenth edition of *Science and Health* published.

	September	Gill becomes *Journal* editor.
1887	January	Wiggin replaces Gill on *Journal*.
	February 8	Dresser lectures on Quimby.
	August	*Christian Science: No and Yes* published.
	October 19	Mental Healers' Convention, Boston.
	November	Glover family descends on Boston for six months. *Rudiments and Rules of Divine Science* published.
	December	Move to 385 Commonwealth Avenue, Boston.
1888	March	*Unity of Good and Unreality of Evil* published.
	June 12	Defection of Boston students.
	June 14	Speech at Central Music Hall, Chicago.
	August	Visit to New Hampshire.
	November 5	Ebenezer J. Foster adopted as son.
1889	February	Bailey made editor of *Journal*.
	February 15	Address at Steinway Hall, New York.
	May	Leaves Boston for Barre, Vermont. Resigns pastorate of Boston church.
	June	Gives *Journal* to National Christian Scientist Association.
		Moves to 62 North State Street, Concord, New Hampshire.
	September 23	Christian Scientist Association dissolved.
	October 29	Massachusetts Metaphysical College dissolved.
	December 2	Church formally disorganized.
1890	May 27	National Christian Scientist Association adjourns for three years.
	June– December	Climax of work on major new revision of textbook.

1891	January	Landmark fiftieth edition of *Science and Health* published
	May	Moves to Roslindale, Massachusetts.
	June	Returns to 62 North State Street, Concord.
	November	*Retrospection and Introspection* published.
1892–1910		Completes founding of Church and becomes world figure.

The kind of cosmological and ontological issues to which *Science and Health* in its own way addresses itself have engaged the human intellect from the pre-Socratics to Whitehead, Heidegger, and the physicists of the Max Planck Institute. Such issues, however, were far from being at the center of interest in the Darwinian decades of the last century. Only after the successive emergence of relativity and quantum theory could even the most rudimentary conceptual bridges be thrown between, for instance, Mrs. Eddy's explanations of mind, matter, and causation and those of the more philosophically-minded natural scientists.

To many philosophers and scientists, indeed, "metaphysics" remains a dirty word. It signifies that which lies not merely beyond physics but beyond the pale of respectability—a speculative, prescientific realm where hypotheses which are clearly not susceptible to experimental verification are bandied around. It is, as they see it, a pseudodiscipline in which language games replace the strict criterion of predictable and repeatable results. Wittgenstein's dictum, "The world is everything that is the case," sums up this attitude of noninquiry.

Meanwhile, however, the "case" has changed. While molecular biology and other scientific disciplines have come closer to the controls and exactitudes of physics, physics itself has introduced new questions which undermine some of the old scientific certainties. As the neurologist, for instance, leans more heavily on the biochemist and biophysicist, he seems to be "materializing" intelligence; but at the dead end of his theory, where consciousness becomes electrical circuitry, the quantum physicist takes over, and presto! a subatomic world opens up, where an electron is not a "thing" and the uncertainty and complementarity principles demand an entirely new kind of thinking about causality and objectivity—and thus, by inference, about consciousness itself. In his *Physics and Beyond* (New York: Harper & Row, 1971) Werner Heisenberg tells how Einstein's statement, "It is the theory which decides how we can observe," helped the younger man to formulate the uncertainty principle, and he quotes Niels Bohr as saying:

> The objective world of nineteenth-century science was, as we know today, an ideal limiting case, but not the whole reality. Admittedly, even in our future encounters with reality we shall have to distinguish between the objective and the subjective side, to make a division between the two. But the location of the separation may depend on the way things are looked at; to a certain extent it can be chosen at will.

It remains a question whether the addition of biological concepts to quantum mechanics will necessarily demand an extension of the latter, but it is conceivable that in the organic world every life situation is in some degree influenced by the mental state (*i.e.*, theory, observational situation, psychological expectation, linguistic formulation) of the observer. The study of chemical or electrical processes in nerve conduction, for instance, necessarily operates on the assumption of a kind of causality equally appropriate to inorganic matter. This way of looking at things is a limitation on—but at the same is limited by—the teleological concepts which are a necessary part of the biologist's approach to the nervous system. This latter approach in turn stands in a similar complementary relation to that of the psychologist, and his in turn to that of the metaphysician. The metaphysical overview that can take into account the whole hierarchy of modifications of yesterday's naive scientific determinism is most often found at present (in scientific circles) among physicists who have seen matter in its subatomic form dissolve into a set of mathematical relationships to varying observational situations. Quantum physics over several decades furnishes impressive evidence that the interplay of metaphysical concerns (existential or idealist) and scientific disciplines (experimental and mathematical) can stimulate in first-class mentalities the development of immensely fruitful new ways of looking at nature.

This is the point at which Mrs. Eddy's concept of metaphysics as a scientific discipline rather than a speculative luxury has relevance. Obviously there is a considerable distance between Einstein's comment to Heisenberg, quoted above—or Bohr's observation about the subject-object relationship—and the synoptic statement of *Science and Health* (p. 86), "Mortal mind sees what it believes as certainly as it believes what it sees," or the even more basic proposition (p. 484), "Physical force and mortal mind are one." But the *concerns* are similar, and the physical scientists—no less than, though in a different way from Mrs. Eddy—live in a cosmos in which subjectivity is no longer an intruder. For them, too, matter "in the old sense" has ceased to exist.

310

Matter in the new sense is, literally, another matter—one end of a mind-matter or psychosomatic spectrum which defines the character of the phenomenal world accessible to scientific observation and manipulation. Mrs. Eddy, in comparable fashion, refers to matter as the unconscious substratum of mortal mind and speaks of the body as the objectification of mortal thought. The important division for her is not between mind and matter—a division which may be located almost at will, as Bohr half-seriously suggests—but between mortal mind and divine Mind. It is this metaphysical distinction that robs of ultimate importance the changes promised (or threatened) by the new genetics and by psychobiology. "The elements and functions of the physical world," she writes, "will change as mortal mind changes its beliefs." (*Ibid.*, p. 124 f.) In several places she seems to anticipate some of the changes already taking place today, but always maintains a clear distinction between the effective agency of the divine Mind and the imitative efforts of the human mind. This point is made explicit in a passage in *A Century of Christian Science Healing* (p. 254):

> In the nature of things the propositions of Christian Science cannot be affected by new developments in natural science—for instance, the possible discovery of other forms of life on other planets or the synthetic creation of human life on this planet. For if reality is pure Spirit, material existence at best can be only a series of attempted approximations of reality. As Mrs. Eddy puts it, "Whatever seems to be a new creation, is but the discovery of some distant idea of Truth; else it is a new multiplication or self-division of mortal thought, as when some finite sense peers from its cloister with amazement and attempts to pattern the infinite" (*Ibid.*, p. 263).

On these terms, each attempt to "pattern the infinite" may as easily take a destructive as a constructive form. If indeed there is nothing new "under the sun," there is no cause for surprise when Heisenberg (*op. cit.*, p. 214) speculatively allows room in the scientific world picture for a sort of demonology. Pointing to the confusions (*e.g.*, Nazism) which historically obscure man's relatedness to a "central order"—an order nevertheless discoverable in the subjective as well as the objective world—he writes:

> Demons can be let loose and do a great deal of mischief, or, to put it more scientifically, partial orders that have split away from the central order, or do not fit into it, may have taken over. But in the final analysis, the central order, or the "one" as it used to be called and with which we commune in the language of re-

ligion, must win out. And when people search for values, they are probably searching for the kind of actions that are in harmony with the central order, and as such are free of the confusions springing from divided, partial orders. The power of the "one" may be gathered from the very fact that we think of the orderly as the good, and of the confused and chaotic as the bad.

While such an observation is hardly to be classified as either Christian Science or natural science, it usefully suggests the area of implication within which the post-positivist search for values may go on.

Abbreviations Used in Notes

A.   Archives of The Mother Church.
CSJ.   *The Christian Science Journal.*
L.   Longyear Historical Society.

Unpublished writings of Mary Baker Eddy:

A&M.	Articles and Manuscripts.	35 vols.
L&M.	Letters and Miscellany.	94 vols.

Published works of Mary Baker Eddy:

S&H.	*Science and Health with Key to the Scriptures*
Man.	*Manual of The Mother Church*
Mis.	*Miscellaneous Writings*
My.	*The First Church of Christ, Scientist, and Miscellany*
No.	*No and Yes*
Ret.	*Retrospection and Introspection*
Rud.	*Rudimental Divine Science*
Un.	*Unity of Good*

Unless otherwise indicated, the references to Mrs. Eddy's published writings are always to the latest editions.

1. The details and quotations throughout this section are drawn from a circumstantial account written by Mrs. Godfrey's daughter (A. Reminiscences of Mary Godfrey Parker). Mrs. Parker states that her mother consulted not one but several doctors in regard to her infected finger.

2. For the past forty years the house has been open to the public as a historical site, and thousands of visitors each year climb to the "little attic room" famous in Christian Science history.

3. A. Reminiscences of R. A. Nash and Flora Glover Nash Duff. The latter gives 1876 as the year of her birth, but the Lynn city records show that she was born at 8 Broad Street on October 1, 1875, a date which accords with Mrs. Parker's account. After two or three years at that address the family moved to Utica, New York. Although they never became Christian Scientists they remained friendly with Mrs. Eddy and always visited her when they came back to Lynn and Boston.

4. A. Parker reminiscences. In later years Flora became a medical nurse herself. She comments (A. Duff reminiscences):

> My mother often related the following experience [which occurred] in the Lynn household. I was sick, and my mother called a medical doctor. The physician gave my father a prescription to fill at a drugstore. While he was gone Mrs. Glover came in. She stopped at the door and listened to my mother's fears about me. Mrs. Glover said, "Put away the medicine. Flora is all right." When my father returned with the medicine, I was playing on the floor, perfectly well. . . . I have been well all my life. I have nursed all kinds of contagious cases without fear.

The incident seems to show that Mrs. Glover did on occasion "interfere" in her tenants' affairs.

5. The following incident is related in his daughter Mary's reminiscences:

> A carpenter came to our house, for some reason, who had his arm in a sling. Father asked him what the trouble was and he said he had strained the ligaments and paralysis had set in. The arm was partly withered and all the physicians said that it would continue to wither. . . . Father told him about [Mrs. Glover] and asked him if he went to her to come and tell him the result. About a week later the carpenter came to the house to tell father that he was completely healed. . . .
>
> I might add that when this man came to see Mrs. Glover she was too busy to come down to talk with him and just opened a window in her parlor

room on the second floor and called down to him. Father never told me any details of this experience other than those I have related, but so far as I know this was the only conversation Mrs. Glover had with the man and he came away healed.

6. Cf. *S&H*, p. 412:28–11. According to Mary Godfrey, the croup never returned.

7. A. Parker reminiscences: "I was small for my age, and though she was not a robust woman, it never seemed to tire her to have me play around or sit in her lap." The rocker has been given a perhaps undeserved fame by Mrs. Eddy's critics as well as by her admirers. See, *e.g.*, F. O. Matthiessen, *American Renaissance* (New York: Oxford University Press, 1941), p. 368: "From the weaker aspects of Emerson's thought, the rocking chair of Mary Baker Eddy is only just around the corner."

8. Several biographers have claimed that it was Daniel Spofford who introduced Asa Eddy to Christian Science and who healed him before he even met Mrs. Glover. This rests on the unsupported statement of Georgine Milmine in her *Life of Mary Baker G. Eddy* (New York: Doubleday, Page, 1909). Edwin Franden Dakin remarks ironically in his *Mrs. Eddy* (New York: Scribner's, 1929), p. 120: "The preferred tradition among Mrs. Eddy's followers is that Mr. Eddy went to Mrs. Glover via Mrs. Godfrey." There is good reason for preferring this account, since it is supported by all the evidence. Mrs. Eddy herself wrote in a letter to a Mrs. Kingsbury on January 12, 1877: "Last spring Dr. Eddy came to me a hopeless invalid. I saw him then for the first time, and but twice. When his health was so improved he next came to join my class" (A. *L&M* 61–8737). On May 9, 1882, Mrs. Godfrey wrote Mrs. Eddy, "I feel as if I owe you a debt which will never be paid when I look at my thimble finger of my right hand"—but, she added, perhaps she had paid part of it "when I sent A. G. Eddy to you for I don't believe you could have found a better one anywhere." (A.)

9. A. Mrs. Eddy's account book shows that there was just one other student in this class. Though the regular price for tuition was $300, Asa Eddy paid only $150 and Miss Mary Putnam $200.

10. Printed in Lynn by Thos. P. Nichols. In the early versions of this essay Mrs. Glover called her teaching Moral Science; in the 1876 version she calls it Metaphysical Science, while retaining the earlier title of the treatise. The term Christian Science was already being used and soon gained ascendency over all others.

11. The "great general" was Ulysses S. Grant, at that time fighting a losing battle against scandal in his second term as President of the United States. Tyndall had lectured in Boston in 1873.

12. Others are said to have gone to Queen Victoria, Thomas Carlyle, and the Archbishop of Canterbury. Possibly it was Alcott who suggested sending one to Carlyle.

13. *The Journals of Bronson Alcott*, ed. Odell Shepard (Boston: Little, Brown, 1938), p. 467. A full discussion of Alcott's relations with Mrs. Eddy and Christian Science is to be found in Robert Peel, *Christian Science: Its Encounter with American Culture* (New York: Holt, 1958), pp. 47–96.

14. A. Handwritten review, anonymous but obviously clerical.

15. With more grace than some, the clergyman followed his criticism with the words: "It is with feelings of delicacy that I present you with the above review,

because from the apparent sincerity and earnestness, and decision of character of the authoress I presume my criticism may strike you as unkind. . . . But I trust you know enough of my heart to believe that I have none but kind feelings toward Mrs. Glover."

16. A. Handwritten review, signed A. S. C. Minutes of the Christian Scientist Association for April 11, 1878, refer to the author or speaker as the Reverend Mr. Silver of the New Jerusalem Church, Boston Highlands. Mrs. Glover was frequently confounded with mediums in those days, despite her vocal opposition to spiritism. Mrs. Alice Swasey Wool, who was living in Beverly, near Lynn, about 1876–77, tells in her reminiscences (A.) of suffering from abdominal pains from which the doctors were unable to relieve her. A friend proposed she should go to Lynn to consult "the 'medium' who healed without medicine." On her arrival, Mrs. Eddy "talked with me a few minutes and then said, 'Now we won't talk any more.' She closed her eyes and sat with her hands in her lap for about ten minutes and then she said, 'You will not have that trouble any more' and I said aren't you going to rub me—or do anything—and she said, 'You are healed' and I was." It was common practice for healing mediums, like practitioners of animal magnetism, to rub the head or affected part of the body.

17. A. Letter of March 22, 1876.

18. A. Letter of March 24, 1876. Letts finally did study with her in 1878.

19. A. Though her charge was nominally $300 for the course, her account books show that from the fourteen students she taught in 1876 she received a total of $1,140 only, or an average of $81.40 per person.

20. Cf. S&H, p. 225:5–6, and Church Manual, p. 48:16–21.

21. A. Undated letter, apparently spring of 1876.

22. See, e.g., John I. Ladd's testimony of healing of his daughter Clara, attested by pastor of Congregational Church, two deacons, and another friend, published in Lynn Transcript, November 11, 1875. Another widely publicized healing effected by Spofford was that of Etta Richardson. But when Mrs. Richardson's friend, Laura Jane Smith (A. Laura Jane Smith Goodwin reminiscences) took her two-year-old son, who was suffering severely from catarrh, to Spofford, he was unable to help the child. Mrs. Smith thereupon bought a copy of Science and Health and during her study of it, the catarrh "suddenly and completely" disappeared.

23. Journals of Bronson Alcott, p. 467.

24. Lynn Transcript, November 25, 1876. Other contributions by her to the Transcript in that year included a poem "Spring" (April 22); poem "Woman's Rights" (May 6) which had already appeared many years earlier in the New Hampshire Patriot and the Portland Advertiser; poem "Rock of Ages" (May 20) which was also a third reworking of a poem already twice published; article "A Query" (June 3)—attack on the "clap-trap chicanery of one of our sermonizers"; article "Spiritualism" (December 30), condemning the fraud and credulity of mediumship.

25. Quoted in Del Brown, The Year of the Century: 1876 (New York: Scribner's, 1966), p. 295.

26. The poem is now known as "Communion Hymn."

27. A. J. Henry Jones reminiscences.

28. A. Elvira F. Newhall reminiscences.

29. A. Charles Otis reminiscences. The florist's comment on his regular customer was: "[She] was not a woman looking for the bad in anyone, but the good."

30. A. Mary Godfrey Parker reminiscences: "I remember there were stacks of calla lilies. . . . Mrs. Glover occasionally took me on the balcony with her and then I thought I was just about in heaven."

31. See Sibyl Wilbur, *Life of Mary Baker Eddy* (Boston: Christian Science Publishing Society, 1933), p. 253. Miss Wilbur got her description from Clara Choate and other early students of Mrs. Eddy.

32. A. Grace Choate Huse reminiscences.

33. Several biographers have suggested that the tenants moved out because they found Mrs. Glover impossible to live with. On the contrary, with two exceptions, they all expressed unusual regard for her in later years. The exceptions—Mrs. Lucy Bixby and James Howard—were students of hers, and it was as students, not as tenants, that they quarreled with her.

34. A. Huse reminiscences.

35. A. Helen M. Grenier reminiscences. This incident may belong to a period a year or two later, after Mrs. Glover had married Asa Eddy.

36. A. Emma C. Shipman reminiscences.

37. This attitude was by no means universal. Orville A. Clough told of seeing her come out of 8 Broad Street one day holding a small child by the hand. He had often admired the sign outside the house, with its symbol of a cross and a crown. "You have a most beautiful sign there," he commented. In the brief conversation that followed, Mrs. Glover remarked, "We all have the cross but each one must become as this little child before he can have the crown." That was Clough's only contact with her (although he became a Christian Scientist more than forty years later) but it was apparently sufficient to inoculate him against neighborhood gossip. (A. Luella A. Clough reminiscences.)

38. A. Newhall reminiscences.

39. Victoria Woodhull and her sister Tennessee Claflin started their spectacular careers giving backwoods spiritistic exhibitions and demonstrations of animal magnetism, telling fortunes in an itinerant medicine show, etc. They later came to the attention of Cornelius Vanderbilt, who set them up as successful stockbrokers in New York. There they launched *Woodhull and Claflin's Weekly* which, in addition to its advocacy of women's rights and free love, provided the first American publication of the *Communist Manifesto*. In 1872 Victoria Woodhull announced that she was a candidate for the presidency of the United States. Shortly afterward she launched the sensational charges against Henry Ward Beecher which led to his trial for adultery and her own and her sister's temporary imprisonment. Both sisters ended as wealthy and successful members of English society.

40. A. A total of $2,200 was paid before publication, $1,700 by Barry and Miss Newhall. The remaining $500 was probably furnished by one Edward Hitchings, who seems to drop out of the picture after 1875.

41. Alma Lutz, *Susan B. Anthony* (Boston: Beacon Press, 1959), p. 224.

42. A. *L&M* 54–7649.

43. In *S&H* (3rd ed.), p. 15, Mrs. Eddy attributed this episode to a "mesmeric" influence which she did not then understand. She described Barry as suddenly manifesting "mental symptoms foreign to his constitution, and wholly unlike himself." She also quoted a sentence from "one of his last letters" to her: "Since the tie of friendship must be broken, let me thank you for past favors." In her view, the explanation for his action was not a simple psychological one; rather, she saw him acting compulsively under an unrecognized external mental influence.

44. See Robert Peel, *Mary Baker Eddy: The Years of Discovery* (New York: Holt, Rinehart and Winston, 1966), p. 244 f.

45. *L&M* 54–7649. This statement appears to be connected with the phenomenon described on pp. 23 ff. and p. 34 of this book.

46. A. *L&M* 70–9897. There is no record of Hattie Baker's views.

47. A. Shipman reminiscences. Her tenant, Mrs. Gatchell, reported that Mrs. Glover one day asked which of the two men she preferred and seemed pleased when she said Gilbert Eddy. Spofford boarded at 8 Broad Street during much of 1876.

48. A. *L&M* 55–7809.

49. A. *L&M* 55–7810.

50. A. Dittemore interview with Bancroft.

51. This statement, made by several biographers, has been questioned by others. However, it is supported by the Spofford family itself. According to Mrs. Helen Dyer, only daughter of Spofford's daughter Constance, Daniel (confident of the successful outcome of his divorce suit) actually proposed to Mrs. Glover, but she refused him. The incident is recounted in an unpublished paper by Mrs. Dyer's son Charles (A. "Daniel Harrison Spofford—Doctor of Christian Science," written for a history course at Phillips Academy, Andover, Massachusetts). The family tradition, according to this breezy prep school research paper by Spofford's great-grandson, is that Grandfather "Dan" was so upset by Mrs. Glover's refusal that he "pulled out a gun and threatened her with it." The account continues: "Keeping her usual cool she said, 'Give that to me, Daniel.' And Daniel did."

52. The witness was Spofford's mother. Mrs. Glover attributed the sudden change to the influence of her disaffected student Richard Kennedy. (*S&H* [3rd ed.], II, p. 8.)

53. Her letters after the later break with Spofford express her relief at having the hidden antagonism brought out into the open.

54. A. Dittemore interview with Bancroft. The latter was ignorant, however, of Spofford's desire to marry Mrs. Glover.

55. A. *L&M* 55–7811. The quotation from *S&H* (1st ed.) to which she refers reads in part as follows:

> Sin is thought before it is deed, and you must master it in the first, or it conquers you in the second instance. Jesus said, to look with foul desire

on forbidden objects, breaks a moral precept; hence, the stress he laid on the character of a man that is hidden from our perception. . . .

The atmosphere of impure desires, Like the atmosphere of earth, is restless, ever in motion, and calling on some object; this atmosphere is laden with mental poison, and contaminates all it touches.

56. The tone of his proposal can be inferred from an undated letter which he wrote her immediately afterward. The chronology of events is more obscure. The letter implies that he does not expect to see her again until the next regular Thursday meeting (January 4). Spofford later reported that when Eddy told him on Sunday night (December 31) that he and Mrs. Glover were to be married the next day he added that he himself had known nothing about it until the night before. It seems more likely that if he proposed on December 30 he did not know the answer for certain until the next morning. He may then have written her the letter in question (which begins, "Good afternoon, Mary Dear"), and the decision to get married the following day may have been taken that evening just before his calling on Spofford.

57. A. Clara Shannon reminiscences.

58. A. *L&M* 71–10093.

59. By an odd coincidence this was the tenth anniversary of Spofford's unhappy marriage—a fact which he can hardly have failed to brood over.

60. Samuel Putnam Bancroft, *Mrs. Eddy As I Knew Her in 1870* (Brookline: Longyear Foundation, 1923), p. 36 f.

61. February 10, 1877. The shower itself was on January 31.

62. A. Clara E. Choate reminiscences.

63. He was born in 1832 on a farm near Londonderry, Vermont. As a young man, he left home to become a spinner in a cotton mill (or, according to some accounts, a weaver in a woollen mill) and eventually, by a natural transition, an agent for the new sewing machines that were helping to revolutionize American domestic life. This unprepossessing history gives little hint of the "reserve force" on which some of his contemporaries commented.

64. A. Choate reminiscences.

65. A. *L&M* 39–5141.

66. No event in Mrs. Eddy's life appears to have disturbed her critics more than this entry. It is possible, even probable, that Gilbert Eddy did not know her exact age at that time, since she was not in the habit of talking about it and most people judged her to be considerably younger than she was. It is even more likely that the clerk, confronted by Gilbert's passive resistance, simply slapped down for both of them a good round number that would satisfy the requirements of probability.

67. L. S. P. Bancroft to Mrs. Longyear. Quoted in her *Asa Gilbert Eddy*, p. 20.

68. L. Arthur True Buswell to Mrs. Longyear. Quoted in her *Asa Gilbert Eddy*, pp. 17–19.

69. A. *L&M* 55–7812.

70. A. Letter to "Dear Teacher" dated "Friday Night."

71. A. *L&M* 16–2015.

72. In the first of several letters on the subject Mrs. Eddy gave as her reason for wanting a stenographic copy: "I think this is to be my last class and I have a great gift to leave my successor in this mission." The stenographer was Mrs. Eddy's old friend Sarah Crosby from Albion, Maine, who was hardly prepared for the new tone of authority she found in Mrs. Eddy's teaching. She left finally in a towering rage over the pay she received for her work. Before coming, she had written in regard to the terms she was asking, "Dear Mary, I feared you would feel that your Sarah had grown worldly & sordid." Mrs. Eddy ended by feeling just that.

73. H. A. L. Fisher, *Our New Religion* (New York: Jonathan Cape & Harrison Smith, 1930), p. 60.

74. A. Dittemore interview with Bancroft.

75. A. Plaintiff's Bill of Particulars, *Barry vs. Glover,* Superior Court, Essex, September Term, 1877.

76. This phrase occurs in Mrs. Eddy's definition of "Adam" in *S&H*, p. 580: "The name Adam represents the false supposition that Life is not eternal, but has beginning and end; that the infinite enters the finite, that intelligence passes into non-intelligence, and that Soul dwells in material sense; that immortal Mind results in matter, and matter in mortal mind; that the one God and creator entered what He created, and then disappeared in the atheism of matter."

77. *S&H* (2nd ed.), p. 80.

78. Cf. G. B. Caird, *The Revelation of St. John the Divine* (New York: Harper & Row, 1966), pp. 147–150:

> In the folklore of many nations there are found stories of the usurper who, doomed to be killed by a prince as yet unborn, attempts to cheat the fates by killing the prince at birth. The prince is miraculously snatched from his clutches and hidden away, until he is old enough to kill the usurper and claim his inheritance. . . .
>
> John rewrites the old pagan myth deliberately to contradict its current political application. . . .
>
> The woman is the mother of the Messiah, not Mary, but the messianic community . . . By the birth of the Messiah John means not the Nativity but the Cross. . . .
>
> The dragon's attempt TO DEVOUR the child may include the temptations and dangers of Jesus' earthly life, but its primary reference is certainly to the crucifixion.

Caird's learned and subtle exegesis fails to *universalize* the Revelation account as Mrs. Eddy does (*S&H*, p. 561): "The woman in the Apocalypse symbolizes generic man, the spiritual idea of God."

79. Even in her most anguished references to the dragon's persecution of the woman and her child, she clung to the promise of ultimate victory implicit in the symbolic account.

80. A. *L&M* 55–7811.

81. A. *L&M* 55–7814 and 7815.

82. A. *L&M* 55–7816.

83. A. Letter of May 30, 1877. It was unusual for him to sign himself Daniel, since Mrs. Eddy called him Harry. It is the first sign of a mystical streak in him which caused him to identify himself with the Daniel of the Old Testament. As late as 1922 he wrote a small pamphlet entitled *Light: Reflected by the Words of Daniel.* See note 86 below.

84. The dispute was tied up with Spofford's handling of the first edition. He had legally contracted on April 17, 1876, to pay her a royalty of ten per cent of the net list price of the book, to render her a monthly list of the sales, and to pay royalties twice yearly. None of these conditions had been observed and Mrs. Eddy had received no royalties whatever. Spofford had ploughed $500 of the earnings back into advertising the book and had earmarked the remaining $600 for George Barry and Elizabeth Newhall as a partial return on their original investment. He had given considerable time to promoting the book, but since most of the sales were through patients and inquirers he had not had to worry about the usual large discount to booksellers.

Ernest Sutherland Bates and John V. Dittemore state in their *Mary Baker Eddy* (New York: Knopf, 1932) that Barry and Miss Newhall lost over $2,000 on the first edition and Spofford about $500. Actually Barry and Miss Newhall lost just over $1,000 and Spofford paid the $500 in advertising costs out of the book's early sales. His account book (L.) shows that in his agreement with Barry and Miss Newhall on April 11, 1876, he had contracted to pay them a total of $1,700 *from any sums accruing beyond $1,200.* Hence he was not obligated to pay them the $600 he did in July, 1877, whereas he was legally obligated to pay Mrs. Eddy the royalties which he withheld from her.

The net result of this action was that when Mrs. Eddy badly needed money to publish the second edition, she found herself without a cent for all the time and labor she had put into the first. As a consequence she told Spofford firmly that she would require a twenty-five per cent royalty on the new edition. In an ordinary commercial publishing venture this would have been unthinkable, but Mrs. Eddy saw the issue in crusading terms. The ensuing dispute involved not merely the normal difference of viewpoint between an author and a publisher, or between a feminine and a masculine approach to business, although both these elements entered into it. More profoundly it was the difference between viewing the publication of *Science and Health* as a spiritual commitment and as a commercial risk.

Mrs. Eddy wrote Miss Newhall on July 8, 1877 (*L&M* 20–2551), "I only regret that those who paid for the first edition should not have reaped the benefit of that and other editions." But since they declined to continue their interest into the "other editions," the loss was inevitable. Realistically, the lack of continued faith and of financial return was closely linked.

85. *The Interpretation; or, The Birth of Jesus of Nazareth and the Birth of the Son of God* (Newburyport: William H. Huse & Co., 1877).

86. Spofford's symbolic identification of Mrs. Eddy with Mary the mother of Jesus is clear from two strange letters he wrote—one in 1901 to Mrs. Eddy and the other in 1921 to Mary Beecher Longyear. In each he gave a brief genealogy tracing his descent from his great-great-grandfather, who, by coincidence, was the same man

on both the paternal and maternal sides and who bore the name of David. This childish tomfoolery was clearly intended to show Spofford as the "son of David" or the man-child born of "the woman" in Revelation. In both letters he indicated that he felt he had been born "spiritually" of "Mary"—*i.e.*, he had found his true spiritual selfhood through the teachings of Mrs. Eddy. This whole elaborate game involved a claim on his part to be Mrs. Eddy's spiritual successor.

87. A *L&M* 17–2048.

Notes: *Chapter II*

1. *Learned Lady: Letters from Robert Browning to Mrs. Thomas FitzGerald 1876–1889*, ed. Edward C. McAleer (Cambridge: Harvard University Press, 1966), p. 64 f.

2. Cf. Augustine, *Confessions*, Book VII, Chapter xii: "All things which are corrupted are thereby deprived of some good. But if they are deprived of all good they must altogether cease to exist. . . . Evil, then, the origin of which I had been searching out, has no being of its own, for had it a being it would be good."

3. *The American Scene: 1860 to the Present*, ed. William J. Chute (New York: Bantam Books, 1966), p. 226 f.

4. Hanover P. Smith, *Writings and Genius of the Founder of Christian Science* (Boston, 1886), pp. 43, 45 f.

5. *S&H* (3rd ed.), II, p. 38.

6. *S&H* (2nd ed.), p. 140.

7. A more basic analogy might be drawn with the fact that a mathematical system can be constructed on any set of internally consistent postulates without its necessarily having any correspondence to the way things are in the external universe. Similarly, even the internal consistencies of evil in human experience, in Mrs. Eddy's view, rested on postulates inconsistent with reality as revealed by divine Mind. This did not obviate the necessity, in her view, of analyzing and exposing the operations of evil within its own hypothetical power systems.

8. Bancroft, *Mrs. Eddy As I Knew Her*, p. 39.

9. Mrs. Eddy for some years used the term "Moral Science" to describe what she later called Christian Science, and for her the moral or ethical use of mental power remained the crucial test of Christian healing. Any use of mental power to harm rather than heal was therefore "immorality." Fortunately she soon abandoned this usage of the word in public.

10. A. Atkinson and Spofford letters.

11. A. *L&M* 91–13466.

12. A. The letter was written by Gilbert Eddy but conveyed Mrs. Eddy's instructions.

13. A. *L&M* 59–8294.

14. A. January 27, 1878.

15. A. c. January 28, 1878

16. A. *L&M* 78–11162.

17. A. April 23, 1878.

18. *S&H* (3rd ed.), II, p. 34 f.

19. A. The original of this document was stolen from Mrs. Eddy's files a year later. See p. 54.

20. Defendant's Answer in case of *Glover vs. Kennedy* filed on March 5, 1878.

21. Answer filed April 29, 1878.

22. One of the Bible lesson subjects which is found twice yearly in the *Christian Science Quarterly* is entitled "Ancient and Modern Necromancy, *alias* Mesmerism and Hypnotism, Denounced."

23. Ralph Waldo Emerson, *Lectures and Biographical Sketches* (Boston: Houghton, Mifflin, 1904).

24. Barrett Wendell, *Stelligeri, and other essays* (New York: Scribner's, 1893). Three-quarters of a century later a rather chichi revival of interest in witchcraft would be one of the oddities of the Age of Aquarius, but at a level of serious scholarship there would also be a reexamination of the Salem phenomena. In his coolly reasoned, carefully documented, and psychologically sophisticated *Witchcraft at Salem* (New York: George Braziller, 1969), Professor Chadwick Hansen comes to the conclusion: "One cannot fully understand any aspect of the events at Salem without a recognition of the genuine power of witchcraft in a society that believes in it." Wendell's more impressionistic and speculative essay goes beyond Hansen's detailed empiricism to suggest further implications that deserve scientific exploration, but Hansen at least points in the same direction in his flat statement: "There was witchcraft at Salem, and it worked. It did real harm to its victims and there was every reason to regard it as a criminal offense."

25. Cf. Hansen, *Witchcraft at Salem:* "There was an outbreak of epidemic hysteria in Salem Village which originated in experiments with the occult. And the hysterical hallucinations of the afflicted persons were confirmed by some concrete evidence of actual witchcraft and by many confessions, the majority of them also hysterical." See also Michael Polànyi, *Personal Knowledge* (London: Routledge & K. Paul, 1958), p. 168:

> The destruction of belief in witchcraft during the sixteenth and seventeenth centuries was achieved in the face of an overwhelming, and still rapidly growing body of evidence for its reality. Those who denied that witches existed did not attempt to explain this evidence at all, but successfully urged that it be disregarded. Glanvill, who was one of the founders of the Royal Society, not unreasonably denounced this proposal as unscientific, on the ground of the professed empiricism of contemporary science. Some of the unexplained evidence for witchcraft was indeed buried for good, and only struggled painfully to light two centuries later when it was eventually recognized as the manifestation of hypnotic powers.

Polànyi was rushing things a bit in suggesting that a connection between witchcraft and hypnotic powers is now generally recognized.

26. The present emphasis seems to have shifted from the somewhat discredited Rhine type of approach (with its extrascientific background of belief in the "psychic") to a naturalism which, ironically enough, relates telepathy to a literal and physical "animal magnetism." This is especially the case in the Soviet Union, where as early as 1920 Professor B. B. Kazhinsky was doing telepathic experiments with animals, and where the more recent work of Vasiliev, Terentiev, and others has built on Kazhinsky's concept of "biological radio," or telepathy as a residual animal faculty. "We should confess it to Mesmer's injured memory that animals do produce magnetism, and that magnetism can have effects resembling hypnotism." (John Williamson, "Animal Magnetism," *The Spectator* [London], January 13, 1961). Whether it is given a psychological or a biophysical interpretation, telepathic communication seems destined for considerably more scientific investigation —and practical application. It is interesting that Vasiliev's *Suggestion at a Distance* was issued by the Moscow State Publishing House in "a huge paperback edition." (Anthony Lejeune, "The Telepathic Curtain," *The Sunday Times* [London], July 7, 1963.) Freud has written in connection with extrasensory perception: "It is a familiar fact that we have no notion of how the communal will of the great insect states comes about. Possibly it works by mental transference of this direct kind. One is led to conjecture that this may be the original archaic method by which individuals understood one another, and which has been pushed into the background in the course of better phylogenetic development. . . ." (Brian Inglis, *Fringe Medicine*, London: Faber & Faber, 1964, p. 266.) Cf. Arthur Koestler, *The Sleepwalkers* (London: Hutchinson, 1959):

> Thus for the last thirty years an impressive body of evidence has been assembled under strict laboratory conditions which suggests that the mind might perceive stimuli emanating from persons or objects without the intermediary of the sensory organs; and that in controlled experiments, these phenomena occur with a statistical frequency which invites scientific investigation. Yet academic science reacts to the phenomena of "extra-sensory perception" much as the Pigeon League reacted to the Medicean stars; and it seems to me for no better reason. If we have to accept that an electron can jump from one orbit into the other without traversing the space between them, why are we bound to reject out of hand the possibility that a signal of a nature no more puzzling than Schroedinger's electron waves should be emitted and received without sensory intervention.

This is a far cry from "witchcraft," but it may form the necessary theoretical springboard for any genuinely scientific investigation of the latter phenomenon.

27. *S&H* (2nd ed.), p. 47.

28. L. *Light: Reflected by the Words of Daniel.*

29. Quoted in *Newburyport Herald*, May 16, 1878.

30. Bates-Dittemore, *Mary Baker Eddy*, p. 188.

31. A. May ?, 1881.

32. *Boston Globe,*

33. The plaintiff, under Arens' direction, then appealed the case which was set for a hearing before the full bench in November, but on November 6 the appeal was waived.

34. It was heard on June 4, 1879, at the probate court in Salem.

35. See Peel, *Encounter*, p. 87.

36. *Peabody Reporter,* July 2, 1878.

37. *Ibid.,* July 16, 1878.

38. A. Clara Choate reminiscences.

39. *S&H* (2nd ed.), p. 145. This is the only edition in which the chapter "Metaphysics" appeared.

40. *Ibid.,* p. 147. "The conception of Jesus was spiritual, if Joseph was not his father. The superior spirituality of Mary might have been the transparency, through which immortal Mind reflected, somewhat, the idea of God, giving the better likeness of Truth and Love, in the good and pure Jesus." Cf. the final edition (p. 332): "Jesus was the son of a virgin. . . . Mary's conception of him was spiritual, for only purity could reflect Truth and Love, which were plainly incarnate in the good and pure Christ Jesus."

41. A. Mrs. Eddy used a number of copies of the Bible through the years, and made entries in many of them. Normally she studied the King James Version, though consulting other translations from time to time.

42. L. The wickedness is not specified, but Kennedy complains of her bringing villainous accusations "against those who are her betters in every respect." Cf. letter from the Reverend Joseph Williams of the Baptist Tabernacle in Boston to Mrs. Eddy on April 19, 1880: "I am sorry anyone should attempt to malign your fair reputation; and whatever Mr. Richard Kennedy may have said to others, to me he bore unqualified testimony in your favor as a virtuous lady, and upheld you as a model of chastity and virtue." (A.)

43. The photograph of young Kennedy published in McClure's Magazine in May, is not that of an amiable, extroverted Irish lad. The heavily underlidded eyes, compressed lips, and sharply intent air suggest rather the wariness which seems to have marked his dealings with later investigators. In an 1873 letter to Sarah Bagley he wrote: "I am not as fond of going about as the general class of people. I have neither found but few acquaintances." (Peel, *Discovery*, p. 357.) Mrs. Calvin Hill (A.) who met him a number of times in his last years comments on his marked reserve, and almost nothing of his personal life seems to have come down through the wall of silence he built around himself. See also note 46 below.

44. A. Milmine collection. Letter of January 7, 1907.

45. A. Powell collection. Letter of June 8, 1907. Mrs. Eddy drew a sharp distinction between Kennedy and Spofford. The former she regarded as a deliberate connoisseur of evil, the latter as a victim of Kennedy's influence who for a time allowed his mind to be tyrannized by hatred of her and her cause.

46. He refused to show Milmine, Wilbur, or Powell any of Mrs. Eddy's letters to him, and toward the end of his life he destroyed them all. Fortunately Mrs. Eddy kept copies of one or two of them .

47. There may be significance in the fact that Kennedy was afflicted with spermatorrhea when Mrs. Eddy first knew him and spent the last few years of his life in a mental hospital.

48. This phrase, used to characterize Iago, has also been extended to the Luciferian element in mortal nature—that self-destroying hubris which aspires to be God. Dostoevsky in his notebooks on *The Possessed* defines the demonic as "an incomprehensible immediate power, searching for rest, excited to the extent of pain which throws itself with delight into monstrous deviations and experiments until it finds peace." See Wolfgang M. Zucher, "The Demonic from Aeschylus to Tillich," *Theology Today*, April, 1969. As Mrs. Eddy saw it, a person was particularly open to the demonic when he had discovered the immense, unsuspected power of mind without observing the crucial distinction between mortal mind, capable of every sort of depravity, and divine Mind, capable only of good. With the revived interest in satanism and witchcraft today, even the ancient superstition of devil possession has come up for re-examination and reinterpretation. An article in the Jesuit weekly *America* for November 16, 1968, quotes Karl Rahner:

> The meager data which we have from the Old and the New Testament does not permit us to conceive of Satan as an opponent of God, nor to depict the character and doings of the devil as popular piety does. In view of the seriousness of saving history, it would be untheological levity to look on Satan and his devils as sort of hobgoblins knocking about the world. Rather it may be assumed that there are powers of the world, insofar as this world is a denial of God and a temptation to man. This view preserves the personal nature of devils, which is laid down by Scripture and the magisterium, since every essential disorder of the world is personally realized. Jesus Christ overcame sin; however real the powers of war, tyrants and so forth are in the world, they are stripped of all real power.

The writer of the article, Herman S. Hughes, concludes that evil "is personal in the evil person." Mrs. Eddy's thinking in 1878 had not yet developed to the point where she made the "impersonalizing" of evil the necessary condition of "nothingizing" it.

49. Scientific orthodoxy's continued scorn of parapsychology (not to mention metaphysics) as a discipline deserving serious attention illustrates Koestler's observation in *The Sleepwalkers* that "the materialist philosophy in which the average scientist was reared has retained its dogmatic power over the mind, though matter itself has evaporated." Meanwhile, in the less hard-headed "other" culture, the mythologies of psychoanalysis in its various permutations seem to be the preferred surrogate for yesterday's religious orthodoxies.

50. A. *L&M* 84–12422.

51. A. *L&M* 90–13376.

52. See p. 287.

53. This item of news may have been furnished to the *Lynn Item* by the detective who arranged Spofford's "absence."

54. Philbrick's part was little more than nominal. He had been brought into the case at the last minute by Pinkham, who was the moving spirit throughout.

55. None of the papers hesitated to prejudge the case before it even came to the municipal court for a preliminary hearing. Cf. the *Boston Advertiser* on the same day: "The affair seems to have been instigated by Mrs. Eddy in pursuance of the spirit of revenge against Spofford."

56. October 30, 1882. This story, like the similar ones in other papers, was evidently based on information furnished by Pinkham. In thus trying the case without troubling to verify the alleged facts or considering the possibility of alternative explanations, the Boston papers only anticipated the Milmine approach to the same episode.

57. A. The letter shows no loss of the calligraphic perfection that was as characteristic of Gilbert Eddy as was the immaculate neatness of his appearance. In some ways he foreshadowed the "representative'" Christian Scientist of later days.

58. Useful reports of the hearing can be found in the *Lynn Item* for November 8 and 9, 1878. It may not be coincidental that the appeal on the "witchcraft" case was waived on November 6.

59. *S&H* (3rd ed.), p. 22.

60. The anomalous nature of the evidence has been strangely underplayed by some historians. Bates-Dittemore, *e.g.*, are at pains to quote the testimony at some length (there was, of course, no defense testimony at this hearing) and make a great show of "analyzing" the case on the basis of this testimony, but its most suggestive features seem to have escaped their attention entirely. Having commented that Pinkham "was a good deal of a disappointment in his testimony, being apparently as stupid as members of his profession are commonly supposed to be," they apparently feel excused from paying any further attention to his key role in the drama. Their "disappointment" with his performance raises interesting speculations.

61. November 8, 1878. The story in the *Newburyport Herald* of November 11 illustrates again the lack of inhibition in the reporting of a case still before the courts. Kennedy had been "a willing victim" of Mrs. Eddy, who "artfully played upon his feelings," etc. There was a certain shrewdness, however, in their observation that "Mrs. Eddy seems to have had more trouble with pupils than with patients."

62. This lecture, which is reputed to have been given by him six thousand times and to have sold in the millions as a published essay, stands together with Andrew Carnegie's *The Gospel of Wealth* as an expression of the capitalistic ethos of the Gilded Age. It urged the acquisition of wealth as a moral duty and the godliness of riches as a form of Christian stewardship.

63. *Philadelphia Evening Bulletin,* March 5, 1907. Conwell characteristically admired "her unerring judgment" in the real estate affairs which he conducted for her through the 1870's. In 1908 a Christian Scientist sent Conwell a copy of Sibyl Wilbur's *Life of Mary Baker Eddy.* Conwell's secretary replied: "I am requested by Dr. Conwell to thank you. . . . He says that he has read the book through and considers it a faithful and accurate history of Mrs. Eddy, and it presents her character truthfully as he knew it." (A.) This has a special interest in view of the fact that Miss Wilbur devoted a full chapter to the conspiracy-to-murder case.

64. A. Collier, who was a black sheep in a respectable lower-middle-class family, had been persuaded by his family to confess.

65. A. December [17?], 1878. Conwell added, "As we have Collier's written confession, it is of no consequence to us anyway to prosecute him."

66. A. May 12, 1881. The only testimony given was that for the prosecution, since the testimony for the defense was not presented to the grand jury.

67. February 23, 1879.

68. Janet, *Psychological Healing* (London: Allen and Unwin, 1925), p. 64. The Reverend Leslie D. Weatherhead, in his *Psychology, Religion and Healing* (London: Hodder and Stoughton, 1951) repeats Janet's story, then remarks blandly, "Frankly, it seems to me that here Janet . . . may well be exaggerating." This gentle tap on the wrist illustrates the lack of seriousness with which even the more benevolent of Mrs. Eddy's fellow Christians have approached her life.

69. The highly inaccurate *Boston Globe* story of October 30, 1878, in regard to the alleged murder conspiracy, states that Arens was arrested on June 24, 1876, for being concerned in a "swindling transaction in Lynn with the famous Gremlaw-White gang." Research in the newspapers of that period has so far brought to light no further information regarding the episode.

70. *Op. cit.*, p. 201.

71. A. Powell collection.

72. The heavily slanted interpretations of the news stories prior to the Municipal Court hearing could hardly have emanated from anyone but Pinkham since Spofford was not then available for interviews. See, *e.g.*, the *Boston Globe* story: "It is claimed [by whom?] that Spofford was more successful in the treatment [of the sick] than Mrs. Eddy and that last spring, in order to get rid of her rival, the Eddy woman and her friends. . . . ," etc.

73. A. *A&M* 22–10604 and 10611.

74. Spofford held Kennedy responsible for the estrangement of his wife, and this could hardly have made for cordiality between the two men.

75. *Op. cit.*, p. 141.

76. A. Choate reminiscences.

77. *S&H*, p. 410.

Notes: *Chapter III*

1. In *Ret.*, p. 15, Mrs. Eddy speaks of "the Baptist Tabernacle of Rev. Daniel C. Eddy, D. D." Dr. Eddy was not, however, pastor at the time she lectured there.

2. Fisher, *Our New Religion*, p. 61.

3. A. Richard Armstrong letter, November 8, 1906.

4. A. Choate reminiscences.

5. A. *A&M* 22–10604.

6. A. George Clark reminiscences. Also Bancroft, *Mrs. Eddy As I Knew Her*, p. 15.

7. *S&H* (2nd ed.), p. 166.

8. A. *L&M* 20–2463.

9. *Man.,* p. 17. The *Manual* account telescopes the events of several months.

10. L. Buswell reminiscences.

11. *Ibid.*

12. A. Letter of September 15, 1879.

13. June 14, 1879.

14. A. Powell collection. Letter of August 30, 1907. It should be noted, however, that $1,000 in 1878 was a heavy drain on a young man's purse; it was roughly the wages of a Lynn shoe worker for an entire year.

15. Milmine, *Life,* p. 145.

16. *Ibid.*

17. *Mis.,* p. 31. In *S&H,* p. 450:1–8, Mrs. Eddy describes two classes of thinkers of which Stanley and Kennedy appear to be the prototypes.

18. June 14, 1879. The *Item* also recorded the testimony of Mrs. Flora Bowker that Stanley had told her he studied with Mrs. Eddy because the latter had restored his wife and son to health and that he thought highly of her method.

19. A. Referee's report in *Eddy versus Tuttle et al.*

20. See page 11.

21. A. *A&M* 22–10616.

22. A. *L&M* 86–12621.

23. A. Letter of October 25, 1879.

24. A. *A&M* 9–10357 and 10–10367.

25. A. Letter of November 11, 1879. This letter completely demolishes the Milmine story, repeated by Dakin and Bates-Dittemore, that Mrs. Eddy sent Buswell to Cincinnati, then "abandoned" him there without funds or moral support. It is evident that he entirely supported her staying in Boston and that he took full responsibility for his Cincinnati venture.

26. Peel, *Discovery,* p. 341, note 85.

27. A. Parker reminiscences. Actually, this incident probably refers to Glover's later visit in 1887, but it serves equally well to illustrate the impression he made on Bostonians at both times.

28. A. Minutes of the Christian Scientist Association. Cf. reminiscences of Eva Thompson, who knew the Glovers well in 1905–07: "Mr. Glover often spoke of the benefits he had received in Christian Science, and how he had been protected many times from accidents. He felt that his mother's protecting thought was always hovering over him. He always carried in his pocket the little locket containing his mother's picture which she had given him when he was a baby."

29. A. Eugenie Paul Jefferson reminiscences.

30. *New York World,* March 3, 1907.

31. A. The letter was written for Mrs. George Glover, who was herself illiterate.

32. A. Billings reminiscences. Quoted also in Clifford P. Smith, *Historical Sketches* (Boston: Christian Science Publishing Society, 1941), p. 70 f.

33. A. Choate reminiscences.

34. A. July 9, 1879.

35. A. December 9, 1879.

36. A. *L&M* 32–4080.

37. A. Howard letter to Mrs. Eddy.

38. A. Cf. Gilbert Eddy's letter to Ackland on February 22, 1880: "I am looking forward to the time when we may through the press speak to the millions instead of the few that we now address."

39. A. Communion or Sacrament services are now held twice yearly in Christian Science churches. Cf. Mrs. Eddy's statement in a sermon of this period (*A&M* 22–10624):

> In communion with Christ bread and wine can only stand for the thoughts they express. . . . Could I only give you a new and vivid sense of the faith and love the greatness and truth of which they tell you would receive an exhilaration and conscious nourishment that no material element can supply. Then would you understand what our communion service is designed to be and what it is to commemorate Jesus in spirit and in truth.

40. A. Choate reminiscences, quoted also at length in Lyman P. Powell, *Mary Baker Eddy: A Life Size Portrait* (Boston: Christian Science Publishing Society, 1950), pp. 297 ff.

41. *Christian Healing, A Lecture,* by Mrs. Glover Eddy (Cambridge: University Press, 1880).

42. A. Letter of June 28, 1880.

43. A. *L&M* 20–2478B.

44. A. Letter of July 19, 1880.

45. A. *L&M* 87–12923.

46. Deltus M. Edwards. *The Toll of the Arctic Seas* (New York: Holt, 1910), pp. 200 ff. A macabre extension of the analogy with Mrs. Eddy's experience is to be found in the fact that the exhumation and autopsy of Captain Hall's body ninety-seven years after his death revealed that his death had been caused by poisoning, as he himself claimed before he died—not by natural causes, as common-sense historians had maintained. Tyson's suspicion of deliberate malice at work in the situation was thus objectively justified.

47. *Mis.,* p. 222 f. The incident recounted in *Ret.,* p. 37 f. refers not to this "research" but to her earliest observations of mental malpractice.

48. *A. L&M* 87–12923.

49. A. *L&M* 32–4077.

50. A. Mrs. Eddy's visions, like those of the Old and New Testaments, lend themselves to Freudian or Jungian interpretations, where the reader is disposed toward one or the other of these orthodoxies. The same visions are also open to a more direct and practical connection with Mrs. Eddy's immediate religious experience, if the reader is one who finds Freud's Moses, for instance, less persuasive than the Moses of Hebrew and Christian faith.

51. *Mis.*, p. 284.

52. *S&H* (3rd ed.), II, pp. 39.

53. *S&H*, p. 405.

54. *S&H* (3rd ed.), I, p. 104 f.

55. *S&H*, p. 234 f.

56. Brian Inglis. *The Case for Unorthodox Medicine* (New York: G. P. Putnam's Sons, 1965), p. 159.

57. A. Mrs. Eddy's Notebook. Cf. René Dubos, *Pasteur and Modern Science,* New York: Anchor Books, 1960.

58. Experiments of R. Rosenthal and colleagues in 1960–61. See Naomi Weisstein, "Kinder, Küche, Kirche as Scientific Law," *Motive,* XXIX, 6 & 7, March–April, 1969, pp. 78 ff.

59. Koestler's *The Sleepwalkers* and *The Act of Creation* contain interesting examples of experiments pointing in this direction, but the issues involved become more sophisticated every year. See Appendix B.

60. A. *L&M* 17–02095.

61. A. August 22, 1880.

62. A. *L&M* 61–8659.

63. A. August 7, 1880.

64. A. *L&M* 61–8661.

65. A. October 16, 1880.

66. A. *L&M* 55–7686.

67. A. *L&M* 36–4661. This letter to Ellen L. Clark, who studied in the same class with Miss Bartlett, goes on to say: "I feel for you all that Mother love that enjoys more to see you grow in the likeness . . . of Christ than from any other source. . . . My prayer is always, God bless and feed my lambs."

68. Mrs. Eddy urged both women to have more charity toward each other.

69. A. *L&M* 61–8651.

70. A. *L&M* 32–4085.

71. A. June 16, 1881.

72. A. *L&M* 20–2487b.

73. R. K. Noyes, M. D., *The History of Medicine for the Last 4000 Years* (Lynn, Mass., 1880), p. 7.

74. A. *L&M* 85–12510.

75. Two further charges of the same sort were brought against him subsequent to Mrs. Eddy's break with him. On the last occasion he was found guilty and sentenced to five years' imprisonment.

76. A. Delia S. Manley reminiscences.

77. A. *L&M* 61–8657.

78. William Dana Orcutt, *Mary Baker Eddy and Her Books* (Boston: Christian Science Publishing Society, 1950), p. 19.

79. *Ibid.*

80. *Ibid.*, p. 18.

81. *Ibid.*, p. 13.

82. In letters to her later editors she commented on this a number of times.

83. John Wilson, *A Treatise on English Punctuation* (New York: Potter, Ainsworth & Co., 1871), p. 183.

84. *S&H* (3rd ed.), I, p. 169.

85. *Ibid.* As it appears in her last revised edition (p. 468), the statement reads: "There is no life, truth, intelligence, nor substance in matter. All is infinite Mind and its infinite manifestation, for God is All-in-all. Spirit is immortal Truth; matter is mortal error. Spirit is the real and eternal; matter is the unreal and temporal. Spirit is God, and man is His image and likeness. Therefore man is not material; he is spiritual."

86. *S&H*, p. ix.

87. A. *L&M*.

88. *S&H* (3rd ed.) II, p. 31.

89. A. Alfred Farlow, "Facts and Incidents Relating to Mrs. Eddy," p. 170.

90. A. *A&M* 63–9055.

91. (3rd ed.) I, p. xi f.

92. A. Letter of July 8, 1881.

Notes: *Chapter IV*

1. A. Nadia Swartz Williams reminiscences.

2. This is the evidence sedulously collected by Georgine Milmine and her *McClure's* associates; anyone who gave opposite testimony was automatically excluded

by Miss Milmine as a prejudiced witness. Actually, both kinds of evidence need careful sifting. The great German church historian, Karl Holl, wrote of the Milmine *Life* in his *Gesammelte Aufsätze*, III, pp. 450–479, that despite the verifications adduced, most of the accusations included were "readily recognizable as gossip and slander." On the other hand, Pierre Janet, the eminent French psychologist, not only took them at face value but also on their basis constructed a portrait of Mrs. Eddy as a classic hysteric.

3. Sibyl Wilbur, "The Story of the Real Mrs. Eddy," *Human Life,* Vol. IV, No. 10 July, 1907), p. 7.

4. A. Williams reminiscences. In later years Nadia, then Mrs. Williams, became a Christian Scientist. In 1902 her brother-in-law took her to Concord, where she had a visit with Mrs. Eddy, who greeted her with pleasure and a quick recollection of the trivial incidents which had meant so much to Nadia.

5. A. Laura Jane Smith Goodwin reminiscences.

6. This concept does not appear explicitly in the first two editions of *S&H.*

7. The exception is to be found in *Mis.* 367:19–20: "Infinite Mind knows nothing beyond Himself or Herself."

8. *S&H* (3rd ed.), II, p. 119.

9. See p. 282.

10. In its sensational attacks of October 28–30, 1906, on Mrs. Eddy (cf. Hugh A. Studdert Kennedy, *Mrs. Eddy,* San Francisco, 1947, chapter 46), the *New York World* quoted one of her defected students as saying, "She talked so much about the evil eye and devils that she caused one of the younger children of James Howard, who lived in the lower part of her house, to have fits." For the credibility of this picture of Mrs. Eddy lecturing the Howard baby on demonology, see note 26, page 335.

11. Spofford was divorced by his wife at Knoxville, Tennessee, in 1880, upon his failure to appear in court to contest her action. Later that year he married Ellen Carter of Newburyport, Mass., and settled down to a more tranquil existence than he had had since first falling in love with Mrs. Glover. He himself in a letter to Mrs. Longyear on June 27, 1921 (L.) gave 1877–81 as the period of tension between himself and his former teacher. In a signed statement written two weeks earlier (L.) he had declared: "This is to certify that during my acquaintance with the aforesaid Mary Baker Glover I never perceived by word or act of her aught but the most rigid compliance with what is universally conceded as moral law." After 1881 Mrs. Eddy herself seems to have refrained from all further criticism of Spofford and to have regarded his enmity as a temporary aberration rather than a settled attitude.

12. A. Choate-Howard statement of March 17, 1881.

13. A. Eastman statement of July 19, 1881. Also interview in *Boston* Globe, June 4, 1882.

14. Wilbur in *Human Life,* July, 1907, p. 7.

15. Cf. the charge of "ebullitions of temper" (p. 96) with Julia Bartlett's state-

ment in her reminiscences (A.), "I have seen students come from her room . . . softened and chastened and in tears, saying they never saw such love."

16. A. *L&M* 20–2457.

17. A. Mrs. Choate added that she was thirty-one years old that day.

18. A. Letter of July 31, 1907.

19. A. September 19, 1881.

20. *S&H* (3rd ed.), II, p. 2.

21. *Ibid.,* p. 38 f.

22. A. Minutes of Christian Scientist Association.

23. A. *Ibid.* Also records of Church of Christ, Scientist.

24. Mrs. Eddy called on Mrs. Rice in particular for Christian Science treatment on many occasions when she felt under particular stress. See, *e.g.,* Peel, *Discovery,* p. 255.

25. A. Letter of July 14, 1881. Hanover Smith wrote Buswell on November 16, "I was at Mrs. Eddy's house most of the Summer . . . and I know her life and example was Christian and their reports utterly false." Gilbert Eddy wrote Ackland on December 1 that "a few days before . . . they had been treating Mrs. Eddy with the utmost affection and Mrs. Durant . . . had up to ten days before . . . absolutely refused to be satisfied in paying Mrs. Eddy what she asked her but insisted on paying . . . her full tuition three hundred dollars." A month later Mrs. Eddy wrote Ackland (*L&M* 16–2025) of her surprise at Mrs. Rice's finding "fault with me *now* when I have deserved it much more at some other time."

26. Two years later Mrs. Rice moved to San Francisco and opened classes on Christian Science, presenting it as more or less her own discovery and seasoning her presentation with sharp attacks on Mrs. Eddy. Several members of these classes (A. Letters of Mrs. J. A. Root, Mrs. James G. Smith, and Frances L. Babcock) wrote that the attacks convinced them not of Mrs. Eddy's unreliability but of Mrs. Rice's. When (out of curiosity and despite Mrs. Rice's warnings) they read *Science and Health,* each of them in turn decided that Mrs. Rice could not be taken seriously either as a proponent of Christian Science or as an opponent of Mrs. Eddy. Evidently poor Mrs. Rice herself felt some sort of inadequacy, for in 1887 she tried to smarten herself up with a course of study under Mrs. Eddy's volatile apostate student Emma Hopkins, who was then lecturing in San Francisco. This heady mixture appears to have been too much for the disoriented ex-Lynn housewife, and shortly afterward she was consigned to a mental hospital for a time. Upon her release she returned to Lynn but did not attempt again to teach or practice healing. Later she became the source for some of the most sensational charges relating to the Lynn period published by the *New York World* in 1906, including the story that Mrs. Eddy was responsible for the Howard baby's convulsions.

Mrs. Rice was also authority for the claim that Mrs. Eddy was addicted to the use of morphine during the 1870's. The *World* reporters, for all their muckraking zeal, were unable to find anyone in Lynn who both knew Mrs. Eddy and accepted this story of Mrs. Rice's except for the latter's friend Ellen Locke. No evidence was produced to support the claim of "addiction," and the charge that morphia "made her [Mrs. Eddy] crazy" is directly contradicted by the evidence of Alvin

M. Cushing, M.D. in connection with her accident in 1866. What may lie behind the story is indicated by Mrs. Eddy's statement in 1885 (*Mis.*, p. 248 f.) that in the late Lynn period she "experimented" several times with large doses of morphine in connection with the "poison" of mental malpractice and found that the drug had no effect on her. (Cf. the account by Otto Anderson, M.D. [page 110] of Buswell's similar experiment a little later.) Even if carried on under stress, as Mrs. Rice claimed, these "experiments" seem to have led to positive conclusions. If the narcotic effect of a powerful drug could be nullified by spiritual power, then toxic action—whether induced by drugs or by suggestion—could be understood better from the level of psychology than of biochemistry. In Mrs. Eddy's conceptual scheme, this meant understanding the crucial distinction between the self-defeating action of the human mind and the restorative action of the divine Mind. Human life itself was a kind of laboratory experiment, as she saw it, and this in itself may be enough to explain Mrs. Rice's ultimate bafflement.

27. A. *L&M* 20–2492.

28. A. Quoted in Ackland letter of January 1, 1882.

29. Cf. letter of November, 4, 1881, from George Chase of Newburyport: "I think they are a set of bedeviled fools and will come to their senses soon." (A.) Instead, Chase himself withdrew the following year after the movement had suffered another setback.

30. The defecting members were not present at the meeting, as most biographers have assumed.

31. A. There are two or three slightly different versions based on the notes made by Gilbert Eddy and the students present. I have not confined myself to any one version but have selected the passages that seem best to convey Mrs. Eddy's thought. "Absalom" stood obviously for Howard. The name occurs also in one or two of the night visions which she had at this period and which Gilbert Eddy recorded for her.

32. A. Julia Bartlett reminiscences. Miss Bartlett arrived just after Mrs. Eddy had uttered these words, but learned of them from the others there.

33. *Ibid.*

34. Of the others, only Mrs. Anna Newman continued to operate as an independent healer. For Louisa M. Alcott's subsequent experience with Mrs. Newman see Peel, *Encounter*, p. 108 f.

35. Among these was the gentle Mrs. Frothingham, who wrote Mrs. Eddy on December 20, 1881, "Please accept my heartfelt thanks for your every kind word, thought and deed in my behalf—now for valid reasons I withdraw my name from the Christian Scientist Association." No further explanation was given.

36. The resolutions were printed in the *Lynn Union*, February 3, 1882 (after Mrs. Eddy had gone to Washington).

37. A. Bartlett reminiscences.

38. A. *L&M* 55–7689.

39. A. *L&M* 20–2495.

40. A. Choate reminiscences.

41. A. *L&M* 55–7689.

42. A. *L&M* 90–13359.

43. A. November 1, 1880. Later Alice Sibley became a professional singer.

44. A. *L&M* 90–13356.

45. A. *L&M* 90–13357.

46. A. August 3, 1881.

47. A. August 9, 1881.

48. A. *L&M* 78–11204.

49. A. August 24, 1881.

50. A. *L&M* 90–13360.

51. A. *L&M* 86–12625.

52. A. *L&M* 20–2496.

53. A. This was augmented by a circular announcing that Mrs. Eddy, President of the Massachusetts Metaphysical College, would conduct "Parlor Lectures on Practical Metaphysics."

54. A. *L&M* 20–2497.

55. Cf. *Brooklyn Sunday Eagle,* June 4, 1882. "Mrs. Potter is a frequent visitor in Washington, where she has many friends who recall with pleasure her attractions as one of the household of President Pierce, and as a most agreeable hostess in the absence of Mrs. Pierce, who was an invalid."

56. She apparently intended to take a course at the Massachusetts Metaphysical College, but never did, though she later came to see Mrs. Eddy there and was listed on the college prospectus as an official "Visitor."

57. The *Washington Post* had spoken of Mrs. Potter as being descended from Sir John McNeil, a piece of misinformation that she passed along to Mrs. Eddy as a McNeil descendant. Though both women could trace their ancestry back to a remote John McNeil of Edinburgh, this was not the Sir John McNeil that Mrs. Potter supposed. She also presented Mrs. Eddy with a copy of the McNeil coat of arms, under the impression that they were both entitled to use it on their stationery and otherwise (see *My.,* p. 311). Her interest in matters genealogical and heraldic is suggested by an unidentified and undated newspaper clipping (A.): "Mrs. Fannie McNeil Potter . . . has painted for the Garfield Memorial Fair, now in progress in the Capitol at Washington, the coat of arms of every state in the Union on a background of white satin." Her misinformed enthusiasm in regard to the McNeil coat of arms did an inadvertent disservice to Mrs. Eddy, who was later criticized for both vanity and presumption in believing that she was entitled to use it. As someone who was frequently pictured by her critics as "an ignorant woman from New Hampshire," she obviously took pleasure in Mrs. Potter's assurance that she was "of truly noble birth," and she was not in a position to question that lady's facts.

58. A. *L&M* 39–5140.

59. A. *L&M* 20–2499.

60. *Mis.,* p. 112. The whole Guiteau case hinged on the hotly debated medico-legal question of "moral insanity." This differed considerably from Mrs. Eddy's concept of moral idiocy. "In legal contexts the term 'moral insanity' implied an inability to conform to the moral dictates of society—as a consequence of disease, not depravity, and despite the absence of traditionally accepted signs of mental disturbance." (Charles E. Rosenberg, *The Trial of the Assassin Guiteau,* Chicago: University of Chicago Press, 1968, p. 68). A moral imbecile or monstrosity was, according to Edward C. Spitzka, the New York neurologist who testified for Guiteau, "a person who is born with so defective a nervous organization that he is altogether deprived of that moral sense which is an integral and essential constituent of the human mind." Mrs. Eddy, on the other hand, saw moral idiocy not as a congenital defect of the brain but as the culminating effect of a deliberate abandonment to evil as an end in itself. One expert witness who refused to accept Guiteau as a case of moral insanity but saw his crime as "the culmination of uncontrolled wickedness" was the New York alienist Allen McLane Hamilton. Twenty-five years later Hamilton would examine Mrs. Eddy's mental condition in connection with the much-publicized Next Friends' Suit.

61. A. *L&M* 90–13364.

62. A. *L&M* 20–2499.

63. A. *L&M* 17–2056.

64. A. *L&M* 17–2057.

65. A. Bartlett reminiscences.

66. A. *L&M* 55–7690.

67. A. February 20, 1882.

68. A. *L&M* 20–2499.

69. Her letters at this time show her close association with Josephine Curtis Woodbury, who was one of the two women in Christian Science history—Augusta Stetson being the other—who would later rival the invidious eminence of Kennedy and Arens.

70. A. *L&M* 84–12625.

71. A. *L&M* 20–2500.

72. A. *L&M* 32–4088.

73. She disavowed any special interest in the suffrage movement in a letter to Mrs. Mary Ellis in 1872. (A. *L&M* 43–5668) Cf. *S&H,* p. 68.

74. A. *L&M* 55–7690. Nine years later she signed a letter to her student Carrie Snider in the same way, then crossed out the word Mother and added the explanation: "I erase the above word! *God* has just shown me it will not do to use it for it will create a *schism.*"

75. *My.,* p. 303.

76. A. *L&M* 86–12626.

77. March 26, 1882.

78. April 2, 1882.

79. A. *L&M* 17–2058.

80. A. April 22, 1882.

81. When the fashionable Corey ladies of Beacon Hill, in *The Rise of Silas Lapham*, ventured into the South End to visit the Laphams, their coachman professed to be wholly at sea in such alien territory. This amiable poke at Beacon Hill snobbery by William Dean Howells is in the same class with J. P. Marquand's in *The Late George Apley*, where he has his blue-blooded protagonist commend the democracy of the volunteer services in World War I in which his Beacon Hill wife and daughter work every week side by side with women from the Newtons. Such refinements of satire are lost on the non-Bostonian who may not know that the South End in 1882 and the Newtons in 1916 contained many well-to-do citizens of very solid standing, taste, and education.

82. A. The two doctors were dropped within a few months and a list of Visitors substituted. These were Rev. William R. Alger, D. D. (Boston), Rev. Richard S. Rust. D. D. (Cincinnati), Rev. William F. Adams (Melrose), Rev. Charles D. Barbour (Plymouth), General Nathaniel Banks (Boston), Mrs. F. McNeil Potter (Washington).

83. See p. 237.

84. November, 1882. See p. 341, note 6.

85. A. *L&M* 91–13467. This seems to be the meaning of a later reference by Mrs. Eddy to their spending hundreds of dollars to extricate Arens from a peril that his own conduct had brought upon him.

86. A. Letter of Mrs. E. D. Smith, November 19, 1932.

87. A. Delia S. Manley reminiscences.

88. Mrs. Eddy was teaching a class at the time, and Gilbert Eddy sat in on the sessions when he was well enough. Several of the students in the class have left written reminiscences which confirm the fact that he kept assuring his wife that he could handle his case himself. What happened in moments of crisis is described in Wilbur, *Life of Mary Baker Eddy*, p. 269, on the basis of another student's verbal reminiscence: "Sitting by him, Mrs. Eddy would lay her face close to his and murmur, 'Gilbert, Gilbert, do not suffer so,' and under her silent treatment he would be relieved for a time and sleep."

89. A. Addie Towns Arnold reminiscences.

90. A. Manley reminiscences. This testimony and Mrs. Arnold's throw doubt on Milmine's circumstantial accounts of Gilbert Eddy's settled fear of mesmerism.

91. A. A signed statement of Eastman declares that he examined Mrs. Eddy on July 19, 1881, and found her suffering from gastritis caused by poison. He also listed some of the symptoms. In the copy of Jahr's *New Manual of Homeopathic Practice*, which she had kept from the days of her interest in that subject, Mrs. Eddy

marked twenty-five of the symptoms of poisoning listed by Jahr under Arsenicum Album which occurred in her own or her husband's illness. The fact that a number of these same symptoms are to be found in connection with various cardiac troubles has formed the basis of many a murder mystery.

92. E. J. Arens, *Old Theology in Its Application to the Healing of the Sick,* Volume I (Boston: Alfred Mudge & Son, 1884), p. 126. Cf. his pamphlet, *Theology, or the Understanding of God,* published a year earlier in question-and-answer form. Question 12 asks, "Is it the arsenic that kills?" and Arens answers that mind, not arsenic, produces death. Question 13 continues, "In what way is mind the cause of death which is said to be produced by poison?" Arens answers:

> Materia medica and physiology teach that poison kills. It is indeed a universal thought admitted as a fact in every mind. Now thought is action; and this thought, produced and accepted by mind, acts upon the mind and life of the [victim] and produces confusion therein. This confusion produces unconscious fear; this unconscious fear in the [victim's] mind heats the blood, causing the first conscious action; this disturbs the pulsation. A chemical action takes place in the system, and the result of this action is death.

93. Mrs. Eddy's correspondence with her students as well as their later reminiscences provide scores of examples of her ability to sense currents of thought and troublesome situations of which she had no explicit knowledge. Although she repudiated clairvoyance in the usual psychic meaning of the word, she did believe that spiritual intuition should forewarn one of special needs that required one's attention. Susie M. Lang, who was in her class of May, 1882, tells of receiving a message from her later that summer saying, "If you cannot come to me I shall go to you." On turning up, Miss Lang was amazed to discover that Mrs. Eddy had sensed her sharp need in a situation of which she (Mrs. Eddy) had no knowledge and had reached out at once to help her. (A. Lang reminiscences) Cf. *S&H,* p. 94:24–11.

94. A. Hermann F. Arendtz interview with Lucia C. Warren, April 5, 1929. Arendtz, though he spelled his name differently, was the son of Edward J. Arens.

95. A. William Lyman Johnson material.

96. A. Bartlett and other reminiscences.

97. A. *L&M* 16–10402.

98. A. *L&M* 91–13467.

99. *Boston Globe,* Sunday edition, June 4, 1882.

100. In a joint public statement the two doctors announced that the heart and lungs had been diseased but that the body showed no evidence of poison. To add to the confusion, Eastman made out a separate certificate giving bronchial catarrh as the primary cause of death and emphysema as the secondary. However, in the *Boston Post* of June 9, 1882, Eastman still maintained that "the case before death gave full evidence of arsenical poisoning."

101. June 5, 1882.

102. A. Manley reminiscences.

103. *Ibid.*

104. A. *L&M* 17–2059.

105. Mary Beecher Longyear, *The Genealogy and Life of Asa Gilbert Eddy* (Boston, 1922), p. 77.

106. A. *L&M* 32–4089.

107. A. *L&M* 55–7691.

108. A. *L&M* 32–4090.

109. A. *L&M* 75–10643.

110. A. Cf. Peel, *Discovery*, p. 127 f.

Notes: *Chapter V*

1. A. *L&M* 63–8946.

2. A. *L&M* 31–4885.

3. A. At the annual meeting of the church on December 12 Mrs. Eddy told them: "I never felt more encouraged than now. I never loved my students as now." (Church records.)

4. A. Minutes for January 31, 1883.

5. A. David S. Robb and William Bradford Turner reminiscences.

6. One aspect of the past which was completely eliminated was the connection of Noyes and Eastman with the Massachusetts Metaphysical College. In the fall of 1883 the right of their Bellevue Medical College to confer degrees under the terms of its organization came into question and as a result of the ensuing inquiry the institution folded up. The good reputation of Noyes survived the collapse of the enterprise and he remained a highly respected member of the Massachusetts medical community for some years to come, but he could afford no more connection with heterodox ventures and quickly severed his association with Mrs. Eddy. The bad publicity did more damage to the far more vulnerable Eastman, and as soon as the questionable nature of the Bellevue venture became known to her, Mrs. Eddy wrote and asked for his resignation from the board of trustees of her own college.

7. A. Anna M. Swan reminiscences.

8. This is the Bates-Dittemore thesis, which requires an equally ruthless exclusion of a vast body of evidence to the contrary.

9. Bancroft, *Mrs. Eddy As I Knew Her*, p. 18.

10. Over the years Mrs. Eddy received many letters from students thanking her for vigorous reprimands which they felt had stirred them to new efforts. An interesting glimpse into her methods is given in (A.) Mary E. Foye reminiscences: "During the opening exercises Mrs. Eddy was unusually solemn, which prepared us for what followed. Such a denunciation of evil I have never heard, and how

the guilty one could reply,—which she did,—was hard for a beginner to understand. Then our teacher's manner changed, showing that she felt no resentment; and such expressions of love, compassion, and tenderness came from her lips, that all but the obdurate one were in tears."

11. A. *L&M* 17–2060.

12. From the start the *Journal* carried advertisements of recognized Christian Science practitioners. The first issue contained fourteen; a year later there were twenty-eight; ten years later three hundred and eighty-five.

13. *CSJ*, I, August, 1883. Later Mrs. Eddy prohibited the use of any uncharitable references to doctors or ministers.

14. Reprinted in changed form in *Mis.*, p. 7.

15. A. *A&M* 16–10407.

16. In the first three editions of *S&H* and in other early documents Mrs. Eddy gave that year as the date of her first glimpse of what she later called Christian Science, and her healing of Miss Mary Ann Jarvis in 1864 is cited in *S&H* today (p. 184 f.) as an example of metaphysical treatment. Only through a gradual process did she come to the recognition of her healing of February, 1866, as the great watershed in her spiritual development, though it is evident that elements of Christian Science were in her thought before that date and elements of Quimby's thought continued to influence her for several years afterward.

17. *Mis.*, p. 24.

18. See Peel, *Discovery*, pp. 230 ff.

19. *Ibid.*, p. 270.

20. A. It seems hardly likely that a simple soul like Sim would have written such a letter if the question it raises had not been planted in his mind by someone else. Kennedy is the most obvious candidate (see p. 130).

21. A. This contradicts George Quimby's constant reiteration in later years that he would not publish his father's manuscripts because the world was not "ready" for them.

22. A. Cf. George Quimby's statement that Mrs. Eddy heard many of his father's essays read and wrote many of her own which she submitted to him. (Peel, *Discovery*, p. 342, note 106.)

23. A. From this time on, Spofford began to claim that when he first knew Mrs. Eddy she freely attributed the origin of Christian Science to Quimby—a claim which is, however, contradicted by his own earliest references to her. See, *e.g.*, Peel, *Discovery*, p. 286.

24. The second edition was incomplete, the third not yet printed.

25. *S&H* (1st ed.), p. 373 f.

26. Milmine, Dakin, Bates-Dittemore, etc., miss the fact that after 1881 Mrs. Eddy ceased to feel active opposition from Spofford and dropped all further reference to him.

27. A. *L&M* 32–4080.

28. A. *L&M* 31–3928.

29. A. Miss Ware's reference to Quimby's "theory" supports the repeated statements of George Quimby and the Dressers that Quimby himself habitually referred to his "theory" or "the truth," and this is the way it was almost always referred to in his lifetime. Later writers—including reputable historians and sociologists—have claimed loosely that it was "called" or "known as" the Science of Health, the Science of Christ, even as Christian Science, but the contemporary evidence gives no support whatever to such a claim. These terms occur in the Quimby manuscripts (the term Christian Science in only one place) but they were not used to designate his theories even by the Quimby coterie. Cf. Peel, *Discovery*, pp. 183, 189, 337 (note 20).

30. A. Letter undated.

31. "A.O." tells of recently "speaking with a gentleman" who was intimate with Quimby. This seems to be Dresser's rather roundabout way of referring to himself. He goes on to say, "This gentleman informs me that Dr. Quimby did a great amount of writing on the subject of mental healing, or his theory, which he termed 'Science of Health.'" Cf. George Quimby's statement in the *Belfast Republican Journal*, January 10, 1889: "To develop this 'theory' or 'the Truth,' as he always termed it, was what he labored for. . . . He used to say: 'Wait till I get my theory reduced to a science. . . .'"

32. Mrs. Eddy included in her letter an anecdote intended to show the basically mesmeric nature of Quimby's power:

> He, Dr. Quimby, told us one evening, on our way to a lecture at the city hall in Portland, that he would exhibit some of his power to us in the hall. Accordingly, after we were seated, he said to us I shall set them to coughing, and immediately one after another commenced coughing until the assembly in general joined in chorus, longer or shorter, according to direction. Then all of a sudden the coughing stopped, but our laughter was not over, for immediately the people commenced sneezing as if a sudden coryza had seized them, and pocket handkerchiefs were in quick requisition.

Other accounts have come down of feats of mental suggestion and clairvoyance performed by Quimby in the Portland years after he had supposedly advanced beyond mesmerism. Dr. E. F. Brush, brother-in-law of Calvin Frye and mayor of Mount Vernon, New York, described such an exhibition in the *Portland Sunday Telegram* of April 3, 1910. About 1860 Brush had been a bellhop at the International Hotel in Portland where Quimby lived and carried on his practice, placing his patients under "a kind of hypnotic control." One evening about ten o'clock Quimby came down to the hotel office to relax and got into a discussion with "the Davenport brothers" about clairvoyance. As a result, he asked E. H. Elwell, editor of the *Portland Transcript*, and Judge Kingsbury, a local notable who was also present, to write out a question each. Kingsbury wrote his question in Greek, Elwell wrote his in English. Both were enclosed in an envelope, heavily sealed, and locked in the hotel safe, to be made available only to the entire group in ten days. On the ninth day Quimby gave the two men copies of their questions; the next day the originals were taken undisturbed from the safe. Brush recalled the amazement of all when they found Quimby's two questions to be identical with the ones in the sealed envelope. Like the incident described by Mrs. Eddy, this belongs more to the world of the stage hypnotist and conjuror than to the serious history of religion.

33. February 24, 1883. Cf. George Quimby's statement dictated to Edward H. Hammond on June 30, 1883 (A.): "Dr. Quimby . . . had no pupils whom he taught his method with the exception of the Misses Ware of Portland who have never practiced." Also Emma Ware statement in letter of January 9, 1883, to Arens regarding the knowledge she derived from Quimby "and my want of success in making that knowledge practicable or even intelligible."

34. Dresser, in his previous letter in the *Post*, had quoted from the letter Mrs. Eddy wrote him on February 15, 1866, but had not quoted from his reply to her. Mrs. Eddy in this final *Post* article gave the explanation which can be found in Peel, *Discovery*, p. 198 f.

35. (1) *Plato's Best Thoughts*, ed. C. H. A. Bulkley (New York: Scribner's, 1883), p. 257. (2) William H. Alger, *The Friendships of Women* (Boston: Roberts Brothers, 1882, p. 102.) Alger was Theodore Parker's successor as pastor to the Society of Liberal Christians, lectured at Alcott's Concord School of Philosophy, and was listed on the prospectus of the Massachusetts Metaphysical College as a Visitor.

36. *S&H*, p. 124.

37. A typical example is the urgent plea she addressed in separate letters to Kennedy and Spofford in 1878 just before the conspiracy-to-murder case broke—letters written out of an obvious sense of impending crisis. See also note 93, page 340.

38. The exception occurs in her correspondence with George Choate while he was in Portland in 1880.

39. A. Frye diaries.

40. A. Minutes of February 14, 1883.

41. E. J. Arens, *Christianity, or the Understanding of God* (Boston: Caleb Rand, 1883), Preface.

42. A. Letter of June 19, 1883.

43. A few copies were also in the hand of Quimby's widow, while a few of Quimby's original manuscripts—in his own hand with his distinctive phonetic spelling—were still extant, though George Quimby's general rule had been to destroy the originals.

44. A. June 6, 1883. This is possibly the most puzzling fact in the history of the Quimby manuscripts. On all other occasions over a half-century period, George Quimby guarded the manuscripts with a jealousy that would not let them out of his hands for one minute. In this same letter he wrote Arens, "I have had many calls before and therefore do not make an exception in your case as I have invariably refused to let them go, but now they are going abroad." Three years earlier, in her letter to George Choate, Mrs. Eddy had intimated that Kennedy had an interest in both the manuscript material and Emma or Sarah Ware in Scotland—to whom George Quimby, by his own account and for unknown reasons, had now sent the whole carefully guarded cargo. A further complication arises here, how-

ever. George Quimby writes that Emma Ware has just sent or is just about to send the manuscripts to her sister in Scotland, whereas George Choate—back in Boston from Portland—had written Mrs. Eddy on August 26, 1881: "K has been gone [from his Boston office] some time and his sign is taken down. Can it be that he has gone to Scotland after those papers. I shall write to Bethel tomorrow and see what I can find out." Had George Quimby sent the manuscript to Sarah Ware on two separate occasions, and if so, why?

In addition to his desire in 1883 to get the material out of the country so that he could not be compelled to produce it as evidence in the Arens case, another possibility suggests itself. Mrs. Eddy is known to have done a good deal of writing in 1864, commenting on and interpreting Quimby's theories, and there is some evidence that Quimby may have been influenced by her views quite as much as she was influenced by his. (See Peel, *Discovery*, pp. 179–183 and 342 f.) Lyman Powell, who knew George Quimby well and kept up a friendly correspondence with him, intimates that George (barely out of his 'teens in the early 1860's) resented the influence of this newcomer: "To him his father was a finished product. George was jealous for his father's reputation, and fearful lest the most arresting personality he had ever met might endanger it. That was the boy of it. To himself, of course, no man is ever finished." (*Mary Baker Eddy*, p. 98.) Now that the issue had flared up into public discussion in 1883, George may have felt that a slight precaution would enable him to deny any influence by Mrs. Eddy on the development of his father's ideas or the presence in the manuscript material of any glosses by her on his father's writings. By the simple expedient of having some of the later material recopied and possibly predated by the original copyist,—that is, dated prior to Mrs. Eddy's arrival in Portland in October, 1862—his father's originality could be protected. The two Ware sisters might well feel that so small a deception in so worthy a cause was ethically justified. Cf. (A.) George Quimby's letter of October 17, 1907, to Lyman Powell: "You *may* think that I have stretched the truth a bit, in saying that I *had read the proof*. I *did read part*, and you read a bit to me. I don't think as a *parson* you will think I lied very badly, and if I have 'tis in a good cause." Also his comment in a letter of August 19, 1904, to Minot J. Savage, writtten with something of the sardonic panache of a Mark Twain: "I know what a lie is, for I judiciously lie some myself, so I consider it our best gift, but one wants to use it as one does liquor,—with fear and trembling and not become a common lie 'drunkard.'" By 1883 both the Ware sisters and George Quimby had been persuaded by Arens and Dresser (and possibly Kennedy) of the total dishonesty of Mrs. Eddy.

This motive would at least explain the sending of the manuscripts to Scotland and the anomalies which any close study of the present dating of the manuscripts discloses. If George Quimby's conscience was entirely clear, it is hard to see why he did not welcome the opportunity—at no financial cost to himself—to have the manuscripts produced in court, together with witnesses who were ready to swear to his father's authorship of them. It is true that the manuscripts would not have supported Arens' contention that *Science and Health* and *The Science of Man* were plagiarized from them, but the occasion would still have provided an unparalleled chance to establish the manuscripts as bona fide copies of Quimby's actual writings—if, indeed, there were no equivocal factors in the background to be concealed. A similar question arises about George Quimby's firm refusal to the end of his life to have the manuscripts published, even after Mrs. Eddy's demise. His explanation was that the world was not "ready" for them, yet he had written Spofford in August, 1878, that his father would undoubtedly have had them published if he had lived—and the world seemed ready enough to give a hearing to Mrs. Eddy, not to mention the mind-curers who were far closer to Quimby's position. There are many questions in this situation which have remained not only unanswered but even unasked.

45. October 3, 1883.

46. A. *L&M* 17–2062.

47. These night visions usually occurred at times of particular stress or crisis, and Mrs. Eddy often felt that through them she got either an answer or new insight into the problems besetting her. Many of the visions had to do with water, and she told the Christian Scientist Association on March 28, 1883: "Water corresponds to unconscious mind. All thought unconscious is in solution: when it comes to the surface it is dry land. The Red Sea spoken of in Scripture is figurative of fear in unconscious mind." See note 50, p. 332.

48. A. Frye diaries.

49. It had been the subject of correspondence between her and Spofford in 1877.

50. This may have been suggested to her initially by a *Dictionary of Correspondences* (Boston, 1847) drawn from Swedenborg's writings, but most of the alleged resemblances between that book and Mrs. Eddy's "Glossary" break down under examination. (See Peel, *Discovery*, p. 348 f., note 52.) The most persuasive argument that she was familiar with the *Dictionary of Correspondences* is the unusual inclusion of the preposition "IN" as a term for metaphysical definition in both books, though the two definitions are entirely different.

51. Dakin, Bates-Dittemore, and other writers have stated categorically that J. H. Wiggin persuaded Mrs. Eddy to remove the personal material from the chapter on demonology, but she did this in the sixth edition two years before she even knew Wiggin. For the probable basis of their misunderstanding, see p. 189, but even there Wiggin presents as Mrs. Eddy's own the decision not to include any fresh personal material in the new edition.

52. *S&H* (6th ed.), p. 5. On April 18, 1883, a Mrs. F. N. Wilbur of Boston, applying for admission to the Massachusetts Metaphysical College had written her: "I cannot but think it would be better for you and your cause if you would *entirely ignore* this Arens, especially in public. I have heard a number of people who believe in the principles of your book say that they did so much wish it had been written without any allusion to this man. Do you not intensify his power by speaking of him? do you not, *in a way, advertise* him when you speak of him? . . . You know, *principle* is lasting and *personality* soon gone, whether for good or evil. I have so much admiration for the cause you espouse . . . that I cannot bear to see it marred by anything."

53. Her statement that Quimby "commenced miscellaneous writings after we saw him" is in accord with her statement (A. *A&M* 16–10408) that when she first asked him to show her his writings, all he produced was notes on the individual cases he was treating, including her own. It also accords with her hope expressed in the *Portland Courier* of November 17, 1862, that he would develop his theory more fully in writing: "May it be in essays instead of notes! say I."

54. *S&H*, p. 66.

55. A. Buswell reminiscences. Writing of one such evening, Buswell mentions Mrs. Eddy's "keen sense of humor in observing the singular pranks of Cupid in a threatened love affair between a temporary resident in the person of a young Episcopal clergyman who was contemplating entering the practice of Christian Science, and a handsome young school mam who was present as our guest for the evening."

56. A. *L&M* 37–4885.

57. Some of these have all the starkness of a nightmare recorded at the moment of waking but are accompanied by metaphysical comments dictated by Mrs. Eddy a little later. On September 20, 1883, for instance, Frye records the mesmeric argument directed to her, "You can see the image of Dr. Eddy's[;] it follows you day and night and you are dying of the same disease"—then adds Mrs. Eddy's subsequent dictated comment, "If we had no fear though all the world was against us it could not hinder our work." Some three weeks later he recorded her account of a vision in which he himself had been one of the dramatis personae: "Thought K and A were telling me how sick I was. . . . Frye was with me and he said, 'How fortunate that you can hear them talk, for you aren't afraid of them now.'" No diary by Frye for the years 1885 to 1892 has come to light.

58. She returned from the mental hospital where she had been for some years and led a normal, active life again, but died a few years later during a sudden relapse.

59. For some the problem remains today.

60. A. Letter of July 14, 1881.

61. A. December 22, 1881.

62. A. Buswell diary, April 14, 1883.

63. *Ibid.*, April 24, 1883.

64. A. Frye diary, June 8, 1884.

65. *Ibid.*, March 3, 1883.

66. Milmine, *Life,* p. 303. An additional detail which Miss Milmine did not include is that during an earlier discussion as to who should introduce the famous Dr. Peabody on Sunday, Buswell had said, "Such a prominent man needs no introduction." (A. Milmine material.) He probably took no pains to hide the fact that he felt Frye woefully incompetent for the task, and when the latter felt himself tongue-tied from sudden stage fright as the great moment came, a quick look down from the platform at Buswell's sardonic faec would be all that was needed to set the later little drama in motion.

67. A statement (A.) signed by Buswell, Frye, and Julia Bartlett on January 25, 1883, reads: "We the undersigned hearby promise to keep a close guard on our thought and action and never by word or deed knowingly influence a resident of this College, or any one, to a wrong result." When Buswell was finally dropped from the Christian Scientist Association in December, 1885, he wrote Mrs. Eddy, "I cannot possibly admit that I am *consciously* guilty of deliberate plotting in malice as intimated." He went on to say with "profound sorrow" that he did, however, find much error in his thought, "especially in the manner of judgment of yourself. Now I see you and mankind in a different light than ever before and

I am bound to uphold your ascended being whatever may be our personal relations in time and sense." This last comment referred to a mystical vision of her that he had had a few nights before in which the whole world seemed to be embraced in her love and influence. "I see now the petty feelings which I have from time to time been governed by surely vanishing in the grand sequel of this vision. I see now the beauty and truth of man in you as never before."

After his formal expulsion on December 16, Buswell wrote Mrs. Eddy again, "Until you hear from me, noble woman, think of me, I pray you, as one in search of whatever things are true. . . ." Writing to Ackland more than a year later (*L&M* 75–10645), she commented: "Your ideas and mine on friendship coincide very nearly. I think [Edward] Young expresses just my thought in this sentence, 'Judge before friendship then confide till death'. . . . Your old friend [Buswell] is a good specimen of the friendship that I value, that has some stick to it." After some years of silence, Buswell wrote her on October 20, 1897, that he had in the meantime taken both a theological and a medical course, that he had married and now had a little son, and that he had never lost the vision of her that came to him at the time of his break with the Christian Scientist Association.

When *McClure's Magazine* began its highly critical series of articles against Mrs. Eddy in 1906, however, Buswell seems to have caught the muckraking fever and wrote in to the magazine, volunteering to provide Miss Milmine with the most damaging sort of "inside" information. The offer was accepted with alacrity, and he thereupon joined Spofford, Mrs. Rice, and others of the more hostile defectors in contributing to the emerging *McClure's* picture of Mrs. Eddy as an irascible, unstable personality bent on domination. After the excitement stirred up by these articles and the *New York World* attack died down, he seems to have reverted gradually to his earlier estimate—as Spofford did also, though with more reservations. Fifteen years later Buswell wrote out for Mary Beecher Longyear a detailed, balanced account of his association with Mrs. Eddy which is supported by his letters of that earlier period. In the end his "vision" of Mrs. Eddy seems to have won out over his wounded feelings.

68. A. Ellen Brown Linscott letter of January 21, 1899, to Carol Norton. See also *Un.*, p. 7.

69. *Rud.*, p. 2 f.

70. See letter to the editor, *CSJ*, I, February, 1884: "A few weeks ago a certain Mr. C. of this city [Chicago] went to Boston for the purpose of studying the science. The result was he studied with a certain Mr. Arens. Last evening a copy of your journal . . . accidentally fell into my hands. In it was that article 'Infringement of Science and Health' which told of Mr. A's offences and accounted for the stories against Mrs. Eddy, which Mr. C———— had brought directly from Mr. A————."

71. A. *L&M* 20–2529.

72. A. *L&M* 20–2530.

73. *Ibid.*

74. A. *L&M* 20–2522.

75. A. *L&M* 20–2519.

76. A. December 12, 1883.

77. A. *L&M* 20–2520.

78. A. Ashley and Crosse affidavits.

79. *S&H* (3rd ed.), p. 39.

80. A. *L&M* 32–4094.

81. A. *L&M* 77–10966.

82. A. *L&M* 18–10437. *Mis.*, p. 350.

83. This is the assumption to be drawn from the rumors that grew up about the "P. M. [Private Meeting] Society," as it came to be dubbed, though Mrs. Eddy's directions to Ellen Brown as to how to hold a similar meeting show that the whole purpose was to heal and not to harm. See also *Mis.*, p. 350.

84. *Mis.*, p. 283.

85. A. *L&M* 20–2528 and 17–2065.

86. A. *L&M* 20–2527.

87. A. January 7, 1884.

88. A. This was one of the occasions when Mrs. Eddy wept freely at a meeting of the Christian Scientist Association. Among her students she was far from maintaining an attitude of rigid stoicism.

89. A. January 21, 1884.

90. A. February 6, 1884.

91. A. Minutes of March 5, 1884.

92. A. Minutes of March 18, 1884.

93. A. Bartlett reminiscences.

94. *Ibid.* Also Walter W. Watson reminiscences.

95. *Ibid.*

96. A. Quoted in *A Century of Christian Science Healing* (Boston: Christian Science Publishing Society, 1966), p. 9.

97. A. Bartlett reminiscences.

98. *Ibid.*

99. *Ibid.*

100. The Sawyers had hoped to have Mrs. Eddy come on to Milwaukee from Chicago and were put out at her refusal to do so. However, they and several others got to Chicago for the last five lessons of the course and their ruffled feelings were then quieted.

101. A. *L&M* 32–4095. Like Buswell, who had been so active in his opposition to her, Mrs. Choate went through several different stages in her subsequent attitude to her teacher. She soon started a rival "college," writing to Mrs. Eddy for advice from time to time and alternating between protests of continued devotion and

evidences of deep antagonism. Twice during the 1890's she sought reinstatement in the church and was finally readmitted in 1904. For all the extravagant praise of her later reminiscences of Mrs. Eddy, one suspects a certain ambivalence in her attitude to the end.

Notes: *Chapter VI*

1. A. Lewis Prescott reminiscences.

2. See, *e.g.*, testimony of Henry A. Littlefield quoted in Smith, *Historical Sketches*, p. 65, and Hopkins account in *CSJ*, II, February, 1885, p. 5. There are a number of references in reminiscences and letters in A. to similar healings observed by the respective writers. See *A Century of Christian Science Healing*, p. 9, for account of Mrs. Eddy's healing of a cripple on Boston Common, possibly on her way to or from Hawthorne Hall.

3. A. *L&M* 88–12981.

4. Stacy Fowler, "Christian Science," *Homiletic Review*, August, 1885. Cf. (A.) Walter W. Watson reminiscences: "She gave a brief sermon, speaking with animation and friendly warmth which drew the audience to her. . . . [Her] manner and presence were so convincing that you felt she spoke with authority and you were bound to listen." Also Harold S. Bangs reminiscences: "As a small boy I accompanied my parents to the Christian Science services in Hawthorne Hall. . . . During these services the spiritual light that seemed to radiate from [Mrs. Eddy's] face made such a lasting impression on me, even as a child, that it has remained with me [1931] down through the years." See note 47, p. 358.

5. This remarkable personage at the age of three was racing through full-length books of every description, reading them as easily upside down as right side to. At seven he memorized the entire Bible with scarcely any effort. At nine he was teaching classes in arithmetic and writing his cousin, "I am perfectly satisfied that Colburn's Arithmetic is founded on an excellent plan, and that it will be of great use in instructing those who know nothing of Arithmetic." At twelve, when already proficient in Latin, Greek, French, and German, he was admitted to Harvard College. He was deeply loved by several generations of Harvardians, and a plaque in Appleton Chapel announces that "for thirty-three years he moved among the Teachers and Students at Harvard College and wist not that his face shone."

6. In his book *The Rising Faith*, published in 1872, Bartol had struck the note of Transcendental prophecy almost for the last time in print.

7. The Christian Scientist Association on May 7, 1884, passed a resolution tendering Bartol "heartfelt thanks" for his sermon, recognizing "his moral courage, his being the first pulpit to fully and to fearlessly utter itself" on behalf of the new faith.

8. *Boston Morning Journal*, May 10, 1884.

9. Useful sidelights on this attack are to be found in William Lyman Johnson, *The History of the Christian Science Movement* (Brookline: L., 1926) II, pp. 304 ff.

and Raymond J. Cunningham, "The Impact of Christian Science on the American Churches, 1880–1910," *American Historical Review*, April, 1967.

10. In a sermon on November 10, 1884, Mrs. Eddy described her healing of a blind woman the week before and told of a visit she had just had from a man whom she had healed of violent insanity in her early days in Lynn. (A. *A&M* 2–10038. Also Smith, *Historical Sketches*, pp. 71 f. and 81 f.) A little earlier in 1884 she healed Eugene H. Greene of Portland, Maine, in one visit of what his wife later described as tuberculosis of ten years' standing, and while he was in her November class he was also healed of a hernia. (A. Grace A. Greene reminiscences.) At this time she had several former doctors as students, including S. J. Avery of Chicago and Luther Marston of Boston, and others came to talk with her about her methods. One of these wrote later: "In preparing my graduation thesis in 1884 from the Boston University School of Medicine I sought Mrs. M. B. G. Eddy on account of an unusual interest in the metaphysical side of medicine. She very kindly gave the larger part of an afternoon to me in research on the subject, which I shall always hold in fragrant memory." (A. Letter of January 6, 1916, from Frank Clifford Walker, M.D., 10 Milk Street, Boston.)

11. Quoted in *CSJ*, II, March, 1885, p. 1.

12. Cf. Abraham J. Heschel, *The Prophets* (New York: Harper & Row, 1962), Chapter 26.

13. *Mis.*, p. 320.

14. *S&H*, p. 313.

15. *CSJ*, III, April, 1885, p. 14.

16. A. Bartlett reminiscences.

17. Reprinted with slight changes in *Mis.*, p. 245 f.

18. *Homiletic Review*, August, 1885.

19. *The Times* of London, May 26, 1885.

20. Reprinted in changed form in *Mis.*, p. 238 f.

21. See *A Century of Christian Science Healing*, pp. 18–23. Mrs. Eastaman in her reminiscences speaks of her husband's father as being a Barcelona merchant, but several of his friends refer to his "Portuguese" background.

22. *Ibid.*

23. A. Jennie Sawyer reminiscences.

24. A. February 18, 1884.

25. A. January 21, 1884.

26. A. July 18 and September 1, 1884. Caroline Noyes, writing Mrs. Eddy on June 19 about the Swartses' activities in Illinois, had exclaimed with a sudden reversion to her Maine austerities, ". . . this west is a queer place[;] give me staid old Boston." Replying eight days later, Mrs. Eddy had written with equal New England fervor, "I agree with you that *clean* staid old Boston is the place for *home*." (*L&M* 41–5410)

27. A. September 1, 1884.

28. A. May 19, 1884.

29. See Ary Johannes Lamme III, "The Spacial and Ecological Characteristics of the Diffusion of Christian Science in the United States: 1876–1910," doctoral dissertation, Syracuse University, 1968.

30. A. Marian McDonald reminiscences.

31. Johnson, *History*, I, p. 11 f.

32. *Ibid.*, p. 80 f.

33. Friedrich Nietzsche, *Beyond Good and Evil* (Chicago: Great Books Foundation, n.d.), p. xv.

34. Mrs. Eddy, as a nineteenth-century Bostonian, is unlikely to have encountered Marx's writings. *Science and Health*, on the other hand, is reported by an early Zurich Christian Scientist (A.) to have been one of the books that Lenin borrowed from the Central Library during his days of exile in that city. The same report, unconfirmable at this late date, states that Lenin himself drew friends' attention to the fact that the book's "scientific statement of being" represented the precise opposite of the basic propositions of dialectical materialism. Cf. Stalin's *Leninism: Selected Writings* (New York: International Publishers, 1942), p. 416:

> . . . if nature, being, the material world, is primary, and mind, thought, is secondary, derivative; if the material world represents objective reality existing independently of the mind of men, while the mind is a reflection of this objective reality, it follows that the material life of society, its being, is also primary, and its spiritual life secondary, derivative, and that the material life of society is an objective reality existing independently of the will of men, while the spiritual life of society is a reflection of this objective reality, a reflection of being.

35. *S&H*, p. 25.

36. *CSJ*, III, March, 1886.

37. L. Buswell reminiscences.

38. *Ibid.*

39. See, *e.g.*, p. 159.

40. *Rud.*, p. 15.

41. *Op. cit.*, p. 40.

42. A. Sermon by Rev. H. Slade quoted in his letter to her of June 20, 1887.

43. A. *L&M* 88–12883.

44. *We Knew Mary Baker Eddy*, Second Series (Boston: Christian Science Publishing Society, 1950), pp. 8 ff.

45. See also *A Century of Christian Science Healing*, p. 8, for a comparable experience by another of Mrs. Eddy's students.

46. *S&H*, p. 48.

47. A. April 18, 1884.

48. A. July 29, 1884.

49. A. Janette B. Weller reminiscences.

50. A. Ladora D. Trahn reminiscences.

51. A. *L&M* 17–2066.

52. *Mis.*, p. 15.

53. Cf. A. *L&M* 28–3834: "A Christian Scientist is not made in 12 lessons. Prayer, watchfulness, defeats and victories make a Christian Scientist, after they are duly instructed into the letter and shown the Christian side of this great subject."

54. Written at great speed, they are almost always completely legible, while the punctuation and syntax often suffer from her haste. Interlineations and crossed-out words are frequent, but the general effect is of decisiveness combined with informality. The letters written to her are a different matter. To one correspondent she wrote, "I will accept you for a student in my normal class notwithstanding your penmanship!" (*L&M* 71–10065) Quite a few of her correspondents still followed the old practice of "crossing" their letters, to the despair of the modern reader.

55. A. November 27, 1883.

56. A. October 20, 1884.

57. A. November 17, 1884.

58. A. June 4, 1885. At the top of an earlier letter from Dorman, Mrs. Eddy wrote in pencil, "My favorite little boy." After going through the Normal class, he wrote her that he wished the sixth lesson (the last) had been the first. It was the only one to deal with animal magnetism and he felt it had opened his eyes to the subject:

> I never saw mortal mind in regard to mesmerism so clearly before. . . . *I* needed it, for either I am to blame or someone else in getting off the *watch* and letting that creep in that I have no use for. That 'sense of wrong' spoken of is valuable to me. . . . I need to be on the *watch* most of the time, or I am too much like myself, as mortal.

In view of the charges made by Dakin, Bates-Dittemore, and others that Mrs. Eddy's classes at this time were devoted almost exclusively to the subject of animal magnetism, this letter has evidential value in showing that in her six-day Normal class the subject did not even arise until the last day.

59. A. Chevaillier reminiscences.

60. A. May 3, 1889.

61. A. March 30, 1900.

62. Quoted in *CSJ*, VI, April, 1888.

63. A. *L&M* 27–3374.

64. A. February 17, 1885.

65. A. Undated letter.

66. The evidence is contradictory as to whether she was for a day or two in the class that was interrupted by Gilbert Eddy's death in 1882, but in any case she did not take a full course until two and a half years later.

67. A. The word occurs in statements both by her own students and by strangers who barely knew her, as, *e.g.*, in Lucia Coulson reminiscences.

68. This little-known fact was told by Mrs. Woodbury's non-Scientist brother, General Wendell P. Battles of Concord, New Hampshire, to Antoinette M. Mosher (A. Mosher reminiscences). The unsympathizing brother added that Mrs. Woodbury "went into Christian Science to 'rule or ruin' as she expressed it, saying 'I will have Mrs. Eddy's place or pull the whole thing down upon their heads.' " While his remarks throw light on some of the later events of his sister's career, they do not suggest the more genuine qualities in her which Mrs. Eddy persistently sought to appeal to and strengthen.

69. A. *L&M* 21–2633.

70. A. January 19, 1886.

71. Augusta E. Stetson, *Reminiscences, Sermons and Correspondence* (New York: G. Putnam's Sons, 1926), p. 15 f.

72. A. January 14, 1884.

73. *CSJ*, II, October, 1884.

74. Bates-Dittemore assert that it was Mrs. Hopkins' "inquiring mind" and wide range of reading which caused Mrs. Eddy to drop her as editor, but the fact is that it was immediately after the publication of this article in the *Journal* of April, 1884, that Mrs. Eddy made Mrs. Hopkins acting editor.

75. Bates-Dittemore make the curious statement that under Mrs. Hopkins' editorship the *Journal* ran riot with articles on mesmerism. The reader who searches the issues in question will have to hunt hard to find the two or three brief articles on mesmerism that lurk obscurely among dozens of variegated articles on theological, metaphysical, biblical, medical, organizational, and other topics. If anything got special attention in these issues it was the clerical critics of Christian Science who were beginning to raise their voices in anxious outrage.

76. A. Lathrop correspondence with Mrs. Eddy.

77. A. At this time Mrs. Plunkett was back in Detroit telling the practitioner who had first healed her that unless Mrs. Eddy let her take the Normal class and made her head of the movement in all the territory west of Buffalo, "I will sweep her off the face of the earth." (Annie M. Knott letter to Mrs. Eddy, May 15, 1889, and later reminiscences).

78. Mrs. Hopkins continued to use the term "Christian Science" in her teaching over a number of years, and this caused a good deal of confusion in her own day and to some extent still does.

79. A. Letter to Emma A. Estes.

80. A. December 25, 1886.

Notes: *Chapter VII*

1. A. Chevaillier reminiscences.

2. This paper was also published as the leading article in the September, 1885, issue of the *American Journal of Dental Science.*

3. Matthew Arnold, *Culture and Anarchy* (London: Smith, Elder & Co., 1869), p. 116.

4. Mrs. Eddy would later speak of herself as having been editor of *CSJ* for several years. Her active editorship lasted only one year, but during the years 1884–88 she kept careful watch over policy, while leaving the selection and editing of content to various acting editors.

5. This is the article called "Taking Offense" in *Mis.*, p. 223. An example of a completely transformed borrowing is to be found in the "Prospectus" in the first issue of *CSJ*, reprinted in changed form in *Mis.*, p. 1. As a girl, Mary Baker pored over Edward Young's long, lugubrious "Night Thoughts" and verbal echoes from it are found in many places in her writing, but nowhere more strikingly than in this passage:

"Prospectus"	"Night Thoughts"
Humility is the stepping-stone to a higher recognition of Deity. The mounting sense gathers fresh forms and strange fire from the ashes of dissolving self, and drops the world. Meekness heightens immortal attributes only by removing the dust that dims them. Goodness reveals another scene and another self seemingly rolled up in shades, but brought to light by the evolutions of advancing thought, whereby we discern the power of Truth and Love to heal the sick.	I gaze, and as I gaze, my mounting soul Catches strange fire, eternity! at thee; And drops the world—or rather, more enjoys: How chang'd the face of nature! how improv'd! . . . It is another scene! another self! And still another, as time rolls along; And that a self far more illustrious still. Beyond long ages, yet roll'd up in shades Unpierc'd by bold conjecture's keenest ray; What evolutions of surprising fate!

6. A. April 10, 1885. Cf. reader's letter in *CSJ*, V, April, 1887: "I shall also rejoice if more attention is paid . . . to grammar, and to minor matters of taste, in the wording and typography of the contents of the *Journal.*"

7. Milmine *Life*, p. 332, and Orcutt, *Mary Baker Eddy and Her Books*, p. 34.

8. *My.*, p. 317.

9. A. William B. Reid reminiscences. Quoted also in Orcutt, pp. 24 and 29 f.

10. *My.*, p. 317.

11. A. *L&M* 18–2159.

12. A. *L&M* 18–2160, 18–2168, 18–2173, 18–2169.

13. Cf. *My.*, p. 318: "In almost every case where Mr. Wiggin added words, I have erased them in my revisions." This is demonstrably clear in regard to the quotations he added.

14. *S&H*, p. 125.

15. There is no evidence that Mrs. Eddy was familiar with Pascal, although she did write that "God is at once the centre and circumference of being." (*S&H*, p. 203 f.) There seems to be no direct indebtedness here. Cf. her related statement about the healing power of Truth: "It lives through all life, and extends throughout all space." (*Ibid.*, p. 146) This echoes a passage of Pope's upon which Mrs. Eddy drew in several different contexts—namely, his description of God as the universal Soul which

> . . . Lives through all life, extends through all extent,
> Spreads undivided, operates unspent.

16. Appropriately enough, a number of Christian Scientists would play prominent roles in the development of atomic and space programs in the next century. See, *e.g., Christian Science Sentinel* September 5 and 12, 1970. See also Appendix B.

17. See Peel, *Discovery*, p. 17 f.

18. A. Phare Pleigh, *Christian Science and the Bible* (Boston: S. H. Crosse, 1886), p. 60.

19. *S&H*, p. 561.

20. Many writers have stated categorically that Wiggin persuaded Mrs. Eddy to cut down the chapter on demonology as it existed in the third edition, but she had already done this (see p. 135) two years before she became acquainted with Wiggin. What she thought of adding to the sixteenth edition was apparently a denunciation of Arens as outspoken as John viii:44.

21. Phare Pleigh, *Christian Science and the Bible*, p. 65.

22. Milmine, *Life*, p. 338. Wiggin, who was not slow to claim credit, did not state that he persuaded her to take these pages out but that "she wished" to take them out. This throws doubt on the later Livingston Wright account of the episode. More important is the fact that through the interplay of influences and the manifold demands of experience she was constantly gaining better insights into the nature of Christian Science. God might speak to her daily and directly from the Bible, as she always maintained, but—being Mind—He could also speak to her occasionally through Wiggin or the grocery boy, as she also acknowledged.

23. The *Journal* of February, 1886, noted what was evidently a slight uncertainty in Mrs. Eddy's manner and proposed an explanation of its own: "January 24, the pastor, Mrs. Eddy, preached for the first time in several months. The hall was full, despite the cold snowstorm. [Her text was] Revelation xxi:16, 'The city lieth

four-square.' . . . In leaving home, the speaker was so unfortunate as to mislay her manuscript, but she bravely overcame this embarrassment, and spoke to such acceptance that many will be glad to know that the pith of the sermon is embodied in a chapter of the forthcoming edition of her book, Science and Health." The pith would have been more acceptable without this gratuitous excuse, probably furnished by Mrs. Woodbury, who regularly reported Mrs. Eddy's sermons for the *Journal*. See also p. 28.

24. In an undated letter (A. *L&M* 18–2164) to Wiggin at a time when he was feeling rather ill, Mrs. Eddy told him that she was sending a carriage and coachman to take him for a drive through the suburbs, then added: "Remember the City lieth four square and every side is *safe, harmonious.* This City is the kingdom of Heaven already within your grasp. Open your spiritual gaze to see this and you are well in a moment." This illustrates graphically the difference between her use of the city metaphor and Wiggin's treatment of it as an academic exercise.

25. *CSJ,* III, March, 1886.

26. For his later attitude see pp. 280 ff.

27. A. *L&M* 18–2176. Before he entered the class she warned him that she could not *teach* Christian Science to a mere spectator. Teaching required an actual contending with the student's opinions, and Wiggin's mere sitting with the class should not be considered the test of what he could learn as her student. When it became clear that he had no intention of changing his opinions, she wrote him: "You were wise in your conclusions about not entering the class at present as a student, and I will do as you sagely suggested, viz., pass you by with my questions and that will elicit no debate."

28. A. April 16, 1886.

29. A. April 21, 1886.

30. A. Letters of May 4, June 14, June 22, July 1.

31. This did not mean that she took an obscurantist attitude toward such subjects. Cf. *S&H.,* p. 195: "Whatever furnishes the semblance of an idea governed by its Principle, furnishes food for thought. Through astronomy, natural history, chemistry, music, mathematics, thought passes naturally from effect back to cause."

32. A. Addie Towns Arnold reminiscences.

33. A. November 5, 1886.

34. A. *L&M* 35–4479 and 77–11003. To Mrs. Larminie she also wrote, "I see the need of educating students in common branches before we can fill the important posts for our Cause."

35. Cf. her letter to Emma McDonald (A. *L&M* 77–10581): "Give yourself no care over my doubting one of my christian students. It takes me a long time to doubt sinners or get my eyes open to what they do. Much less can any hypocrisy in others cloud my vision of you." Mrs. McDonald, who visited Boston that fall or winter, wrote back to her family in Green Bay, Wisconsin: "Then we stayed to church and heard Mr. Gill, liked him very well. I think he will have to be toned down a little, but Mrs. Eddy will do that."

36. A. Janette B. Weller reminiscences.

37. A November 25–26, 1886.

38. A. *L&M* 20–2555.

39. A. November 27, 1886.

40. A similarly named article which appeared in the March, 1887, *Journal* is combined with the earlier one in the present version in *Mis.*, pp. 359–368.

41. A. February 5, 1887.

42. A. *L&M* 77–11007. Earlier she had written to her student George Wickersham asking him if he could send her an *honest* man to preach or edit the *Journal,* then adding: "I seem fated to have those who take these places work for some hobby of their own and in this way it makes it such a care for me and so hazardous for our cause."

43. A. Undated letter. The ban on ministers in her classes was only temporary, and on November 14, 1888, one Charles A. Roberts, after attending one session of her class, wrote his wife (A.): "There were twenty-five in the class and a bright thoughtful lot I assure you. . . . Two of the men were ministers . . . and I tell you . . . these ministers could ask questions, and she could answer them. It would be a splendid thing if her classes could be all ministers; how Christian Science would spread."

44. *Message to The Mother Church for 1902,* p. 2.

45. It was a circular advertising Oberlin College which in 1834 announced: "Where this Institution is beginning to diffuse the cheerful beams of Christian Science, less than one year since was the darkness of a deep Ohio forest without inhabitant."

46. *CSJ,* IV, May, 1886. Adams uses the phrase to describe what he felt about *Science and Health* after having previously studied the metaphysical works of Warren F. Evans.

47. A. April 29, 1886. Cf. comment in a letter by a little boy, Ernest, to his father, Winslow C. Fisk, after hearing Mrs. Eddy preach a year or two later: "The sermon was *beautiful,* more beautiful than I could explain. . . . When Mrs. Eddy came out on the platform she looked so motherly & calm & when she came in it was as still as could be untill it was through with."

48. A. May 14, 1886.

49. A. November 16, 1886. Adams, for his part, wrote Mrs. Eddy two weeks later: "I find Miss Brown just what you told me, a true, loyal Scientist, excelled by none here that I know of, but with an ego so large and a temper so near the surface, that the sloping over sometimes puts my gentleness and patience to the utmost tension."

50. A. *L&M* 56–7866.

31. *Message for 1901,* p. 15 f.

52. *Ibid.,* p. 32 f.

53. A. *L&M* 33–4203 and 77–11000.

54. Mrs. Eddy's strictures against plagiarism have often been held up ironically against her own literary borrowings (see note 5, p. 355). But an intensive study of all her references to the subject suggests that her basic concern was not a literary one at all—not a matter of either literary ethics or literary prestige. What she seems to have feared was a dilution or pollution of the "purity" of her teachings. As her terminology and phrasing were bandied around by writers with little taste for metaphysical precision, it became evident that they tended to take on a "lower" meaning, to lose the sharp distinctions which to her were all-important. The end product of such a process is to be seen in such flamboyant parodies of Christian Science as the "prayer for a dyspeptic" by "Dr." Jean Hazzard, head of the so-called "New York School of Primitive and Practical Christian Science":

> Holy Reality! We BELIEVE in Thee that Thou art EVERYWHERE present. We *really* believe it. . . . We know, Father and Mother of us all, that there is no such a thing as a really diseased stomach, that the disease is in the Carnal Mortal Mind given over to the World, the Flesh and the Devil; that the mortal mind is a twist, a distortion, a false attitude, the HAMARTIA (Off-the-Trackness) of Thought. . . . Help us to stoutly affirm with our hand in Your hand, with our eyes fixed on Thee that we have no Dyspepsia, that we never had Dyspepsia, that we will never have Dyspepsia, that there is no such thing, that there was never any such thing, that there never will be any such thing. Amen.

When James M. Buckley in an article in the *Century Magazine* in 1887 quoted this piece of bathos from a man who had almost nothing of Christian Science but the name and a few appropriated terms, the *Journal* expostulated that it was surely not fair "to adduce Mr. Hazzard's extravaganza prayer 'as an example of Christian Science.'" An additional fact worth noting is that Mrs. Eddy ruled out the use of formula prayers or treatments from the practice of Christian Science.

55. A. February 25, 1887.

56. A. February 28, 1887.

57. A. *L&M* 56–7892.

58. *Chicago Christian Scientist,* I, October, 1887.

59. A. An undated letter from M. C. Spaulding to Mrs. Eddy gives an amusing account of a sermon by Adams delivered at the Hopkins College. Invited to preach to them because of his broad-mindedness, he threw them into a state of alarm by his strictures on organization:

> Adams had no sooner seated himself than up jumped Gesterfeld and shouted that standing there as the representative & champion of Mrs Hopkins he could not let any such disloyal sentiments as the speaker had uttered go forth as the creed of that assembly that he believed in organization, meaning the Hopkins organization. . . . "Rev" Adams seeing that he had kindled quite a good sized blaze—quickly touched the "brother" and began to hem & haw. . . .Each of the speakers grew red in the face—and the audience began to take side & squirm—but finally a truce was effected and the Doxology was sung. . . .
> Here [Adams] was denouncing personality in others and making a first-class exhibition of it himself. He pursued the same course while in your class—consuming more time than any one or three others in airing his

theological notions and making it so much more difficult for you to lead the others into the way of Truth.

60. A. June 3, 1887.

61. A. Letter of June 7, 1886.

62. A. *L&M* 32–4181.

63. *S&H*, p. 135.

64. *My.*, p. 318.

65. *Ibid.*, p. 179.

66. *S&H*, p. 1.

67. *Mis.*, p. 214.

68. See p. 34:18–28 of this little book as revised and renamed *No and Yes* for a typical example of the book's double-edged approach to traditional theological questions, in this case the doctrine of the sacrificial blood of Christ.

69. Mrs. Eddy had Wiggin's assistance on the early versions of these books but not on the later revisions when they were renamed *Rudimental Divine Science* and *Unity of Good.*

70. This tendency grew on Mrs. Hopkins with the years and became a marked characteristic of the New Thought movement in which she later played a prominent part. After hearing her preach, Joseph Adams wrote Mrs. Eddy that he could find no fault with what Mrs. Hopkins said except for "what you refer to yourself viz., the absence of Christianity or that spirituality which cannot fail to be recognized if there." On the other hand, some of Mrs. Hopkins' later students attempted to meld her essentially non-Christian mysticism back into conventional Christianity. One such student was a young Episcopal clergyman, John Gayner Banks, whom she taught in California and who later founded the Episcopalian Order of St. Luke. As late as the 1960's the order's official organ *Sharing*— widely read by Episcopal and Anglican devotees of spiritual healing—ran occasional advertisements of Mrs. Hopkins' printed lectures on "High Mysticism." The July, 1963, issue reprinted an earlier article by the Reverend Dr. Banks which illustrates the way in which Hopkinsian elements have entered into the stream of Episcopal homiletics:

> The life of Christ's Spiritual Body is the Holy Spirit, just as our animal vitality is the life of our natural bodies. And as the animal magnetism streams forth from the natural body and has an intangible influence outside of it, so does the Holy Spirit, which Christ breathed into His Church and then sent down in fullest measure at Pentecost, stream from His Spiritual Body and work as a vitalizing Principle in the spiritual bodies of His members.

This obviously bears no relation to Christian Science, but it does have affinities with Warren F. Evans.

71. *S&H* (16th ed.) p. 259.

72. A. *L&M* 70–9936.

73. A. July 25, 1887. The high estimate Mrs. Eddy put on Mrs. Noyes' potentialities —and the rugged demand she made on her most committed students—is illustrated by a recorded incident. (Edith Lunt Smith reminiscences). Mrs. Noyes came from Chicago to Boston on one occasion to consult Mrs. Eddy about a difficult situation she was facing. When Mrs. Eddy came into the room, she did not even ask her visitor to take off her wraps but listened in silence to her tale of woe. At the end, Mrs. Noyes said plaintively, "One thing, I have done the best I could," to which Mrs. Eddy replied emphatically, "Oh, no, you haven't. Go right back and do better." That concluded the interview, and Mrs. Noyes returned to Chicago—and did better.

74. A. October 18, 1885.

75. *Rud.*, p. 17. (final version)

76. *Un.*, p. 9 f. (final version) Of this book she wrote Ellen Brown (*L&M* 61–8753) that it "was needed or it would never have taken about six months to get [it] published. The way is always blockaded in proportion to the weight of good that is to be carried over it."

77. Julius A. Dresser, *The True History of Mental Science* (Boston: Alfred Mudge & Son, 1887), p. 14 f. George Quimby allowed him to copy extracts from the manuscripts.

78. *Ibid.*, p. 11.

79. It was first of all printed in the March and April, 1887, issues of the *Mental Healing Monthly*.

80. Annetta G. Dresser, *The Philosophy of P. P. Quimby* (Boston: George H. Ellis, 1895), p. 87.

81. Born the day after Quimby's death, Horatio became a student of Josiah Royce and William James at Harvard and the leading expositor and historian of New Thought. It was through his association with James that the latter gained an acquaintance with New Thought and was led to confound it with Christian Science in his *Varieties of Religious Experience*. By lumping both New Thought and Christian Science together as "religions of healthy-mindedness," James missed the fact that his own basic distinction between the "once-born" and the "twice-born" pointed to essential differences of viewpoint between New Thought optimism and Christian Science emphasis on regeneration.

82. See, *e.g.*, Peel, *Discovery*, p. 336, note 7.

83. *S&H*, p. 332.

84. This was done in a long series of books including *Health and the Inner Life* (New York: Putnam's, 1906), *A History of the New Thought Movement* (New York: Crowell, 1919) and, as editor, *The Spirit of the New Thought* (Crowell, 1917) and *The Quimby Manuscripts* (Crowell, 1921).

85. It stretches credulity very far to accept the date of 1859 for the following passage (*The Quimby Manuscripts*, ed. Horatio W. Dresser, New York: Crowell, 1921, p. 186)—if, indeed, one can accept it as Quimby's at all:

> True life is health, knowledge, and happiness. Death is disease, error, misery and pain; all in this belief. Each of the above is called our knowledge,

and to believe in one is to disbelieve in the other, for our life is in our belief. Death is the destruction of the one, and the life of the other, or the
disbelief of the one and the belief of the other. Christ came to destroy death
or belief, and bring life and immortality to light, and this life or belief was
in Christ.

On the face of it, such a passage has all the earmarks of a gloss by Mrs. Eddy
on Quimby's writings, or even an addition by a later copyist. Cf. a typical passage
from a manuscript of Quimby's attributed to 1856 (*ibid.*, p. 72):

> I then became a medium myself, but not like my subject. I retained my
> own consciousness and at the same time took the feelings of my patient. Then
> I was able to unlock the secret which has been a mystery for ages to man-
> kind. I found that I had the power of not only feeling their aches and pains,
> but the state of their mind. I discovered that ideas took form and the
> patient was affected just according to the impression contained in the idea.
> For example, if a person lost a friend at sea the shock upon their nervous
> system would disturb the fluids of their body and create around them a
> vapor, and in that are all their ideas, right or wrong. This vapor or fluid
> contains the identity of the person.

On the other hand, too much should not be made of George Quimby's admissions. There is sometimes a tendency to read more of a disclaimer than he
meant into his statement (*ibid.*, p. 436):

> The *religion* which [Mrs. Eddy] teaches *is hers,* for which I cannot be
> too thankful; for I should be loath to go down to my grave feeling that my
> father was in any way connected with "Christian Science". . . . In [Quimby's
> method of] curing the sick religion played no part. There were no prayers,
> there was no asking assistance from God or any other divinity. He cured by
> his wisdom.

86. *CSJ,* V, June, 1887. Seven months earlier the *Journal* had published a signed
statement by Mrs. Emma A. Thompson of Minneapolis, together with a corrobora-
tive statement by her father, mother, and aunt, which provides an interesting additional bit of evidence. In 1862 Mrs. Thompson, then Miss Morgan of Portland, had
received treatment from Quimby and continued as a patient for two or three
years without even getting a real healing. During that time she had met Mrs.
Eddy, then Mrs. Patterson, through Quimby. Two decades later she heard of
Christian Science and began its study, not connecting it with Quimbyism in any
way. When she came to the Massachusetts Metaphysical College to take the
Primary course in September, 1886—the only one of Quimby's patients to have
done so—she was astonished to find (A. Thompson reminiscences) that Mrs. Eddy
was the Mrs. Patterson she had met twenty-four years before in Portland. She could
see no resemblance between the two systems and bore spontaneous testimony to
this fact during one of the class sessions. She told also of her father's offer of one
thousand dollars to Quimby if he could explain his method of treatment and of
Quimby's reply, "I cannot; I do not understand it myself." This was the basis of
her attested statement in *CSJ,* November, 1886, and of her more detailed affidavit
in 1907. See Peel, *Discovery,* pp. 164 f., 180, 339 (notes 39–41).

87. See Peel, *Discovery,* 189 f., 268 ff., 301 ff

88. This is confirmed in an article by A. J. Swarts in *Mental Science Magazine,*
March, 1888.

89. A news item in *CSJ*, V, September, 1887, pointed out that the show window of the *Banner of Light* office on Wadsworth Street, Boston (a spiritist publishing company) contained a picture of Quimby with a card beside it reading:

The
Late Dr. P. P. Quimby
Magnetic Physician
of
Maine

90. A copy of Evans' professional card for 1883–84 in A. reads:

MIND AND BODY
Magnetism in its higher Applications,
and School of Psychological Medicine.
Dr. W. F. Evans
44 Chandler Street,
Cor. of Berkeley,   Boston.

91. W. F. Evans, *The Primitive Mind-Cure* (Boston: H. H. Carter & Co., 1885), p. 307.

92. W. F. Evans, *The Divine Law of Cure* (Boston: H. H. Carter & Co., 1881). The preface promises "a theoretical and practical system of phrenopathy, or mental-cure, on the basis of the idealistic philosophy of Berkeley, Fichte, Schelling, and Hegel"—which was as near as Evans ventured to come to Mrs. Eddy's doctrine of matter. But that he remained essentially an exponent of animal magnetism is evident from such a passage as the following (p. 276) justifying manual manipulation:

> The hand was used in order that through the sensation of touch (which is only in the mind of the patient) your thought, to which is given a healing intention, may be communicated to his soul, and through this affect the body. In this condition of mental contact with him the physician *thinks, imagines, and believes* for the patient, and if he is highly susceptible his mind will *vibrate* in harmony with yours; if not fully impressible, it will create a *tendency* towards your line of thought and feeling.

93. *The Primitive Mind-Cure*, p. 68 f. as quoted by Gordon. Again and again Evans identifies his method of healing with "the science of magnetism." Charles S. Braden, in his *Spirits in Rebellion* (Dallas: Southern Methodist University Press, 1963) makes the astonishing statement (p. 96): "Whether this was his own method is not stated. He may only have observed it as practiced by another." From his first book on mental healing to his last, Evans repeatedly, explicitly, and proudly identifies his healing as magnetism.

Notes: *Chapter VIII*

1. See Peel, *Discovery*, pp. 31. and 215 f.

2. A. George W. Baker statement.

3. A short time before, Mrs. Eddy, together with one of her students, had visited Tilton in order to see the monuments which she had had erected in the local

cemetery to Gilbert Eddy and to her mother and father. While there, they had been caught in a storm just as they were passing Abigail Tilton's home. Rather than take refuge in a house where she was not welcome, Mrs. Eddy and her companion stepped into the adjacent barn and waited there until the downpour was over.

4. A. August 18, 1885.

5. A. An obituary in the *People and New Hampshire Patriot,* September 16, 1886, told of her numerous charities: a new parsonage to the Episcopal Church in Tilton, $10,000 to aid in founding St. Mary's School in Concord, $1,000 to the Home for the Aged in Concord, $5,000 each to the parish and for the poor of Tilton, etc.

6. A. Letter to Mary Baker Glover Billings, April 22, 1924.

7. Samuel and his wife accompanied Mrs. Eddy on her first visit to Quimby in 1862 but did not take to that gentleman. Samuel died in 1869.

8. On August 20, 1901, Mrs. Baker wrote Rev. Irving C. Tomlinson a letter (later printed in Alfred Farlow's little booklet *Christian Science: Historical Facts,* Boston, 1902, pp. 25 ff.) which reads in part:

> Whether logical as truth, or otherwise, Christian Science is her faith, sincerely embraced after long years of faithful study of the Bible; and according to her belief it is intelligently taught. She is now, and has been for thirty-five years, hard at work in the cause she espoused. With her means she is carrying blessings to many a needy one, and she works on, seeking the good of all. Whatever differences of belief the public may entertain concerning any of her doctrines, they cannot justly ignore the fact that hers is an earnest, generous and noble life—the legitimate outgrowth of a noble soul. . . .
>
> Her great kindness to me can never be forgotten. I pray God to sustain and keep her from all harm. A difference in theological views does not call for such treatment as she has received from some who disagree with her.
>
> My standing in the Orthodox church will vouch for the truth of every word I have written in this letter. Perhaps I should say that I was educated for missionary work, and early became a member of the American Board of Commissioners of Foreign Missions. I went out as a missionary to labor among the Choctaw Indians at Pine Ridge Seminary, Indian Territory, where I was principal of that institution. I continued in the missionary field of labor until the failure of my health. In these many years of Christian activity I was associated with Rev. I. C. Strong and wife, Revs. Kingsbury and Hotchkins, and other well-known Christian workers.

9. A. Janette B. Weller reminiscences.

10. Mrs. Eddy uses this phrase in a number of different contexts.

11. A. *L&M* 88–13086.

12. A. *L&M* 77–11014.

13. A. *L&M* 17–2085.

14. A. *L&M* 17–2089. A little girl who lived two miles from the Glovers just after

they moved back to the Black Hills described Mrs. Glover later (Ethel Grow reminiscences) as "a thin, colorless . . . woman, never tidy . . . and her children were not well cared for." She talked a good deal to the small girl about Mrs. Eddy's wealth and earning capacity and complained that she "let her son work and gave HIM nothing"—a fact which, to the child "seemed dreadful." Another view of Mrs. Eddy was held, however, by her youngest granddaughter, who wrote her on December 11, 1889, during a spell of sickness:

> Dear Grandmother, you must not worry about me for it makes me quite happy to be able to write to you these few lines. Oh Dear I must tell you we have a darling baby boy he has eight teeth and can say lots of words real plain he is fat and strong he is very handsome.
>
> I only wish you could see him you would laugh to here him call papa to the top of his voice. . . . From your little Grand daughter
>
> Evelyn Tilton Glover
>
> God bless you.
> God bless you fore ever.

15. A. August 23, 1886. For explanation of the term "M.A.M.," see p. 229.

16. A. March 7, 1887.

17. *Gage County Democrat,* May 7, 1887.

18. A. *L&M* 13–1575.

19. A. April 25, 1888.

20. *S&H,* p. vii.

21. She actually made him her "assistant" at the college but did not want him to advertise the fact until he had proved himself more thoroughly.

22. A. Kate Davidson Kimball reminiscences.

23. A. *L&M* 70–9912.

24. A. Knott reminiscences. *We Knew Mary Baker Eddy,* Third Series (Boston: Christian Science Publishing Society, 1953), p. 82 f.

25. A. January 31, 1888.

26. A. Form letter sent out at the end of March, 1887.

27. A. *L&M* 14190.

28. Quoted in Johnson, *History,* I, p. 178.

29. Luther M. Marston, M.D., *Essentials of Mental Healing,* Boston, 1886. Preface.

30. *Mental Healing Monthly,* I, April, 1887.

31. *S&H,* p. 380.

32. *Rud.,* p. 1: "*How would you define Christian Science?* As the law of God, the law of good, interpreting and demonstrating the divine Principle and rule of universal harmony."

33. *S&H,* p. 23.

34. Mrs. Eddy always insisted that God is not *within* man and that, on the contrary, man has his entire being from God.

35. On August 14, 1887, he adjured her in a letter to *hold fast:* ". . . you are pointing out the way and are grounded on the rock which many will have to fly to for safety." But when the *Journal* eleven months later published a letter from a Denver reader gently taking Dorman to task for the metaphysical immaturity of his answers to letters in the columns of his own magazine, Dorman's vanity was touched and he flew to Mrs. Plunkett for what looked like safety but turned out to be demolition. See p. 259.

36. A. Knott reminiscences.

37. The large if dispiriting literature of mind-cure bears overwhelming testimony to this chaotic situation. In June, 1886, after another well-meaning sermon by Cyrus Bartol, the *Journal* commented: "When Dr. Bartol, in his kindly way, bids Christian Scientists live in friendly unity with these *isms,* he asks the impossible. In charity, Yes,—in oneness with every holy purpose; but in unity of opinion, No. Oil and water mingle not. Material mind-cure, corporeal spirits, bodily mesmerism, are not outgrowths of the Christian Science of the Bible."

Alfred Farlow in a letter of November 9, 1888, commented that it was all very well to be charitable but one couldn't take the mind-curers into one's house simply because they expropriated the family name. They desire, he wrote, "to sail under the banner of Christian Science and at the same time . . . denounce the mother of Christian Science. If I did not desire to be known as a horse-thief and did not respect the business I would not call myself a horse-thief but take some other name." Mrs. Eddy, more temperately but with equal decisiveness, wrote Ellen Brown (*L&M* 77–11008), "Unless a great and radical change is effected by *pure* Christianity our Cause will disappear and the schools of Gnosticism and Theosophy . . . will take the place of Chr. Sci."

38. A. *L&M* 56–7867 and 88–12982.

39. A. Letter of Captain John F. Linscott, March 27, 1887. One E. A. Robbins wrote in the February, 1888, issue of *Mental Science Magazine:* "Those who feel that Mrs. Eddy estimates at too high a price her knowledge of 'Christian Science,' should see as I have, in the neighboring towns and cities of Chicago, how the imperfect teaching, stating of facts without proof or explanation, and the temporary healing (mostly free) by students [who have been taught by low-priced pretenders] is bringing distrust and contempt upon the Science." This statement seems a little anomalous in Swarts's magazine.

40. *Truth, A Magazine of Christian Science,* I, November, 1887.

41. *Mental Healing Monthly,* II, November, 1887.

42. *CSJ,* V, November, 1887. Also *Mis.,* p. 269.

43. A. *L&M* 35–4552.

44. Many later writers have incorrectly extended the use of the term (and the abbreviation) back into the 1870's and early 1880's. Marston in the *Mental Healing Monthly* for June, 1887, noted the linguistic switch from mesmerism to animal magnetism then taking place among Mrs. Eddy's followers. The first use of the abbreviated M. A. M. I have noticed is in Farlow's letter of August 23, 1886

45. *My.*, pp. 210 ff.

46. In some cases it was not so much ambivalence as oscillation.

47. *CSJ*, V. June, 1887.

48. L. Letter of January 16, 1841.

49. A. Letter of Henry A. Reynolds, August 18, 1887.

50. *Mis.*, p. xi f.

51. To Sue Ella Bradshaw she wrote in 1886 (A. *L&M* 36–4833): "Drop your present argument. My students cannot yet carry out my directions on this question[;] every time it is tried they increase the hate instead of *destroying* it. Take *only* this way. God is *all* and He is *Love*."

52. Among theological writers of the twentieth century it is, curiously enough, Simone Weil who comes closest to Mrs. Eddy in understanding Providence as the working of impersonal law. Vastly different though the two were as women and as thinkers, the mathematically-minded young Hellenic-Hebrew-Catholic mystic at least shared with Mrs. Eddy that passionate metaphysical logic which saw that an infinite love that was also infinite intelligence must operate as law.

53. *L&M* 87–12804.

54. See *e.g.*, Irving C. Tomlinson, *Twelve Years with Mary Baker Eddy* (Boston: Christian Science Publishing Society, 1945), p. 59 f.

55. A. July 24, 1884.

56. *Chicago Inter-Ocean*, January 2, 1887.

57. A. *L&M* 87–12898.

58. A. This was the first of several attempts by different writers to produce a popularized version of *Science and Health*, but these have uniformly ended up in the dusty depths of obscure secondhand bookshops. Whatever difficulties it may offer, *Science and Health* has continued to sell in phenomenal quantities through the twentieth century. (Orcutt, *op. cit.*, p. 3.)

59. Ursula N. Gestefeld, *Statement of Christian Science*, Fourth Edition (New York, 1887), p. 3.

60. *S&H*, p. 1.

61. Gestefeld, *Statement*, p. 114.

62. A. *A&M* 27–11052. Cf. Bonhoeffer's, "What do we really believe? I mean, believe in such a way as to stake our whole lives upon it?" And Barth's, "What the people want to find out and thoroughly understand is *Is it true?* . . . Let us not be surprised that this want of theirs seldom or never meets us openly with such urgency as I have indicated. . . . They expect us to understand them better than they understand themselves. We are misled . . . when we think that when they come to us they may really be put off with next-to-the-last and less-profound answers." (Karl Barth, *The Word of God and the Word of Man*, New York: Harper Torchbooks, 1957, p. 108 f. Quoted also in DeWitt John, *The Christian Science Way of Life*, Englewood Cliffs: Prentice-Hall, 1962, p. 33.) Susie M. Lang

in a letter to J. V. Dittemore on June 13, 1917 (A.) tells how she was puzzled during her first class with Mrs. Eddy by the question of evil's origin and could get no solution, though Mrs. Eddy patiently analyzed it for her three times. Ashamed to ask again before the class, Miss Lang approached the teacher privately afterward and was answered in "four powerful words"—we can only guess at what they were—but they "stirred my consciousness to its very depths, keeping it in a state of fermentation for several hours, and then the inward voice spoke to me so clearly, so emphatically, the mystery was solved and I stepped out, as it were into another world."

63. Emma Curtis Hopkins, *Twelve Lessons in Christian Science*, Chicago, 1891.

64. *CSJ*, VI, October, 1888.

65. Ursula N. Gestefeld, *Jesuitism in Christian Science* (Chicago, 1888), p. 15. Mrs. Eddy made many references to "mad ambition," but without applying the words explicitly to Mrs. Gestefeld.

66. Ellen Linscott wrote on January 27, 1889, "*Mrs. Gestefeld* WANTS to be excommunicated. This means mischief, so we must go slow." The action two months later was, however, unanimous when it came.

67. *S&H*, p. 581.

68. A. *L&M* 18–2208.

69. See Peel, *Encounter*, p. 77 f. for an example of Mrs. Eddy's own handling of such a case.

70. A. *L&M* 60–8546.

71. A. *L&M* 88–12966.

72. A. December 28, 1887.

73. One example just preceding the notorious Corner case is recounted in a letter to Mrs. Eddy (A.) by Charles F. Kinzel of Atchison, Kansas, written on April 4, 1888. At the end of the Primary class which he had completed with her just a week or two before, Kinzel had come to her and told her that his wife would be having a baby shortly after he arrived back in Kansas. Mrs. Eddy had told him to have no fear, she would give the case her prayer and support. Now he wrote that the birth had been swift and easy. Four hours later his wife had risen and dressed the child, and twenty hours later she had got up for good. If it were not for the healthy little newcomer, it would be difficult to realize that anything had happened. Twenty-two years later Kinzel wrote Mrs. Eddy confirming the incident and telling her that the daughter, now a healthy young woman, was studying in Boston.

74. Before the trial Mrs. Eddy offered to pay to have a medical expert brought in to give evidence, but Mrs. Corner's counsel declined the help, assuring her that no more witnesses were needed.

75. See *CSJ*, vol. 85, p. 607 f. and *Christian Science Sentinel*, vol. 70, p. 1790, for representative examples. Also *A Century of Christian Science Healing*, p. 83 f. and pp. 106–112 for related types of healing.

76. A. James E. Brierly reminiscences.

77. The natural birth movement in this century can be traced in part to the innumerable examples furnished by Christian Scientists over the years, as many medical men who have espoused it have readily acknowledged, including the chief English proponent, Dr. Grantly Dick-Read. A Christian Scientist seeking an obstetrician has for guidance Mrs. Eddy's words in her early sermon *Christian Healing* (p. 14): "Great caution should be exercised in the choice of physicians. If you employ a medical practitioner, be sure he is a learned man and skilful; never trust yourself in the hands of a quack. In proportion as a physician is enlightened and liberal is he equipped with Truth, and his efforts are salutary; ignorance and charlatanism are miserable medical aids." A doctor who is "liberal" in this sense is one who will permit the mother to rely on prayer entirely and who will limit his services to the mechanics of the delivery.

78. *Boston Herald,* April 29, 1888.

79. The first Committee on Publication had been formed in the spring of 1885 to reply to the many attacks and uninformed comments on Christian Science that were suddenly sprouting up in the public press. Like many of Mrs. Eddy's most effective moves, the formation of the committee came in response to a concrete, immediate need rather than as the result of long-range planning. It was not until the end of the century, however, that she found in Alfred Farlow the man with the vision, steadiness, and developed capabilities to develop this corrective and informative work effectively.

80. *Boston Herald,* April 29, 1880.

81. This is a matter which belongs more to the history of Christian Science— and the social history of the past century—than to a biography of Mrs. Eddy, but it is a matter which needs careful, impartial study. Not only is one likely to find here fresh light on what has often been called the overdefensiveness of Christian Scientists but also on some of the scientific myths of our time.

82. A. *L&M* 70–9970.

83. This was an important decision for the future of Christian Science. If the church were to take financial and moral responsibility for all the mistakes of its members, it would be at the mercy of every bungler and dabbler. Mrs. Eddy's decision, however, did not rule out the church's going to the rescue when justice and humanity clearly demanded official support.

84. From the correspondence that ensued it appears that those who were most insistent that the church should help to pay Mrs. Corner's legal fees contributed nothing themselves when they had the opportunity.

85. A. June 7, 1888.

86. At a meeting of the Christian Scientist Association six months before, Mrs. Crosse had read an essay on the need for united effort "in her calm quiet and impressive manner," as the official minutes put it, and "held the large audience captive, and attentive listeners." Charles Troup, the secretary who wrote the minutes, was one of those who followed Mrs. Crosse out on June 12.

87. *Boston Traveler,* June 23, 1888; Chicago papers of June 15; *The Chicago Christian Scientist,* July, 1888; reminiscences and letters in A; Smith, *Historical Sketches,* p. 74.

88. *Mis.*, p. 102. This is from the abridged and revised version of the talk prepared by Wiggin for the *Journal*, which differs considerably from the imperfect stenographic account in *The Chicago Christian Scientist*. Mrs. Eddy labels it the "substance" of her talk, and it certainly represents the substance of her thinking on the topic she had to choose so quickly. If her Chicago audience did not hear these exact words, they heard something very close to them from a speaker who habitually started her teaching from this premise.

89. Wilbur, *Life*, p. 311.

90. Johnson, *History*, I, p. 151.

Notes: *Chapter IX*

1. A. *L&M* 56–7870. Despite Mrs. Eddy's objection to Filbert's taking a three-year theological course, other evidence indicates that she did not reject the usefulness of historical scholarship. At the close of the obstetrics course in October, 1888, for instance, she told Mrs. Knott to prepare herself to hold services and preach sermons and recommended as aids Archbishop Trench's *The Miracles of Our Lord* and *The Parables of Our Lord*, Conybear and Howson's *The Life and Epistles of St. Paul*, and John S. C. Abbott's *The History of Christianity*.

2. Reprinted in *Mis.*, pp. 277 ff.

3. The Fabyan House had a large Jewish clientele, and it is unlikely that many of them were attracted by the name "Christian Science" at that time. Later, as Christian Science healing became better known, a considerable number of Jews became Christian Scientists. It was largely to counteract this tendency that Rabbi Morris Lichtenstein started the movement known as Jewish Science. In a paper that was both an analysis and a warning, read before the Central Conference of American Rabbis at Baltimore on April 15, 1912, Rabbi Maurice Lefkovits made a point that many of Mrs. Eddy's fellow Christians had failed to grasp:

> Christian Science is more than a mere healing association. It is primarily a religious organization. It is a church. . . .
> And it is a Christian religious organization. It is a Christian church community. . . . Its central figure is Christ Jesus. . . . It is he who is the original source and supreme sanction of Christian Science. There is hardly a page in "Science and Health" . . . on which the name of Christ Jesus does not occur once or more often. . . .
> Christian Science does not believe in the deity of Jesus, but it does believe that he was the offspring of Mary's self-conscious communion with God; and it supplements this belief with the statement that thus far only he, and no one else, has had such consciously divine descent. Christian Science rejects the belief that the blood of Jesus atones for the sins of those professing faith in him, but it emphatically upholds the belief that he, of all men, was the Wayshower, that he, infinitely more than any one else, manifested the Christ spirit, and thus he pre-eminently pointed and still points man's way to salvation.

In the light of these later developments Mrs. Eddy's comment in an 1888 letter to Mrs. Nellie Eaton [*L&M* 36–4698] takes on special interest: "But dear you should not have told the poor Jewess that you could not heal her unless she believed in Christ[;] you should have healed her and thus brought her nearer to Him and then she might have seen him as 'trees walking' like the blind of old."

4. A. Knapp memoirs.

5. *Ibid.*

6. A. June 8, 1889.

7. See *We Knew Mary Baker Eddy* (all three series) and Smith, *Historical Sketches* (chapters 11, 13, 15) for excerpts from typical reminiscences in A.

8. A. Lathrop reminiscences.

9. *Mis.*, p. 54.

10. See, *e.g.*, Carter and Thompson healings in Smith, *Historical Sketches,* pp. 66 f. and 75 f.

11. An example of this in A. is a letter of December 13, 1886, from Mrs. E. C. Heywood thanking her for the good she had done Mrs. Heywood's teen-age daughter: "The eve she called to see you at the College, she said, the minute you came into the room it seemed as though an electric shock went all over her and she seemed to be lifted beyond the earth. Since then she has appeared like another child and since coming to Worcester people will ask what she has done to herself and she says, 'I've seen Mrs. Eddy.' " Mrs. Heywood went on to say that the girl had had a slight impediment in her speech which entirely disappeared that night.

12. Typical examples of these are to be found in the last hundred pages of *S&H,* but Mrs. Eddy's correspondence is laced with healings, direct and indirect, recounted by her students. Mrs. A. M. Harvey wrote her on May 31, 1886, after returning to Cincinnati from Primary class with Mrs. Eddy, that she found her patients all healed: "I was so delighted to see them so happy, it is wonderful (they said) that you could make us so strong and well and us here in Cin." (A.)

13. A. *L&M* 32–4110.

14. Other teachers continued to give twelve.

15. A. Martha H. Bogue reminiscences.

16. See full account in Norman Beasley, *The Cross and the Crown* (New York: Duell, Sloan and Pearce, 1952), p. 191 f.

17. In May she gave the first lesson to a new Primary class, then took off for Barre, Vermont, and left Foster Eddy to give the remainder of the lessons. He also conducted a Normal class which followed shortly after.

18. A. *L&M* 88–13090.

19. A. *L&M* 86–12782.

20. *Mis.*, p. 279 f. This slightly revised version of the contemporary *Journal* report makes the final metaphor a little clearer.

21. A. *L&M* 86–12782.

22. A. Late August, 1889.

23. A. Bartlett reminiscences.

24. The letter was received and acted upon the same day it was written. Mrs. Eddy was stopping temporarily at 385 Commonwealth Ave.

25. Foster Eddy was made president of the organization and was the dominant figure at the convention the following year.

26. A. *L&M* 41–5465.

27. The first Christian Science church in the world had been built in Oconto in 1886. The pastor of the church, a former clergyman named Lanson P. Norcross, later became pastor of the Boston church. Laura and Victoria Sargent were sisters who married two brothers and thus had the same married name.

28. *Mis.*, pp. 355 ff.

29. A. *L&M* 55–7700.

30. December 2, 1889. It continued, however, to retain its name and hold services.

31. A. Johnson letter to Board of Directors, July 1, 1925.

32. The low price has given rise to speculation that there was something irregular about the sale, but there is no evidence to support such a theory. The auction was advertised in the Boston papers on July 11, 18, and 25. An affidavit was made by Mrs. Eddy's lawyer, Baxter E. Perry, to the effect that the property was sold on August 3 at public auction conducted on the premises by Amos W. B. Gooding, a duly licensed auctioneer, as required by the power of sale in the mortgage. This affidavit was recorded with the Suffolk Registry of Deeds on August 6, together with the deed itself. It is common and accepted practice in Massachusetts for real estate transactions to take place through a "straw" or agent, such as the younger Perry (and, later, Ira Knapp). Thirty-six years later, however, Frederick W. Peabody in a raging polemic entitled *The Faith, The Falsity, and the Failure of Christian Science* (New York, 1925) made an unsupported allegation that no auctioneer had appeared on the appointed day and that the sale had taken place privately in the elder Perry's office. Such an action would certainly have stirred a protest among Boston real-estate dealers at the time, but there is no record of any such protest. On the contrary, Alfred Lang, one of the three trustees to whom Mrs. Eddy later conveyed the land, wrote her on March 18, 1892 (A.) that the trustees' lawyer—whom he described as "the best conveyancer in the State"—had assured them that "the foreclosure of your mortgage was legally executed." Though the trustees questioned several defects in the title they had been given, at no point was any question raised as to the full legality of the sale on August 3, 1889.

33. *Mis.*, p. 139 f.

34. *Ibid.*

35. Mrs. Eddy had asked Perry to have the notice in the Sunday *Herald* of December 8, but it did not actually appear until Monday, December 9. This gave the dissidents only twenty-four hours to act before Knapp purchased the lot for Mrs. Eddy. When complaints reached her about the speed of the transaction, she

wrote Murphy and Charles Crosse (husband of Sarah) promising to sell the lot to either or both of them on condition that they would use the land for the purpose of building a church open to all Christian Scientists, and for no other purpose. This reduced them to astonished silence; the offer (or the responsibility) was apparently more than they had bargained for.

36. A. *L&M* 92–13585.

37. These two forms, masculine and feminine, both appear in the words of Jesus to Peter recorded in Matthew 16: "Thou are *petros,* and upon this *petra* I will build my church."

38. *CSJ,* VI, April, 1888.

39. *Man.,* p. 17.

40. *S&H,* p. 583.

41. *Man.,* p. 19.

42. More often than not, these thrusts were clearly pointed at Mrs. Eddy but did not name her. The same thing is true of the criticisms in other mind-cure publications. They seem to have felt that to attack her by name was somehow to acknowledge her pre-eminence and belittle themselves. No such caution inhibited her critics in the traditional churches.

43. *International Magazine of Christian Science,* III, January, 1889

44. *International,* III, December, 1888.

45. *Ibid.,* August, 1888.

46. *S&H,* p. 56.

47. *International,* IV, July, 1889.

48. Quoted in Johnson, *History,* I, p. 211.

49. Mrs. Hopkins had been feeling a growing sense of independence, and before long she dropped any further use of the words Christian Science. Before then she taught Charles and Myrtle Fillmore of Kansas City, who had studied also with Joseph Adams and who proceeded to start a movement and a magazine of their own. The latter they entitled *Christian Science Thought* but soon changed it to *Modern Thought.* Mrs. Hopkins went on to become a peripatetic but leading light in the New Thought movement of the 1890's, while the Fillmores became founders of the highly successful Silent Unity movement with its headquarters in Kansas City.

50. The "literary" quality introduced by Miss Chevaillier marked the end of the crude but catchy exuberance of the magazine and clearly foreshadowed its early demise.

51. *CSJ,* VII, June, 1889. Also *Mis.,* pp. 285 ff.

52. Dakin and other writers have confused the issue by quoting her words "legalized lust" as though they were her summing up of marriage instead of her description of what marriage becomes on a completely materialistic basis. See *My.,* p. 5.

53. A. *L&M* 77–11012.

54. A. *L&M* 90–13430.

55. A. *L&M* 94–14070. It was to Mrs. Robinson (later Mrs. Weller) that in 1884 she told the story of her marriage with Daniel Patterson (see p. 170). This suggests that she had sensed in Mrs. Robinson a need to have a more charitable estimate of her own husband.

56. Letter dated February 18, 1888, but quoted in the December, 1889, issue of the *International*.

57. A. *L&M* 77–11013.

58. *The Chicago Christian Scientist*, II, October, 1888.

59. Quoted in *Chicago Christian Scientist*, II, November, 1888, with Mrs. Eddy's permission.

60. A. November 9, 1888. Cf. letter of James E. Brierly on January 2, 1888: "I do not hold to the personality of Mrs. Eddy for the Truth . . . but I must say, she is dear to me as a teacher for she has shown me the way to understand the Truth that Jesus taught."

61. *Mis.*, p. 105.

62. A. *L&M* 77–11061.

63. *CSJ*, VII, April, 1889.

64. A. *L&M* 82–11937.

65. *CSJ*, VI, March, 1889.

66. A. *L&M* 35–4469. Cf. her explanation to Julia Bartlett (*L&M* 55–7695) that she will not entertain organizational questions because "under the counteracting mental influence, if I do this, my counsel is liable to be either carried out too late, or misunderstood, or carried out only in part, and because of all these things the wisdom and necessity of it is not seen nor the good it might do accomplished and many will say 'she is a hard master.' I have borne this many years and think at this period of my retirement it should be seen that this is why I left the field."

67. A. *L&M* 85–12444.

68. A. *L&M* 87–13026.

69. A. *L&M* 75–10750.

70. On January 2, 1890, she wrote to Eugene and Grace Greene (*L&M* 43–5736): "The test of my dear students this year in following by faith the order of Science is so sweet so comforting to me that but for this it would have seemed insupportable to have borne the cross of the old year."

71. This is the keynote of her writings from this time on. Cf. *My.*, p. 343:22–30.

72. A. *L&M* 55–7752.

73. A. *L&M* 78–11173.

74. A. *L&M* 75–10695.

75. Some of these are to be found in her small book *War in Heaven*, Boston, 1897.

76. Mrs. Woodbury had just been on a return visit to Montreal, and it was this visit that elicited Clara Shannon's letter to Mrs. Eddy. Mrs. Woodbury herself had written Mrs. Eddy from Montreal on January 3 with apparent sincerity:

> I have come now to defeat and forgive my enemies, undo my mistakes, and so far as my life has become corrected, to bless my dear students here. . . . You have been surgeon as well as mother to me, and have proved your love by doing the thing that was hardest for both mother and child. . . . May you . . . receive the comfort that should come to you from a loving, grateful child, who thus far has done but little to merit your great tenderness.

77. A. Letter to Mrs. Larminie, January 18, 1890.

78. *War in Heaven*, p. 50. Mrs. Woodbury already had a thirteen-year-old daughter and a twelve-year-old son.

79. A. *L&M* 90–13430. A fourteen-year-old boy who attended the Sunday School at Chickering Hall in the 1880's later recalled (W. L. G. Perry reminiscences) "the screeched tirades against everything carnal" by Mrs. Woodbury, who taught a neighboring class. His own teacher he regarded as "a dear," but she did not have the faculty of sensing what was puzzling or troubling the students as Mrs. Eddy did when she occasionally conducted his class.

80. *War in Heaven*, p. 51 f.

81. Mrs. Eddy evidently took very seriously her own statement in *S&H*, p. 448:5–7.

82. Ira Knapp had brought Mrs. Eddy a similar message in the summer of 1888 when Mrs. Woodbury was stopping in New Hampshire (see p. 176).

83. A statement in full accordance with Mrs. Eddy's actual views on the subject had appeared in *CSJ*, VI, November, 1888, in an article entitled "The Immaculate Conception" by Julia Hunt. The article made the popular mistake of using the phrase "immaculate conception" as a synonym for virgin birth, but the substance of what it said was unequivocal. It was irrational for a Christian Scientist to believe in a repetition of the virgin birth, Mrs. Hunt stated. That event had served its unique purpose in history, and would no more need to be repeated than Christian Science would need to be discovered again and again.

84. A reminisecnce (A.) by Jenny M. Lowell tells of a visit she made with a friend to a meeting at 571 Columbus Avenue about 1885. Neither girl was a Christian Scientist, but the meeting made a strong impression on Miss Lowell, who later wrote:

> A rather gross looking German asked if there would ever be another immaculate conception. Mrs. Eddy rebuked him and said very positively, "No." She said there could be but one "only begotten of the Father."
> Mrs. Josephine Curtis Woodbury was present at that gathering. She was very flippant. My friend was frightened at her flippancy. My friend was afterwards a very good Christian Scientist. Mrs. Eddy's attitude towards Mrs. Woodbury was one of perfect indifference.

85. *S&H*, p. 56.

86. A. *L&M* 21–2552.

87. Mrs. Woodbury did not hesitate to threaten her students with dire ills if they left her, and this also played a part in her magnetic hold on them. A number of them did break away, however, and their accounts of her mental methods do not make pleasant reading. The evidence suggests that Mrs. Woodbury really did do some of the things Mrs. Eddy was accused of doing, and this lends credence to her brother's characterization of her as determined to "rule or ruin."

88. A. *L&M* 21–2552.

89. "Christian Science and Its Prophetess," *Arena*, May, 1899. This was composed of two parts, the first written by Horatio Dresser, the second by Mrs. Woodbury.

90. A. Undated letter, but probably written between 1891 and 1896.

Notes: *Chapter X*

1. *S&H* (3rd ed.), II, p. 119.

2. A. *L&M* 60–8565. Quoted in *We Knew Mary Baker Eddy*, Second Series, p. 25.

3. A. *L&M* 88–13007. To General Bates she wrote in August, 1890 (*L&M* 94–13960), "I want to remain with you on earth long enough to see my revised edition of Science and Health published, I need say no more."

4. Some of her women students, though few of the men, had noted the signs of artificial coloring, less taken for granted in her day than in ours. But while Concord encouraged the grandmotherly look, it produced one opposite phenomenon. Some time after her retirement, Mrs. Eddy laid aside the reading glasses she had used for some years and found she could read fine print with ease. On one occasion prior to this healing she remarked to several of her students as she put them on, "When I have more time I will have to look after Mary." (A. Knott reminiscences.)

5. A. *L&M* 17–2098. In another letter of the same period Mrs. Eddy wrote that she did not know the cause of her losing so much weight but that the Concord climate seemed to sap her strength. Before long she had regained her normal energy, but she remained light as a feather to the end of her days.

6. *Mis.*, p. 248. Miss Anthony, who found Christian Science too metaphysical for her taste, never met Mrs. Eddy but wrote her once or twice and sent her a copy of her history of woman suffrage.

7. A. Belisle reminiscences.

8. A. *L&M* 47–6393.

9. A. *L&M* 34–4341.

10. A. *L&M* 56–7855.

11. A. *L&M* 27–3472.

12. A. *L&M* 45–6060.

13. *Mis.*, p. 137.

14. The Christian Science Convention held in 1893 in Chicago as part of the World's Parliament of Religions was regarded as an adjourned meeting but was not held for deliberative purposes.

15. When the Sawyers were studying with Mrs. Eddy, the latter one day illustrated a point by relating an unhappy incident involving a "disloyal" student. In the middle of it she suddenly stopped and said, "Now I've gone and spoiled it by naming him—and error is neither a person, place, nor thing!" Then, with a kind of pleased surprise, she added: "That's *good!* That's going into my next edition of *Science and Health*." (Related to me by one of Jennie Sawyer's students in the early 1950's.) Ironically, the statement in question had, as it happens, already appeared in the first edition of *Science and Health*—a fact that adds a dimension of psychological interest. The scriptures and seminal works of all faiths have in common the quality of involvement in life—an interaction between statement and experience which starts with the author and continues with the reader so that the book becomes, in a sense, a piece of life itself.

16. Concordances to Mrs. Eddy's works as well as to the Bible are standard equipment for Christian Scientists. It is not unusual for them to give hours or even days of study to her use of a single word. While those who study Christian Science in other languages have been hampered by a lack of concordances in their respective languages, the availability of computerized methods makes it likely that in the future a concordance to *Science and Health* can follow more quickly upon each new translation of the book itself.

17. On several occasions she took him to task for doing more than this. Her gratitude to him was sufficient, however, to impel her to have a contract drawn up, giving him and his heirs a substantial royalty on future editions of *Science and Health,* but he turned this down with a sense of its being quite undeserved. Whereupon she asked him to sign a release absolving her from any further financial responsibility for his work, and this was signed on August 28, 1889.

18. A. *L&M* 75–10691 and 82–11974.

19. A. *L&M* 75–10681.

20. A. On December 12, 1888, Foster Eddy wrote Bailey that Mrs. Eddy felt that perhaps he should stop until he had grown to the work: "As it is it puts too great a burden upon her and makes it just about as hard as if she had to do the work alone."

21. A. *L&M* 82–11985.

22. A. Bailey reminiscences.

23. A. Belisle reminiscences.

24. *Mis.*, p. 92. The full statement reads, "Centuries will intervene before the statement of the inexhaustible topics of that book become sufficiently understood to be absolutely demonstrated."

25. *My.*, p. 115.

26. A. *L&M* 32–4134.

27. The periods of closest association were 1885–1889 and May, 1890 to January, 1891, but they were intermittently in touch beyond 1892.

28. A. July 1, 1888.

29. A. *L&M* 18–2213.

30. Milmine, *Life,* p. 337.

31. See p. 189.

32. She did not drop her own development of the metaphor of the city foursquare, which now appears on pp. 575 ff. of *S&H.*

33. A. May 11, 1890.

34. *Ibid.*

35. A. *L&M* 18–2217.

36. A. May 16, 1890.

37. A. *L&M* 18–2218.

38. A. November 8, 1890.

39. Orcutt, *Mary Baker Eddy and Her Books,* p. 34.

40. A. September 1, 1890.

41. A. *L&M* 18–2253.

42. A. *L&M* 18–2226.

43. A. *L&M* 18–2227.

44. Milmine, p. 338.

45. *My.,* p. 319. The account of Wiggin's friend, Livingston Wright, appeared first in the *New York World* of November 6, 1906, and was later reprinted as a brochure, *How Rev. Wiggin Rewrote Mrs. Eddy's Book.* Mr. Wright claimed to have written his account in 1901, the year after Wiggin's death, and in 1903 he showed it to Mark Twain, who was impressed by it at the time but did not see fit to refer to it, even obliquely, in his book *Christian Science* published in 1907. As in the case of the Quimby claim, which Twain had carefully looked into for ammunition, the great humorist obviously decided in the end that there was no point in spoiling a high-spirited argument against Mrs. Eddy's authorship of *Science and Health* by citing weak evidence. The decision is a tribute to his canny instincts, if not to his magnanimity, for the Wright account is full of details and circumstances which are belied by the actual correspondence between Mrs. Eddy and Wiggin. The accounts of Mrs. Eddy's supposed first "visit" to Wiggin, for instance, and of the "conversation" between them about "Wayside Hints," need only to be held up against the facts revealed in the letters (see, *e.g.,* pp. 187 and 281) to show Wright's penchant for fictionalizing whatever he remembered of Wiggin's verbal reminiscences. How much of the cynicism in the account is his own and how much is Wiggin's no one can say for sure. Wright's confident style has led some biographers to quote his account as though Wiggin himself had written it or as though it were a verbatim report of his words. The assumption

that it reports Wiggin accurately can be made only at the cost of turning that pompous but distinguished gentleman into a common garden variety liar.

46. The chapter on demonology had been cut down in the sixth edition from forty-six to thirteen pages. It had been renamed "Animal Magnetism" in the sixteenth edition but remained the same length. In the fiftieth edition it was cut to its present length of seven pages. In 1910 Mrs. Eddy renamed it "Animal Magnetism Unmasked."

47. This came to a climax in the *Journal* of March, 1889, just after Bailey had become editor, with Carrie Snider's account of her husband's death. The reaction of the readers to this sensational though opaque account is a measure of the distance that had been traveled since Gilbert Eddy's death in 1883.

48. *S&H*, p. 252.

49. *CSJ*, VI, December, 1888.

50. A. July 1, 1910.

51. *CSJ*, X, July, 1892, p. 155 f.

52. A. *L&M* 75–10663.

53. A. Tomlinson notes.

54. A. Minutes of May 9, 1883.

55. A. *L&M* 42–5493.

56. *CSJ*, VII, May, 1889. Also *Mis.*, p. 284.

57. By a different path, Mrs. Eddy arrived at some of the same conclusions as the behaviorist in regard to the interlocking mechanisms of individual and social life-attitudes. But her inferences were utterly different. Cf. *S&H*, p. 176: "When the mechanism of the human mind gives place to the divine Mind, selfishness and sin, disease and death, will lose their foothold."

58. *S&H*, p. 570.

59. A. Norcross had done the indexing of the book, the task that Wiggin had performed for the sixteenth edition. This time Wiggin worked on the marginal headings which were introduced into the book for the first time.

60. *CSJ*, VIII, March, 1891.

61. A. June 13, 1891.

62. This was the Boston of Van Wyck Brooks's *New England: Indian Summer,* and it has been a temptation to the sociologist and historian to ensconce Mrs. Eddy so firmly amidst the knickknacks of that gilt and plush period as to lose sight of both the iron in her formative years and the steel in the thrust of her thinking. See Appendix B.

63. The chapters were moved around in each major revision of *Science and Health.* While this chapter made a logical opening for the book—"In the year 1866 I discovered the Science of Metaphysical Healing, and named it Christian Science"— it was abrupt, to say the least. The next sentence went on to speak of God's

graciously preparing the author through many years for the reception of this revelation, and in the years to come she recognized the need of preparing the reader in a similar way. The introductory chapters in the final edition do this.

64. *S&H* (50th ed.), p. 3.

65. Another small change of a different sort is the substitution of the word "demonstration" for "experiment," reflecting her change in emphasis from "trials" to "victories."

66. During the 1890's and with the growth of the New Thought movement, the term gradually began to be used less loosely. Within Mrs. Eddy's lifetime a general recognition grew up that it properly referred to her teaching and to the movement represented by the Church of Christ, Scientist.

67. Johnson, *History*, I, p. 336 f.

68. *Chicago Christian Scientist*, IV, January, 1891.

69. A. *L&M* 18–2264.

70. A. *L&M* 18–2268.

71. A. *L&M* 60–2563.

72. *CSJ*, IX, July, 1891.

73. *Chicago Christian Scientist* (Truth Gleaner), V, September, 1891.

74. *Man.*, p. 34.

75. *Ibid.*, p. 43 f.

76. *Ret.*, p. 30.

77. A. *L&M* 55–7810.

78. A. *L&M* 36–4667.

79. A. *L&M*.

80. *My.*, p. 249.

81. See, *e.g.*, *S&H*, p. 272.

82. "Love Your Enemies." I have used the slightly revised version in *Mis.*, pp. 8 ff., of the article published in *CSJ*, VIII, April, 1890. Cf. Janet Colman reminiscences in A: "I can say one thing truthfully that if I were asked today after all my experience with our Leader [1914] which was the greatest of them to me I would say this: I always found her loving her enemies, always ready to do them good, always would see those who had injured her if she could help them even before one who had been loving and kind to her."

83. *Mis.*, p. 135 f.

84. A. *L&M* 59–8392.

85. A. *L&M* 19–2342.

86. A. *L&M* 19–2344 and 2345.

87. Her second cousin, Fred N. Ladd of Concord, later reminded her with some amusement of her remark as a small girl to his mother, Clarinda Baker: "Oh, I wish I could cut my thinker off!" (A. Ladd reminiscences)

88. A. *L&M* 82–8896.

89. Farlow sent her a book on the subject which she read and passed along with her comments to Wiggin. Various students sent her books which they thought would interest her, or drew her attention to them. M. C. Spaulding, for instance, wrote her about Amiel's *Journal* (just translated by Mrs. Humphrey Ward), which he felt came as near to the border of Christian Science as Moses did to the Promised Land, with "thoughts that breathe and words that burn."

90. A. *L&M* 18–2228. She also commended highly Drummond's *The Greatest Thing in the World.*

91. She had read and marked *The Light of Asia* and had sent Arnold a copy of an early edition of *Science and Health,* but she never joined in the swell of enthusiasm for that versified life of Buddha which presaged the later flood tide of popular Orientalism in America.

92. Ten years later she sent Tolstoy a copy of *Science and Health* and received a polite but noncommittal letter of acknowledgment from his son Sergei. The French mathematician, W. Rivier, in his philosophical work *Les Deux Chemins* (Brussels: Editions du Temple, 1950) picks Tolstoy and Mrs. Eddy as two outstanding interpreters of Christianity, Tolstoy stressing the element of sacrifice in it and Mrs. Eddy its "caractère essentiellement raisonnable."

93. A. *L&M* 36–4644.

94. A. *L&M* 27–3384.

95. A. *L&M* 89–13114.

96. A. *L&M* 45–5962.

97. A. *L&M* 27–3403.

98. A. *L&M* 34–4346.

99. A. *L&M* 27–3477.

100. A. *L&M* 56–7826.

101. The nucleus of this work had been published first in 1885 under the title *Historical Sketch of Metaphysical Healing.* Since then it had been issued in several variant versions under slightly changed titles, but *Retrospection and Introspection* had a good deal of fresh material and a new dimension of thought. The 1891 text is essentially like that of the present version, but a few variations in content and arrangement can be seen from the passages I have quoted from the first edition. The small book illustrates its own thesis in a striking way. The opening section, which deals with the author's ancestry more in the spirit of Walter Scott romance than of sober genealogical research, is labeled "Ancestral Shadows," and later the writer breaks off the chronological narrative to exclaim: "It is well to know, dear reader, that our material, mortal history is but the record of dreams, not of man's real existence, and the dream has no place in the Science of being. It is 'as a tale that is told,' and 'as the shadow when it

declineth.' " For the early retrospective portions she relies on memory rather than on a careful checking of names, dates, and factual details, and with the "discovery" of 1866 she obviously moves with relief into the new world of which she now feels herself a native. In the last part of the book the author's vision of reality entirely supersedes her recollections of the past; it is clear that her real interest is in the spiritual ancestry and destiny of her child, Christian Science.

Index

Abbott, Francis E., 190
Absalom, 98, 336
Ackland, James, 64, 66, 79, 86, 97, 104, 105, 108, 110, 118, 335
"Acres of Diamonds," 54
Adam, 321
Adams, Mrs. J. A. D., 200
Adams, Rev. Joseph, 198–205, 227, 263, 265, 268, 291, 293, 359
Adams, Mary, 223
Aesop, 124
Alcott, A. Bronson, 7, 10, 44, 99, 153, 316
Alcott, Louisa M., 336
Aldrich, Lou, 223
Alger, William R., 339, 344
Allen, Edward E., 186
Allen, George, 79
American Academy of Dental Science, 184
Amiel, H. F., 381
Anderson, Otto, M.D., 110, 336
animal magnetism, 35, 93, 122, 125, 126, 132, 144, 160, 169, 170, 176, 208, 210, 211, 228, 240, 265, 285, 287, 293, 317, 325, 353, 363, 366; malicious animal magnetism (M.A.M.), 36, 75, 219, 288; "Animal Magnetism," 188, 189, 229, 284. *See also* hypnotism, mesmerism, mental malpractice
Anselm, 165
Ante-Nicene Fathers, 299
Anthony, Susan B., 15, 223, 276
anthropology, 138, 206
Appleseed, Johnny, 161
Aquinas, Thomas, 8
Arens, Edward J., litigious character, 38–40, 43, 44, 67; conspiracy case, 50–57, 329, 339; defection and plagiarism, 72, 84–87, 93, 106, 108, 112; "mental murder," 113–115, 340; Quimby campaign, 126, 128, 129; copyright suit, 133–135; hostility, 145, 146, 188, 198, 202, 271, 345, 348; publications, 85, 86, 113, 134, 340
Armstrong, Joseph, 219
Arnold, Edwin, 299, 381
Arnold, Matthew, 184, 298
Arthur, Chester A., 172
Associated Charities of Cincinnati, 110
astronomy, 187, 193, 194, 206, 357
Atkinson, Adelma ("Dell"), 37, 38, 85
Atkinson, Benjamin F., 37, 38, 63, 85, 115
Augustine, 31

Austin, David, 55

Bagley, Sarah, 40, 47, 49
Bailey, Joshua P., 264, 267, 269, 278, 279, 280, 281, 282, 284, 290, 291
Baker, Albert, 105, 230
Baker, George Sullivan, 216
Baker, George W., 216
Baker, Hattie, 16
Baker, Henry Moore, 105, 106
Baker, Martha Rand, 215
Baker, Mary Ann Cook, 216, 217, 364
Baker, Samuel, 216
Bancroft, Lawyer, 44
Bancroft, Samuel Putnam, 10, 17, 19, 22, 36, 37, 82, 95, 96, 99, 123
Banks, John Gayner, 360
Baptist Tabernacle, 61, 63, 326, 329
Barbour, Rev. Charles D., 121
Barry, George, 10, 14, 15, 22, 23, 27, 37, 39, 46, 47, 67, 68, 95, 96, 108, 233, 234, 318, 319, 322
Barth, Karl, 367
Bartlett, Julia S., 79, 80, 98, 100, 101, 107, 108, 114, 117, 118, 123, 139, 146–148, 157, 160, 163, 170, 179, 180, 256, 374
Bartol, Cyrus A., 154, 226, 366
Bates, E. S., 57, 322, 328, 330, 342, 346, 353, 354
Bates, Edward P., 219, 252, 295
Bates, General Erastus N., 252
Battles, General Wendell P., 354
Beecher, Henry Ward, 318
Bellevue Medical College, 81, 82, 341
Benson, Nancy, 4
Berkeley, George, 24, 363
Bernard, Claude, 77
Bernheim, Hippolyte, 124, 229
Bertram, W. H., 240, 241, 247, 253
Beyond Good and Evil, 164
Bhagavad-Gita, 187
Bible, 6, 47, 52, 67, 97, 100, 118, 169, 190, 196, 205, 208, 218, 234, 252, 278, 281, 287, 290, 299
Billings, Josh, 124
biology, 77, 225, 309, 310
birth, 236, 237, 238, 368, 369
Bixby, Lucy, 318
Blackman, C. Lulu, 168, 169
Blackstone, William, 45
Blavatsky, Helena P., 190, 207, 210
Bohr, Niels, 310, 311
Bonhoeffer, Dietrich, 367

Boston Christian Scientist, The, 263, 264

Boston College of Metaphysical Science, 225

"Boston Craze," 138

Bostonians, The, 172

Bowker, Flora, 330

Braden, Charles S., 363

Bradford, George H., 199

Bradford, William H., 241

Bradshaw, Sue Ella, 223, 299

Brahmanism, 225

Brierly, James E., 238, 374

Brooks, Phillips, 153, 154, 174, 263

Brooks, Van Wyck, 153, 379

Brotherhood of the New Life, 173, 260

Brown, Ellen. *See* Linscott, Ellen Brown

Brown, Lucretia L. S., 25, 42, 43, 101

Browning, Robert, 31

Brush, E. F., 343

Buckley, James M., 359

Buddhism, 178, 210, 225, 381

Buffalo Bill, 11

Bunyan, John, 122

Buswell, Arthur True, 63, 64, 65, 68, 69, 96, 97, 110, 111, 117, 137–139, 143–145, 160, 167, 330, 335, 347, 348

Caird, G. B., 321

Carlyle, Thomas, 32, 316

Carnegie, Andrew, 328

Carter, Ellen, 334

Cartesianism, 77

Centennial Exhibition, 11

Central Music Hall, 242

Century of Christian Science Healing, A, 311

Chamberlain, Dr. Willie, 172

Channing, William Ellery, 187

Charcôt, J. M., 124, 229

Chardon Street Convention, 228

Charles, George B., 141

Chase, George, 336

Chase, Stephen A., 219

chemistry, 357

Cheney, Florence, 10

Chevaillier, Alzire, 172–174, 177, 183, 260, 261, 263

Chicago Truth Gleaner, The, 293

Chicago Christian Scientist, The, 203, 227, 263, 265, 291

Chickering Hall, 163, 192, 195, 199, 217, 289

Choate, Clara, 45, 48, 61, 62, 71–75, 79, 80, 93, 94, 96, 99–101, 104–109, 117, 118, 121, 127, 141–146, 149, 175, 228, 318, 349

Choate, George, 45, 71, 72, 73, 108, 117, 121, 129, 344, 345

Choate, Grace, 13, 14

Choate, Judge, 65, 66

Choate, Warren, 71, 73

Christ, 17, 27, 33, 62, 96, 100, 125, 142, 143, 157, 166, 169, 198, 200, 203, 204, 207, 208, 242, 257, 259, 265, 292, 296, 297, 302, 331, 360, 362, 370, 371

Christian Healing, 73

Christianity, 6, 22, 25, 33, 34, 51, 62, 66, 87, 99, 132, 138, 143, 154, 156, 157, 167, 176, 192, 194, 198, 202, 204–206, 225, 231, 247, 258, 263, 271, 284, 360, 366, 381

Christian Science (magazine), 259

"Christian Science and its Revelator," 266

Christian Science and the Bible, 190

Christian Science Committee on Publication, 220, 239, 240, 369

Christian Science Journal, The, 124, 183, 185, 190, 227, 231, 253, 263

Christian Science Monitor, The, 301

Christian Science: No and Yes, 230

Christian Scientist Association, 11, 28, 37, 38, 42, 50, 62, 63, 70, 74, 85, 86, 95, 96, 98, 99, 121, 122, 133, 173, 195, 197, 224, 240, 241, 244, 253, 287, 296

Church of Christ, Scientist, 63, 68, 72, 79, 95, 96, 97, 98, 193, 221, 240, 253, 257, 259

Church of the Divine Unity (Scientist), 208, 225, 226, 227

Claflin, Tennessee, 318

Clark, Ellen L., 332

Clarke, James Freeman, 175, 187

Clarke, Miss Sarah J., 291

Cleveland, Grover, 184

Clough, Orville A., 318

Colles, Marjorie, 223, 266, 297

Collier, George, 52, 55, 56, 328

Colman, Janet, 161, 206, 219, 380

commitment, 7, 142, 163, 171, 206, 226, 296

Committee of Relief, 50, 287

Concord School of Philosophy, 153, 344

Conwell, Russell H., 54, 55, 328

Cook, Rev. Joseph, 155, 156

Corner, Abby H., 237, 239, 240, 241

Cozzens, Phoebe, 223

Crabtree, Addison D., M.D., 184

Crosby, Sarah, 321

Crosse, Sarah J., 121, 144, 148, 179, 190, 239, 240, 241, 253, 257, 263, 280, 373

Cullis, Dr. Charles, 138
Culture and Anarchy, 184
Cushing, Dr. Alvin M., 336

Dagon, 17, 18
Dakin, E. F., 58, 316, 330, 342, 346, 353, 373
Damnation of Theron Ware, The, 204
Damon, Mary A., 98
Darwin, Charles, 124, 156, 188
Day, Rev. George B., 203–205, 242, 248, 267, 268
Defence of Christian Science, 155, 185
Deists, 31
Deland, Margaret, 204
demonology, 41, 48, 62, 76, 94, 122, 135, 144, 188, 270, 311, 327
Descartes, René, 165
Dexter, H., M.D., 9
Dick-Read, Dr. Grantly, 369
Dictionary of Correspondences, 346
Dittemore, J. V., 57, 322, 328, 330, 342, 346, 353, 354, 368
Divine Law of Cure, The, 210, 211
Dixon, Hepworth, 184
Dodge, Annie, 223
Donne, John, 376
Dorman, Albert B., 172, 227, 259, 260, 353, 366
Dostoevsky, Feodor, 32, 48, 204, 327
Dresser, Annetta, 126, 129, 208, 343
Dresser, Horatio, 208, 209, 361, 376
Dresser, Julius, 126, 129–131, 133, 180, 202, 208–210, 227–230, 343, 345
Drummond, Henry, 299
Dudley, Rev. J. A., 44
Dunshee, Margaret J., 96
Durant, S. Louise, 96
Durfee, George, 105
Duvalier, 94

Eastaman, Capt. Joseph S., 159, 242, 249, 277, 283, 286–288, 301
Eastman, Charles J., 81, 82, 111–113, 115, 116, 339–341
Eaton, Nellie, 371
Eddy, Asa Gilbert, meets Mrs. Glover, 5–7, 10, 14, 15, 316; marriage, 18–23, 25, 319, 320; Spofford feud, 37–39, 44; teaches class, 45; conspiracy case, 51–57, 61; married life, 63, 65, 68, 69, 73, 75, 111, 136, 138, 335; champions *S&H*, 82, 86, 87, 106, 135; illness and death, 111–117, 121, 143, 217, 339, 364; character, 16, 20, 21, 222, 286, 320, 328
Eddy, Daniel C., 329

Eddy, Ebenezer J. Foster, 221, 222, 242, 250, 252, 254, 269, 276, 282, 286, 300
Eddy, Mary Baker, previous history, 6, 7, 12, 39, 40, 62, 69, 78, 101, 125, 126, 170, 171; discovery of Christian Science, 6, 12, 68, 69, 130, 133, 166, 207, 290, 342; early healings, 3–6, 13, 23, 58, 71, 72, 315–317; early leadership, 10, 15–17, 26–28, 46, 99, 100, 137; appearance, 12, 20, 21, 61, 170, 249; reputation, 4, 8, 9, 13, 14, 318; marriage, 7, 16–21, 320; revision of *S&H*, 16, 23, 25, 28; Spofford break, 17, 18, 21, 22, 25–28, 37, 38, 322; Barry suit, 22, 23, 27, 46, 47; teachings, 32–36, 42, 45, 46; Salem case, 39, 40, 43–45; Kennedy-Spofford crisis, 46–50, 326; conspiracy case, 50–58, 328, 329; preaching, 61–63, 68, 69, 80; church founded, 62–65, 68, 72, 73, 79, 331; Stanley case, 65–67, 330; family involvements, 69–71, 78; Concord "research," 73–77; college founded, 81, 82, 103, 111, 112; work on *S&H*, 83, 84, 87, 92–95; trouble from Arens, 84–87, 93, 113, 115, 339, 340; Lynn rebellion, 91–98, 334–336; "transfiguration" and exit, 97–101; feminine friendships, 91, 92, 101–104, 105, 107–109; Washington visit, 104–106, 338; Boston return, 109–111; loss of husband, 112–118, 121, 135; new energies, 121–125; Quimby redivivus, 125–129, 135, 342; Dresser-Arens campaign, 129–132, 133, 343, 344; copyright suit, 133–135, 344–346; life at college, 136–140, 347; Choate break, 142–145, 149, 349; Chicago class, 140–142, 146, 148, 149, 349; Boston preaching, 153, 154, 156, 167, 189, 350, 356, 358; embattled orthodoxy, 155–158, 211; healing work, 140, 154, 159, 194, 249, 250, 351, 371; college teaching, 160, 161–171, 178, 191, 251, 252, 353, 357, metaphysics, 164–167, 190–193, 195–197, 233, 234, 236, 367, 368; care of students, 122, 123, 171–177, 224, 341, 342, 361, 380; Hopkins defection, 145, 177–180; editorship, 183–185, 190, 355; revision of *S&H*, 186–189, 356; Gill episode, 192–198, 357; Adams unloosed, 198–204, 265, 293, 359, 360; Christian revelation, 166, 167, 204–208; rejects occultism, 205–207, 210, 211, 360; Dresser controversy, 208–211, 227, 229, 361–363; family relations, 215–218, 276, 287, 363–365;

Eddy, Mary Baker (*cont.*)
  new students, 219–224; mind cure rampant, 225–228, 366; Gestefeld take-off, 231–234, 248, 368; love of children, 13, 236, 237; obstetrics, 111, 237–239, 250, 368, 369; Corner case, 238–240, 368; Boston insurrection, 240, 241, 243, 244, 253, 369; Chicago triumph, 241–243; uncertain future, 247, 248; health, 248, 249, 276, 376; organization dissolved, 252, 253, 255, 256, 277, 374; Concord retirement, 254, 275–277, 299; church building plans, 240, 256–259, 295, 372, 373; attitude toward marriage, 260–263; troubles with Bailey, 264–266, 281, 284, 290, 291; and Day, 248, 267, 268; Woodbury problem, 268–271, 325, 326; revision of *S&H*, 278–284, 286, 289, 295, 378–380, 384; M.A.M., 284, 285, 287, 288, 296; Stetson trouble, 291–293, 297, 298; search for home, 299–301; retrospect, 301, 302, 381, 382
Edison, Thomas A., 264
Edwards, Jonathan, 201
Einstein, 309, 310
Eliot, George, 261
Emerson, Ralph Waldo, 31, 32, 87, 124, 137, 225, 228, 254, 316
Emma Hopkins College of Christian Science, 203, 359
Esoteric Buddhism, 210
Esoteric Christianity, 210
"Essay on Man," 185
Essentials of Mental Healing, 225
Evans, Warren F., 126, 210, 211, 360, 363
evil, problem of, 31–33, 35, 36, 48, 75, 94, 114, 165, 192, 195, 196, 233, 234
Ewing, Ruth, 223
Ezekiel, 166, 174

Fabyan House, 248
faith healing, 138, 226
Farlow, Alfred, 219, 220, 265, 289, 366, 369
Felt, Lavinia, 91
Fichte, J. G., 24, 363
Filbert, John P., 247, 252
Fillmore, Charles and Myrtle, 373
Finney, Charles G., 199
Fiske, John, 190
Fluno, Ella, 236
Fluno, Francis J., M.D., 236
Formgeschichte, 188
Foster, Ebenezer J. *See* Eddy, Ebenezer J. Foster

Fowler, Rev. Stacy, 157
Frederic, Harold, 204
free love, 14, 262
Freud, Sigmund, 124, 325, 332
Frothingham, Sarah, 61, 336
Frye, Calvin, 97, 136–139, 142, 148, 160, 222, 241, 242, 253, 254, 265, 279, 282, 283, 300, 343, 347

Gale, Frank, 275
Gardner, Mrs. Jack, 153
Garfield, James A., 102, 106
Gaskell, Mrs., 187, 319
Gatchell, Mary, 13, 319
General Association for Dispensing Christian Science Literature, 292, 293, 297
geometry, 191, 193, 194
Gestefeld, Ursula N., 231, 232, 234, 235, 248
Gifford, Rev. O. P., 155, 157, 166, 167
Gill, Mrs. W. J., 195–197, 202
Gill, Rev. William I., 192–199, 202, 205, 216, 227, 228, 263, 357
Glover, Evelyn Tilton, 365
Glover, George, 69, 70, 71, 78, 117, 215, 217, 218, 222, 276, 287, 330
Glover, Mary Baker. *See* Eddy, Mary Baker
Glover, Mary Baker (granddaughter), 71
Glover, Nellie, 71, 217, 218, 365
gnosticism, 91, 211, 366
Godey's Lady's Book, 185
Godfrey, George L., 4, 5, 286
Godfrey, Mrs. G. L., 3, 4, 5, 6, 7, 286, 315, 316
Godfrey, Mary, 4, 5, 70, 315, 316
Gordon, Rev. A. J., 155–157, 211
Graf-Wellhausen, 188
Grant, Ulysses S., 316
Gray, Judge Horace, 44, 45
Greene, Eugene H., 351, 374
Grenier, Helen M., 13
Guiteau, Charles J., 106, 172, 338

Hahnemann Medical College, 222
Hale, Edward Everett, 175
Hall, Captain Charles F., 74, 331
Hall, Minnie, 223, 288
Hall, Nettie, 223
Hamilton, Allen McLane, 338
Hanna, Judge Septimus J., 173
Hansen, Chadwick, 324
Harris, Edward N., 184
Harris, Thomas Lake, 173
Harte, Bret, 218

Harvard College, 159, 162, 163, 350
Harvey, Mrs. A. M., 371
Hawthorne Hall (Rooms), 68, 153, 154, 156, 163
Hayes-Tilden election, 11
Haymarket Riot, 184
Hazzard, Jean, 359
Hegel, G. W. F., 17, 363
Heidegger, Martin, 309
Heisenberg, Werner, 309, 310
Hershey Hall, 149
Heywood, Mrs. E. C., 371
Hickok, Wild Bill, 69
Historical Sketch of Metaphysical Healing, 185, 381
History of Medicine for the Last 4000 Years, 81
Hitler, Adolf, 41
Holl, Karl, 334
Homiletic Review, 157
Hopkins, Emma, 145, 170, 177–180, 183, 200, 202–206, 211, 227, 228, 234, 235, 259, 260, 335, 354, 360, 373
Hopkins, Mark, 159
Hopkins, Mrs. Mark, 223
Horticultural Hall, 240
Howard, James C., 72, 73, 74, 75, 78, 79, 82, 85, 92, 93, 95, 96, 98, 99, 108, 318, 334–336
Howard, Sarah, 92, 93
Howe, Julia Ward, 187
Howells, William Dean, 32, 339
How Rev. Wiggin Rewrote Mrs. Eddy's Book, 378
Human Life, 48
Huxley, T. H., 11
hydropathy, 64
hypnotism, 41, 90, 124, 176, 229, 285, 324. *See also* mesmerism

Ibsen, Henrik, 32
International Christian Scientist Association, 259
International Magazine of Christian Science, The, 259, 260, 261, 263
Isaiah, 290, 292

Jahr, 339, 340
James, Henry, 172, 221
James, William, 153, 361
Janet, Pierre, 56, 329, 334
Jarvis, Mary Ann, 342
Jeremiah, 133, 138
Jesuitism in Christian Science, 234
Jesus, 22, 24, 27, 52, 68, 69, 72, 91, 92, 107, 113, 125, 154, 156, 166, 204, 205, 255, 257, 258, 263, 266, 270, 296, 302, 326, 331, 370, 373
Jewish Science, 370
Joan of Arc, 91
Job, 191
Johns Hopkins University, 11
Johnson, William B., 162, 163, 241, 242, 244
Johnson, William Lyman, 162, 163, 244, 256, 350
John Ward, Preacher, 204
Journal of Christian Science, The. See Christian Science Journal, The
"Joy Cometh in the Morning," 248
Judas, 22, 198
"Judge Not," 260
Jung, Carl, 206, 332

Kafka, Franz, 94
Kazhinsky, B. B., 325
Kennedy, Richard, defection, 35, 108, 319; enigma, 47–49, 326; *Glover vs. Kennedy*, 39, 40, 53, 54, 67; conspiracy case, 57, 58, 329; Stanley case, 65, 66, 330; Glover confrontation, 70, 287; "demonology," 74, 78, 79, 84, 85, 93, 94, 135, 178; relation to Quimby, 126–129, 344, 345
Kimball, Edward A., 219, 220, 221, 222
Kimball, Kate, 221, 222
Kinzel, Charles F., 368
Klebs, Edwin, 124
Knapp, Flavia, 174–176, 248
Knapp, Ira O., 174–176, 248, 257, 276, 300, 301, 372
Knott, Annie Macmillan, 223
Koestler, Arthur, 325, 327
Kreutzer Sonata, The, 299

Ladd, Fred N., 381
Lang, Alfred, 241, 258, 372
Lang, Susie M., 340, 367, 368
Larminie, Hannah, 194, 223
Lathrop, Laura, 178, 223, 224, 237, 249, 276, 300
leadership, 99, 100, 112, 137, 256, 269, 297–298
Lefkovitz, Rabbi Maurice, 370
Lenin, Nikolai, 352
Letts, Colonel J. M., 9
Lichtenstein, Rabbi Morris, 370
Light of Asia, 299, 381
Light of the World, 299
Linscott, Captain John F., 262, 275
Linscott, Ellen Brown, 140, 141, 144, 149, 154, 160, 168, 194, 198, 200, 202, 228, 262, 263, 267, 275

Livermore, Mary A., 102
Locke, Ellen, 335
Locke, John, 164
logic, 33, 137, 164, 165, 191, 204, 233, 278, 284, 367
Longfellow, H. W., 187
Longyear, Mary Beecher, 322, 334, 348
Lowell, Jenny M., 375
Luther, Martin, 143, 281

MacDonald, Jessie, 53
M.A.M. *See* animal magnetism
"Man for the Hour," 219
Manley, Delia S., 113, 116
Manual of The Mother Church, 293
Mark Twain, 109, 345, 378
Marquand, J. P., 339
marriage, 15, 18, 170, 261, 262, 263, 270, 373
Marston, Luther M., M.D., 225, 227, 228, 229, 230, 259, 366
Marx, Karl, 164, 352
Mary Magdalene, 165
Mary (mother of Jesus), 27, 68, 69, 92, 277, 322, 326, 370
Mason, Frank E., 221, 239, 240, 242
Massachusetts Metaphysical College, 81, 82, 103, 111, 158–161, 175, 199, 203, 225, 227, 255, 289, 296
materialism, 16, 17, 25, 99, 139, 140, 156, 209, 327
matter, 17, 23, 24, 132, 140, 158, 205, 208, 293, 309–311, 321
Max Planck Institute, 309
McClure's Magazine, 48, 326, 333, 348
McDonald, Emma A., 161, 162, 357
McLaren, George, 9
McNeil, General John, 105
McNeil, Sir John, 105, 337
Memorial Church, 295
Mental Healing Monthly, 225, 227, 229, 259
mental malpractice, 35, 43, 45, 66, 70, 75, 93, 94, 99, 115, 136. *See also* mesmerism
Mental Medicine, 126
Mental Science Magazine, 180, 225, 227,
mesmerism, 22, 28, 35, 38, 42, 43, 45, 46, 62, 65, 113, 116, 122, 130–132, 144, 159, 172, 173, 207, 208, 324, 343, 354, 366. *See also* animal magnetism, hypnotism
Messenger of Truth, 227, 259
metaphysics, 4, 17, 33, 36, 45, 46, 82, 84, 86, 107, 111, 178, 193, 209, 211, 226, 228, 236, 243, 309, 310, 367

Milmine, Georgine, 47, 48, 61, 316, 328, 333, 334, 339, 342, 347, 348
mind cure, 160, 199, 206, 220, 226, 366
Mind-Cure Journal, 180
miracle, 10, 17, 140, 191, 204
Miscellaneous Writings, 230
Moody, Dwight, L., 7, 11, 243
Moore, Maryann McNeil, 105
Morgan, Martha, 253
Mormonism, 184
morphine, 110, 111, 335, 336
Morrill, Dr. Ezekiel, 254
Morton, Joseph, 85, 86
Moses, 332, 381
Moslem philosophy, 178
motherhood, 92, 216, 222
Munroe, Marcellus, 258
Murphy, J. M. C., 240, 241, 247, 253, 257, 373

Napoleon, 77
Nash, Flora Glover, 4, 315
Nash, William, 3, 4
National Christian Scientist Association, 224, 241, 242, 248, 253, 259, 266, 269, 277
Natural Law in the Spiritual World, 299
Neo-Platonists, 8
new birth, 171, 236
Newhall, Elizabeth, 15, 27, 37, 318, 322
Newhall, Elvira, 14
Newman, Anna B., 96, 173, 260, 336
New Manual of Homeopathic Practice, 339
New Thought, 360, 361, 373, 380
Newton, Isaac, 126, 234
Nietzsche, Friedrich, 32, 164–166
"Night Thoughts," 185, 355
Nixon, William G., 258, 280, 282, 291, 292, 295
Norcross, Lanson P., 289, 295, 372
Norton, Carol, 297, 298
Noyes, Amos, 44
Noyes, Caroline D., 141, 146, 149, 160, 206, 351, 361
Noyes, Rufus, King, M.D., 81, 82, 111–113, 115, 116

obstetrics, 111, 237, 238, 250, 267
Old Theology in Its Application to the Healing of the Sick, 113
Oliphant, Laurence, 174
ontology, 33, 82, 114
Orcutt, William Dana, 83, 283
Osgood, Anna, 248
Otis, Ann, 254

Palmer House, 243
pantheism, 157, 158, 211
Paradise Lost, 187
parapsychology, 41
Parker Memorial Hall (Building), 63, 228
Parmenides, 24
Parmenter, Judge William, 40
Pascal, Blaise, 188, 356
Pasteur, Louis, 77
Patterson, Dr. Daniel, 19, 170, 222, 374
Paul, Saint, 8, 115, 184, 185, 197, 202, 207
Peabody, Rev. Andrew P., 154, 347
Peabody, Elizabeth, 153
Peabody, Frederick W., 372
Perry, Baxter E., 257, 258, 372
Perry, George, 256
Peter, Saint, 257, 298, 373
Phare Pleigh, 188, 190
Philbrick, Detective, 51
Phillips, Fannie, 91
philosophical idealism, 17, 33, 125, 156
Philosophical Realism, 192, 194, 195, 197
philosophy, 9, 24, 164, 197
phrenology, 64
physics, 234, 309, 310
Physics and Beyond, 309
Pierce, Franklin, 105, 230, 337
Pilsbury, Ellen, 78
Pilsbury, Martha, 78, 215
Pinkham, Hollis C., 51, 52, 53, 55, 56, 57, 58
Pippa, 31
plagiarism, 134, 201, 345
Plato, 17, 132, 184
Plunkett, Mary, 178–180, 200, 203, 227, 228, 235, 259, 260, 261, 262, 354
"P.M. (Private Meeting) Society," 349
Polanyi, Michael, 324
Pope, Alexander, 185, 356
Popular Science Monthly, 285
Possessed, The, 48, 327
Potter, Carrie, 80
Potter, Fanny McNiel, 105, 106, 337, 339
Powell, Rev. Lyman P., 48, 57, 65, 345
"Prayer and Atonement," 180, 188, 295
Prescott, George, 38, 39
Pre-Socratics, 309
Prime, Sarah T., 94
Primitive Mind-Cure, The, 210, 211
"Prince of Peace," 270, 271
"Private Directions for Treating Disease Metaphysically," 86
prophecy, 68, 156

psychoanalysis, 327
psychology, 36, 41, 48, 115, 171, 229, 285, 288

Quakerism, 264
Quimby, George, 126–129, 134, 209, 342–345, 362
Quimby, Phineas Parkhurst, 125–135, 180, 202, 208–211, 229, 342–345, 361–363

Rahner, Karl, 327
Rasputin, 94
Rawson, Dorcas, 10, 14, 42, 43, 96, 98, 99, 100
Relief Committee. *See* Committee of Relief
Retrospection and Introspection, 185, 301
revelation, 6, 12, 17, 25, 27, 47, 98, 171, 188, 204, 205, 236, 290, 321, 380
Rice, Miranda R., 10, 51, 58, 96, 98, 99, 100, 335, 336, 348
Rimbaud, Arthur, 32
Ritschl, 190
Rivier, W., 381
Robert Elsmere, 204
Roberts, Charles A., 358
Robinson, Fred A., 262
Robinson, Janette E., 170, 171, 262, 374
Rosenberg, Charles E., 338
Royce, Josiah, 361
Rudiments and Rules of Divine Science, 205, 207
Rust, Richard S., 339

Salvation Army, 34
Sargent, James L., 52, 54, 56
Sargent, Laura, 254, 276, 300, 372
Sargent, Victoria, 254, 276, 372
Satan, 36, 156
Sawyer, Jennie, 146, 149, 159
Sawyer, Dr. Silas J., 141, 145, 149, 159, 160, 224
science, 11, 12, 77, 130, 309, 310, 311, 312
Science and Health, 47, 58, 93, 99, 155, 180, 185, 186, 201–203, 218, 227, 228, 232, 234, 252, 260, 266, 279, 291, 293, 295, 330, 358, 377, 381, quoted, 58, 77, 136, 187, 321, 333, 357, 379; first ed., 6–9, 14, 15, 18, 20–22, 35, 46, 64, 85, 126–128, 134, 262, 322, quoted, 15, 317, 319; second ed., 9, 16, 22–27, 45, 46, 50, 64, 82, quoted, 24, 35, 42, 46, 62; third ed., 73, 75, 82, 83, 87, 92, 107, 112, 138, quoted, 34, 39, 77, 84, 93, 94, 95, 144; sixth ed., 135; six-

Science and Health (cont.)
teenth ed., 187–189, 205, 228, 378; fiftieth ed., 278, 282, 289, 295, 379, 380, quoted, 290; *Key to the Scriptures,* 25, 135, 188, 346
"Science and Philosophy," 197
Science of Man, The, 6, 83, 85, 134
"scientific statement of being," 83, 84, 279, 333
Scott, Walter, 381
Shakerism, 184
Shakespeare, 187
Shankara, 24
Shannon, Clara, 223, 268, 269, 270, 375
Sherman, Bradford, 141, 146, 149, 160
Sherman, Mattie, 146
Sherman, Roger, 141, 146, 149, 160
Sibley, Alice, 101–104, 106, 117, 118, 121
Silent Unity, 373
Silsbee, Fannie, 141, 146
Sim, Peter, 126
Sinai, 299
Smith, Colonel Eldridge J., 27, 105, 106, 110, 117, 121, 124, 135
Smith, Hanover, P., 72, 103, 107, 114, 122, 168, 219, 335
Smith, Laura Jane, 92, 317
Smith, Melissa, 146
Smith, Sydney, 124
Snider, Carrie, 277, 338
Society for the Advancement of Science, 138
Spaulding, M.C., 198, 359, 381
Spinoza, Benedict, 164, 178
spiritism, 41, 153, 155, 158–160, 199, 207, 226, 317
Spofford, Daniel Harrison, promising aide, 10, 14–17, 316, 317; disappointed suitor, 17, 18, 21, 319, 320; final break, 25–28, 322; warfare, 35–38, 46, 47, 49, 50, 74, 84, 326; court cases, 40, 42–44, 50–58, 329; relation to Quimby, 126–128, 342; fading of antagonism, 93, 334, 348
Standish, Myles, 64
Stanford, Mrs. Leland, 223
Stanley, Charles S., 40, 44, 65, 66, 67, 330
Statement of Christian Science, 232, 234, 248
Stavrogin, 48
Steinway Hall, 251, 260, 261
Stetson, Augusta E., 176, 177, 184, 224, 264, 291, 292, 294, 297, 298, 338
Stevens, Oliver, 56
Stewart, Rev. Samuel R., 19
Straw, Jane L., 86, 96

Streicher, 94
Stuart, Elizabeth G., 86, 87, 93, 96, 98, 228
suggestion, 95, 124, 125, 128, 132, 169, 229, 285, 288, 343
Swarts, A. J., 160, 178, 180, 184, 202, 206, 211, 225, 227, 228
Swartz, Nadia, 91, 92
Swedenborgianism, 8, 264, 346

"Taking Offense," 185, 355
Teilhard de Chardin, 77
theism, 209
theology, 8, 27, 48, 158, 171, 190, 267
Theosophical Society, 206, 231
theosophy, 155, 190, 206, 207, 226, 366
Thompson, Emma A., 362
Thoreau, Henry, 137
Tilton, Abigail, 78, 215, 364
"Timely Issue, A," 124
Titcomb, Sarah E., 190
"To Loyal Christian Scientists," 247
Tolstoy, Leo, 299, 381
Townsend, Luther T., 155, 157
Treatise on English Punctuation, A, 83
Tremont Temple, 155, 156
Trial of the Assassin Guiteau, 338
Trinity Church, 133, 134
Troup, Charles, 369
True History of Mental Science, 208, 227
"True Philosophy and Communion," 193
Truth (magazine), 227, 228, 259
Truth Healing, 293
Turgot, 124
Tuttle, George H., 40, 44, 65
Tyndall, John, 6, 10, 316
Tyson, Captain George E., 74

Unity of Good and Unreality of Evil, 205, 207
University Press, 82, 83, 186, 283, 286
Upanishads, 178, 205

Varieties of Religious Experience, 361
"Veritas Odium Parit," 157
virgin birth, 27, 46, 68, 270, 326, 370, 375
visions, 75, 97, 98, 135, 174, 250, 332, 346, 347, 348
Vyr, Hector, 260

Wagner, Richard, 302
Ward, Mrs. Humphrey, 204, 381
Ware, Emma, 126, 129, 133, 134, 209, 345

Ware, Sarah, 126, 129, 134, 209, 344, 345
"Way, The," 255
"Wayside Hints," 189, 281, 378
"Ways That Are Vain," 229
Weatherhead, Leslie D., 329
Webster, Elizabeth, 223
Weil, Simone, 367
Wendell, Barrett, 41
White Mountain House, 248
Whitehead, A. N., 309
Whiting, Abbie, 97, 99, 107
Wickersham, Robert, 300
Wiggin, James Henry, 186–193, 204, 205, 218, 236, 263, 278, 280–284, 288, 289, 299, 346, 356, 357
Wilbur, Mrs. F. N., 346
Wilbur, Sibyl, 48, 318, 328, 339
Williams, Joseph, 61, 63, 326
Wilson, John, 82, 83, 186, 282, 283, 286
witchcraft, 4, 14, 40, 41, 42, 45, 324, 325, 327
Witchcraft at Salem, 324
Wittgenstein, Ludwig, 309

women, position of, 15, 108, 109, 183, 223
Woodbury, E. Frank, 175, 270
Woodbury, Josephine Curtis, 175–177, 239, 240, 262, 268, 269, 270, 271, 338, 354, 375, 376
Woodhull, Victoria, 14, 178, 318
Wool, Alice Swasey, 317
Wordsworth, William, 235
Work While Ye Have the Light, 299
Worthington, A. Bentley, 260, 261, 262
Wright, Livingston, 356, 378
Writings and Genius of the Founder of Christian Science, 168

Young, Edward, 185, 348, 355

Zend-Avesta, 178
Zeno, 190
Zion's Herald, 155, 157, 192
Zola, Emil, 32
Zoroastrianism, 85